Also by Robin Hemley

Invented Eden

Invented Eden

The Elusive, Disputed History

of the Tasaday

Robin Hemley

Farrar, Straus and Giroux ✌ New York

Farrar, Straus and Giroux
19 Union Square West, New York 10003

Copyright © 2003 by Robin Hemley
All rights reserved
Distributed in Canada by Douglas & McIntyre Ltd.
Printed in the United States of America
First edition, 2003

Library of Congress Cataloging-in-Publication Data
Hemley, Robin, 1958–
    Invented Eden : the elusive, disputed history of the Tasaday /
Robin Hemley.— 1st ed.
        p.   cm.
    Includes bibliographical references (p.) and index.
    ISBN 0-374-17716-3
    1. Tasaday (Philippine people)—Social life and customs.   2. Tasaday
(Philippine people)—Public opinion.   3. Impostors and imposture—
Philippines.   4. Anthropological ethics—Philippines.   I. Title.

    DS666. T32 H46 2003
    959.9'7—dc21

                                                        2002032547

Designed by Jonathan D. Lippincott
Map designed by Jeffrey L. Ward

www.fsgbooks.com

10   9   8   7   6   5   4   3   2   1

For Bret Lott and David Shields,
and with love to Margie

Contents

A Note on Spellings

Over the years there have been various spellings of the names of the
Tasaday and their neighbors. For the sake of consistency and accu-
racy, I have used the spellings provided to me by linguist Lawrence
Reid.

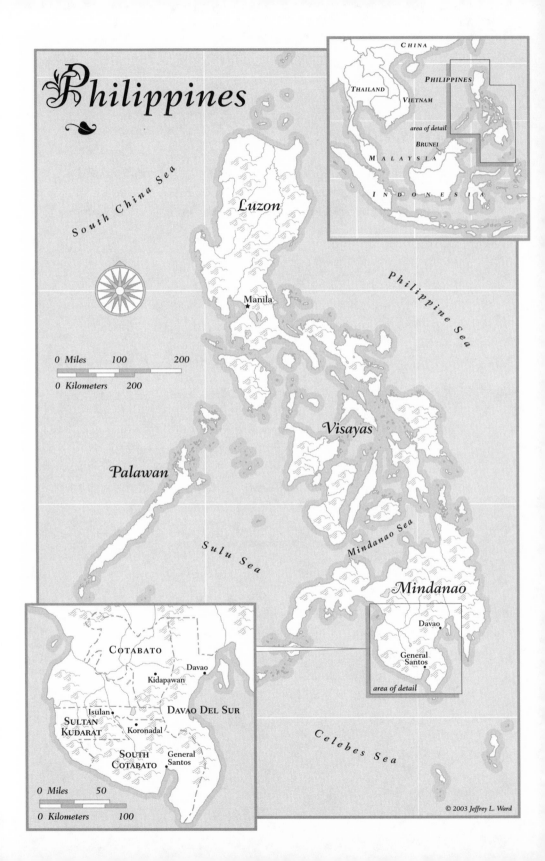

Philippines

South China Sea

Luzon

Manila ★

Visayas

Palawan

Philippine Sea

Sulu Sea

Mindanao Sea

Mindanao

Davao

General
Santos

area of detail

Celebes Sea

CHINA

THAILAND

VIETNAM

PHILIPPINES

area of detail

BRUNEI

MALAYSIA

INDONESIA

0 Miles   100   200

0 Kilometers   200

COTABATO

Davao

Kidapawan

Isulan

SULTAN
KUDARAT

DAVAO DEL SUR

Koronadal

SOUTH
COTABATO

General
Santos

0 Miles   50

0 Kilometers   100

© 2003 Jeffrey L. Ward

Invented Eden

1

A Meeting Between Centuries

Mercy, mercy me. Ah, things ain't what they used to be.
　　　　　　　—Marvin Gaye, "Mercy Mercy Me (The Ecology)"

Toward the end of the *NBC Nightly News* on July 16, 1971, David Brinkley announced in his oddly measured way, "The outside world . . . after maybe a thousand years has discovered a small tribe of people living in a remote jungle in the Philippines. Until now, the outside world didn't know they existed . . . and they didn't know the outside world existed. Their way of living is approximately that of the Stone Age. Their society is so primitive they don't even know about fighting wars . . . or even about fighting among themselves."

A map of the Philippines, the only graphic on the news report besides the stock market graph, showed a spot in southern Mindanao labeled "Lost Tribe," as Jack Perkins narrated a report from correspondent Jack Reynolds. "Numbering only a few dozen people," Perkins said, "it was easy for the Lost Tribe to stay lost until a month ago when officials from the Philippine government discovered them." A shot taken from a helicopter showed seemingly endless expanses of mountainous jungle as Reynolds and Perkins related to the audience the discovery of this lost tribe called the Tasaday, which, Reynolds reiterated, had been isolated in the dense jungle for at least five hundred years and probably more than a thousand.

He told a little about their life in the dense rain forest, how they lived by stream beds and gathered small crabs and tadpoles for food. They were shown huddled tensely together, their arms hugging their knees. A couple jumped from rock to rock in a stream bed with a baby or toddler hanging from its mother's neck. They looked like refugees of some sort, displaced, uncomfortable, fearful, unsure of what was happening around them. They looked vulnerable at least, if not peaceful. Only the children looked at the camera. The others averted their eyes. If not for this obvious discomfort the first glimpses we had of the Tasaday would be in line with the youth of the world; with their pale bronze skin and clothing consisting only of leaves, they looked like extras from a Tarzan movie or, more appropriately, a shell-shocked group from Woodstock who'd gone back to nature.

The first physical attribute Reynolds mentioned was that both men and women wore their hair long. This of course was of interest and relevance to the audience. Hair represented social critique and rebellion in the sixties and seventies; long hair was decidedly antiestablishment, anticapitalist, proequality of the sexes. *Hair* had even been the title of a smash musical on Broadway a couple of years earlier.

Reynolds reported that their only tools were made of edge-ground stone, a type of implement dating back more than six thousand years. Their clothes were made of palm leaves. Reynolds went on to explain that a hunter from a local tribe, named Dafal, had given them their first iron tools and some earrings and had taught them how to make crude shelters. Dafal, Perkins explained, had found the Tasaday five years earlier and had relayed his discovery to Manuel Elizalde, Jr., the head of tribal affairs, known to the hill people as Tao Bong (Good Man).

A young curly-headed Elizalde was shown with dark glasses and a cigarette dangling from his mouth. Perkins reported that Elizalde and an anthropologist named Robert Fox had gone into the mountains to meet the Tasaday. "It was a meeting between centuries," Perkins said. "Between the ages." This wasn't true, of course. The Tasaday were as much of this time as we were, but that wasn't how we would view them.

Fox had something of the look of Ernest Hemingway, with a thin white beard that framed his cheerful and chubby face, and he stood in a clearing excitedly stammering the story of his encounter with the

Tasaday. He said that "our coming was like lightning for them." When asked what they wanted, Fox incredulously explained, "They don't seem to want anything. They don't ask us any questions about the outside world."

A group of human beings who didn't want anything, who had no innate curiosity. This indeed must have struck the *Nightly News* audience as both bizarre and delightful. The grinding materialism of the workaday world had worn the American psyche thin; the American dream had been tarnished by war, riots, assassinations, the killings at Kent State, and a government that seemed to regard its young people as enemies.

Fox explained that the Tasaday had stories of a *diwatà* or a deity that they were expecting, and Elizalde had apparently met their expectations. "As you know, he gave them many things when he was first here," Fox said, chuckling.

If Elizalde looked a little like a deity, it was of the Greek or Roman variety, a petulant human writ large, with the whims and cruelties of a Zeus, able to mix with mere mortals, but wreaking havoc among them as well. In those days he often wore a yachtsman's cap. He was in his thirties, sloe-eyed and sullen-looking, often manic, puffing on a cigarette.

Fox explained that the Tasaday were named after a mountain they called Tasaday, a day's hike from the forest clearing where Fox and Elizalde met them. They called their language Manobo, which Fox asserted was "a distinct language" related to other languages in the area. They had been isolated for an awfully long time. They had no word for "sea" or "boat" (though the sea was roughly twenty-five miles away) or "iron" or any cultivated crop. No word for "rice" ("although all the people around them are rice growers," Fox said), "corn," "gabi," or "sweet potato."

"Now that their separation, their isolation, has ended," Perkins concluded, "two things will happen. One, anthropologists will begin the most fascinating studies of the Stone Age culture of these people. And two, it is inevitable, these people will begin to change." There was some resignation and sadness in Perkins's voice as the camera closed in on various Tasaday, including a child named Lobo, a boy with delicate features and long, straight hair and a winning smile who was soon to become world-famous. But that would pass too.

Whenever I tell the story of the Tasaday, that is more or less how I begin. When I tell people this story, I watch closely as a light of recognition slowly registers in my listeners. Sometimes I can almost see them tipping back into time, falling as if into a pool of spring-fed water. In my own case, I keenly remember at the age of fourteen or so seeing an NBC television special on the Tasaday, the narrator, Jack Reynolds, dressed in jungle regalia sitting near the main cave, surrounded by several sweet-looking boys my own age, dressed in leaves, as Reynolds intoned a few of their words and they giggled in response.

I remember shots of them in the dense jungle gathering food, bathing in a rushing stream, the sounds of birds all around, and I remember feeling awed by the idea that such a group might exist. I wanted of course to *be* one of them, to know their happy, simple life. Romantic, of course, but this was TV, and I was fourteen. I wasn't alone. Millions of Americans ogled the Tasaday from their BarcaLoungers, their dinner tables, their beds, their poolsides. Lawrence Welk, *Bonanza*, *Bewitched*, all offered comfortable alternate realities to lose oneself in, but none as enticing as the Tasaday. These people were real. They lived in Eden. Viewers felt they had visited a fantastic place that made the Vietnam War vanish, that made the modern state vanish, that made the past ten thousand years of human progress (which seemed at times more like human decline) vanish.

The Tasaday were the antithesis of the Yanomamo Indians of South America, whom anthropologist Napoleon Chagnon made famous as the "fierce people," a group that supposedly preferred war to peace. The Tasaday seemed as close to our human ancestors as any group imaginable, the Stone Age come to life in the eyes of the world media, and what's more, if this group* represented who we had once been, then who we had *become*, a collection of squabbling, barbaric nations on the brink of nuclear devastation, was not a foregone conclusion.

When I tell the story of the Tasaday, I notice in some listeners an altogether different reaction to those innocents from mine at four-

---

*I use the term "group" instead of "tribe," itself a rather slippery term. To call the Tasaday a tribe is a misnomer. At best, they fit the term "band," which anthropologists use for small groups of hunter-gatherers.

teen. In some, I discern a glint of caution, a glimmer of knowing irony, that terrible affliction of the overeducated. They listen, not as though they want to fall backward, but tipped forward, expectant, as though ready to leap from their chairs to spout a punch line to a joke they've heard before.

After their "discovery," the Tasaday became, for a time, worldwide celebrities. Lobo graced the cover of *National Geographic* in one of the magazine's best-selling issues in its history. By 1972 camera crews had choppered in with dizzying frequency to the Tasaday's forest enclave, reporters sometimes outnumbering the small group of cave dwellers. Celebrities, famed aviator Charles Lindbergh and Italian actress Gina Lollobrigida, visited them as well.

I can usually expect a laugh when I come to this part. The names Charles Lindbergh and Gina Lollobrigida conjure up anything but the forest primeval, and here the ironists' antennae begin to quiver. The romantics in the audience feel uneasy at the thought of this human zoo.

Then, in 1976, after a few aborted scientific studies, Elizalde closed the forty-five-thousand-acre reserve President Marcos had set aside for the Tasaday. A presidential proclamation made trespassing into the area without permission punishable by deportation or prison. And no one received permission.

In 1986, as the corrupt Marcos government was toppled in one of the most uplifting and peaceful public revolts in history, a Swiss reporter, Oswald Iten, acting on a tip, hiked into the Tasaday Reserve unannounced in the company of a Filipino activist and reporter, Rizal "Joey" Lozano. With Lozano acting as his interpreter, several Tasaday reportedly told Iten that they had been coerced into pretending to be cavemen, that they were in fact farmers from a neighboring tribe, that they lived near Tasaday Mountain but that in fact no such group as the Tasaday existed. They posed in T-shirts and Levi's. Here usually several people in the audience laugh, as though the Tasaday had somehow betrayed themselves by appearing in garb other than leaves, other than what we would wish them to wear. Some audience members look vaguely alarmed, and I'm quick to point out that after fifteen years of acculturation, posing in Levi's proves nothing. While Iten rushed home to Switzerland to develop his photos and file his story, a pair of reporters from the German magazine *Stern* made the same trip as Iten and Lozano, but with an important difference. They hiked in accompanied by the Tasaday's original "discoverer," the hunter Dafal.

The same Tasaday dressed in Western attire Iten had met a week earlier had miraculously reverted to the "Stone Age" and now wore only leaves.

Obviously, this transformation showed that the Tasaday were a hoax. Much of the world reacted to Iten's scoop with the same zeal as they had twelve years earlier to the tribe's discovery. Of course, we too had changed quite a lot in those dozen years. In the wake of Watergate, we did not so easily believe what government officials told us. If the seventies had been a decade of hope, the dawning of the Age of Aquarius, the eighties were a decade of cynicism, and the idea that the Tasaday were nothing more than a Marcos ploy to put a good face on the Philippines in the wake of martial law seemed more than a little plausible.

A scientific conference at the University of the Philippines was hastily organized by hoax proponents, followed by a conference in 1988 in Zagreb, Yugoslavia (by all accounts a media circus), and finally the American Anthropological Association held a session on what was now a brewing controversy. Meanwhile the media followed apace. ABC's 20/20, Britain's Central TV, the BBC, and PBS all did documentaries on the Tasaday, some in support of the hoax proponents, others favoring those who claimed the Tasaday were "authentic," though the word "authentic" leads to the question, Authentic what? This book, then, is an investigation not only of the Tasaday controversy but of the language we use to describe others. The story of the Tasaday is as much about us (the industrialized world), who we perceive ourselves to be, as it is about a band of twenty-seven or so souls in the Philippines who became stand-ins for the world's hopes, dreams, and fears.

I became reacquainted with the Tasaday in May 1997, two weeks after the death of Elizalde. By the end of my initial research I wasn't sure what to believe. At times the people called Tasaday seemed the victims of a twisted man obsessed with the usual lures of fame, power, money, and sex. At other times they seemed victims of cynical journalists and academics. The more I investigated the Tasaday phenomenon, the more fascinated I became, even to the point of obsession, like so many others before me.

Inevitably, when I finish speaking about the Tasaday, someone always approaches me and asks, "So what was it? A hoax?"

The following is my answer.

2

Protector of the Primitive

Were man but constant, he be perfect.
　　　　　　　　　　—William Shakespeare, *Two Gentlemen from Verona*

he Philippines, at the time of Manuel Elizalde's birth, November 8, 1936, still retained more than a pinch of the feudal trappings the Spanish had created during their three-hundred-year occupation of their seven-thousand-island colony. The Spanish had been vanquished and then replaced by the Americans in 1898 after the Spanish-American War. The unsuspecting Filipino independence movement sided with America, thinking that America, founded on democratic principles, would help free them from the Spanish yoke. Instead, after the defeat of Spain and the ceding of the Philippines to America, a conscience-stricken U.S. Congress realized that Filipinos were not yet ready for the responsibilities of independence and desperately needed to be "Christianized" (though they were by this time overwhelmingly Catholic, apparently the wrong type of Christian). What followed was a protracted, bloody guerrilla war, a proto-Vietnam with altogether different results, a war for independence that the United States still refuses to call a war. The United States has never apologized for putting down this unlawful "insurrection," much to the continuing chagrin and dismay of many Filipinos.

Filipinos, who, like most long-oppressed peoples, have keen

9

senses of humor, sometimes characterize their occupations by first Spain and then the United States as spending three hundred years in a convent followed by fifty years in Hollywood. While few Filipinos speak Spanish now and increasingly few speak English—the official national language is Filipino*—Spanish and American cultures have left a considerable residue. Most Filipinos have Spanish last names, which were assigned by Spanish administrators in the nineteenth century, and these names do not reflect the ethnic makeup of their bearers.† Perhaps Spain's most striking legacy, Catholicism has long been the official religion of the Philippines, the only Asian nation with a majority of Christians and one of a handful of countries in which divorce is illegal. Economically, the Spanish left their imprint, too, in the form of hacienda culture, vast landholdings of an elite gentry, upon which tenant farmers struggle to eke a living. The Philippines has long been an oligarchy, controlled by the Roman Catholic Church, a few families, and a few corporations, such as Dole, whose landholdings make those of the wealthy hacienda owners look like forty acres and a mule.

Manda, as Elizalde was known, was the product of both of the Philippines' colonizers. His mother, Mary Cadwalader, was a Boston Brahmin, and his father, known as Don Manolo, was one of five brothers from the Basque region of Spain, one a diplomat, one a well-known conductor, one an alcoholic and a bit of a ne'er-do-well, one executed by the Japanese for his activities with the Manila underground, and Manolo, the businessman, all fanatical polo players, except for the conductor, who presumably couldn't afford to hurt his fingers.

The Elizaldes' vast business holdings included at various times rope manufacture, weapons, paint, rum, shipping, radio and newspapers, and if not for World War II, Manda perhaps would have grown up without ever knowing deprivation of any kind. Manolo and his wife and children, Manda, Freddy, and Mary Ruth, sat out the war in California and, after the defeat of the Japanese, returned to a Manila devastated by the fierce bombings by the Americans to recapture it

*A language based on Tagalog, the language of Manila.
†Commonly, Filipinos are said to be of Malay stock, but this is misleading. Prehistorically, Filipinos predated Malays by several thousand years. Migration was from the north to the south and east.

from the obstinate Japanese. When the war was over, hardly a building stood in the once-lovely city, known before the war as the Pearl of the Orient.

Don Manolo trained both his sons as sportsmen. Manda excelled at tennis and his younger brother, Freddy, at swimming. To Manolo, being a sportsman was not simply a matter of excelling in a sport. It also meant having a sportsmanlike attitude. One should be fiercely competitive, but compassionate toward one's defeated opponents. Above all, temper should be controlled. Don Manolo published an issue of a magazine in the early fifties as a kind of advertisement for the sports accomplishments of his sons. Mustachioed, eyes hidden by shades, mouth grimly set, Don Manolo graces the cover of the magazine *Sports Review*. The caption reads, "Sportsman Manolo Elizalde/ 'Give the kids a break!'" Ads for various Elizalde companies run throughout the journal: Yco Wax, Elizalde Rope Factory, Samar Mining, Tanduay Distillery, Manila Steamship Company, Metropolitan Insurance Company, La Carlota Sugar Central, Elizalde Paint and Oil Factory, and others. Manda figures prominently in photos throughout. In one, his head is cropped into the shape of a tennis ball, along with three other "Yco Entries" displayed on the mesh of an illustration of a tennis racket. The copy says: "At every tournament, sportsman Elizalde has always reminded his Yco contestants of the first commandment in tennis 'control of temper' and he now reminds contestants again that, 'A man who cannot command his temper can never become a man of tennis.'"[1]

That lesson would always be lost on Manda. Nearly anything could send him into a rage, and if you were the unfortunate recipient of his fury, not only would you receive a tongue-lashing, but you might well be beaten, or somehow abused, by either Manda or one of his ever-present goons.

Manda could be charming, gracious, and generous and then megalomaniacal, hot-tempered, malicious, and manipulative. Certainly, it didn't help that Don Manolo spoiled him and would never tolerate an ill word spoken about his favorite son. For a rich kid growing up in the 1950s, Manila presented few restrictions. You could order a drink as soon as you could see over the bar, and Manda early on developed a taste for scotch. By the time he left for Harvard he seemed headed for a profligate and dissipated life. He ran up traffic violations by the dozen for driving under the influence. He thought nothing of renting out a railway car for himself and his friends, and once he set fire to his books in a Harvard courtyard and ran off nearly naked through the snow with a security guard giving chase.[2]

After graduating in 1958, he circled the globe several times before finally settling back in the Philippines. Business did not suit him; he needed something that could provide him with the sense of adventure he sought, something grand. In 1964 he married a beautiful Spaniard named María del Carmen Martí. On their honeymoon on the island of Mindoro, the story goes, Manda and María came upon a "negrito boy" whose leg was mutilated. Manda carried the boy to their camp, then radioed for a nurse. This was the beginning of his "crusade." "I guess I suddenly found myself," he observed in a 1972 *Reader's Digest* article. "All those years I had been looking for something. Now I had the key." Using family money, Manda outfitted a yacht (much to the dismay of his father's business associates) with medical equipment and started making forays around the islands with medical personnel, treating, by his count, more than a million and a half people. But what was a playboy like Manda Elizalde doing traipsing around the jungles, fixing people's teeth and treating them for ringworm? There must be something in it for Manda, people thought; he never did anything selflessly, it seemed to his friends and acquaintances.

Eventually Manda attracted the attention of First Lady Imelda Marcos and, through her, Ferdinand Marcos, who on August 10, 1967, appointed Manda presidential adviser on national minorities. The post was subsequently elevated to cabinet rank, and on December 17, 1968, Manda was appointed presidential assistant on national minorities (PANAMIN). At the same time, Manda created a private foundation, also called PANAMIN, but standing for, in this case, Private Assistance for National Minorities. PANAMIN now existed as two entities, first as a private foundation and second as a government body, with Manda at the helm of both.

At home in Manila in elite Forbes Park and in PANAMIN headquarters (a historic mansion, formerly General MacArthur's headquarters), he filled the rooms with tribespeople, many of whom were children he "adopted" from the various ethnolinguistic groups of the Philippines. He also funded the education of many boys and girls from these groups. Other tribal people performed dances for Manda's wealthy friends at elaborate parties called *ati-atihan*. Manda at the time lived adjacent to the Manila Polo Club, and his neighbors did not share his appreciation of tribal people. When Manda's native guests started shooting arrows at the polo horses, Manda was asked to move or to get rid of his houseguests. He chose to move. His guards wrecked the mansion, which he had rented, as Manda and his entourage picked up stakes. Only reluctantly, on the urging of his right-hand man, Vince Revilla, did he pay damages.

If you wanted to see Manda, you went to his new mansion in the fashionable White Plains district of Quezon City. He slept most of the day and operated at night, so if he could meet you at 11:00 p.m., that was when you met him. When Manda walked by, the people he kept at his house, forced to wear "authentic" garb, would bow to him or kiss his hand, and the sea would part. "If you sit inside those walls at White Plains long enough," a friend recalls, "and people are kissing your feet, I guess you start to believe it." After Elvis Presley died, Manda announced, "I'm just like Elvis Presley, kind of a magical person."[3]

Jim Turner, an American who has lived in the Philippines since the early sixties, worked for Manda's brother, Freddy, and regularly visited White Plains on business. Once he was kept waiting there for four or five hours. At one point a native man in a tribal G-string strolled over and said, "Can you tell me where I am?" Manda had plucked him from his place in the mountains and brought him to Manila. Turner told him how to get to the road where he could catch a cab, but he doubted anyone would pick up someone dressed in tribal garb. Turner gave the man some money as well as directions to the bar Turner owned. A couple of days later the man showed up, dressed in street clothes and with a companion in tow. Turner gave them both money for a trip back to their home province.

During this time Manda's drinking grew worse, and his marriage, which gave him two sons and a daughter, crumbled. His drinking got so bad in the sixties that he developed delirium tremens and had to be hospitalized. His doctor told him to swear off drinking, which he did, switching to prodigious amounts of soda instead. Before, he'd have bottles of scotch airlifted to him in the jungle; now cases of soda borne by porters followed him into the deepest jungle. From then on his code name in radio transmissions was SODA.

A 1972 *Reader's Digest* article gushed that Manda was a champion of the underprivileged: "Manda Elizalde has achieved staggering results. Yet, being a realist, he accepts that PANAMIN still stands at the 'end of the beginning.' 'We still have an awfully long way to go. Our needs sometimes seem infinite,' he says. But, intense and passionately committed, Manuel Elizalde, Jr., will not rest until his awesome mission is accomplished."[4]

The previous year *National Geographic* had also featured him in a laudatory article titled "Help for the Philippine Tribes in Trouble." The truth was that the Philippine tribes *were* in trouble. A Catholic priest and longtime resident of Mindanao told me in 1999 that in the mid-sixties some members of the Philippine Congress, fearful of Elizalde's power and intentions, had approached a prominent bishop to help the tribal communities, but the bishop had declined, believing that the church needed first to help the lowlanders moving into Mindanao. Into this void, the priest told me regretfully, Elizalde had stepped, and he had been a disaster.

In the late sixties and early seventies, Mindanao, the second-largest island in the Philippines, had the well-earned reputation as the wild, wild south. It was rich in natural resources and less populated than the northern islands of the country. Settlers were invited by the government to help "civilize" Mindanao after World War II. But the island contained a volatile mix of peoples and a history of unrest that only worsened as the settlers moved in. The Mindanao coasts were lined with communities that had been converted to Islam long before their northern neighbors had known Christianity. The Muslims, or Moros, as the Spanish called them, had a reputation as fierce and implacable warriors, who had never been vanquished, not by the Spanish, not by the Americans, not by the Japanese. When Elizalde came on the scene, the Muslims had a new enemy, the Ilagas (Rats), a group of marauding settlers largely from the Visayan region of the Philippines who were engaged in a vicious take-no-prisoners war with the Muslims and other ethnic minorities.

A 1972 PANAMIN pamphlet states that four million Filipinos belonged to some "60 ethnolinguistic groups considered 'national minority groups.' "[5] Quite a number of them lived in Mindanao; among them were the T'boli, the Manobo, the B'laan, the Ubu, the Mandaya, the Mamanwa, and the Higaonon.* As land-grabbing settlers as well as miners and loggers moved in, the tribes retreated to the highlands. Even there they found no safety; if they resisted those who wanted their lands, their houses were burned, their families murdered. In one instance a Higaonon chief, Datu' Manpatilan,† had hidden in the forest for two years after he killed several lumbermen who had raped and killed his granddaughter and niece, shot his son, and killed another boy. Elizalde persuaded him to surrender to President Marcos and flew him to Manila, where Marcos heard his story and was moved to grant him amnesty. In another case the Ubu chief Ma Falen had resisted the lowland settlers, and one day in 1970 a group of lowlanders attacked his ridgetop settlement with rifles and machine guns. The Ubu, using homemade rifles and spears, were able at first to beat back their attackers, though Ma Falen's eldest and favorite daughter, Kining, was mortally wounded. The girl's mother, sobbing, begged Elizalde for justice as she recounted holding the girl's shattered body. John Nance, who became the chronicler of the Tasaday in the early days, describes in his 1975 best-seller *The Gentle Tasaday* a stricken Elizalde listening to the girl's brokenhearted mother: "Ye Elen's voice broke with sobs as she recounted the story. Then she tearfully pushed the slain girl's rings onto Elizalde's fingers. 'Tao Bong' [Good Man], she said. 'Wear her rings . . . you must wear them always. Remember Kining. Remember . . . and tell your world that justice belongs also to the innocent.' Elizalde pulled the sobbing Ye Elen against himself and kissed her hair. 'I won't forget. Tell her . . . Tell her I won't forget.' "[6]

The central Philippine government at the time was more or less powerless in the south. Manila is a long way off from Mindanao, and the tribes had not only the Ilaga and miners and loggers to contend with but also a mounting Muslim insurgency pressing for an inde-

*For more up-to-date information, see the Philippines section of The Ethnologue (*www.ethnologue.com*), which lists 170 separate languages.
†When *datu* is part of a name, as in Datu' Manpatilan, it is best represented as Datu', but when it's written in an English sentence, such as "He was a *datu*," the mark is omitted, according to Lawrence Reid.

pendent Muslim state led by the Moro National Liberation Front (MNLF) and a Communist insurgency led by the New People's Army (NPA).

In response, Elizalde began to arm a small PANAMIN militia that escorted him on his jungle forays and medical missions. The words *Tao Bong* were emblazoned on the side of his helicopter. Once, when Manda's helicopter landed in the hills, he was disappointed by the lackluster reception, so he told the few people on hand that he would leave for an hour and he expected a proper reception on his return. If they wanted his favor—meaning food, medicine, and, in many cases, weapons—they had to comply. When the helicopter landed again an hour later, a crowd had formed, and they carried him off on their shoulders.

Perhaps Manda's most favored tribe was the T'boli, who live near the shores of Lake Sebu and on high mountain ridges. Very few tribes in the Philippines or elsewhere can compete with the T'boli in terms of artistry and material culture. For ceremonial occasions they wear colorful costumes woven from bark. They are highly skilled at making brass, and the women adorn themselves with brass earrings and bangles and most notably heavy brass belts festooned with hundreds of bells that ring as they walk to scare away evil spirits. T'boli traditionally prefer horse fighting to cockfighting, a more ubiquitous Filipino sport, and you can consider yourself lucky to witness T'boli dancers on a hilltop enclave dancing to a rhythm drummed on an overturned Clorox bottle.

Mostly the T'boli lived in solitary huts until PANAMIN's arrival. PANAMIN gathered them, as they did other tribes, into collective service centers, partly to protect the traditionally scattered tribe against Ilagas and other marauders and partly to enable such social services as food, medicine, and education to be more evenly distributed. But the service centers concentrated disease and also had the effect of creating reservations from which the tribes could be more easily controlled by the central government, a boon for Marcos.

For a Marcos crony, life was a withdrawal slip. Take Manda's tin-plating plant (Elisteel) for instance, which the government bought from him (for 1.4 billion pesos) for no reason except that it wasn't doing well.[7] Or Manda's armament plant, licensed by Colt, which had a locked-in deal with the military. Says one associate: "He told me at the time, I think they were making assault rifles, 'We got all the plans, so we don't need Colt anymore.' So they dumped Colt."[8] And then turned around and sold guns to Indonesia, a deal to which Colt had objected.

Despite what the priest had told me, Manda had not stepped into a vacuum when he arrived in Mindanao. The Catholic Church, in the person of an American priest, Father Rex Mansmann, of the mission at Lake Sebu, already had a foothold among the T'boli, and Father Rex resented and feared Manda's intrusion. Manda had little but contempt for the church, and he and Father Rex clashed for the next twenty years.

Another power broker in southern Mindanao was Mayor Joe Sison of Surallah, whose interests lay squarely with Christian settlers and loggers. Mayor Sison loathed Manda and tried to kill him on many occasions.

If Manda had a number of enemies, he had powerful friends in equal measure. In the late sixties he had befriended famed aviator Charles Lindbergh, who, now in his seventies, had become interested in the Philippines. Lindbergh, like Manda, was a man of contradictions, famous first for his solo flight across the Atlantic, then infamous for his anti-Semitism and his efforts with the America First organization to ally the United States with Nazi Germany, and now, late in his life, known as a conservationist. Drawing worldwide attention to the endangered tamaraw and the monkey-eating eagle, Lindbergh struck up a friendship with Manda based on their mutual concerns. Manda gave him a brief tour of some of the tribal settlements throughout the country, and in 1969 Lindbergh rented a plane and flew anthropologist Robert Fox to northern Luzon, where the pair lived among the Agta tribe, sleeping on the beach in a lean-to. While there, Lindbergh learned of the Agta's plight, which was the plight of most, if not all, tribal Filipinos: Their land was being stolen out from under them. In 1970, Lindbergh lived with other tribes, this time bringing with him *New York Times* reporter Alden Whitman. As A. Scott Berg writes in his biography of Lindbergh, the war against the tribal peoples of the Philippines wasn't only a war of land-grabbing but a cultural war as well, "a war of shame" in which the ethnic minorities were taught that everything about them was ugly and without value. "Elizalde's policy," Berg says, "was to encourage the tribes to

LIBRARY
THE UNIVERSITY OF TEXAS
AT BROWNSVILLE
Brownsville, Tx 78520-4991

partake in legal services if they wished to remain separate from the rest of the country or in social services if they wished to assimilate."[9] Lindbergh agreed with Manda's policies and joined the board of the PANAMIN Foundation, adding international luster to Manda's efforts. In June 1970, Lindbergh, traveling in Mindanao with Manda and his men, found himself surrounded by a hundred of Mayor Sison's men who stopped Manda's bus. A tense standoff ensued, Manda grasping his pearl-handled revolver and Lindbergh at the ready with a submachine gun.* But no one fired that night, and the bus was finally allowed to proceed.

Manda also gathered allies among the tribes. One young man named Mai Tuan particularly caught his attention. A T'boli, Mai had been educated with his brothers, Fludi, Yani, and Dad, by missionaries, and when Manda met him, Mai was helping a group of Protestant missionaries from the Summer Institute of Linguistics (SIL) translate the New Testament into T'boli. Manda offered Mai what seemed like a better deal: In exchange for Mai's help in advancing PANAMIN projects among the T'boli, Manda would help make Mai a rich man, a world traveler, and an undisputed leader among his people. Manda and Mai made a powerful team. Manda gave Mai and his people rifles, and they provided security for him as he traveled Mindanao's dangerous roads or flew in low among the trees to some distant mountain outpost where trouble brewed among the different peoples.

Mai was a short man, but imposing in his own way. A winning smile showed through his beard and mustache, and though his voice was high-pitched, he spoke with passion and intensity. But Manda was a true orator. Even when he spoke in English or Tagalog and his audience couldn't understand him, he mesmerized the crowd, preaching self-determination.

The national policy toward the tribal minorities before Manda and PANAMIN had integration into the larger society as its aim, but Manda said he wanted the tribes to have a choice: integration, if that

---

*This episode is described in greater detail in The Gentle Tasaday, as well as in Scott Berg's Lindbergh.

was what they wanted, or the preservation of their land, their resources, and their customs. He wanted, above all, the tribes to feel pride in their traditions and to resist being bulldozed, literally and figuratively, by the larger society. This message found receptive audiences among the minorities. Manda praised his listeners, but he also chastised them for surrendering too easily. Unfortunately, Manda's rhetoric of tribal pride often transformed into a kind of enforced primitivism.

Manda fetishized primitivism, and he insisted that tribal people conform to his vision of them. Not only were houses bulldozed in PANAMIN reserves that weren't "native" enough, but if the minorities wanted his help, then they had to dress like minorities. A church report of the time by Father John Doherty explains: "Dole-outs of medicine, food (canned goods) and clothing characterized these visits. Hordes queued up to receive gifts. But Elizalde's orders were that only natives, scantily-clad or attired in tribal wear, would be eligible for the presents. Full-clothed or lowland-attired natives were rejected, or forced to remove their clothing. 'Of course,' [a former PANAMIN employee reported], 'many people got wise. Even if you weren't a native, as long as you looked like one, you got the goodies.' "[10]

PANAMIN was a pyramid-shaped organization with little in the way of self-determination for the people whose interests Elizalde was supposed to serve. The church report remarks: "PANAMIN's actual practices contradict its stated objectives. It claims to promote the dignity of the tribes and help them cultivate pride in being themselves, and yet PANAMIN's policy of top-to-bottom planning stifles the natives' freedom and ability to participate in decisions. They are treated like wards . . . and PANAMIN assumes the role of paternalistic *datu* [chief]."[11]

In some cases, natives were hardly given a choice about the reserves but were threatened and cajoled into moving onto them. When one reserve was established in Simod, Manobo "living outside the area complained that PANAMIN people threatened to have them declared as 'rebeldes' and driven out of the area, unless they joined PANAMIN."[12] While the ethnic minorities were certainly losing their land at an alarming rate to settlers and agribusiness alike, the reserves were an imperfect solution at best and sometimes had the effect of benefiting large agribusinesses more than the tribes. One anonymous

regional PANAMIN official remarked: "A reservation is the only answer to the land problem. The tribes will be forced to give up their
nomadic ways. That way, too, they will no longer be considered squat-
ters [on agribusiness land]. It's really very hard to deal with companies
and big corporations. Our only answer is to compromise. We resettle
the natives in reservation land which we manage for the natives. From
then on, any company who is interested in the land deals with us."[13]
In effect, what this meant for many tribal people living on some
PANAMIN reserves was that they would become peasants, working
for a feudal master, whether PANAMIN or a nearby agribusiness.

But Elizalde's concern for tribal traditions went only so far. Where
his libido was concerned, he trampled on traditional tribal modesty. In
1983 the London-based Anti-Slavery Society, documenting the Marcos regime's various abuses, recounted a story of Manda in the mountains asking two teenage girls to dance topless for him and then
offering the parents of one girl 1,250 pesos, an enormous sum, to bed
her. When the parents refused, he burned the money in front of
them.[14]

Manda collected women much as he collected tribal people. Some
were from indigenous tribes; others came from Spain or the United
States. A friend of his from college would "procure" these women,
mainly small-town beauty queens, from far and wide. He'd gather
them, about ten or so, and bring them over. Manda placed them in
luxury hotels around Manila, the Mandarin and the Penn, and had
them delivered (that's probably the most accurate word) to White
Plains as needed. Some who had been lured to Manila with promises
of modeling and acting jobs hadn't bargained that part of the deal involved sleeping with the boss.

"We kept our distance from him," said a pastor from the mountainous Cordillera Region. "He was rotten to the core. A vicious dunce."
Elizalde, the pastor said, didn't dare go to the Cordillera because people there had taken vows to kill him. "He tried to rape the sister of one
of my friends," the pastor claimed. The young woman was one of
Manda's "scholars." One evening Manda sent a driver to pick her up,
and when he "made his proposal," she said, "If you want your face to
look like anything in the morning, you won't touch me." She opened
her fist and showed him her long fingernails. Manda backed down, but
he told her not to tell anyone. "My helicopters know where your parents are, and you'll never see them again if you do."

To the tribes Manda appeared larger than life, as he did to the foreign press and to the throng of reporters who eagerly tagged along as he landed on a burning hillside, negotiated the surrender of a bandit, transported a bullet-riddled patient to a clinic, or peered out the darkened window of a bus, tightly grasping his pearl-handled revolver. Manda made good copy. Young, curly-haired, with moody good looks, a yachting cap perched on his head, he had the world press infatuated; almost no one wrote a critical word. But as he garnered attention outside and inside his country, inevitable jealousies emerged; Manda's affection was haphazard and capricious. To some he gave great amounts of assistance and money. To others he gave less or nothing. And while he traipsed around down south, the rumor mills of Manila churned busily. What was he up to? What were his true motives? Was he trying to stake mining claims on tribal lands in the guise of helping the tribes?

For some, talking about Elizalde is like a wake or an exorcism. Among the misdeeds recounted to me were that he had looted his sister Mary Ruth's money, attempted to bribe a geologist at the North Davao Mining Company, roasted a T'boli man alive in an oil drum, stolen jewelry from his mother on her deathbed, intentionally torched one of his yachts and the PANAMIN offices, smuggled jewels, committed his wife to a mental hospital so he could get custody of the children, and run guns to Indonesia.

Of Manda's motives, Lindbergh said: "I think he's an extraordinary person. And I'll tell you, I think you've got to be very careful, *very careful*, about looking into motives. Why does anyone do anything? If you ask too many questions about this, you begin to be compelled to find an answer, produce one—whether it's the right one or not. But it's very rare that you can accurately say what is going on inside another person. I have my own ideas, of course, but I don't *know* what motivates Manda. And it doesn't really concern me much. What does concern me is the kind of job he does. And I think he does an excellent job. Yes, I have no doubt, an excellent job."[15]

3

The Center for Short-Lived Phenomena

[T]heir *history* as a people begins with our visit on June 7, 1971.
—Manuel Elizalde, Jr.

umors of a group of wild people living in the rain forest to the east of the mountain village of Blit had been reaching Elizalde and his staff for a year. Sometimes, while out hunting, villagers caught fleeting glimpses or came across sites where *natek*, a starch extracted from the pith of the caryota palm, had been prepared or where animals had been butchered. No one had gone deeper into the forest than the hunter Dafal, who was said to walk "through the forest like the wind." A scrawny little man with jutting features and pop eyes, Dafal enjoyed telling stories and exaggerating, but he insisted when he spoke to Elizalde that he knew some wild people whom he'd run across while hunting. He'd traded with them, taught them how to smoke meat and set traps, given them little scraps of cloth (they were virtually naked) and brass earrings and bolo knives. He had stayed with them a few nights and called them Tasaday. He insisted they'd had no agriculture, no cloth, and no metal tools when he first contacted them, and they hadn't even known how to hunt.

In late May 1971, Elizalde made plans to try to survey by helicopter the mountains of the Blit region, partly to plan a PANAMIN development project for the area and partly to see if contact could be made with the forest people of whom Dafal had spoken. Dafal volunteered to try to reach these people and assemble them, if possible, at a clearing where a helicopter could land. While the rain forests of southern Mindanao do not come close to the immensity of the Amazon, in 1971 the forests still seemed formidable and expansive. Visitors surveying them by helicopter were awed by mile upon mile of unbroken forest canopy. But loggers owned "concessions" throughout the area, and the rain forest was rapidly shrinking.*

A week after he went into the forest Dafal returned to report that the group was willing to meet Elizalde.

In early June† a helicopter transported Elizalde and PANAMIN staffers, including bodyguards, to the clearing that had been made near the edge of the forest. Four men emerged from the trees and shivered in the windy wake of the chopper blades.

To Elizalde, the group seemed timid and terrified and responded hesitantly to the many questions of a local tribeswoman named Igna, whom Elizalde had brought along to serve as translator. Elizalde thought they might simply be some ragtag group planning an ambush.[1] They did, after all, have bows and arrows.

Elizalde gave them grains of rice, which they put in their mouths raw and spit out. Fearful of sugar and salt, one man asked, "Perhaps it is poisonous?"[2]

During that afternoon and on the following day, twenty other members of the group, now including women and children, visited the clearing. It was difficult to extract information from them at first. Igna estimated that she understood "less than half" their responses. First, the Tasaday would say something, which Igna with Mai Tuan's help would translate into Blit Manobo or Tagalog and then into English as best she could. (Dafal didn't have the patience or interest in translation work.)

They talked about the *fugu*, a sickness some of them had memo-

---

*Between 1962 and 1968, when the Philippine government conducted a national forest inventory, 91,564 hectares of forest disappeared annually, and by 1980 only 20 to 40 percent of the provinces of South Cotabato and Sultan Kudarat remained forested.
†Elizalde kept poor records at first. He reported June 7 as the date he met the Tasaday, but it has also been reported as June 4. Some say the meeting never happened at all.

ries of, and Elizalde speculated that perhaps this helped explain why there were so few old people among them and why they were so afraid of outsiders. He later explained, "When they were questioned about what they fear the most, it was not evil spirits, even the inexplicable aircraft which they see flying over their forest domain, but *fugu* or epidemic sickness."[3] A cholera plague was at the time sweeping Asia, Elizalde noted, and could wipe out the Tasaday if they came into contact with it.

Among the Tasaday there was one elderly couple who were deaf and mute and an albino child with so many sores on his body that no one had much doubt he would eventually die. Manda had brought along a doctor, Doc Rebong, to attend to their ailments, but for the most part they seemed remarkably healthy.

A young man of about twenty named Belayem stood out. He wanted a wife and asked Elizalde for his help. Elizalde later explained: "[Belayem] expressed great fears about his future role as a husband and father. According to him, there were no marriageable young women among the Tasaday. On our first visit, we suggested jokingly that we would help him find a wife something to the effect of, 'If we run across any forest maidens, we'll let you know.' "[4]

Elizalde and Mai Tuan discussed the group at length that night. Mai Tuan said the T'boli had never heard of the Tasaday and "they agreed the Tasaday were unique and possibly very significant."[5]

The next day Elizalde excitedly wired Robert Fox, a fifty-three-year-old American anthropologist from the National Museum and head of PANAMIN's research department. Fox, a longtime resident of the Philippines, was one of the country's most respected anthropologists. He had worked on a variety of important projects over the years, from forensic identification of World War II remains in the 1950s to more recent excavations of the Tabon Caves in Palawan. A hard drinker (Manda airlifted cases of scotch into the jungle for him), he was an equally hard worker.

Elizalde waited impatiently for a response and finally heard back not from Fox but from an unnamed associate at the National Museum.[6] "Technically, there is no such thing as a lost tribe but only more isolated than other known tribes," the message began in a reasonable tone. The staff member went on to suggest extensive interviews with the Tasaday and comparative studies with other tribes. Fox replied later that same day in a somewhat more excited fashion: "New group of great importance anthropologically. Have been expecting that you and chopper would find such group. Lost tribe simply means new tribe. If they are truly food gatherers with no agriculture among world's rarest people."[7]

After starting his message by saying that a lost tribe meant a new group, Fox was using a similar term, "lost groups," by the end of the message and stating that such groups were extremely important to the modern world. He wondered too if they were without agriculture, what the extent of their foraging was, whether they used stone tools, whether they lived in caves. This tribe was a tantalizing discovery, something akin perhaps to the twenty-two-thousand-year-old* culture he'd been excavating at the Tabon Caves on the island of Palawan.[8]

As it happened, *National Geographic* had been filming a special on Manda and PANAMIN in the main T'boli settlement. Before Fox or any other anthropologists had arrived, Manda fetched the crew to film the Tasaday.

Robert Fox arrived on the sixteenth and spent two days with the Tasaday. He started compiling a genealogy of the twenty-four Tasaday and a word list. The group consisted of four married couples, one widower, the bachelor Belayem, and fourteen children. The largest family was that of Bilengan and his wife, Etut, and their four sons. The Tasaday indicated that two other forest groups of which they spoke, the Tasafeng and the Sanduka, were slighter larger in number, but it had been some time since anyone had seen them.

Such encounters as Elizalde and Fox had with the Tasaday were rare but common enough that the Smithsonian Institution had created an organization with the fanciful title the Center for Short-Lived Phenomena, the short-lived phenomenon in this case being the world's ever-shrinking and marginalized hunter-gatherers.

The Elizalde-Fox report to the Center for Short-Lived Phenomena was based on only two brief contacts with the Tasaday, but even so, it made bold claims about the group. There were good reasons to rush the report. Elizalde and Fox thought the group needed protection. "The initial contacts with the Tasaday dramatically illustrate the deep moral and humanistic commitments which PANAMIN has to the mi-

*According to C14 dating of a skull fragment in the cave.

nority people of the Philippines and now to the Tasaday, for the survival of these singularly unique people is being threatened by plans of loggers to drive roads into their great forest sanctuary."[9] From the air, one could see logging roads pushing ever closer to the domain of this small group.

The report floated some tentative theories about who the Tasaday were and where they'd come from. The first theory was that they'd simply broken off from a larger Manobo group relatively recently, fleeing an epidemic. The second theory, which they favored, claimed the Tasaday were a splinter from a much older proto-Manobo group and retained many of its characteristics. If this was true, the report claimed, then one could learn something about how the early Filipinos lived. It's not difficult to see why they liked this theory, though there was little to base it upon except the beginnings of a word list, the stone tools, and a few days of observation.

If Elizalde and Fox thought that such groups as the Tasaday could provide a window into the past, they were not alone. In 1965 the Origin of Man Conference convened at the University of Chicago, and the next year the Man the Hunter Conference was its logical follow-up, bringing together for the first time the leading anthropologists whose specialties were the small-scale societies around the world that still lived, at least partly, by hunting and foraging as our ancestors had ten thousand years ago.

Prior to Man the Hunter, our ancestors were said to have lived lives that were "nasty, brutish and short" in the words of Thomas Hobbes. Now anthropologist Marshall Sahlins proposed a new model, the original affluent society. This paradigm dominated the field for the next two decades.

Sahlins argued that we cannot judge Paleolithic man by our own standards of affluence. If we define affluence instead by the number of hours one spends in food production in relation to one's hours of leisure time, many hunter-gatherer societies are better off than we. Modern man, he said, stands "sentenced to a life at hard labor. It is from this anxious vantage that we look back on the hunter . . . having equipped the hunter with bourgeois impulses and Paleolithic tools, we judge his situation hopeless in advance."[10] Far from nasty, brutish, and short, hunters and gatherers "had it made." Instead of the endless pursuit of large TVs, cars, and houses, the hunter-gatherer spent several hours in food production and the rest sleeping or enjoying his life in other ways.

The Tasaday seemed to fit the Sahlins model perfectly, a peaceful life without worry or want. With the excitement of treasure hunters who've stumbled upon a gold-laden galleon, Elizalde and Fox described the "factors" that made the Tasaday of "such great importance in reconstructing early Filipino cultures." The Tasaday retained "ancient behavior, beliefs and tools." They had lived in "geographical and social isolation over a considerable span of time." They lived a "life based on food gathering and trapping in a forest environment with only very primitive tools of stone and bamboo." Moreover, their "linguistic differences" indicated the "Tasaday have been separated from other peoples for a great length of time. It is not possible with the data available to state when this separation took place, but it was certainly not during this century and probably not within Spanish times, that is, within the past 400–500 years. One is tempted to argue that the Tasaday are the actual descendants of a people using only stone tools, and that their separation took place some 1500–2000 years ago."[11]

Elizalde immediately recognized the Tasaday's dramatic potential: Here was a group that had lived in complete isolation, a lost tribe threatened by loggers in a diminishing rain forest. If handled right, they could become poster children for other tribal minorities in the Philippines. The Tasaday held "great potential—as subjects of scientific study, as a means of dramatizing the cultural minorities of the Philippines and their problems, and as a way of publicizing the work of PANAMIN and its personnel."[12] Elizalde's list, it later turned out, placed the ranking of their importance to him in reverse order.

Whatever belied their primitiveness was conveniently set aside. If one examines the photos and statements of how the Tasaday appeared when contacted by Elizalde, they seem not so unusual. The women "wore only faded cloth wrapped around their hips. Brass rings dangled from their ears."[13] In the December 1971 issue of the *National Geographic*, photos of the Tasaday appeared under the heading "First Glimpse of a Stone Age Tribe," presumably from that first meeting. In the photos the Tasaday look strategically arranged to hide their clothing, young children standing in front of their squatting parents or cradled in their parents' arms. To the inexperienced eye, they look "primitive." In one photo a woman sits apparently naked, playing with a monkey's skull for the amusement of the toddler in her lap. On the opposite page a Tasaday man plays a mouth harp (made of cultivated bamboo and cut with metal).

But these discrepancies were easily explained. Before Dafal met them, Elizalde claimed, the Tasaday had none of the accouterments of Metal Age culture. Dafal brought them everything and taught them everything. And so their anthropological significance depended on one thing primarily, belief. You had to believe Dafal first of all, and you had to believe the Tasaday.

And you had, above all, to believe Elizalde.

4

Message from the Stone Age

I intended no harm, would tread carefully, respect their sensibilities, seek truth, serve the public interest. . . . But as the Tasaday became people with names, faces, feelings, it all became more complicated.
—John Nance, *The Gentle Tasaday*

lmost thirty years later the Portland, Oregon, Art Museum sponsored an exhibit of John Nance's Tasaday photographs. Actually, it wasn't at the art museum per se, as Nance had told me, but in a small gallery at the adjoining Pacific Northwest College of Art. Nance was a tall, pale man with rugged features and an attitude that was by turns intense, earnest, and sometimes supercilious when angered or exasperated. In his sixties, he was still lean and energetic, almost bursting with nervous energy. No one else was at the gallery, and he left the room to let me examine the photos alone. The small exhibition was titled "Survival of the Tasaday." A placard read: "About this exhibit: these photographs are arranged chronologically from 1971 to 1997 and run counterclockwise from this point around the room. The pictures offer a glimpse of the Tasaday, a people of Mindanao, Philippines, over their first quarter century of contact with the modern world."

Nance is the person most associated with the Tasaday, even more so than Elizalde, though it was Elizalde who gave him access to the group. And it was Nance's association with Manda that eventually tainted his career. But it's Nance's original account in *The Gentle Tasaday* that we must rely on for much of our understanding of the outside world's early infatuation with the group. Virtually no one had more frequent contact with them. A former Associated Press photographer and bureau chief, Nance gave up his livelihood to become a devotee of the Tasaday and their main chronicler.

Nance was a professional photographer, and the photos, especially the early ones, depicting what seemed like an idyllic existence, were nothing if not alluring: The Tasaday man Udelen sat in a mountain stream as water cascaded off his body; children climbed trees and swung on vines. Young Lobo, son of Bilengan, played with a pet bird. Udelen tied a vine to a butterfly as a leash for his son to hold, and Lobo looked for nectar in a flower's petals.

The accompanying text mentioned the controversy surrounding the Tasaday, but this was John Nance's show, and here his version of events prevailed: "In June of 1971, this small group, less than 30 persons, was dying out and began a struggle for survival that would take them from a Stone Age style of life in an ancient tropical rain forest to the law courts of metropolitan Manila and home again to a new way of being." A photo showed Elizalde with several Tasaday children all looking up. Five children crouched with him, looking at a helicopter about to arrive.

I gravitated to the book of guest comments and flipped through its pages to see what impact this exhibit had on the people who viewed it.

Excellent sequence. The first two walls blow you away. Then civilization hits. But let's be hopeful, though. Really a wonderful experience.

Interesting. Glad to see the Tasaday were not portrayed as "the Noble Savage," trying to ward off Westernization.

What a heart Elizalde had for these people. I love the smiles on the Tasaday people. So beautiful. Much appreciation.

If one were to see just this exhibit, the evidence for the group's "authenticity" would seem almost incontrovertible. Only three comments were not positive.

Survival?

Believers have become the takers corrupted by the takers.

This whole exhibition is a hoax covering up a larger hoax.

Nance pointed out this last person didn't even sign the register. I had the feeling John might have phoned the person to argue if the comment had been signed. Time and again Nance had doggedly tracked down his detractors, traveling half the globe when necessary to counter the arguments of those who would label the Tasaday "fake."

In a glass case near the entrance to the exhibit, Nance had arranged various documents attesting to the veracity of his claims: *Tasaday* by Carlos Fernandez and Frank Lynch; *Further Studies on the Tasaday* by Douglas Yen and John Nance; *Lobo of the Tasaday: A Stone Age Boy Meets the Modern World*, written and photographed by John Nance; and *The Gentle Tasaday* and *Discovery of the Tasaday, a Photo Novel* by John Nance.

The materials in this case include some of the key documentation of the Tasaday and their experiences of the 1970's when they first met modern society. . . . Included in the case also is an issue of last month's January '98 *Reader's Digest* and a copy of its article entitled, "The Greatest Hoaxes of All Time." In it, the Tasaday are described as a naked lie about which "most anthropologists do not dispute the Tasaday's cave life, limited diet, and isolation were all falsified." The author of the article, Michael Farquahar, said in a recent phone conversation that he had read that the Tasaday were a hoax in "several books," but he could not recall the names of the books. Asked whom he had spoken to about the Tasaday, he said, "Nobody . . . just the books."

Actually, Farquahar *did* have a source other than the books, but he wasn't going to divulge this person's name, certainly not to Nance.

In early July 1971, something small caught John Nance's attention. It was a tiny article buried on page 14 of the *Manila Daily Mirror* and headlined: LOST TRIBE FOUND IN C'BATO. "Ostensibly described as food gatherers and trappers, the so-called 'lost tribe' of Tasaday Manobo has puzzled anthropologists for having survived in that forbidding forest area with virtually no contact with the outside world."[1] Elizalde was quoted in the article as saying that the tribe still used stone tools and their discovery was "of great scientific interest."[2]

Nance wondered why with Manila's abundance of news sources (there were no fewer than sixteen daily papers) no one else had reported the story. And why was the story buried on page 14? Nance had traveled to the area the year before with Elizalde and knew something of its dense jungles and mountains, but a lost tribe discovered only "a few miles inland from the Celebes Sea" and fifty miles from the town of Surallah?

Before he ever heard of the Tasaday, John Nance made his career as a reporter in Vietnam with the Associated Press. In Peter Arnett's autobiography, *Live from the Battlefield*, he writes of Nance's experience: "AP photographer John Nance was stumbling through the sticky mud of rice paddies along the Saigon River with First Infantry Division troops when mortar shells slapped in among them, creasing him on the arm and sending him sprawling as a machine gun opened up on the patrol, killing several soldiers around him. Nance had placed his heavy metal camera case on the paddy dike for added protection and a Vietcong gunner apparently thought it was important because he kept firing at it, six bullets bursting through the metal and over Nance's head, which was pressed for safety into the warm mud."[3]

Fed up with the war, his wife eight months pregnant, Nance decided he'd had enough close calls, seen enough of his friends die. The AP created a job for him in Hong Kong, and he became a kind of roving reporter. Three days after his wife gave birth, the AP sent him to Singapore to cover the shah of Iran's visit, then up to Bangkok, and then he was asked to "spell" someone in Vietnam. So he and Peter Arnett caught a plane to Saigon, which turned out to be the last commercial plane in or out of the city for some time. Arnett, Nick Ut, Nance, and several other well-known Vietnam reporters were playing cards when someone burst into the room and told them to get to the embassy quick. The Vietcong had launched a full-scale surprise attack on the South over the Vietnamese holiday known as Tet. During the Tet offensive, ten thousand Vietcong fanned out across Saigon, and a force of nineteen captured the grounds of the U.S. Embassy and held it for six hours, after surprising and killing a number of embassy guards.

Hurrying to the embassy, Nance and Arnett discovered a bullet-ridden car in the middle of the street, its driver dead inside. Hiding behind the car, Nance was driven back by gunfire, but he returned again as U.S. soldiers stormed the embassy, grenades exploding, automatic weapons firing.

The Tet offensive reinforced Nance's weariness and disillusionment with his work. The job he'd wanted, being a roving reporter and photographer based in Hong Kong, traveling around—none of it seemed so great anymore. Every time someone wanted a leave of absence, grew ill, got wounded, he knew he'd be tapped.

"I realize this isn't in your game plan," the general manager of AP, Wes Gallagher, said to him one day, "but would you be willing to take over the bureau in Manila?"

Nance had never been to Manila, but that didn't matter. After a second's thought he said, "Yes! Yes! Yes!"

Manila took him out of the thick of the war, but his responsibilities widened. As South Asia Bureau chief he was responsible for not only his own reports but the reports of others as well. When the pope visited Manila, Nance, sorting through the chaos of the crowds and various reports from his correspondents, had to wire dispatches to New York at a frantic pace, trying to scoop the other news services. A report came in that an attempt had been made on the life of the pope by a Bolivian man dressed as a priest and wielding a knife. None of the other services had this news yet, but was it true? Nervously Nance wired a story back to New York. Then another reporter who'd only been standing a few feet from the pope insisted nothing had happened. The pope was fine. But the news had already gone out across the wires. Then . . . confirmation. An attack had occurred. The pope had been grazed by the knife. The Bolivian man was in custody. The Vatican was trying to play it down.

This was Nance's life. This is what he'd signed up for, at least until he noticed the unassuming article on the "lost tribe" in Mindanao. In *The Gentle Tasaday*, Nance writes of his first reactions to the Tasaday story: "Several years as a newsman had conditioned me against the ploys and entreaties of politicians and various kinds of promoters when they wanted something publicized. I began to wonder if the historic discovery was a mistake or a hoax. The more I thought about it, the more suspicious I became—a people isolated for centuries from towns and civilization only forty or fifty miles away. Incredible!"[4]

Nance had dealt with Elizalde before, and this only made him more skeptical. Elizalde was not an easy man to figure out; arrogant and aloof, he was also charming and idealistic. The only constant was his hunger for publicity.

Nance arranged a meeting with Elizalde and Fox to discuss the Tasaday. In the living room of Elizalde's mansion, Nance read the Elizalde-Fox report while maids and aides hovered around and brought them drinks. Nance had some questions about the way the story had been divulged to the media.

"You don't believe it?" Elizalde said.[5]

"Well, it's hard to believe," Nance said. "I mean, I don't know. I'm not an anthropologist. But it's pretty hard to believe."

"Why's that?" Elizalde said.

"The way the story came out. Nobody else had it."

"I know it's not a full story," Elizalde told him. "We had to do this because of the loggers. . . ."

Elizalde told Nance they were going back.

"You're going down there?" Nance said. "I'd like to go."

"Absolutely," Elizalde said. "I'll see to it."[6] He promised that Nance would be among the first reporters to make a trip to see the Tasaday.

After that, Nance checked daily with PANAMIN Executive Director Oscar Trinidad for updates on the trip, but Manda had either forgotten his promise or never intended to keep it. One day Trinidad told Nance, "He's gone. He left this morning—with the *Reader's Digest* guy [Christopher Lucas], and he's going to meet Jack Reynolds [of NBC]."

That day the former president of the AP and head of Gannett papers was coming to visit, and Nance told a colleague, "Have my second guy meet him. I'm leaving."

"It was just like some magnet," Nance recalls. "I told the general manager of the AP. He said, 'Don't go [to see the Tasaday]. Send Billy Mann.' I said, 'Never got this message,' and left."

Nance flew to Davao, the largest city on Mindanao, where he ran into Jack Reynolds who had flown in advance of his camera crew from Tokyo. Reynolds had arrived in Vietnam just as Nance was leaving, and all the AP guys (they were all "guys" back then) who knew him liked him. So Nance approached Reynolds, and after he had explained the situation, Reynolds invited Nance to hitch a ride with him and his crew. He was able to squeeze Nance in the small plane to Surallah, the closest airport to the settlement at T'boli, where Manda and his entourage of reporters, scientists, and PANAMIN staffers were gathering in preparation for their Tasaday expedition.

Nance found Elizalde at his enormous house on a hill overlooking T'boli. In his characteristic yachting cap, and surrounded by his fawning staff and servants, Manda seemed unruffled, even happy to see Nance.

Early the next morning the PANAMIN helicopter ferried Nance and Chris Lucas of the *Reader's Digest* to the settlement of Blit, a half hour's journey over rugged mountains. From Blit, the chopper flew Nance, Lucas, Igna (the translator), and others in shifts to the clearing at the edge of the forest, a ride of only two minutes or so.

Soon another chopper arrived carrying the rest of the visitors, the scientists Robert Fox and Jesus Peralta and the NBC film crew. Peralta, a soft-spoken but unflappable man, was a graduate student who had been working with Fox doing Paleolithic archaeology in the Cagayan Valley of northern Luzon. Oddly, Fox introduced him not as an anthropologist but as a scientific illustrator. Peralta swallowed his surprise and went along with the ruse. "Manda Elizalde then was very selective about who goes in," Peralta recalls. "I think he got the ire of some anthropologists simply because of that. He screened people out. . . . He [Fox] told them that I was a scientific illustrator, so I wasn't supposed to be doing research. He just told me to keep observing things. So that's what I did."

In the dark and humid forest, they clambered up and down steep hillsides for about half an hour, tripping over roots and following a stream bed over which sunlight trailed through the dense jungle. They followed a brook for a while until they came to a bend where Elizalde sat on a log beside several Tasaday, wisps of smoke drifting around them from a small fire. The tableau seemed posed to Nance. The Tasaday sat serenely around the fire, their light brown bodies covered in green leaves, the men wearing leaf G-strings, the women wearing leaf skirts. Where the Tasaday stopped and the forest began, Nance could hardly distinguish; these people seemed to him as he came upon them almost the living embodiment of the trees, the cries of the birds, the flowing water, the dense foliage. Yet he still felt guarded. He wondered if Elizalde hadn't simply preselected this dazzling spot to introduce the Tasaday to the reporters. Nance asked what had happened to their clothes. He remembered there being cloth in the photographs. " 'We asked them this morning to dress like they used to before they met Dafal or us,' Elizalde said. 'And when we got down here a little while ago, this was it—leaves. They must have left the cloth scraps upstream somewhere.' "[7]

Nance was hooked, but doubts still lingered. He wondered what would happen now that they had been placed in the spotlight. He wanted to know what was going on in their minds. Certainly, all this commotion must be confusing. Here they were, isolated for centuries perhaps, the depths of the forest the only place they'd ever known. They'd never seen other people besides their forest neighbors. They'd never seen a helicopter, never seen a cigarette or a camera. They'd never tasted rice. What did they think of all these new things and new people? Nance called over Mai and Igna and said he wanted to ask the Tasaday a few questions: " 'How do they feel about what has happened to them the last few weeks? What are their feelings about all the new things and new people they have seen?' They addressed Belayem, and, as the question passed from Mai to Igna and into Tasaday, a frown crinkled across Belayem's forehead. He put his fingertips to his cheek and blinked and held them there for several seconds before saying in a soft, clear voice: 'It is like lightning. It has come to us without warning.' "[8]

While Manda held forth in front of reporters and camera crews, Jesus Peralta, unnoticed, walked around and talked to people and saw a man using a small "opaline quartz thumbnail scraper." The man was polishing a stick, probably one used for making fire. Manda was displaying two tools, a hafted* stone hammer and a hafted edge-ground tool that he said were the only two tools that had been found. Peralta blurted out, "I just saw [another] one!" Elizalde didn't believe him. He insisted all the stone tools the Tasaday were using had already been gathered up. But Peralta was trained in archaeology, and Manda was not; he knew what he'd seen. The high-angle opaline quartz scraper was exactly of the kind that he and Fox had excavated in Cagayan. Annoyed, Elizalde asked one of his men to fetch the tool. When the man returned a couple of minutes later with the tool, which he must have

---

*The hafting is the rattan (in this case) binding and handle into which the stone is fitted.

snatched out of the Tasaday man's hand, he turned it over to Fox, who examined it closely. Peralta had been right. What made the find significant to Peralta was that no one, not even Fox, had known of the scraper's existence until he brought it up, and no one except the two of them would have been able to recognize its value.[9]

Fox was astounded by Peralta's find and the other two tools that the Tasaday had shown them. " 'These tools are simply incredible,' Fox moaned, with a shake of his head. 'Every time I see that edge-ground scraper I want to faint. Fascinating. You see, the scraper is so fundamental that without it man could not survive. It's the primary tool for working bamboo or any wood. We've found thousands in Philippine Paleolithic sites, tens of thousands of years old—but this is the first scraper ever discovered here actually in use.' "[10]

To the scientists the stone scraper might have been a find, but Manda saw Peralta as an annoyance. Peralta asked a lot of questions and voiced some mild skepticism; soon he found himself excluded from the group, ignored by Manda and his men. Taking the hint, he packed up and returned to Manila. The press was more important than the scientists to Manda in any case.

The press included Nance, Jack Reynolds and his three-man TV crew, and Christopher Lucas from *Reader's Digest*. The *National Geographic* film crew had also returned for a second peek. The scientists included Fox and Teodoro Llamzon, a priest who was a professor of linguistics at the prestigious Ateneo de Manila University. To Fox's chagrin, Manda had also invited along Frank Lynch, another priest and a professor of anthropology.[11] By the end of July 1971, a mere month after their "discovery," the Tasaday had been visited by two TV crews, Nance and Lucas, Jack Foisie of the *Los Angeles Times*, and more than a dozen Filipino reporters. Letters from the world over, but mainly from industrialized Europe and America, started pouring in, most expressing concern for the Tasaday, urging their protection. A small mountain of news clippings had of course preceded these letters.

Momo' Dakel Diwatà* Tasaday, the Tasaday called Elizalde now,

---

Diwatà is of Sanskrit origin and can be found throughout the Philippines, but it was the only such word the Tasaday ever used, and later Manda insisted the word was not the Tasaday's but a translator's or Dafal's. *Diwatà* has been translated as "god" by some, but Austronesian language specialist Lawrence Reid thinks it more likely means "benefactor." He translates *Momo' Dakel Diwatà Tasaday* as "Big Uncle Benefactor of the Tasaday."

or sometimes Momo' Bong, a fusion of the Tasaday *Momo' Dakel* and the T'boli *Tau Bong*. The Tasaday said their ancestors had told of the coming of a man like Momo' Dakel, and now he was here. They seemed truly drawn to Manda, hugging and nuzzling him, and he responded in kind. Elizalde had always loved the jungle. He was a different person here, calmer, soft-spoken, and kind, and his affection for the Tasaday seemed genuine to observers. Whatever else the Tasaday might be, they seemed infatuated with Elizalde, and protective and concerned, he hovered over them.

John Nance and I sat in the small dining room of his duplex in Portland, Oregon, the TV set tuned to a football game. He fixed me a bowl of homemade soup and asked if I wanted a cup of tea. "Did I show you the film I made? We should look at it while you're here. It's only sixteen minutes."

We chatted for a while and eventually got around to the film he'd made for students, *A Message from the Stone Age*. He threaded the film through a projector, turned off the lights, and aimed the projector toward the wall. The image, nothing distinct, fluttered before me, and a high-pitched sound pierced my ears as though the projector were keening, a horrible banshee wail. What a forlorn message from the Stone Age! John turned the projector off and tried again, and this time the keening slowly turned into the sounds of birds chirping—a little distorted, but recognizable. Next came the sound of water. Then John's voice, a bedtime story voice: "In the tropics of Southeast Asia, on the island of Mindanao in the southern Philippines, lies one of the earth's last great unexplored rain forests. For millions of years, the forest has flowed like an inland ocean across jagged mountains and down to the banks of shining rivers, covering the steep slopes and deep valleys with dense jungle. Dark rain clouds often added to the aura of mystery and foreboding. Fearful folk living outside believed wild beasts and savage spirits inhabited the forest depths. Few people ventured inside. . . . Within this luxuriant undergrowth lived people, a people who knew not how or why they'd come into this forest . . . it was their world, their universe."

The loud calls of jungle birds dominated. The film enchanted me. John's photos, accompanied by that soporific narration, were hypnotic. The sound of a mouth harp punctuates the sounds of running water, the pictures of idyllic life in the jungle. The Tasaday boy Lobo gazes quizzically at a bird perched on his thumb, Udelen squats in the stream, looking contemplative as white water cascades off his body. Even a photo of Belayem focusing the lens of a camera beckons, seeming somehow more miraculous than ordinary people focusing camera lenses. John narrates quietly, as though speaking any louder might scare away the jungle folk: "The people's soft smiles and gentle embraces spanned thousands of years of cultural time and technology. The communion of Stone Age and space age folk acknowledged differences but affirmed that human beings, wherever and whoever they may be, are vastly more alike than different. . . . The Tasaday are us and we are them, all members of the human family. In their simplicity and peacefulness and love the Tasaday invite us to join them in calling all men one man, all women one woman." The film ended, and the clatter of the projector brought me out of a stupor.

It was a fairy tale. And as a fairy tale it was enchanting. If it didn't deal with real people, my response would have been simple, but it wasn't. The film seemed to me as close to being inside John's mind as one could get. It wasn't meant as a piece of ethnography, he told me. It was meant as a way to get students to think about cultural differences and similarities. He defended his language in the film as well. The way the Tasaday lived, he said, was the way our ancestors *might* have lived, not definitely how they lived. "I never said this was who we were. This is an idea of who we *might* have been, preagriculture. And I said that Dafal was *one* of the rare outsiders. I didn't say he was the only one. I don't know those things. I'm careful. That's why I get so angry at these people [his critics]!"

A study guide accompanied the film:

In a class play about outsiders meeting the Tasaday, help students devise alternatives to what actually happened:
   a. What objects would they provide the Tasaday?
   b. What objects would they withhold?
   c. Would they come in a helicopter?
   d. Might they decide not to contact the Tasaday at all?

Tasaday study questions. The notion seemed silly. I thought I knew the right answers, but wasn't sure. In truth, these questions were the heart of the matter.

Robert Fox floated some initial theories about the Tasaday as well as PANAMIN's plans for them in an article for an English-language magazine titled *The Asian*. He reiterated much of what he and Elizalde had reported to the Smithsonian Center for Short-Lived Phenomena: that the Tasaday had no knowledge of any cultivated plant, had never smoked tobacco or tasted salt or sugar. He explained that their traditional tools were "among the most primitive ever recorded by explorers or anthropologists."[12] Their tools, he believed, could provide archaeologists with "actual data" of how similar tools were made and used thousands of years ago by our ancestors. "The story of the ability of the Tasaday to survive in a damp, high-altitude rain forest without clothing or permanent habitation," he wrote, "with an almost unbelievably primitive technology, and by gathering only wild food plants and river life caught by hand—they also have no traditional hunting or trapping devices—will furnish one of the most fascinating chapters of Man's history and development." He also discussed the Tasaday's clothing, the curculigo leaves that the women wore in miniskirt fashion and that the men wore as G-strings. The social structure was remarkable in that it was nonhierarchical and non-polygamous, though polygamy was widely practiced by their closest neighbors. Relationships between children and parents were "extremely affectionate," and children were carried constantly. The Tasaday spoke of "using rock shelters for habitation," but as of the writing of this article, no one associated with PANAMIN had yet seen where they lived. There was a possible second group, larger than theirs, the Sanduka, of which the Tasaday had spoken originally, but now, "for still unaccountable reasons," they didn't want to discuss them. They also spoke of "Salungal, the owner of the mountain, who lives with the dead and helps them find food." Fox acknowledged that time constraints and language problems made the exploration of Tasaday religious beliefs difficult, but he conjectured that these people lived for the present moment with little concern for the past or the future.

On the basis of the initial findings of the linguist Father Llamzon,[13] Fox thought that the Tasaday had been isolated for perhaps as long as two thousand years. But if so, why, then, were they not succumbing to disease, as had other "lost tribes" when reached by outsiders? The Tasaday by and large were healthy, though they spoke often and with great fear about a *fugu* epidemic. Perhaps their numbers had *already* been decimated just as diseases brought to America by Europeans had wiped out entire Native American villages years before a white man set foot in their territory.

While the world press eagerly lapped up accounts of the "lost tribe," skeptics slowly emerged. Some suspected Manda of political ambitions; others said he was engaged in an elaborate land-grabbing scheme so that he could prospect for "rare minerals."[14] The earliest academic critic was a history professor at the University of the Philippines, Zeus Salazar. His "Comments: Footnote on the Tasaday," written in 1971, raised concerns regarding the lack of original data. "Having happily survived the 'Stone Age,'" the article begins, "through a spate of sensational newspaper reports, the Tasaday have at last become the object of serious scrutiny in the . . . study of Dr. Llamzon, following a more popular study of them by Dr. R. Fox. . . ."[15] The article questioned the methods and conclusions drawn concerning the Tasaday's "isolation" and when they might have split off from a parent Manobo group. In the face of the rampant speculation on the Tasaday Salazar's article was a model of reason and restraint. It criticized Fox for basing his conjecture that the Tasaday had been on their own for two millennia on the stone tools they used.[16] Dr. Salazar thought that the Tasaday had been isolated at most for 150 years. He also questioned the method of glottochronology that Llamzon had used to determine the Tasaday's isolation and was skeptical of the notion that the Tasaday had no words that suggested agriculture. Salazar made valid points, but they were ignored.

Elizalde did nothing to quell suspicions. He vowed to Nance and others that he had no political ambitions whatsoever and denied persistent rumors that he planned to run for the Philippine Senate on the Marcos ticket in the fall elections. But when Nance called Manda's attorney and close associate Oscar Trinidad, he was informed that Manda had indeed been drafted to the Marcos ticket. Less than two months after the Tasaday "discovery," Manda accepted the nomination with the typically grand pronouncement of a seasoned politician: "I have accepted a draft as a senatorial candidate of the Nationalista Party in my desire to bridge the gap between the Haves and the Have-nots and to awaken the social conscience of the people on the sad state of the cultural minorities in the Philippines."[17]

Still, he promised he wouldn't exploit the Tasaday for political gain. During the election he published a little magazine titled *Mindanao Resumé*. It was little more than campaign propaganda. The cover, which featured a photo of Manda, promised such articles as "The Way to Tasaday Was a Demanding Route" and "Help for Philippine Tribes in Trouble" and a reprint of the *National Geographic*'s homage to Manda. In a piece titled "The Visionary Idealist," the anonymous writer declares: "In spite of his concern for the unknown Filipinos living today in the jungles of the countrymen [sic] he would not wish to bring their plight before the Filipino electorate. 'I might be accused of exploiting them,' he explained to us.' "[18]

In a lovely transition, the writer and Manda go on to do just that: "But he did say that the discovery of the existence of the Tasadays whom he had described as 'a long-lost tribe in Mindanao' has brought more fame, more attention to the Philippines than any single event since Independence. Manda is the youngest of the 16 official senatorial candidates of the two major political parties in this country. He will be exactly 35 years old on November 8, just old enough to qualify him for the Philippine senate."[19]

While Manda focused his energies on winning the election, the Tasaday were left without their Momo' Dakel. For months after the initial lightning strike of Elizalde et al. the Tasaday received no visitors.

Nance meanwhile had taken a leave of absence from the Associated Press, a leave from which he never returned. Initially, he planned to write a children's book on the Ubu, though he also hoped that Elizalde would renew his interest in the Tasaday; he was worried that the Tasaday might be upset at being abandoned after having had their lives disrupted. But Manda didn't think the Tasaday were upset. Dafal and Igna's husband had recently visited the Tasaday; they were fine, but they wanted to know when Momo' Dakel would visit again.

In early March, Nance flew to Mindanao and was able to reach the Ubu settlement of Ma Falen with the help of PANAMIN. After four days he received a radio message saying that Elizalde was in T'boli and wanted to know if Nance would meet him there. In due course a PANAMIN chopper picked Nance up and ferried him to

T'boli, where he found Manda slouched on the porch of his staff house. In lieu of hello, Manda said, "How'd you like to go and see the Tasaday with us?"

Manda explained that leaving the election worries to his lawyers, he'd flown down to Mindanao and visited T'boli and Blit. He'd sent Dafal to the forest to find the Tasaday and the next day waited three hours at the clearing before giving up when the sky became dark and threatening. As the chopper lifted off, they noticed a lone figure running towards them at full speed. It was Belayem, a wild chicken in one hand and a pair of deer horns in the other. After the helicopter landed again, Belayem ran up to Manda, laughing and crying at once, hugging him and shoving the gifts at him. "I must have a wife!" he pleaded with Manda through translators. No one else came to the clearing, but Manda promised Belayem he'd return in a couple of days.

In early March, Manda, in the company of Nance, Mai, Igna, and several other PANAMIN staffers, headed once again for the clearing. Nance worried that the Tasaday might not show up, but they did. Asked how they had fared the last seven months, they said they were fine, though they had waited impatiently for Manda's return. Sometimes they heard a helicopter fly overhead and rushed outside, but it never was Manda. Belayem, as he recounted their vigil, said, "We want Momo' Dakel Diwatà Tasaday to stay with us always," and leaned his head on Manda's shoulder.[20]

Storms and high winds had toppled trees and damaged their shelters, Belayem told the visitors, who assumed these shelters were the lean-tos Dafal had taught them how to make. When the visitors asked if the damaged shelters were "buttressed tree roots" or the "rock ledges" mentioned on the previous visits, Belayem seemed confused. They asked if the shelters were bigger than lean-tos. Much bigger, Belayem said.

Were these shelters big enough to hold a hut? When Belayem didn't answer right away, he was asked if the shelters were big enough for a man to stand inside. Oh, yes, he said, they were very high. Could all of them stand inside? Yes. Mai Tuan asked if these shelters were in their mountain, if they went inside the mountains, and he cupped his hand in a half circle. Belayem nodded.

Nance captures this moment, when it all came together, when the Tasaday became the world's perfect Stone Age ancestors:

"Caves! They live in caves!" we exclaimed.

The Tasaday blinked and looked at us as we babbled to each other.

"Of course . . . of course," Manda said. "We never asked them . . . why didn't we think of that? Caves! In their valley. Sure. Perfect. No wonder they say they are safe and warm there."

Our excitement must have puzzled the Tasaday, but then much of our behavior must have seemed odd. They watched quietly as we marveled back and forth . . .[21]

To Nance and the others, this completed the picture. Not only did these people use stone tools and live purely by foraging, wear leaves and live in isolation in perfect harmony with one another and their natural surroundings, but they lived in caves like our ancestors. The Tasaday had become the perfect time machine. It was almost as though humanity could be given another chance, that we could go back in time and visit our ancestors, who were *not* barbaric like us, we could learn from them, we could find out where we'd gone wrong, and the future might at last hold some promise. This made a profound impression on Nance, one that has never faded.

On this visit, nineteen Tasaday had shown up. The others were off making *natek*. The visitors asked the Tasaday if they'd seen any of the other forest people of whom they had spoken. No, they'd seen only Dafal and Igna's husband. Manda asked them if they needed anything. Belayem looked at the helicopter and, after a few moments' pause, asked what it was like inside the big bird. Manda asked if he'd like to go for a ride. Nance worried that this might not be such a good idea, but Elizalde shrugged off Nance's concern, saying it was Belayem's idea. They were curious, he said, and courageous to want to ride in something that had terrified them before. Soon a group of Tasaday, all men, had converged to ride in Momo' Dakel's big bird. Bilengan said if Belayem was going, he'd go too, and Bilengan's son, Lobo, excitedly danced around, wanting to go as well. The chopper took off, flew with a roar, and disappeared in the direction of Blit. The other Tasaday looked up in awe and waited.

This must have been a Copernican moment for the Tasaday. The nature of the world changed before their eyes. Where before they had known the forest only from inside, now they flew above it. The world tilted, and they would have seen mountains and sky and forests in the distance. They had never seen the tops of trees in such number. There would have been the fields of their neighbors in Blit below them, their tiny huts, perhaps a horse, a pig, dogs, and people working in the fields. They had never seen any of these things—no pigs, no dogs, no horses, no fields except for the clearing where they had first met Momo' Dakel.

When the chopper landed, Belayem led the others in a dead run from it. After regaining their composure, chests heaving, Belayem and Bilengan said they had been frightened, but now they were fine. To the Tasaday, in fact, especially Belayem and young Lobo, the helicopter became the centerpiece of all their imaginings of the outside world and Momo' Dakel's power. Who would not want one for himself?

Nance and Elizalde resumed their questioning of Belayem and the others about their forest home. How long would it take for the Tasaday to walk from their cave to the clearing? Belayem said it took a day of hard walking. Manda wondered how long it might take him and the other visitors. Belayem figured it would take them much longer—*if* they could do it, perhaps as much as four days and three nights.[22] Manda asked if the Tasaday would like to continue to meet at the clearing or if they'd like Manda to visit their forest home. It would be good, Belayem said, if Momo' Dakel visited their special place. Manda wanted to hear from the others. Another man said yes, he'd like Momo' Dakel to come, if he could make it. A young mother, Dul, agreed. She said she too would like Momo' Dakel to visit them.

Maybe, Manda said, some friends of his would have to go ahead and make a place in the forest for the big bird to land. This would mean cutting down many trees to make space for the helicopter. Was this also agreeable to the Tasaday? It was.

Manda began preparations for the expedition to the caves. He planned to bring Nance, Charles Lindbergh (who said he wouldn't miss the trip for the world), Kenneth MacLeish, a senior editor at *National Geographic*, and John Launois, a freelance photographer out of New York who would take photos for MacLeish. Nance would document the trip for PANAMIN and for any news articles he might write as a result. After some discussion it was decided that the best way to get to the caves would be by helicopter, but Manda and others worried that creating a clearing so close to the Tasaday's enclave would make them visible by air and vulnerable to discovery by others who might wish them harm. Norman Certeza, PANAMIN's surveyor, suggested a treetop landing pad where a helicopter might land or onto which visitors could jump or be lowered. Lindbergh didn't relish the idea of jumping out of helicopters; he lobbied for clearing a patch of forest or hoofing it. But Manda, Certeza, and Manda's pilot, Ching Rivero, thought the platform could work.

Robert Fox wasn't in on these discussions. He was out. Frank Lynch was in, along with Carlos Fernandez, a Fox protégé and anthropology doctoral candidate from Palawan. Fox had quit PANAMIN. He had not been pleased that Manda had invited Frank Lynch along on the third expedition, a move predicated on Manda's jealousy of the media attention Fox had received.[23] On the day of the opening of the Nayong Filipino Museum in Manila, Elizalde had become enraged with Fox, who had hung on the wall a photo of Dafal with the caption "Discoverer of the Tasadays." Elizalde had ripped the picture from the wall and thrown it away.

Twenty-six men, mostly from the T'boli and Ubu tribes, formed an advance party to create the landing pad for Manda and the other Tasaday visitors. On March 23, 1972, everything was in place. The chopper, piloted by a Vietnam veteran named Bert Bartolo, would make three trips to the treetop platform. Manda had his priorities straight: The first flight would include the reporters Nance, MacLeish, and Launois but not the scientists. While they had been in radio contact with the men who had built the platform, they didn't know its exact location. They flew in over the ridges and mountains, between two peaks that rose above them, and into a valley and along a steep ridge that ran almost the valley's entire length. A flare shot up ahead of them, and Bartolo turned the chopper sharply. The flight had taken only five minutes, "less time than expected," Nance noted.[24] Below the craft swayed the platform, approximately eight by ten feet in diameter, made of saplings lashed together. It stood a dizzying seventy-five feet above the ridge.

As the copter hovered, the men inside slid the door open and unbelted and steadied themselves. Manda jumped first, reeling toward the edge, where he was grabbed by Mai Tuan's brother Fludi, waiting on the platform. Launois went next, and then MacLeish, as the helicopter beat the air above them and hooked a wheel on the rope fence surrounding the platform. The men on the platform flattened themselves while the chopper tried to free itself; they knew if the two-ton machine nudged the platform, it would send them all crashing onto the forest floor below.

The chopper rose again and then swung around to drop John Nance. Manda and Launois gestured frantically; Nance noticed MacLeish already speaking into his tape recorder. Nance jumped and felt himself grabbed and steadied, while a downdraft pounded the platform. He peered over the edge of the platform and saw a sea of green below him; from the ridge below, the valley slanted down another three hundred feet. They started their descent, through a trapdoor and a rope ladder tied to the trunk. As Manda climbed down the ladder, the advance party of T'boli, B'laan, Manobo, and Ubu cheered. Dafal ran up to Manda and said that the Tasaday had made themselves scarce over the previous week, but Belayem had approached Dafal and said that when Momo' Dakel Diwatà Tasaday descended from the big bird, he would guide them to their home, which Dafal himself had never seen.[25] Belayem appeared out of nowhere and hugged Manda, who returned his embrace.

The helicopter returned with Mai Tuan, Igna, and Doc Rebong. On the ridge below the tree, nearly forty people had assembled. Some stayed to guard the site while others proceeded down the ridge into the valley below. Belayem led the way down the steep slope, "skittering down fallen trunks and sliding on vines down almost sheer drops."[26] Manda and MacLeish followed close; the others fell behind, Launois and Nance staying close to the platform so they could take pictures as the others passed. Crashing through untracked foliage, they tried to keep firm footholds on the slippery earth while wading through the dense brush. When they reached a spot with less growth, they careened forward, wary lest they grasp thorny vines as they desperately tried to stay upright. Within an hour they had reached a stream, which they followed for half a mile, hopping from rock to rock. Belayem stopped at a cliff and indicated that was the way, but because Manda thought the rock face impossible to climb, Belayem led them farther, to a slope as steep as the one they had just crashed down. There were no switchbacks, no trails at all. The way was straight up. Crawling, grabbing on to exposed roots to steady themselves, the party made their way in near silence, sweating and panting. Belayem finally stopped. Bare gray rock shone ahead of them. MacLeish described the moment. " 'That's it,' Manda whispered. 'That must be it!' We moved closer. Belayem called out. A voice answered. We stepped into the Stone Age."[27]

A complex of three caves, 175 feet across and 75 feet high, vines hanging around them, sprawled along the cliff face in front of MacLeish and Manda. A large cave strewn with loose boulders was situated lowest, a worn path led up the rock face to the highest cavern, and in between the two was a smaller cave that could be reached by either a narrow ledge or a thin tree that grew in front of it. Chattering birds and a waterfall broke the stillness of the cool air. A number of Tasaday peered at the visitors from the upper chambers of the caves, and Manda suggested they hold up and let the Tasaday "look" at them. The pause also gave the others a chance to catch up. MacLeish was grateful for the break, but not out of weariness. He felt stunned and awed by the beauty of the scene. An old man presently came down to where he sat; the man was naked except for his leaf loin covering. He sat beside the reporter, embraced MacLeish's knee, and "patted it reassuringly."[28]

Into this dazzling scene, one feels reluctant to inject a note of mild cynicism, but one can't completely ignore the *National Geographic*–tinged prurience in MacLeish's admiration for the two Tasaday women who presently showed up: "Two young women followed, leaf-skirted, bare-breasted, shapely. They knelt shyly beside us, smiling briefly in response to a light caress."[29]

But perhaps we should give MacLeish the benefit of the doubt, as warm physicality was one of the Tasaday's hallmarks. Belayem, who crouched beside Manda, sat shoulder to shoulder with him. Manda threw his arm around Belayem, whispering into his ear.

Nance, climbing wearily below heard a shout from above. He followed the sound, but could see nothing but more forest. Clambering to the top of the rise, with yellow light diffused through a stand of bamboo, he found his eyes adjusted. In a crouch he ducked through foliage into a tableau unlike anything he had ever seen. "It seemed as if I were floating within the frame of a gigantic painting," he writes, "that had been hung on a mountainside. We had reached the caves."[30]

The first words Nance heard from Manda were "unbelievable . . . unbelievable," words neither of them could have guessed would be so apt. Nance, overcome by emotion, could only stare, speechless.

A toddler stood at the edge of one of the caves, peering curiously at the strangers. Ten-year-old Lobo, a beautiful boy with fine features and an exuberant smile, soon to become the favorite of photographers, leaped into the tree at the middle cave's entrance and swung back and forth, yelling, "Momo' Dakel!" before sliding down the sapling and dashing to greet Manda, hair dancing behind him.

After allowing the photographers to take some pictures, Manda suggested that the group shouldn't push it. They headed down the slope, out of sight of the caves, and pitched their tents on a terrace in the steep hillside. The visitors remarked that they felt as though they'd stepped back into time, MacLeish telling Nance that the scene was "Neolithic . . . Paleolithic." Yet one of the women wore a wraparound cloth skirt. When Fludi Tuan arrived in camp with a T'boli spear and several arrows that had previously been given to the Tasaday, Manda interpreted this as a possible "rejection" of the ways of the visitors. In the coming months Manda was sometimes hypersensitive to the effect of outsiders on the Tasaday, and at other times he was blithely whimsical, taking the Tasaday on helicopter rides when it suited his fancy or bringing in reporters and, as he did in July 1971, two society page mavens, who stumbled through the jungle in high heels, giggling as they asked the Tasaday idiotic questions. Elizalde had been critical of them, but he after all was the gatekeeper. Now he instructed Mai to tell Dafal to ask the woman with the cloth skirt to "go back to leaves like the others." The other Tasaday were told not to bring out things like beads for a while.[31]

The scientists, who were supposed to follow that same day, were delayed by bad weather and wouldn't arrive for another twenty-four hours. The next morning Manda and his companions visited the caves and were treated to a "vision of time flung backward."[32] About twenty soot-smudged Tasaday sat around fires. The caves held little besides the Tasaday: a few deer horns, a cracker tin brought back from the clearing, firewood, and several stone tools. The Tasaday were asked about their diet. They said they preferred *natek*, the palm starch that Dafal had taught them how to extract, followed by *ubud*, tender palm hearts, and lastly *biking*, the wild yam that had been their staple before Dafal. Belayem proudly displayed a few stone tools, and then Elizalde told the Tasaday that the visitors, who were still learning the Tasaday ways, might make mistakes initially. Were there any things that the Tasaday did not want their visitors to do? The young woman Dul spoke up: There were plants in front of the cave that the Tasaday thought were beautiful, and they did not want these cut. The Tasaday had seen the PANAMIN workers cutting foliage to prepare their campsite a day earlier.

Manda gave strict orders that absolutely no cutting was to be done near the caves. Anyone who violated this instruction would be made to walk out of camp.

Frank Lynch seemed impressed by the Tasaday, but one thing bothered him: The caves seemed too clean. Partly this was due to the fact that Manda had told the Tasaday to put all the gifts given them out of sight; they'd complied and had even exchanged their brass earrings for rattan hoops. Still, Lynch thought the caves might have been frequentation sites—that is, temporary dwellings—rather than a permanent home. However, asked later about other caves, Belayem insisted that there were no others and that the Tasaday never ventured more than a three nights' journey from this cave.

Belayem tried to answer all their questions, but Lynch thought it was necessary for an anthropologist to learn their language before he could get "solid data." By that night, though, he was satisfied that the Tasaday indeed made their permanent home in the caves. Then another mystery presented itself: Where were the Tasaday's forest brethren, the Sanduka and the Tasafeng? Belayem didn't know; he had visited them only as a child with his father. They lived near a stream, but a different stream from the Tasaday's.

The next day Lynch had to return to Manila, but the others, including the other scientist, Carlos Fernandez, stayed. The Tasaday took their visitors on a foraging tour, where they gathered *biking*, small crabs and tadpoles from the stream, and *ubud*, which they sliced with a bolo.

When they returned to camp, they found Lindbergh had arrived, as chipper as could be, having thoroughly enjoyed leaping from the helicopter onto the treetop platform and into the Stone Age. Like the others, he was having the time of his life. The group again visited the caves, and it was on this trip that Carlos Fernandez located the midden—the garbage heap that's part of any long-term habitation site—at the lip of the cave: "Ashes and bits of charcoal and other debris lay on top of the mound which was grown over with leafy plants, bamboo, and rattan that rose higher than the mouth of the cave. The refuse heap was about twelve feet across and extended out perhaps ten feet from the cave. [Fernandez observed:] 'It must go down about sixty feet. . . . See those ashes on top? They apparently just sweep everything out of the cave and that's where it lands.' "[33]

The mystery of the clean caves was settled to the satisfaction of Fernandez, Lynch, and Nance, but Dul's prohibition against cutting plants near the mouth of the cave presented a problem. How could anthropologists respect this prohibition and at the same time learn anything meaningful about the length of time the Tasaday had lived at their caves? They couldn't.

None of these considerations bothered Lindbergh, who, like the others, virtually believed he had traveled back in time. "This is Stone Age," he pronounced, on viewing the Tasaday in their caves. "I don't doubt it for a minute."[34] He also noted that the Tasaday had made no attempt to modify their caves, simply ignoring the fact that Manda had told them to take everything out that made them seem less "primitive."

5

Tourists in Paradise

The only trick in maintaining the fiction was to make sure that no scientist was able to investigate independently. This was accomplished by Elizalde's helicopter shuttle service . . . and by imposing highly controlled conditions for fieldwork.
—Oswald Iten

*M*anda soon became concerned about the impact the visitors were having on the Tasaday's behavior. Although they said they were happy that Momo' Dakel had brought his friends, Elizalde couldn't be sure, and he wanted to see if they were holding anything back. So he instructed Mai and Dafal to leave a tape recorder in the caves. They hid it in some clothes that they said needed to dry by the fire. Elizalde opened himself to criticism—as always—that he was unethically bugging the Tasaday, but he thought the risk worth the benefits. Although Nance at first had some misgivings, he came to agree. Unlike the Tasaday in interview situations, the bugged Tasaday would not tire or grow bored or be intimidated.

The first recording revealed that their private discussions often centered on Elizalde, upon whom they had built a cult of personality based on their ancestors' prophecy. After each session Manda and Igna and Mai made transcriptions. From the recordings they discovered that the Tasaday had not seen the Tasafeng or Sanduka for many years. Manda immediately sent for another recorder from Manila and more tapes.

The visitors had started to learn who was who among the Tasaday.

Besides the ubiquitous Belayem, there were two young mothers. Dul, married to Udelen, was fairly forthcoming, but Dula, married to Mahayag, rarely spoke at all. The others included Etut, the wife of Bilengan; Sekul, the oldest woman and wife of Kuletow; and Ginun, who was rarely around, along with her husband, Tekaf, both deaf-mutes. Of the children, the most visible was Lobo, who enjoyed being the center of attention, and his older brother Lolo'. Their other brothers were Natek (named after the Tasaday staple food), about four years old, and a boy younger than two who had yet to be named. Udelen and Dul's young sons, both under four, were Sius and Maman. Adug and Gintuy, teenagers, were the sons of Sekul and Kuletow. Dula and Mahayag had one daughter of about six named Siyul and a son of about seven named Biking (after the wild yam). Lefonok, a widower, had three young children, Kali, Odo', and Sasa', the last a sickly light-haired child, not an albino, but fairer than the others.

The Tasaday were getting to know their other visitors, too. They had trouble with some names and not with others. They called Manda Momo' Dakel, of course. The word *kakay*, meaning "friend," was an honorific placed in front of everyone's name but Momo' Dakel's and Nance, whom they called Jambangan. Mai they named Mafoko', meaning "short one." Lindbergh was Kakay Shalo or Sharls. MacLeish they simply called Ken. Ching was Ting, and Fernandez was Kalo. Belayem proved to be a good mimic of the visitors, speaking into a pretend microphone to imitate MacLeish, making the sound *tasuk* to imitate the shutter of a camera while making his hands into circles around his eyes.

On one visit Belayem met Sindi', a daughter of the Blit chief, Datu' Dudim, and a friend of Igna's. He and Sindi' seemed to like each other, and before long they became inseparable.

Fueled by Nance's AP dispatches, Lindbergh's presence, and the *National Geographic* crew, a flurry of news reports on the expedition appeared worldwide. Although Elizalde has been criticized, often rightly, for pandering to the press, he turned down the many requests from magazines, newspapers, and television companies that started to pour in, with one exception: Jack Reynolds from NBC was standing by with a crew, waiting to fly down to the Tasaday caves. The group discussed the pros and cons of bringing in the NBC crew. Lindbergh opposed the move. He didn't think much of television, but if Manda wanted to do it, then Lindbergh thought Manda should auction off the rights to the filming and perhaps raise hundreds of thousands of dollars in donations to PANAMIN. Manda didn't think that was a good idea. People would invariably accuse him of being "mercenary," he said, but Lindbergh argued that such transactions were common and aboveboard, as long as the money went to a good cause.[1]

Manda finally decided to allow NBC in for only one day, and if the filming made the Tasaday at all uncomfortable, the crew would be asked to leave. Earlier Manda had asked if there were any kinds of people the Tasaday did not like. People with sharp eyes and loud voices, they answered. Months before, at the clearing, a cameraman, frustrated that he couldn't pose the Tasaday and Dafal as he wanted, started shoving them into position. This enraged Manda, who grabbed the man and told him he'd be on the next chopper to T'boli if he touched them again.[2]

The NBC crew arrived just as MacLeish and Launois were leaving. MacLeish, stunned by his experience, asked Fernandez and Elizalde where they thought these amazing people had come from. It was anyone's guess, but Fernandez had already exclaimed to Nance that the Tasaday were the "most significant anthropological discovery of this century—'and I think we could say of centuries, but at this point I would be conservative.'"[3] Manda told MacLeish that he thought the original suppositions about the Tasaday had been wrong. The idea that they had broken off from a Manobo group long ago to avoid a plague didn't fit. Elizalde believed that it was the opposite way around: The Manobo had broken off from them. He asked MacLeish: "Do agriculturalists forget agriculture? All the surrounding tribes have been agriculturalists for centuries? Do men who have used steel blades forget steel? . . . Does a language change so that many of its words differ from those of the nearest linguistic group in half a century or so?"[4]

The last was a good question. What of this nearly unintelligible language the Tasaday spoke? Igna from Blit could barely understand it at first but was now conversant enough to translate tapes. Was it truly so difficult to understand? And what was this about forgetting steel? The Tasaday had possessed steel since well before their first meeting with Manda; their caves might be stripped of bolos now, but they still presumably knew where their steel was hidden. Manda seemed to want to freeze them in the misty pre-PANAMIN past before Dafal had introduced them to steel.

With supplies running low, the visitors decided to leave, but word reached them that the helicopter needed new parts, which would have to be shipped from France, and this would cause a two-week delay. The alternative possibilities seemed limited: An airdrop of supplies would be difficult, and it would also pinpoint their location to strangers, while hunting for food for the large group might threaten the resources around the cave. Walking to Blit might take a few days, and then they'd have to hike quite a ways farther before they arrived at a spot that could be reached by vehicle. Although Manda didn't relish the idea of being rescued, he sent word to PANAMIN headquarters in Manila to ask the government if they could borrow a chopper. The next day a U.S. helicopter from Clark Air Force Base was sent to pick up the adventurers. News stories soon appeared around the world telling of the dramatic rescue of Charles Lindbergh from a rain forest where the world's only surviving Stone Age tribe dwelled.

Actually, if only they'd tried walking to Blit, it would not have taken them a few days. The village was less than two and a half miles away.* Belayem and his fellow Tasaday could easily have made the trip in a couple of hours. Was this why Manda took the trouble of bringing gullible passengers in and out via helicopter? The flight in from T'boli had taken only five minutes. How long a walk could it be?

The Tasaday, who had not been informed of Manda's imminent departure, were tearful as they said good-bye. What further upset Belayem was that his new paramour, Sindi', was leaving, too. She wanted to stay, but Manda insisted that she get permission from her parents if she wanted to return to be Belayem's wife.

From the tapes Elizalde had learned that the Tasaday were confining themselves to the caves because of his presence. Before he left, according to Nance, he asked them not to do this but to go about their normal routines. He also learned that they were proposing to go in search of the Tasafeng and Sanduka, and he asked them not to do this either. Adding any other group to the mix, he told Nance, might

*As the crow flies.

complicate and delay efforts to get a reservation and would mean greater responsibilities.[5] Lastly, before he departed, he told the Tasaday once again that they needed to protect their forest, that they should cut down trees only to make *natek* or to get *ubud*, but to be careful, or they'd have no forest left.[6]

Five days after the expedition ended, Marcos signed Proclamation 995 setting aside 19,247 hectares (46,299 acres) of rain forest as a Tasaday Manobo Reserve. The land was to be protected from "entry, sale, lease exploitation or other disposition in which the Tasaday and their next-door neighbors, the Manobo Blit, may live as they choose."[7] Marcos proclaimed that he was committed to policies integrating "those minorities who wish to join the mainstream of Filipino national life and protecting the rights of those who prefer to remain and preserve their original lifeways." With Manda looking on, and Imelda too, Marcos said he would rely on Elizalde to carry out this policy.[8]

The people in the area, especially the lowlanders, were more than a little suspicious of Elizalde's motives and his Stone Age "discovery." They claimed there was no such tribe as the Tasaday, that the group was an elaborate concoction of Elizalde's. This was either a land-grabbing scheme of Manda's or a huge publicity stunt to feed his enormous ego, or both. Acting on this belief, the Surallah Municipal Council passed a resolution opposing the Tasaday Reserve. Settlers and loggers and prospectors had crisscrossed the jungles and had seen no such people as described. If anything, the Tasaday were actors or even criminals who had been exiled by their own tribes and recruited by Elizalde to play Stone Age cave dwellers. The lowlander Christian settlers of Surallah were worried and believed that they were "being sacrificed by some big politicians to accommodate the latter's personal interest."

In April, Nance attended a party at which he met Zeus Salazar, who had written the first critique of the Tasaday. Manda had recommended the piece to Nance as one of "the best articles written on the Tasaday,"[9] though he told Nance he didn't agree with all its assertions. Nance and Salazar became embroiled in a heated debate that lasted half the night. Salazar accused Fox and Elizalde of brazen self-promotion and of using the Tasaday as "playthings." Nance, to his discomfort, found himself defending Elizalde. With alarm, he noted that he had lost his impartiality and wondered if he could trust his own interpretations. Increasingly, he felt connected to the Tasaday and swayed by Elizalde's arguments.[10] He worried that such an allegiance might make him overlook "negative aspects."

That same month, in the company of Manda and several others, Nance made another foray to see the Tasaday. The visitors included Sindi', whose parents had agreed to allow her to stay with Belayem. Delighted by this development, Belayem, danced around the visitors, hugging and kissing all takers. As he had told Elizalde, he *needed* a wife. Ostensibly, this was the first instance of a non-Sanduka or Tasafeng's marrying a Tasaday, but as soon as Sindi' moved into Belayem's former bachelor pad cave, she looked as Tasaday as any of them, sporting the same leaf miniskirt.

Something extraordinary had happened in the visitors' brief absence. After hundreds—thousands?—of years the Tasaday had decided to modify their caves. They'd tied a piece of bamboo as a kind of railing for visitors along the path to the upper cave and had also fashioned sleeping platforms out of bark, vines, and branches. Bilengan said they'd copied them from similar platforms the T'boli had made at the tents.[11]

Manda, never fond of criticism, had started to buckle a bit under a new wave of skepticism. He was being accused of keeping the Tasaday to himself. Also, why did he have foreigners like Lynch and Fox in charge of the studies? Why not Filipinos? Fernandez apparently didn't count because he had not yet received his doctorate. Manda remarked bitterly to Nance that everyone had to come down to see the Tasaday for himself or herself to be convinced. Even his associates were skeptical. They included Amy Rara, another protégé of Robert Fox's, who had since joined PANAMIN.

After seeing the caves, Rara allowed that *perhaps* the Tasaday made their permanent home there. Later Manda petulantly told Nance, "Good Christ, what did she think? That we had made all this up? And remember, that's Amy, she works for us. . . . We can't just bring every nonbeliever in here and let him poke around until he is personally satisfied. I tell you, they better be careful or I'll just shut this thing down—tell the Tasaday to go away and that'll be it—I can do that, you know. . . ."[12]

Despite claims to the contrary, PANAMIN had tried from the beginning to get Filipino anthropologists on board the Tasaday expeditions. Fox had aggressively pursued David Baradas, who, at thirty-four, held a doctorate from the University of Chicago and was the wunderkind of Filipino anthropology at the time, teaching at Mindanao State University. However, jungle treks held little interest for him, and he didn't bother to respond to Fox's messages. A year later he had left for Manila; the Moro National Liberation Front's insurgency was on the upswing, and Mindanao seemed too dangerous. Fernandez visited Baradas in Manila and described a recent trip to see the Tasaday; PANAMIN was still trying to figure out how best to approach studying this small group.

Baradas, unlike Lindbergh, did not especially appreciate leaps into the Stone Age. Slender and cosmopolitan in disposition, he felt much more at home in an art gallery or antiques shop than scrambling out of a helicopter. Fernandez had described getting slightly injured when he'd jumped out of the helicopter onto the landing pad, and this made Baradas all the more wary.

"I'm not Tarzan," he told Fernandez. "No, it doesn't excite me. You can hog all the headlines you want, but I'm not a daredevil."

Undeterred, Fernandez returned the following week and said, "David, the helicopter can now land on land. . . . Anyway, it's only for less than a month, a month and a half. . . ." Sensitive to the feelings of the Tasaday, Father Lynch had proposed short bursts of research followed by long periods of inactivity with the proviso that if any scientist bothered or upset the Tasaday, his or her research would be curtailed in some fashion. The priest also expressed the need to conduct research without interference from Manda. It was apparent that whenever he showed up, the Tasaday stopped their normal routine.[13] The secret recordings at the caves showed, time and again, that they wanted to stay at the caves "to please Manda" and to receive gifts from him.[14]

Baradas finally agreed. In mid-May he and Fernandez began what was hoped to be the longest sustained period of fieldwork on the Tasaday to date. In a report Frank Lynch wrote as the fieldwork got under way, he could barely contain his frustration that more had not already been accomplished. Yet the planets, as well as Manda's ego, seemed well enough aligned that some real progress might be made. Lynch was encouraged by Baradas and Fernandez's presence: "As this report is being written this eighth association with the Tasaday is still underway. From the viewpoint of ethnographic information, it should be the most fruitful visit of all. For it promises to be the first time that anthropologists will have stayed with the Tasaday under generally acceptable field conditions. We say this not in complaint, but relief. We understand why these conditions could not be achieved earlier, one main hindrance being the refusal of the Tasaday themselves to be interviewed or observed unless Elizalde were present or somewhere nearby."[15] But, he lamented, the "combined waking time" spent with the Tasaday by scientists up to that point, had been a mere 125 hours.

The idea was for the scientists to spend time with the Tasaday in relative seclusion with a minimal support staff, including a translator. Manda would visit briefly to explain to the Tasaday the scientists' plans. He had also invited, much to everyone's chagrin, a Spanish filmmaker* and his wife. The filmmaker had been prohibited from taking any film footage, but he took still photos with flashbulbs that annoyed the Tasaday. His wife thought the Tasaday were "cute," like "little monkeys."[16] The Tasaday clearly did not like this couple. Sindi', acting as spokeswoman, told Manda that Baradas and Fernandez were fine, but if Momo' Dakel wasn't around and the Spanish couple followed them, the Tasaday would shoot them with arrows. The gentle Tasaday shooting their visitors? No matter, if a remark didn't fit his idea of the Tasaday, Manda explained it away. Sindi' must have introduced the idea to them, he suggested.[17]

Another startling development: Most of the Tasaday had moved out of the upper cave, leaving only Bilengan and his family there. The rest, with the exception of Belayem and Sindi', whose starter home was the small cave to the right, had moved to the large lower cave. Equally startling, the Tasaday had *improved* upon their previous constructions. Nance writes: "Four wooden stands, one tripodal and the rest four-legged, had been erected beside fire areas to hold wood so it could dry and be handy; next to the stands were platforms for sleeping. And all were in the spacious mouth of the lower cave."[18]

*Unnamed by Nance.

The visitors noticed on that first day that the Tasaday seemed unusually glum. The Spanish couple didn't help, but that didn't completely explain their sullenness. It seemed the Tasaday hadn't been expecting Elizalde. They had planned on going fishing, but when Manda showed up, they postponed the fishing trip, and now it was raining. Earlier the Spanish woman had picked a plant in front of the cave, and then it had rained even more heavily. The Tasaday once again explained their prohibition against cutting plants in front of the caves. To make up for this trouble, Elizalde gave them rice, which they had developed a taste for.[19]

The next day the Spanish couple left on the helicopter that brought in Lindbergh. The following morning Baradas woke up to the sight of Lindbergh picking up garbage. The night before, one of the T'boli had secretly thrown some garbage over the ravine. But the wind had since scooped it up and scattered it all over the area. As Lindbergh picked up the trash, he said, "I have very little hope for mankind if we behave in the way we're behaving. There's really very little hope for the earth. We've hardly been here for twenty-four hours and look at the mess we have created." Baradas felt so bad that he crawled out of his sleeping bag and helped pick up the garbage.

That day the Tasaday woman Dul led their visitors to another cave. On an earlier visit Belayem had said the first cave was the only one the Tasaday had, but now here was another. Later Belayem told Manda, Nance, and Mai in a confidential voice that he would show them other caves, "but we would not want the new ones [Baradas and Fernandez] to know about them yet."[20]

This was an intriguing moment. What else were the Tasaday hiding and why? Was it simply the natural reticence of any group toward outsiders learning all their secrets? Or did the existence of other caves dilute their supposed primitiveness? Was Manda ordering the Tasaday to stay at the caves in order to counter Lynch's original notion that the main cave was only a frequentation site? Had the Tasaday constructed their sleeping platforms because they weren't used to sleeping on the hard earth of the cave? Moreover, perhaps their prohibition against cutting the plants in front of the midden was simply a ploy to keep the scientists from poking around a midden that didn't exist. Even such meticulous housekeepers as the Tasaday, supposedly sweeping out their immaculate cave with a leaf broom, wouldn't be able to eradicate the evidence of generations of habitation. Perhaps in Elizalde's mind it was dangerous to let the Tasaday talk to visitors unimpeded. Who knew what might slip out?

Lindbergh questioned them in the new cave about the new things they had experienced over the last year. Was there anything in particular, he wanted to know, that they liked best? He asked them to rank their favorite things: "knives, cloth, medicine, bows and arrows." *Rank* them? Why should they do that? Did that mean that the lower-ranked ones would be taken away? They said they liked them all. The question seemed to confuse them.

The Tasaday clearly had tired of answering things they didn't know or care about. In the midst of Lindbergh's quizzing, one unidentified Tasaday spoke up: "We seem to get a wound inside us when people are asking, asking, asking. They want us to make answers, but we only know what we know."[21] They also complained that Kakay Ami (Amy Rara) asked too many questions and had hard eyes.

"Would you like to have a helicopter of your own?" Lindbergh asked them suddenly.

The Tasaday seemed delighted. Yes, they wanted a helicopter. But they'd also need a pilot. Lindbergh asked what they'd do with a helicopter. After much discussion, Bilengan said they'd wait for Momo' Dakel.[22]

The next day Manda reluctantly departed after once again prohibiting the scientists from sleeping in the caves. He was to be gone to the United States for most of the time the scientists were with the Tasaday. The Smithsonian had invited him to give a lecture in Washington, D.C.; Nance's photographs would be on exhibit as well. Elizalde wouldn't be around to control the scientists directly, so he did the next best thing. He left the scientists in the capable and loyal hands of the Tuan brothers Fludi and fourteen-year-old Dad, as well as a boy named Manuel, to help cook, and the radio operator, whose nickname was Dog Love.

Mai was to stay in T'boli. He was in charge while Manda was in the States. Fludi was told to help the scientists, but his first priority was the "welfare of the Tasaday."[23] To the scientists' dismay, when Manda took off, he left them without the promised interpreter. How were they supposed to communicate with the Tasaday? Apparently Manda had intended Fludi Tuan to serve as the scientists' interpreter, a role he later filled for other scientists. Having stayed in the forest with every expedition, the Tuan brothers had naturally gained fluency in speaking to the Tasaday.[24] But Fludi did not meet the scientists' definition of an interpreter. They didn't necessarily trust him, and they had no way of checking the accuracy of his translations.

It soon became clear that the scientists were not in charge, as they had expected to be, but were instead at the mercy of their helpers. Mai, Fludi, and the others operated in their own orbit, oblivious of the anthropologists. When the scientists radioed for medicine to treat skin ailments of some of the Tasaday children, Mai delivered it personally. His arrival caused almost as much excitement among the Tasaday as Elizalde's arrival and threw them off their "normal behavior." Baradas and Fernandez noticed that every day the T'boli sent out long and detailed radio transmissions in T'boli, which they could not understand.

Otherwise they were able to get by. In the Philippine family of languages one word can reverberate in another language, and between Baradas and Fernandez the pair had the command of eight or nine Philippine languages. Soon they were learning more than two hundred new words each day, drilling each other, and before the week was out, they could speak to the Tasaday in complete sentences.

After a while they made an unpleasant discovery: When they went into the forest, the Tasaday seemed simply to be "visiting." They weren't bringing back anything by way of food—with the exception of a pig they killed.

As it turned out, they didn't need to hunt. The scientists discovered that the T'boli were distributing rice to the Tasaday.

This was the biggest shock of all. The Tasaday were supposedly a food-gathering group, and having food distributed completely distorted their activity. When Baradas and Fernandez complained, Fludi and the others said that if they didn't distribute rice, the Tasaday would be unavailable. They'd be out foraging. But that was exactly what the scientists *wanted* the Tasaday to do. They *wanted* to follow them while foraging. That was the whole point. The doling of rice skewed the data irrevocably. Baradas recalls, "You start to get suspicious because you suddenly realize that here you are, a world-focused scientific inquiry, and there's interference. . . . We're totally helpless to prevent a lot of these things from taking place because they are supposed to provide support assistance for us and their idea of support is not exactly our idea of support."

Back in Manila Frank Lynch wrote optimistically: "From word received at PANAMIN, it seems [Baradas and Fernandez] have established suitable rapport and made great progress with the language. Unlike earlier interviews, which passed through two interpreters in each direction, theirs are now direct communications. It is hoped that many of the ambiguities and uncertainties that mark this report will be clarified and resolved by the observations of these two ethnographers."[25]

Ambiguities, instead of being resolved, in fact multiplied. Early on, Baradas and Fernandez's helpers started to talk about a notorious bandit, a renegade named Kabayo, who, envious of the Tasaday for having been given the forest reserve status by the government, was headed their way to cause trouble.

Part of the hype surrounding the Tasaday suggested that they had no words for "weapon" and "war." But one day someone said they had spotted strangers down by the creek. Suddenly the gentle Tasaday "went into a tizzy," taking up their bows and arrows. Elizalde and Nance could say what they wanted about the Tasaday's lack of aggression, but Baradas observed them differently. He thought their reputation for gentleness was "baloney."

Meanwhile Fernandez started receiving messages from Manila that they shouldn't put "too much pressure" on the Tasaday, who were complaining that Baradas and Fernandez were asking too many questions, a charge that baffled the two. They went to the caves only when invited—Manda had forbidden them to sleep in the caves—and most of their interviews were conducted when the Tasaday stopped by the scientists' tents. Sometimes they encountered the Tasaday by the stream and talked to them there. But they didn't pressure the group; in fact, they rarely teamed up to talk to the Tasaday and never at the caves. Their "house rule" was that if Baradas went up to the caves, Fernandez would stay by the stream, then follow the Tasaday as they went foraging.

To this day Baradas thinks that Manda never wanted the pair to study the Tasaday in the first place but was simply bowing to worldwide scientific pressure. When he left them without a translator, he was trying to keep them in the dark. But the truth was that Baradas and Fernandez had already uncovered a lot: the doling of rice, the relative aggression of the Tasaday. Worst of all, the scientists had broken the linguistic block. Perhaps Manda hadn't counted on the scientists' fluency in so many Filipino languages. Baradas now suspects that the support staff noticed that the scientists were getting on well with the Tasaday and speaking to them directly and reported back to Manda. The expedition had to be disrupted.

Two weeks into the expedition a flurry of shots rang out while Baradas and Fernandez were having dinner in Manda's tent. Fludi was with them, and Dafal was boiling coffee.

Baradas scurried out of the tent. Unfortunately he had forgotten that the tent was pitched on a slope. He started rolling down the hill. He kept rolling in pitch-darkness until a log stopped him. Looking back up the hill into the sky, he could see red tracers whizzing by. After a few minutes he heard somebody rolling toward him. It was Carlos Fernandez.

Frightened, the men separated, feeling their way in the blackness. Baradas fell off a rock and found himself dangling over a steep ravine. He managed to find a ledge, which he worked his way over to. There he felt safe, and after a long time he heard Carlos calling. Fernandez joined him on the ledge for a while, then went off again. Baradas didn't budge. The attack had ended, but Baradas wouldn't move. He spent the rest of the night there while the alarmed staff searched for him, but he had told Fernandez not to let them know where he was. He emerged from his hiding place only when it was nearly daylight. He then noticed something strange. The PANAMIN guards had blithely gone back to their tent and were sitting around chatting with a fully lit lantern illuminating them from the outside.

Baradas, observing from a distance, wondered why any thinking individual under attack by an enemy would sit in a lighted tent, a perfect target, and chitchat as though nothing had happened. The mysterious attackers could not have been more than three hundred feet away, so why wasn't the tent riddled with bullet holes? Moreover, if they had been out there just above the tent, why were there no empty shells? The possibility that this had been a setup was more frightening to Baradas than an actual attack from outsiders was. He and Fernandez started to wonder how safe they were from their own support team. They requested a helicopter to get them out of the area.

They waited all day. The chopper didn't come. Here they were, having been attacked by armed men, and Manda wasn't even concerned enough to send a team to rescue them from danger. If it *was* real danger. As they waited tensely, they decided on a small act of defiance. They'd sleep in the caves. They wanted to rile PANAMIN, but this gave them small comfort. They worried that they'd be assaulted now by their staff. "They could just say the two guys disappeared in the forest, and we can't find them anymore," Baradas recalls. "It's so easy."

Finally they were instructed to go to the landing area. Another day passed. No helicopter. It finally arrived two days later.

John Nance, back in Manila with Manda, tells a different story. In his version the PANAMIN helicopter was undergoing repairs, and Elizalde, far from displaying the nonchalance the scientists attribute to him, was quite nervous and upset about the situation. Nance writes: "His voice was tight. 'About eight o'clock there was a lot of gunfire *right at the tents!* Sounds very bad. We're leaving as soon as possible, setting it up now. You with us?' "[26]

All night repairs were made on the PANAMIN helicopter. Nance, Elizalde, and several others went ahead by commercial jet to Davao, where they learned that the helicopter "had taken off but had to turn back because of a malfunctioning rotor blade."[27] In Nance's account, they finally arrived in the late afternoon:

> Within half an hour the helicopters approached the landing ridge from an unusually high angle—the pilots had been instructed to fly as high as possible because of the chance of sniper fire. The first chopper swooped down and hovered over the ridge as we jumped to the ground—Elizalde . . . Ching . . . Felix, and I. Right behind us, Mai and his group, including Dr. Rebong and Sgt. Roland Daza of the Philippine Constabulary based at T'boli, leaped from the second chopper. When they were off, Fernandez and Baradas, who had been waiting at the landing pad, climbed aboard and flew to T'boli. There had been no chance to talk with them.[28]

Baradas says it happened the other way around. As their helicopter lifted off, they saw another helicopter coming in. It was Manda. They hadn't even realized he was still in the country until that day, and then he couldn't even bother to talk to them. They had had no idea he planned to return to the area. He landed after their helicopter took off and brought them to the T'boli settlement.

Manda was scheduled to go to Davao after visiting the Tasaday, but a storm forced him to go to T'boli as well. He and the scientists shared the PANAMIN staff house. Baradas claims that Manda avoided them completely and seemed uninterested in what had happened. Nance recounts Manda's meeting Baradas and Fernandez briefly on the staff house porch and receiving from them an eighteen-page or so handwritten report, which was never seen again.* Manda should have informed them that he was flying in, the report said among other things. They could have sorted out all their problems on site. They had also "gathered data that challenged earlier findings and beliefs about the Tasaday."[29]

The scientists' major findings were that at least a third of the words previously recorded as Tasaday had actually been imported by Igna and Dafal; the Tasaday weren't so gentle; and they weren't so sedentary either. Some of them stayed away from the caves for great periods of time, and those who stayed had to be coaxed to do so by the doling out of rice. Nance writes: "In general, the reports re-emphasized how little was truly known about the Tasaday. And now, because of misunderstandings between the anthropologists and T'boli, and the attack by intruders, we had more confusion. It struck me that we knew very little about Kabayo, assuming it was Kabayo. . . . Murkiness again. Mysteries. Not for the first time, I wondered what I would have made of these strange events had I not been present and had only heard about them."[30]

Actually he hadn't really been present. He had only heard about the events surrounding Kabayo's attack. Nance reports that Fludi found a shotgun shell the morning of the attack, footprints, and buckshot scars in trees, but he had to take Fludi's word for all this.[31]

According to Nance, Manda met with the scientists twice, both times briefly. After seeing how upset they were, Manda retreated.

*Fernandez and Baradas didn't mention this report to me when I interviewed them in February 1999. They did recall a ten-page handwritten letter to Elizalde that detailed all their complaints.

Nance interpreted Manda's absence as his desire to avoid "angry words" over the incident while everyone was weary and tense.[32] If this was indeed his intention, it backfired.

Baradas and Fernandez felt insulted that Manda wouldn't talk to them in person. They shared the same quarters, Manda's two-story thatched house in T'boli, and he kept sending Nance in as a go-between. The use of go-betweens is typically Filipino, but in this case Baradas and Fernandez wanted to talk directly to the boss.

Nance, for his part, believed that "the anthropologists were leaving many things unsaid."[33] One of those things they left unsaid was that they no longer trusted him.

As for Kabayo, Mai and his men later tracked him down and forced his surrender, offstage, as it were. Nance writes of him that he had seen the PANAMIN helicopter flying back and forth and had vowed to "kill it." He had also wanted to get a "taste" of the Tasaday. Nance adds that Elizalde later met with Kabayo, with Manda's men ready to blow off the bandit's head if he made a false move. At the meeting Kabayo pleaded his case, saying he'd seen the PANAMIN helicopter flying over his territory for years, stopping to help other settlements, but never his people. He just wanted his share. Again, this was someone's story; no disinterested party had witnessed any of these events.

The two scientists' fear persisted, and even after they returned to Manila, they weren't sure how safe they were from PANAMIN. They established a code: When the phone rang at his sister's house next door, David would only answer the phone if the ringing fit a predetermined pattern. If worse came to worst, they figured they could hide out in a tiny beach hut in Batangas Province owned by David's sister, where Baradas was certain no one would find them. Some of what they feared at this point was not physical retribution but a lawsuit. They had signed a contract that stipulated a length of service to PANAMIN, and through the grapevine they'd heard they might be sued. Baradas was prepared to be sued—he planned to countersue PANAMIN for putting his life in peril—but no one bothered them other than Nance, who kept returning because he had now begun writing *The Gentle Tasaday*. They never confided many of their suspicions to Nance because they weren't sure how much would get back to Elizalde. Baradas thought that Elizalde had to give his imprimatur to Nance's account, and because anything "anathema to the outfit" would never find its way to print, why bother mentioning it to Nance?

Since that time Baradas has put the events in the jungle behind him. "For all intents and purposes," he says, "we were not really there as anthropologists. The way I see it is, I was a tourist. What's two weeks worth? My visit there, I've never taken it that seriously, because what can you do in two weeks?"

Although Baradas and Fernandez had come through their ordeal terrified and suspicious of the "foundation," if not Manda himself, they still maintained their connections to Manda and PANAMIN. Things cooled down after a while, and Baradas was asked to run the ethnographic museum Nayong Filipino. The museum's association with PANAMIN was minimal, and no one asked him to go to the jungle again.

One day, while mounting an exhibit in the gallery that included a huge mural of all the Tasaday faces, blown up from Nance's photographs, he noticed a face he didn't recognize at the bottom of the wall. And he knew *all* the faces of the Tasaday. His assistant at the time was Amy Rara. He called her over and said, "Look at this guy. He's not accounted for." Then he called up Nance, who lived only a few blocks away, and said, "John, come to the museum."

"Why?" Nance asked.

"Just come."

At first Nance didn't believe him, figured that it was a mistake and that the boy was really the one named Odo', one of Lefonok's children. Later Nance went to his workroom and pored through the scattered photos on his own. Baradas was right. These *were* two different boys. Nance had to acknowledge his own biases: "Looking over my photographs later, I was embarrassed by my mistake and stubbornness. I blamed it partly on a belief that the Tasaday would not deliberately lie to us or mislead us. The question was simple and clear when we asked Lobo and Lolo' . . . why had they denied knowledge of this boy? Without a blink or a stutter, they had said flatly that there was no such person. What had happened to him? Had he joined another group? Run away? Died? Been traded? . . . killed?"[34] Of course, if the Tasaday had misled Nance and the others about this boy, what else might they have withheld or distorted?

Messages went back and forth now between the Tasaday staff and

Manila. Word came back eventually saying the boy had died and the Tasaday were reluctant to speak of him. According to the reports, he had fallen ill and died after they had returned from their visit to the clearing.

But there was an alternative answer: Perhaps the boy had been included as a Tasaday in the beginning but later hadn't been available or had gone away. Maybe, as Baradas came to believe, someone had made a mistake in counting how many Tasaday there should be. What hadn't seemed to occur to Nance was that it might not be the Tasaday that had misled him and everyone else, but Elizalde.

6

A New Society

In the context of the New Society, when the national image has been of particular importance to the interests of the State, your support of PANAMIN has raised the world's level of regard for our minority peoples and the Nation as a whole from one of concern to that of appreciation and in notable instances, even approbation.   —PANAMIN Report to the President of the Philippines, 1974

At every turn Frank Lynch felt frustrated and stymied by Manda's interference and wanted to come to some kind of understanding about the problems Baradas and Fernandez had faced in the rain forest. He didn't want Manda around, and he didn't want Mai Tuan and his brothers getting in the way either, doling out rice and whatever else they were doing. Elizalde said he was sympathetic, but he felt a "responsibility" to the Tasaday first and science second. His sense of responsibility seemed to include media coverage first and foremost, and John Nance and Jack Reynolds of NBC were still very much part of the picture. Criticism from Lynch and others stung Manda, making him even more petulant. He knew best. Kabayo was one threat. There were undoubtedly others. The region was violent. Land was the most valuable resource, and anyone could come into the reserve and wipe out the Tasaday in a matter of minutes if they wanted. Perhaps, but if there was going to be any significant research done, Manda and his cronies had to stop acting as though the Tasaday were their personal property.

"It seems that I'm the director of Tasaday research in title only," Father Lynch told Nance one day. "Public relations seem to take a higher priority than science."[1] Lynch couldn't even get Elizalde to hand over the cave tapes for analysis.

Even worse, NBC had secured the rights to film a documentary on the Tasaday by donating fifty thousand dollars to PANAMIN, just as Lindbergh had suggested. Filming was to begin at the end of July. This turn of events did not please Lynch at all, especially when he learned from Baradas that the filming would overlap with the field-work of a man named Douglas Yen. If this happened, Lynch said, he would cut off all association with the PANAMIN program.[2]

Yen, a renowned ethnobotanist of the Bishop Museum in Hon-olulu, had been conducting fieldwork in the Solomon Islands when he first received a letter from Robert Fox describing the Tasaday. He remembers reading Fox's exuberant letter describing the Tasaday with both amusement and more than a little curiosity. Fox asked Yen to come look at the Tasaday because he thought they were "ethnobotan-ically fascinating."

"I ended up in Manila a couple of months later on my way home," Yen recalls. "He [Fox] was much saner now."

But Fox was still excited, especially about the Tasaday's stone tools. He told Yen, "Now I see the difference between polished stone tools and the rough-edged ones. There's something ritualistic, cere-monial about these beautiful tools, but these other things they use every day. At last I've been able to see people use them."

"The first time," Doug Yen insists, "I'd struck a deal with Bob Fox. Elizalde was not there. Two to three months later I met Elizalde. By this time Fox had a falling-out with Elizalde, as most people did. Frank Lynch was then in charge all of a sudden."

Manda tried to finesse the conflict between fieldwork and the NBC filming, asking Yen if he'd mind coming a bit earlier so that he could finish ahead of the film crew. Yen told him he'd show up as soon as he could. Jack Reynolds could not postpone the shoot because the contracts had already been assigned and his team assembled, but he assured Elizalde that if the filming overlapped with Yen's fieldwork, the crew would try its best to stay out of his way.

In late July, Elizalde held a dinner at his house attended by nearly all the scientists who had visited the Tasaday up to that point: Fox, Lynch, Baradas, and Llamzon. There were some new faces as well: Doug Yen, linguist Carol Molony, and Richard Elkins, a Protestant missionary with the Summer Institute of Linguistics (SIL), who had lived in the Philippines since the early fifties and was considered a prime authority on Manobo languages. It was an impressive group Manda had assembled. To say that he chose these people, however, is misleading. In every case, either Fox or one of the other scientists had brought his colleagues on board the project.

Llamzon had called Elkins one day and said, "Dick, I've been down with the Tasaday. I've got some linguistic data I'd like you to look at it. Can I come over?"

Elkins had looked at Llamzon's data and said, "Ted, this is Manobo. . . . It looks to me like a dialect of Cotabato Manobo." Fox had claimed that the Tasaday spoke a "unique dialect" related to other dialects of Manobo. Communication had at first supposedly been difficult and frustrating not only for outsiders but for people who already lived in the vicinity of the Tasaday, including Dafal, Igna, and others from Blit. But not apparently for Elkins.

One day he was visited by Fathers Llamzon and Lynch, who said, "Mr. Elizalde wants you to go on an expedition down to the Tasaday."

Elkins was on a special diet for hypoglycemia, and he knew he wouldn't fare well in the rain forest. Even so, Lynch and Llamzon urged him to meet Elizalde. At Elizalde's dinner, after discussing the Tasaday at length with the others, Elkins agreed to go. Like nearly everyone else, he had his doubts. "People not in Elizalde's camp were talking. First time I heard about it I said, 'Listen, I've been all over Mindanao, and I've hiked the hills. If there's a group like that, I'll eat my hat.' That was the attitude among my SIL colleagues and it was my attitude. So when I got the opportunity to go down there, I wanted to go in a hurry."

Elizalde assured him that his special diet was no problem. "You just give my nutritionist a list of what you can't eat, and she'll have everything prepared for you."[3]

Yen visited the Tasaday twice in 1972, from late July to early September and for nine days in December. His friend the Yale-based Philippine specialist Harold Conklin told him, "You don't want to have anything to do with [Elizalde]." Originally Elizalde had asked for Conklin's assistance with the Tasaday, but Conklin had refused, confiding to Yen that he thought Manda was too odd a character.

Yen asked for and received the assistance of two botanists, Hermes Gutierrez, head of the Botany Division of the National Museum of the Philippines, and his assistant, Ernesto Reynoso, as well as Elkins of the SIL. Fourteen-year-old Dad Tuan also assisted Yen in the collection and identification of plants used by the Tasaday. In the first two weeks they collected and named more than two hundred plants, noting their names and uses in both T'boli and Manobo.

When Yen arrived on July 28, 1972, Manda briefed him on events he already knew about. Yen had already heard about the Kabayo incident from linguist Carol Molony, much to the surprise of Elizalde and Nance, who'd thought it had been hushed up.

But this time the expedition was off to a good start. Neither Yen nor Elkins felt controlled by Elizalde, who wasn't even there when Elkins arrived. There remained one rule: to respect the Tasaday and not go to the caves unless invited. Elkins visited the caves several times. He and Yen would ask permission to go up to the caves, and Fludi would relay their request to the Tasaday. "They wanted to leave the Tasaday to live their normal lives without four or five tourist-type people watching them all the time," Elkins remembers. "And we respected that desire for privacy. But Fludi made arrangements and we went up, and I became the special friend of Belayem. He and I really bonded."

Elkins, whose wide-ranging experience with tribal people in Mindanao dated to the early fifties, was amazed by the Tasaday's public shows of affection, something he'd never witnessed in any other group. Although Sindi' was an outsider, she quickly adapted to Tasaday ways. Elkins remembers Belayem and Sindi' hugging each other all the time, though young love and hormones might have had something to do with this. But they weren't the only ones. The young men too sat around with their arms around each other, and this struck him as "very, very different."

Belayem and Sindi' heard that Elkins was not getting proper food. The special diet Manda had promised him turned out to be not so special: rice and pork and beans like everyone else. The scientist's health started deteriorating immediately. One morning Belayem and Sindi' came up to Elkins, who was sitting on a log in the camp. Belayem sat down on his right side, put his arms around Elkins, and gave him a kiss on the cheek. "No tribal man would ever kiss another man like that," Elkins says. Sindi' sat on the other side of Elkins, put her arms around him, kissed him on the other cheek, and said his name, Kakay Dakel Lawa (Brother Big Body). Belayem and Sindi' had been out foraging and brought back some *biking*. "You cook that for him," Belayem told Sindi'. "They're not feeding him." Sindi' built a fire, roasted the yam, and fed it to Elkins.

Elkins's job was to help Doug Yen spell the names of the plants properly. They did a lot of this, and Elkins just sat and listened, but when scientists needed to write down a name, Elkins told whomever was taking notes how to spell it. Yen asked a question once about something supernatural, some of their religious beliefs, and they became upset. They said to Fludi, who was interpreting for them, "You tell these guys if they're going to ask questions about stuff they don't know anything about, we're going home. We're not going to answer any more questions." The scientists apologized and assured them they wouldn't ask any more questions of that nature.

Elkins had studied a Cotabato Manobo dictionary and grammar before the trip and had picked up a lot of vocabulary. After a couple of days he could communicate with the Tasaday and ask them simple questions. But the first time he spoke in a plant identification session was also the first time he opened his mouth in Manobo, and the Tasaday were frightened. "Who . . . taught . . . him . . . to speak our language?" one of them asked.

Elkins turned to Fludi. "What should I tell them?"

Fludi told the Tasaday David Baradas had taught him. Everything was fine then, but it wasn't true.

The Tasaday's forest sanctuary had been invaded by dozens of foreigners, and their last sanctuary, their language, had been breached as well. David and Carlos had picked it up, and now the quiet man they called Kakay Dakel Lawa had opened his mouth and started speaking their tongue. Not only was it strange, but it was obviously frightening, too, and soon they started to speak to one another in a kind of code or pig Latin called *nafnaf* in which each word ended in an *uff* sound. This was a means of communication even their smartest visitors couldn't penetrate.

From the beginning the Tasaday had mentioned their prohibition against cutting plants on top of the midden near the mouth of the cave. "You know there were certain plants that were sacred to the Tasaday, and they didn't want them cut," Elkins remembers. "And [one of the botanists] said, 'Phooey, we don't need to worry about these people. We'll just go ahead and cut them anyway,' and Doug Yen said absolutely not. 'We will not cut down anything that is sacred to them.' "*

Yen asked for a bottle of liquor the next time the helicopter came in so he could smooth things over with the botanist. Dafal got hold of the liquor and drank it all. Roaring drunk, he started swinging his machete around. He also had a shotgun, and as he raved and pointed the gun in people's faces, the Tasaday seemed absolutely fascinated. The men, women, and children hovered around him as though they'd never seen anything like this before. They weren't laughing or scared. They were just amazed. There wasn't another tribe Elkins knew of that didn't know something about liquor and its effect. But the Tasaday really didn't.

Unfortunately Elkins had to leave the rain forest after only four days because of his hypoglycemia and Manda's worthless promise to honor his dietary needs. Linguist Carol Molony, though not a specialist in Manobo, agreed to take his place. Nance, putting the best face on the incident, writes: "Elkins was on a special medical diet and had asked PANAMIN for certain foods, but those supplied disagreed with him and he became ill and had to leave. 'It was really too bad,' Manda said. 'He didn't look so hot.' "4

Had Manda simply forgotten his promise to supply Elkins's diet? He could deliver liquor on a moment's notice, but apparently not food. Was this just another example of his laissez-faire attitude toward researchers in general, or was the neglect of Elkins's special diet something more calculated, a quieter, yet no less effective Kabayo incident aimed at making it seem as though Elizalde were allowing scientific study to proceed while actually standing in its way?

A t the caves Yen realized, as had Baradas and Fernandez before him, that "Tasaday life was not quite the original ideational construction."5 He was most skeptical that the Tasaday could have subsisted on wild yams (*biking*) to the extent reported. Wild yams, Yen

---

*Yen makes the point that " 'Sacred' is a loaded word. Not 'sacred,' but 'restricted.' These were restricted plants on the midden. I never even got a specimen. I didn't want to. I suppose the hoax people would say it was a cultivated plant."

believed, did not grow in abundance in the area, nor were the amounts gathered sufficient to provide what was necessary for them to live. What had they eaten before they met Dafal? Also, was trapping really such a new experience for them? The idealization of the Tasaday hinged precariously on Dafal's stories. The more trade goods they had, the more they might appear just like us, poor souls. *Then* what good would they be? Also, like Baradas and Fernandez before him, Yen learned that rice was being doled out to the Tasaday.

It was difficult to know for certain what the Tasaday's daily calorie intake was. When they went off foraging, they were undoubtedly eating as they foraged and brought home only a token amount to be shared. These and other imponderables (including the doling of rice) made it impossible to calculate accurately what they had subsisted on before they met Dafal. The fact was, they didn't need to subsist as pure foragers anymore, if indeed they ever had. Part of their diet now included the post-Dafal technology of *natek* and meat from the deer they were trapping. Hard enough trying to figure out what the Tasaday lived on in 1972; trying to reconstruct the pre-PANAMIN past was murder. Certainly, there was nothing natural about a camp crowded with PANAMIN staffers (not to mention the NBC crew). But Yen did his best to form at least the beginnings of a study, with the understanding that his findings were in no way conclusive. He had no way of knowing that his preliminary studies would also be the last.

Etut was pregnant and due to give birth in August. To Frank Lynch's dismay, this was also when NBC was scheduled to be at the caves for filming. This should be a forbidden period, he argued, and the film crew should be kept out. Although Nance had known all along that Yen's work and the NBC filming would overlap, Lynch had not understood this and said he would have objected. "You know, the majority of scientists are skeptical about PANAMIN," he told Nance, "and I've failed to change that."[6] Nance offered his opinion that he didn't think NBC intended to film the birth of Etut's child. Lynch said he hoped not, but could one ever be sure with Manda? Lynch believed he had been misled, that promises had been broken, and that Manda was clearly exploiting the Tasaday. "Manda has that candy and is sucking on it, [and he] won't let go."[7]

Despite his considerable misgivings, Baradas took charge of PANAMIN's tattered research program.* In his introduction to the Tasaday articles in the *Philippine Sociological Review*, he expresses a modicum of measured optimism: "PANAMIN now accepts the principle that, barring emergency action, the existence of newly discovered groups will first quietly be brought to the attention of the scientific community."[8] He also writes that Filipinos, where professionally warranted, would be given "the responsibility of introducing their countrymen to the outside world."

The eight-man NBC crew arrived in mid-August followed almost immediately by more journalists, Tillman and Peggy Durdin of the *New York Times*. Peggy Durdin made the sage observation that "One can see, even on a brief visit, that each Tasaday has his own special personality."[9] Hard to accept that such a patronizing comment could have been printed, but it shows as well as any a prevailing attitude in the popular imagination of the time.

When Yen learned of NBC's scheduled arrival, he was "ready to piss off." But the crew stayed out of his way for the most part. Still, no matter how much one is left alone, whether a scientist or a Tasaday, the very presence of cameras alters the landscape. The presence of *any* observer alters the landscape. Some of the sequences that NBC filmed were staged, Yen remembers, though he adds that "their affection for Elizalde seemed genuine to me."

One such sequence involved Belayem, who was "calling out the names of the various members of the film crew for a sequence that might run behind the credits at the end of the show. Belayem was agreeable and it was completed in a couple of minutes. The cameras continued rolling as good-bys were said and all the visitors headed for the camp."[10] There's something more than a little exploitive about this scene, no matter how willing Belayem was to carry out these instructions. He was at this point, if not a paid actor, an actor nonetheless. The scene never made it into the finished film.

*There's some discrepancy in the dates here. In Baradas's introduction to the Lynch-Fernandez report in the *Philippine Sociological Review*, a note states that he became PANAMIN's research director on July 1, 1972. But in *The Gentle Tasaday*, Nance doesn't have Lynch even resigning until early August. It seems likely in this case that Nance's dates are correct, given the main reason Lynch resigned, NBC's arrival in August.

Most of the visitors other than Yen and Manda had been in Vietnam, and now they found themselves in this strange bucolic setting among a group of bubbly leaf-clad people who welcomed them with hugs and warm nuzzles. There were two sets of technicians, two soundmen, and two cameramen. "They felt a tremendous release from this bloody strain of the Vietnam thing," Yen says. "By then John [Nance] was out of Vietnam, but all the reports from there had to go through him [as AP bureau chief]. He could visualize a report the way I couldn't. He could smell the blood. The rich kid, Elizalde, was just as bound up [in the atmosphere at the caves], though he wasn't there very long." At the caves Manda let down his guard and shared moments with the others that had "nothing to do with his wealth and power," sitting around singing Jerome Kern and Cole Porter songs amid the cries of jungle birds.

But there was, as always, trouble in paradise. On the heels of NBC's arrival a Christian family of seven had been butchered in their home near Surallah. The police, aided by the lowland vigilantes the Ilaga (perhaps even one and the same), rounded up seven T'boli and tortured them for four days until they named four other T'boli as the murderers. Held and tortured for more than a month, the T'boli refused to confess. The community of Visayan immigrants in Surallah threatened widespread reprisals against all T'boli, and a small contingent of troops were called in to calm the situation.[11] For the T'boli, this was just one in a string of violent incidents aimed at them.

Manda hired a lawyer to represent the arrested T'boli and get them released on bond. Ever mindful of publicity, he flew in a group of Manila reporters to cover the story.

In early September, Elizalde and PANAMIN staffers (including Nance) met with Mayor Sison and his staff to try to smooth things over. In a remarkable discussion Sison's cohorts lashed out at PANAMIN, criticizing its policy of holding land in trust rather than grant ownership to individual tribal members. Following the establishment of the Tasaday Reserve, charges were repeated from Surallah's city council resolution of that July that the Tasaday were simply a group of Manobo criminals who'd been sent into exile or, variously, that some of the Tasaday had been recognized by residents of Surallah as former neighbors.[12] Elizalde, they said, wanted the Tasaday Reserve for mining.

One man's utopia can be an entire nation's nightmare. The Philippine constitution barred Ferdinand Marcos from seeking a third term. The economic growth of Marcos's first term had given way to a general slowdown, deteriorating cities, poverty, crime, and widespread dissatisfaction with the regime. To add to the public's frustration, the 1969 election was considered one of the most dishonest in the country's history, and there was general apprehension that Marcos might try to subvert the constitution to maintain power.

Marcos in fact had contemplated martial law for quite some time, and when he finally imposed it, there was no great surprise, though some in Congress had tried valiantly to oppose it. In June 1971, as the Tasaday were being "discovered," a constitutional convention was convened. The old constitution had been drafted during the American occupation, and it was agreed the country needed a constitution that had not been imposed by foreigners. Delegates, to be on the safe side, passed a resolution that no matter what the final document looked like, Marcos, as well as any of his family members, would be forbidden to become chief of state. The provision didn't stand in Marcos's way for long; he was able, through means at his disposal, to have the ban dropped the following summer. Even so, as the 1971 midterm elections proved, neither he nor his party held much favor in the Philippines anymore, and polls showed that not he, or Imelda, or even his handpicked successor, Minister of Defense Juan Ponce Enrile, would stand a chance against his most formidable rival, Benigno "Ninoy" Aquino.

On August 21, 1971, a grenade attack during an election rally at the Plaza Miranda in Manila killed ten people and wounded sixty-six, all the opposition Liberal party candidates present at the rally among them. The attack prompted Marcos to suspend habeas corpus, a prelude to the imposition of martial law. Conventional wisdom has it that the attack was instigated by Marcos's agents provocateurs. If so, it backfired in that the Liberal party swept the elections, and many of Marcos's own candidates, including Elizalde, received a drubbing. A member of Marcos's cabinet, Senator Blas Ople, has since suggested that Marcos was in fact "extremely worried by the incident," suspected the Communists, and was, in any case, "quite daunted by the NPA (New People's Army) threat."[13]

On September 21, 1972, Marcos declared martial law. In short order, the military arrested key opposition leaders, including Benigno Aquino, student and labor activists, journalists, and common criminals. Military camps brimmed with thirty thousand detainees. Support in the country was widespread. This seemed a quick fix to the general unrest in the country, and most Filipinos thought martial law would last only a few months. No one dreamed it would last until 1981. A New Society, Marcos called it, dressing up his dictatorship in leaves, in a manner of speaking.

Two months after the imposition of martial law, Elizalde wrote to Marcos that PANAMIN could best serve the New Society in terms of "national security." The president appreciated the offer and ordered Manda to conduct a "special mission . . . to form and maintain tribal militia units called Civilian Home Defense Forces manned exclusively by tribal minorities."[14]

Elizalde wrote a confidential report for Marcos arguing that for the tribal people of the Philippines to resist "subversives," attention needed to be paid to the social ills that made them vulnerable in the first place: "The difficulties in which many tribes find themselves today—losing their land, injustice, lack of security, economic and educational deprivations—make them highly susceptible to the sales pitch of trained subversives who may woo them with promises of solutions. It would be tragic if enemies of the Republic succeeded simply because no one else reached the minorities first. . . . As has been proven elsewhere in Asia, the lasting answer to this problem is in eliminating the just grievances of the people; removing the sources of their alienation from the government; making them truly a part of the nation."[15]

While some of the cures proposed might have been worse than the disease, the tone throughout is earnest. Notably absent is the conspiratorial winking one might expect of two men trying to rob the tribal minorities of their birthrights.

Ferdinand Marcos had long been enamored of tribal Filipinos. For years he had been obsessed with the search for a common Filipino identity, a link with an ur-Filipino. Both he and Imelda were fascinated with anthropology and had visited the Tabon Caves on the island of Palawan. Ferdinand "authored" a four-volume history of the Philippines, *Tadhana* (Destiny), actually ghostwritten by a collection of University of the Philippines professors (including, ironically, Zeus

Salazar and fellow hoax proponent Jerome Bailen). In the mid-seventies, Imelda latched on to the regional myth of Malakas and Maganda (Strength and Beauty), the Filipino Adam and Eve. She became so obsessed with this story that she commissioned a number of paintings of Ferdinand and her in the guise of this primeval couple.

Elizalde asked for a "nationwide extension" of the PANAMIN programs already in place, identifying the various tribes that would make up his constituency. These included some forty-eight groups throughout the country, including the 50,000 members of the Cotabato Manobo, 150,000 T'boli, 12,000 Mansaka, 10,000 Mandaya, and, sandwiched between the Manobo and the T'boli, 27 Tasaday. He divided his strategy into long-term and short-term activities. In the short run he planned medical missions throughout the country, with priority given to those regions that had already been "infiltrated by provocateurs." Elizalde himself would head these missions and disseminate the government's plans, accompanied by a detail of constabulary troopers assigned to him on a twenty-four-hour basis.

He also advocated a public relations initiative aimed not only at the tribes and the domestic audience but at a foreign audience as well. He hoped "to broaden the government's reputation of pursuing advanced policies towards the minorities, which can serve as models for other governments to follow . . . [and] to reinforce the belief held abroad that all Filipinos, including the hill tribes, support the New Society."[16]

Both Elizalde and Marcos recognized the potential of the Tasaday to put a gentle face, as it were, on totalitarianism.

With David Baradas's inevitable resignation and neither Yen nor Fernandez willing or able to commit to the project, sustained study of the Tasaday became less and less likely. The forays to see the Tasaday became ever briefer and continued to include journalists (a film crew from Germany's NDR-TV, a Spanish journalist, a *Time* magazine correspondent, a reporter from the *L.A. Times*), and celebrities, including Mariola Ardid, the granddaughter of Spanish dictator Francisco Franco, and Italian actress Gina Lollobrigida. Douglas Yen and Carol Molony visited the Tasaday once in December 1972 and never returned. Between Yen's final visit and 1974, only one scientist visited the Tasaday, and then only for three days. The German ethologist and filmmaker Irenäus Eibl-Eibesfeldt filmed the Tasaday in 1974 with a trick lens that pointed in one direction and photographed in another.

While people such as Frank Lynch had tried to balance the Tasaday's right to privacy with the scientists' curiosity about them, neither goal was well served. The Tasaday were usually left alone but were also subject to intense, albeit brief, media visits. The scientific trips were too short to do anything but add to the confusion and contradiction and wild theorizing. Yen and Nance, like those before them, certainly seemed unable to contain their own frustrations when they wrote in their Preface to *Further Studies on the Tasaday*: "Notably in common . . . is the reticence of the authors to be definite about the hypotheses that they could derive from their data—and all of them point out the weaknesses of these data derived from short time-spans in the field."[17]

In December 1975 U.S. President Gerald Ford made a state visit to Manila. As Harry Reasoner remarked on ABC News, the visit seemed to give "tacit approval" to Marcos's dictatorship. A grand parade of tribal Filipinos in which every ethnic group would be represented was arranged for Ford. Two Tasaday substitutes were drafted: George Tanedo and Sam Ganguso, T'boli on the PANAMIN payroll. Dressed in leaves and carrying a sign identifying them as Tasaday, they paraded in front of the impressed U.S. president.

Virtually no one visited the Tasaday after 1974. It wasn't that the world had grown bored with them, but Elizalde had. In many ways they had fulfilled their purpose: They had brought positive publicity to Elizalde and the Marcos regime, and they had given Elizalde entrée into Malacanang Palace. His once-private organization now had a national reach, and the nation's ethnic minorities answered to his authority. There had always been jealous anthropologists whom Elizalde hadn't favored with visits and critics who wanted the Tasaday left alone. Ever petulant and possessive, Elizalde gave them what they wanted when, on September 22, 1976, Marcos signed Presidential Decree 1017, "protecting the Tasaday and other unexplored cultural communities from unauthorized entry." In the upcoming ten years no one received authorization, and the world heard little of the Tasaday. Nor did the Tasaday hear much from the world.

7

Passion Play

We feel hurt. We played our part. We did as we were told.
—A translator's response for the Tasaday when asked how they feel now about
Elizalde (from Central Independent Television's *Scandal: The Lost Tribe*)

enigno Aquino spent most of the 1970s in jail, and in 1977 a military court sentenced him to death for subversion. One might be tempted to characterize the fight between Marcos and Aquino as a fight between archenemies, one good and one evil, but that would be simplifying their relationship, even succumbing to fantasy. Actually, Marcos and Aquino were fraternity brothers and addressed each other in private as "brod." Aquino, a legendary womanizer, was also a consummate politician who carefully groomed his image.

Spared after his sentencing by the intervention of the Carter administration, Aquino was subsequently set free in 1980 to seek medical attention in the United States, where he spent the next three years in exile. In 1983 he decided it was time to return home, despite warnings by no less a seer than Imelda Marcos that such a trip might be hazardous to his health (a Communist or even, God forbid, a supporter of her husband might kill him). On August 23, 1983, Aquino returned in triumph to a crowd of supporters gathered at the airport to greet him, while "Tie a Yellow Ribbon Round the Old Oak Tree" played merrily. A small contingent of military personnel boarded the plane and approached the seated Aquino. Two security agents helped him from his seat, at the same time seeming to check if Aquino was wearing a bulletproof vest. He was. Quickly they hustled him from the plane and suddenly closed the door to the stairs in front of the bevy of reporters accompanying him, blocking the journalists' cameras. In full view of the crowd, someone shot Aquino in the head, and he tumbled down the stairs and landed on the tarmac. More shots rang out, and another man lay sprawled on the ground. It was the conveniently dead body of one Rolando Galman, the alleged assassin.

What's still amazing about this assassination after all these years is its audacity. Most people don't believe Marcos himself was behind it because he could have had Aquino killed any number of times had he wanted to. Conventional wisdom lays the blame squarely on the shoulders of Imelda and Marcos's chief of staff, General Fabian Ver. In the hospital at the time, Marcos supposedly went into a rage when he heard the news. Throwing a dish at Ver, he yelled, "Idiot! Now they'll all blame me."[1] Other theories of varying conspirators abound, of course. They include the CIA and even Danding Cojuangco, loyal adviser to Ferdinand Marcos and hated cousin of Aquino's widow, Corazon.

Manda, whose paranoia operated on a hair trigger, must have been greatly alarmed by this development (although one story has him calling his U.S. lawyer on the night of the assassination and nonchalantly inquiring after the purchase of a forward for his basketball team). A close associate, Antonio "Tony" Cervantes, recalls Manda's dread. "If they can kill Aquino, they can kill me," he remarked.[2] A month after Aquino's death, Elizalde fled the country via Philippine Airlines.[3] The first of Marcos's cronies to desert him, he was very stupid or very smart, his friends thought at the time. The government, in response, said nothing, though rumors about Manda's flight circulated madly. One had it that he'd absconded with twenty-eight "tribal maidens" and millions of dollars of pilfered PANAMIN funds on a private yacht.

After covering civil wars and human rights abuses in El Salvador and Guatemala, a Swiss reporter named Oswald Iten arrived in the Philippines in 1985. By that time Marcos's dictatorship was in free fall, and an open civil war with the Communist New People's

Army was taking place in Mindanao and the Cordillera. Iten spent time in the mountains of northern Luzon with one of the Philippines' most wanted men, Conrado Balweg, both a Catholic priest and a commander of the NPA, before making his way to Davao in Mindanao, where a large part of the city was under NPA control. Iten had a number of contacts in the organization and made sure they knew who he was. Otherwise he might be suspected of spying and wind up dead. In a Catholic seminary there, he met Bishop Dinualdo Gutierrez of western Mindanao. As part of Iten's doctoral studies in developmental economics he had taken courses in anthropology and had even lived for a year with the Nuba of Sudan. Since then he'd had an abiding interest in minority groups, and he mentioned this interest to the bishop, who suggested that Iten visit his diocese, which had the most tribal people in Mindanao. Iten had not traveled to this region before. He considered it too dangerous, full of roadblocks and ambushes that reminded him of Central America.

"Isn't that where the Tasaday are living?" asked Iten, who had come across the Tasaday in his studies.

The bishop laughed. "Don't you know that this was a fabricated story? This was a hoax."

When Iten returned to Switzerland, he pored through the most easily accessible publications: the original *National Geographic* article and *The Gentle Tasaday* and discovered "many contradictions." He contacted *National Geographic*, and an editor there told him they *would* be interested in another story on the Tasaday, but they thought it was highly unlikely the Tasaday were a hoax. Knowing a little about Mindanao, Iten surmised he couldn't just walk in the jungle. So through liaisons in Switzerland he informed the NPA of his intentions. The day before he boarded the plane for Manila, he secured a fifty-page paper on the Tasaday written by a German student, Gerd Unger, who had read all the available papers on the Tasaday and had also come to the conclusion that the group was a hoax. Iten brought the paper along and read it on the plane. He thought it was "a wonderful summary by a very bright student."[4]

When Iten landed in Manila, he found himself in the middle of a fast-developing story, the disputed election between Marcos and Corazon Aquino. With each side declaring victory, and U.S. observers appalled by widespread irregularities, the seams of the Marcos regime began separating in quick succession. Computer operators walked off their jobs at the government's Commission on Elections after noticing their figures did not jibe with the official tallies. The church condemned the election as a fraud. While consensus started to build in the various U.S. branches of government that Marcos had to go, Ronald Reagan remained loyal.

On February 22, Enrile and General Fidel Ramos issued a statement demanding Marcos's resignation and barricaded themselves at Camp Aguinaldo and nearby Camp Crame. Cardinal Jaime Sin threw his support behind the rebels and broadcast an appeal for food and supplies on church-owned radio advocating the use of nonviolence to block Marcos's men. Hundreds of thousands of ordinary people responded to the call, flooding EDSA Boulevard in what came to be known as both the People Power Revolution and the EDSA Revolution. Priests and nuns holding Santo Niños stood their ground in front of tanks. No Filipino soldier was going to run over a priest.

During the tense standoff between Marcos and the mutineers, Oswald Iten hunkered down with other foreign journalists at Camp Aguinaldo, watching nervously as low-flying helicopter gunships buzzed the compound. The journalists were told they could leave, but no one did, and to their surprise, the phone lines weren't cut, so they could file their stories. The mutineers of course allowed them to make as many free calls as they wanted.

If there ever was a clear-cut battle between good and evil, the EDSA Revolution seems to fit, but the fact is that as in all elections in the Philippines, there was tampering on both sides.* Conventional wisdom would have it that Enrile and Ramos had had some kind of epiphany and decided to join the good fight. In fact, they had decided to stage a coup against Marcos: The Marcoses would be captured or killed, and Enrile would name himself (not Cory Aquino) the head of a National Reconciliation Council. General Ver got wind of the plan and, instead of arresting Enrile and Ramos immediately, made the tactical error of fortifying Malacanang Palace. His action tipped off

---

*James Hamilton-Paterson quotes O. D. Corpuz in *America's Boy*: "I think Marcos won the last election, but so narrowly he felt it necessary to tamper with the results in order to make it seem like a landslide. . . . [T]here was cheating on both sides . . . as usual" (p. 388).

the coup plotters that their plan had been leaked and that it was only a matter of time before they were arrested. Enrile and Ramos fled to Camp Crame and Camp Aguinaldo respectively, and declared themselves in revolt.

Conventional wisdom has it that evil Marcos would have fired on the crowds of civilians and soldiers, but that good prevailed only because Marcos knew if he'd fired into the crowd, he'd have had nowhere to seek asylum. Actually, General Ver begged Marcos to fire on the rebels, but Marcos staunchly refused.*

Almost immediately the U.S. Senate passed a resolution declaring Cory Aquino the winner, and Edward Kennedy avowed, "Corazon Aquino won that election lock, stock, and barrel,"[5] though he had no firsthand knowledge to shore up his pronouncement. No matter; the United States had anointed Aquino, and when a beleaguered Marcos called Senator Paul Laxalt for advice, Laxalt advised Marcos to "cut and cut cleanly." James Hamilton-Paterson remarks in *America's Boy*:

> Once the Passion play had been cast with Cory as heaven's right hand and Ferdinand as the decrepit prince of darkness, the Americans inevitably appeared as the crusaders in white armour who had enabled good to triumph. It was as though their previous two decades' unflinching support for the prince of darkness were completely forgotten in EDSA's single long weekend. Yet almost no one at the time pointed this out. Everybody was too carried away by the simplistic drama as presented by Cardinal Sin himself. It had nothing to do with politics, said the prelate, for the church never meddled in politics. "The issue was moral. It was a fight between the forces of Good and Evil."[6]

The end of the Marcos regime came with Imelda tearfully singing her theme song on the balcony of Malacañang (first Evita, now Imelda), *"Dahil sa Iyo"* (Because of You), and then boarding a helicopter with her defeated husband and hightailing it to a comfortable exile

---

*Hamilton-Paterson quotes economist Bobby Ongpin, contending that while Marcos was a complete autocrat, he was also "humane to the point of weakness."

in Hawai'i. Soon after, the palace was thrown open, and the public traipsed through it to see for themselves the Marcoses' many excesses, including campy portraits of Imelda and Ferdy in the guise of Malakas and Maganda and, most notably, Imelda's legendary shoe collection. This in fact seems to be what the People Power Revolution has boiled down to in the minds of Americans: Imelda's hundreds of pairs of shoes. This is fitting (no pun intended) because in the end, unlike Russia's Bolshevik Revolution, the EDSA Revolution did not in any way change the status quo but merely relied on images of revolution. The billions of dollars the Marcoses stole from the Philippines have never been recovered. Agrarian reform is still just an empty promise, and the people who were in control during the Marcos years are still in control. After her husband's death Imelda Marcos returned from a few years in exile to the Philippines and, pleading poverty, lived in luxury. In 2000 she presided over the opening of an exhibition of dozens of her shoes, either a sublimely ignorant gesture of self-parody or a shrewd thumbing of her nose to history.

Immediately after Cory Aquino's first press conference, Iten, in the company of his partner, Ursula, headed down to Mindanao. In Davao the people celebrated the Marcoses' departure as euphorically as those in Manila, and no one cared much about the Tasaday. Iten's NPA contacts told him the Tasaday were a hoax, and no one was prepared to guide him to see them. So Iten approached Bishop Gutierrez, who told him that some of his priests knew the so-called Tasaday because they came to the market every now and then at Lake Sebu.

One of those priests, Father James Zimora, told Iten he could organize an expedition, but it would take some time. First, he had to negotiate with the MNLF, the Moro Islamic Liberation Front, and various tribal groups for safe passage through their territory. They all had to know about Iten's plans and be assured he wasn't a spy. He'd also have to give them supplies. After making arrangements, Iten started talking to people in the area about the Tasaday, to the mayor of Surallah (no longer Jose Sison but one Conrado Haguisan), the mayor of Lake Sebu, and the missionaries at the Santa Cruz Mission. He asked questions about the Tasaday, but he didn't tell anyone where he was going.

Father Rex Mansmann, the head of the mission at Santa Cruz and no fan of Elizalde's, told Iten he should leave the Tasaday alone. Iten noted in his diary, "He's one of the first chaps I've met down here who believed in that story."*

Iten thought that his expedition to the Tasaday caves would take upward of three weeks. He had no idea of the trip's duration, and no one could tell him how far it was by foot because in the past everyone had been brought in by helicopter.

While he waited for his expedition to be readied, he thought it might be worth tracking down Dafal. Ursula adamantly opposed this idea. She figured that anyone who'd been instrumental in the hoax in the past wouldn't have any interest in exposing what happened. So Iten decided to wait until he returned from his expedition before confronting people like Mai Tuan and Dafal.

Father James Zimora introduced Iten to Joey Lozano, a Filipino activist and reporter, who was also the editor of the diocesan newspaper, *Concern*. Lozano was to accompany Iten and write an article for the paper. He could also serve as an interpreter. The next morning they started from Ambalgan, where Father James had his parish, about eight miles from Surallah. Father James thought that they would need six porters and that the trip would take six days. He had also contacted the Muslim rebels in order to assure safe passage. Father James carefully chose the porters from among the various ethnic groups: Muslims as well as T'boli and other tribal representatives.

Not long after they set out, they met a man who warned them there were members of the MNLF ahead as well as Lost Commands (groups of disaffected soldiers who had become bandits). During the elections a man had been beheaded by the NPA, and two weeks before the elections two people had been beheaded by Lost Commands. But everyone believed, Iten was told, that the Lost Commands worked for businessmen who wanted to drive out the farmers so they could take over the land for tobacco companies.

Violence was apparent everywhere they stopped. Sitio Mudun, which they reached midmorning, had been attacked by the Ilaga during PANAMIN's days. The school had been burned down twice, and only two years earlier, in 1984, a teacher had been killed there. Soon after Mudun they reached a vast farm of the MNLF's. The fighters

*Oswald Iten read me this, though presumably his diary was in German and he was translating it into English.

were out on patrol, and a nervous guard armed with a carbine, afraid they might be government agents, challenged them. But the porters calmed him.

The next day, after staying overnight with the MNLF guard, they crisscrossed the winding Lawa River some eighteen times and proceeded up a steep, slippery trail. The area had been logged but also cleared by swidden farmers (who use a slash-and-burn method of farming every bit as devastating as logging; only a few big trees remained). It was difficult to advance as they crossed areas that were being logged, and they had to concentrate as they walked among the fallen trees that had been left to dry so they could be burned.

By midmorning they had reached the house of Datu' Boy Datun, a Muslim from Ambalgan who had been granted a hundred hectares of land from Datu' Galang, a mestizo Ubu-T'boli chief from the village of Tubak, not far from the Tasaday Reserve. The politics of land division were intricate here and didn't involve the central government. Datu' Galang had given half his land to settle Muslims, presumably as a peacekeeping gesture. This was T'boli tribal land, but Mai Tuan himself had approved the settlement in 1982. Each family in the settlement had to give the rebels at least a sack of rice a year.

After reaching Tubak the next day, Iten asked Datu' Galang what he knew about the Tasaday and was told that "he hadn't seen the Tasaday as described, only he knew that there were people living there, but not inside the caves."[7] Iten noted how complicated translation was because Datu' Galang spoke an old type of T'boli and his second wife had to translate it into "a T'boli which can be understood by Ilonggo speakers," and then of course Joey Lozano would translate it into English.

Datu' Galang also explained that when Elizalde came to the area, he usually had pictures taken of the T'boli and then distributed rice and arms. Cutting to the chase, Iten asked "whether Elizalde had organized the people to go naked to the caves."

"Yes," Datu' Galang told him. "It is true that Elizalde has ordered some T'bolis to be naked and brought to the caves." This was Iten's first direct corroboration that the Tasaday were a hoax. Datu' Galang added that he was supposed to be one of those people, but he wouldn't go.

Iten then asked if the *datu* knew some of the people who participated in the masquerade, and Datu' Galang said, "Yes. You can meet them."

Had Elizalde posted guards around the reserve and stopped outsiders from going in? Iten wondered. Yes, he was told, and not only that, but Elizalde had offered Datu' Galang twelve Garand rifles and some money, but because he was afraid of Elizalde, he had decided not to participate actively.

"Why should Elizalde have given you guns? What for?" asked Iten, unaware apparently of the Civilian Home Defense Forces Elizalde had organized during martial law.

Datu' Galang said that Elizalde had offered the guns so he and his people could protect themselves in case rebels like the NPA came to the area. But he refused them, fearing "that guns would serve as an attraction for the rebels to come and seize them."

Elizalde had ordered people to tie vines together and climb them, Galang remembered. Then pictures were taken. Approximately thirty T'boli and Ubu were called at one time, and over the next year they were told to go back and forth from the caves. Galang even had blood relatives among the Tasaday.[8]

Everything was beginning to fit together. Now Iten had proof, direct testimony from someone whom Elizalde had actually attempted to bribe. Manda, it seemed, had staged his hoax for myriad reasons: fame, yes, but also the vast natural resources to be tapped. Gold was rumored to be abundant in the Tasaday forest, which itself was ripe for logging.

By the nineteenth, with ten men now in the caravan, Iten could see Mount Tasaday about six miles off. The terrain was difficult, up and down and across rivers, but suddenly they arrived at a small settlement of huts near the caves where Bilengan's family lived.

The first Tasaday Iten met was Bilengan's son Lobo, who told him "that most of the Tasaday actually had been Manobos," but he didn't really remember all the details because he had been a small boy, and he really wanted his father to come tell the story. Lobo and the other Tasaday Iten met that day were dressed in Western clothes: T-shirts and jeans, not leaves. They looked like any other Filipinos, not the Stone Age cave dwellers that *National Geographic* had heralded fourteen years earlier.

Later Lobo explained that his real name was Udol and that he was a T'boli. But the group had consisted of both Manobo and T'boli.

Bilengan wasn't there at the moment, but "Commander Mefalu" would come to join them. He was the "PANAMIN caretaker," son of Datu' Dudim of Blit, and his duty was to keep outsiders away. Natek would also join them, and so would Lolo.

When Bilengan showed up later that day, he introduced himself as a Tasaday. "And then we told him," Iten says, "that Elizalde had left the country."

Bilengan offered to make a deal. "He said, 'Look, I bring out all these Tasaday and I make sure that they come,' but then I [Oswald] should be ready to help support them in the future . . . he was not specific, but being an outsider, being the first white chap coming for a long time, you know, he had a hope that I would be their new protector, something like that. I told him, 'Look, I'm not in a position. I'm not going to promise anything.' "9

They walked in a stream and then took a short trail, which they had to cut with a machete; it was obvious nobody had passed there for a long time. Bilengan said that originally he hadn't wanted to tell Elizalde about the caves. He wanted to keep the caves secret because they had religious significance. Their ancestors had been born there, he said. Iten noted it was fourteen hours' walking time from Ambalgan to the caves. They did it in three days, but one long day might do. So much for the Tasaday's "isolation."

The caves obviously had not been used for some time. The sleeping platforms the Tasaday had built lay in a rotting pile. What had Elizalde's hoax brought the Tasaday? Iten wondered. In return for playing the Stone Age cavemen, they had been sealed off from the rest of the world. Elizalde's promises and all their fame had brought the so-called Tasaday only misery. This dirty ragtag group dressed in stained T-shirts were among the poorest Filipinos Iten had ever seen. The Tasaday had played along, and Elizalde had callously abandoned them. After snapping the pictures of the Tasaday in Western dress, Iten had what he wanted and headed back.

Upon his return, he immediately confronted Mai Tuan about his role in the hoax. Mai, reluctant to talk, was not happy with Iten's questions.

Iten, accompanied by Lozano, next went to see Dafal, but Dafal was not there. As it happened, he was on his way to the caves with some foreigners. No one had come to see the Tasaday for twelve years, and suddenly, within a few days of Iten's trip, journalists were traipsing into the reserve. Foreign journalists. Iten figured out that his competitors were Walter Unger and Jay Ullal of *Stern* magazine. He had crossed paths with them in Manila, but neither he nor they had intimated that their real quarry was the Tasaday. Iten was anxious but figured at least he'd beaten them to it.

Deciding to forget about interviewing anyone else, he left the Philippines on Easter Sunday and waited until he'd returned to Switzerland to develop his film and write his story. He wanted to make sure it would appear in the weekend supplement of the *Neue Zürcher Zeitung*.

That Tuesday he received news from Hamburg that the *Stern* team had been kidnapped. The details weren't known, but the magazine, as alarmed at losing its scoop as much as at losing its journalists, contacted Iten. It wanted to buy his material. This was a big story, and it sent an "emissary" straight away to talk with him. The emissary tried to prevent Iten from publishing his story entirely, but he only agreed to let *Stern* buy the rights to suppress the story in Germany.

It seemed that Dafal, after leading the *Stern* team on a circuitous route, had abandoned them for a day. When he returned, he led them to the caves. At their arrival, the caves brimmed with Tasaday, now all dressed in leaf G-strings. Ullal and Unger glimpsed underwear under some of the G-strings and even a Tasaday cross-dresser, one man attired in not only a leafy G-string but a G-string bra as well.

In a funny reversal, the Tasaday let the *Stern* team stay in the caves at night and went away—to hunt, they said. Or perhaps the rotten sleeping platforms no longer sufficed, and they didn't relish sleeping on the cave floor any more than they had fourteen years earlier. The next day they returned to the caves without game and merrily diminished the German reporters' supplies. When these finally ran out, Dafal offered to buy new supplies. He disappeared, and then the kidnappers came. Belayem had been showing the journalists a couple of stone axes at the time, and Unger told him to hide them deep in the cave. The axes might be important, he thought, and he didn't want the kidnappers to get hold of them. If that had been his only worry, he'd have been fortunate. The pair were threatened and held at gunpoint and made to suffer through a mock execution, then marched over the mountains to the sea. Obviously, they had been kidnapped for one simple reason: They too had suspected a hoax, and Dafal, sensing this, had gone off to tell Mai Tuan, who had responded by sending the kidnappers their way.

After the *Stern* team was freed (the magazine paid a hefty ransom), Iten's story and theirs together made a wonderful pair. Remarkably, Iten had taken a photo of Gintuy and his two wives wearing Western clothes one week, and the next week the *Stern* team managed to take a photo of them in the same pose, but wearing their Stone Age outfits. "This picture," Iten says, "is very important because who has an interest to have all them there like that? And who taught them to be there like that?"

The clear answer was Elizalde and Mai Tuan. Who could doubt after such a spectacle, leaf bras and G-strings over underwear, that the Tasaday had ever been anything more than a complete fabrication? Obviously, they were not the anthropological find of the century but the anthropological fraud of the century. Iten, no doubt exhilarated at having uncovered such a story, must also have felt some grim satisfaction. *National Geographic* had been arrogant in its dealings with him. He had offered to do the story under its auspices, and it had all but dismissed him. It had been so sure the Tasaday were not a hoax, but it had been fooled, hadn't it?

8

"Crimed Up Very Badly"

The idea of the Noble Savage was not invented by the Noble Savage.
> —NBC correspondent Jack Reynolds, *The Today Show*, May 30, 1986

traveled to Manila in January 1999 to spend nine weeks researching the Tasaday. It was the first of several trips. I had spent the last year talking to the various experts on the subject in the States and gathering armloads of documents. Among other people I wanted to meet Joey Lozano, the reporter who had broken the hoax story with Oswald Iten in 1986 and had subsequently led in other journalists to see for themselves. One of these was Judith Moses, who produced a segment for ABC's *20/20*, "The Tribe That Never Was." Moses had given me an earful of hoax evidence, most of it pretty convincing, and she helpfully paved the way for me to travel to Mindanao with Joey as my guide.

Lozano now worked for a nongovernmental organization, the Philippine Association for Intercultural Development (PAFID). When I visited one afternoon, I was buzzed inside the gate and entered a bare courtyard, where I was met by a party of yapping skinny dogs. A mountain bike stood near a shaded table, and on the porch sat a group of men and women deep in conversation. I greeted them and said I was looking for Joey Lozano, and I was directed to the front door. Inside, there was a small warren of hot offices and an air-conditioned room with a sliding glass door where several people sat

99

intent at a bank of computers. Joey emerged from a small room at the end of a hallway and greeted me warmly. His face was bright and youthful. He looked much younger than his fifty plus years, and he had a winning smile and an easy laugh. After exchanging pleasantries, we walked outside to a nearby restaurant, where I bought him lunch, and we started planning an itinerary for a visit to the "so-called Tasaday," as he liked to refer to them.

Back at PAFID headquarters, Joey introduced me to various members of the largely Filipino staff. There was one young Australian woman who was interning with PAFID and an American, Bruce Young, who had served as a Peace Corps volunteer, working and living among the Mangyan people of Mindoro. Joey told me with some amusement that Bruce, when he was home with the Mangyan, went around in a G-string as they did. Joey pointed out a woman in the courtyard who had been an NPA fighter for many years but now worked for PAFID. All were strongly committed to the rights of indigenous peoples. PAFID's staff, using sophisticated Global Positioning System technology and computers, was assisting tribes throughout the Philippines to map out their ancestral domains, utilizing the recently enacted Indigenous Peoples' Rights Acts (IPRA). PAFID's most recent coup was the historic registration of the coastal waters of Coron Island as ancestral domain of the Tagbanua.

Joey showed me a film he had made on the Ati people of the island of Boracay,[1] who had not been as fortunate as the Tagbanua. In the late sixties Boracay had been discovered by the Philippines' elite classes, who prized the small island for its pristine white sand beaches. Within a few years Boracay was billed as the "Number 1 Tropical Beach in the World." Later, it became an overdeveloped paradise with trash littering the beaches and coloforms in the water caused by an overstressed sewage system. The Ati people's ancestral domain has been turned into golf courses and condominiums, and they live on the fringes of the island.

According to an article Joey wrote on the subject, it was none other than Manda who began Boracay's exploitation and corruption: "It is believed that Manuel 'Manda' Elizalde, then president Ferdinand Marcos' chief of the Presidential Assistance for National Minorities, introduced Boracay to the 'outside world.' He had entertained jetsetter friends at the Puka Shell Beach in the early 1970's."[2]

Joey, I learned, tended to pin every known evil in the Philippines on Manda, but here at least he was wrong. Just about every jet-setter in the Philippines seemed to own a piece of Boracay in the seventies, but its actual "discoverer" was Michael Parsons, of a well-known American expatriate family, an actor who had scouted Boracay as the location for the Michael Caine film *Too Late the Hero*.

Still, Judith Moses's admiration for Joey seemed justified to me. Not only did he care deeply for the rights of indigenous peoples, but he was a respected journalist who had earned a citation for one of the ten best investigative journalistic reports of the previous year.

I showed Joey my *Lonely Planet* guide to the Philippines, which distressed him because the Tasaday were not "so-called" in the eyes of the longtime Philippine resident and writer Jens Peters. The Tasaday were part of Peters's section on tribal minorities, and while he acknowledged the controversy, he seemed satisfied that they were a "genuine" ethnic group.

Joey knew that I was in touch with former PANAMIN staffer Amy Rara, who believed the Tasaday were not a hoax. He warned me to keep her at arm's length and insisted I not tell her of my plans. This seemed like sound advice; after all, she had been an associate of Manda's, and he was the bad guy in all this. On Joey's advice, I told Rara I was going to go to the island of Mindoro, to Puerto Galera for a little diving, and proposed that we meet before my trip or after. She seemed fine with that. In any case she was busy with projects of her own with the National Museum and the University of the Philippines Film Center.

Then she called to tell me that Mai Tuan was in town. He was staying at the headquarters of the National Commission for Indigenous Peoples (NCIP). He was having some trouble, she said. The Tasaday controversy, dormant for a number of years, had resurfaced. An attorney in President Joseph Estrada's office, Donna Gasgonia, sought to have Mai removed from his position as a commissioner of the NCIP (he had been appointed at the end of the Ramos administration), using the Tasaday hoax as a strike against him. I couldn't be sure why charges had been brought; corruption and controversy aren't exactly anomalous in Philippine politics, and in fact, Estrada's administration soon toppled, and Estrada himself was jailed for corruption. Joey had confided to me, somewhat gleefully, that he was the one feeding information to Gasgonia, a friend of his. Mai felt beleaguered; neither he nor Amy knew who was supplying Gasgonia with her information or why the controversy had been revived. All they could do was fight the charges by gathering any and all information that supported the Tasaday's "authenticity." The stakes were high, at least for Mai Tuan.

Amy agreed to meet me at the Quezon City Hall, after which we'd travel together to see Mai. It's almost always this way in the Philippines; one works through go-betweens. But after waiting forty-five minutes for her to show up, I called Mai Tuan on my cell phone and explained briefly who I was. He told me to come over.

If you didn't know exactly where it was, you'd easily miss the NCIP, on the second floor of a nondescript concrete building in Quezon City, the front of which is occupied by a Jollibee, the Filipino answer to McDonald's. A gun-toting guard led me through a series of dark and dusty halls to Mai's office. He sat behind a large desk eating lunch, attended by a middle-aged woman with short hair who was introduced to me as Toto'. I recognized Mai, fattened with age, his beard abundantly gray. He spoke a hesitant English that was a little difficult for me to understand. While he talked, Toto' fussed over him, preparing his food, adjusting the fan in the window, and pouring coffee, offering me some as well.

"You are here about mining?" Mai asked, taking a bite of chicken.

This perhaps wasn't the best question he could have asked. Joey had told me about Mai's mining ventures in Kematu, the settlement for T'boli that Manda and PANAMIN had established in 1975. I had seen photos of the open tailing ponds contaminated with mercury that small children played around. No, I wasn't there about mining. I gave him a letter of introduction and reminded him that I had sent him a letter introducing myself and my project on the Tasaday.

"Oh, yes, the Tasaday," Mai said, handing me back the letter, as happy to jaw about the Tasaday as about mining. The stories about them, he said right off, were wrong.

"Robin," he said, "this is what I learned from the Tasaday. . . . Way back in fifth generation, from now to their fifth generation, a woman called Saday was their grandma ancestor, leader of their clan. Died, passed away. And the place in the mountain . . . they called the mountain Ta . . . Saday. Because of this Saday. So they named the mountain Tasaday. These people, I think, have fled away from that certain seas."

"From the seas?" I asked.

"The seas," he said.

"Epidemic," Toto' offered helpfully.

"Oh, from disease," I said. *"Fugu."*

"When you are being contaminated by that *fugu*," Mai told me, "your entire body becomes bubbles."

"Smallpox," I said.

"You cannot lay down just in the floor or in a mat. You have to look for some leaf . . . you will die easily. This Saday with her husband flee to that mountain. The husband of Saday is Lubas. . . . Fangul was the next generation. . . ." Mai led me through the generations until I heard the familiar names of Kuletow and Sikoy in the fourth generation. There were two groups, he told me, the ones that lived at Tasaday Mountain and those at Sanduka. Dul was from Sanduka. Mahayag was the son of Kuletow, and he represented the fifth generation.

"Writers during the first days," he said, "might have committed mistake. They called them Tasaday tribe! To me, in T'boli I am a T'boli tribe. They were about twenty-five to thirty-minutes' flight helicopter to reach this Tasaday. I asked them, 'Were you named as Tasaday tribe long before?' 'No, it's only now. Only now that they call us, when we were discovered they call us Tasaday.' "

"Was it Dafal who called them Tasaday?" I asked.

"I don't know," he said. "I never asked Dafal yet that question. I am being crimed up very badly.* About this Tasaday tribe. That is none of my fault! I am a T'boli. The government come in. They saw us as beautiful tribe. This is Manda: 'Are there some more tribes nearby your tribe that are very poor?' Of course. The hunter Dafal was there with me. He says, 'I know there are some group, very poor. No clothing. No haircut. They live somewhere in the jungle, and they have caves. They do not plant. They do not farm. They do not do business with other tribes. They just stay and stay in that mountain . . .' So Manda said, 'Let's go and visit them.' " Mai suddenly made a very

*I believe that Mai meant that Donna Gasgonia's attempt to remove him from office was a frame-up.

loud and sustained sound like some kind of power tool, a lawn mower or chain saw. It dawned on me he was trying to sound like a helicopter. "We landed. Very poor people. Very touching to the eyes of anybody like Manda. And his friend General Lindbergh. Dr. Fox came in there. Even me, the poorest group I see in my life. It hurts me. It touched me. . . . So pictures, pictures, pictures. Then Manda started, 'Where did you come from?' 'We have a home up there in the interior. It's a cave. We go to the cave.' 'How did you wear clothings in the forest . . . leaves?' They demonstrate how they wear those leaves. Because . . . nothing. Woman all naked. Only a piece of rags with addition some leaves. So they're pictured. They brought us to the caves and see the caves, and perhaps in some ways they instantly— Oh! Tasaday! Tasaday tribe! Tasaday! We have no business to interfere what the writer, what Manda can say. Argue . . . We should not call them Tasaday tribe. Tasaday Manobo. That would be the correct name. Because they speak the neighboring dialect of Manobo."

I took everything Mai said with some skepticism, but what he told me was not inconsistent with the original Fox-Elizalde report to the Smithsonian Center for Short-Lived Phenomena. The Fox-Elizalde report had called them Tasaday Manobo, too.

"Why was it said at first, though, that they couldn't be understood," I asked, "if they were speaking Manobo, a dialect of Manobo?"

"If you want the truth," Mai told me again, "they're Tasaday Manobo. There's no mountain that becomes a tribe!" Here he started rattling off the names of mountains in the Philippines. "Mount Apo! There's no Apo tribe!"

But I wanted to talk about the language. "One thing that doesn't quite make sense to me," I said, "is the idea that people had trouble understanding them at first."

"Yes, that is true," he said.

"They spoke a kind of Manobo dialect. Did Igna [the first translator] really have trouble?"

"No, not so much," Mai admitted. "Not so much."

This was too easy. I asked if people knew they were there.

"People around, I think, know that they were there," Mai said. "They were known. That's impossible for them not to know that there are people there. Like Dafal. Dafal came from a little distance away from the nearby tribe. He know that there are people in the forest."

We talked for a little while about other groups living in the forest. Among the T'boli, Mai said, there were groups of one or two, but the Tasaday were unusual in that they represented more than one family.

"But when you and Manda found the Tasaday, the Tasaday Manobo, at the clearing—" I started to say.

"The edge of the forest," Mai said.

"They were wearing cloth at that time."

"Yes they were. Small."

"But how did they get the idea to—"

"Leaves?" he asked.

"I heard that Manda asked them, 'What did you wear before . . . bark of trees [a kind of cloth can be made from certain barks], leaves?' I think Manda asked them, 'Where are those leaves?' So he asked them to maybe wear leaves or wear what they had worn before."

"Yes, he asked them to wear those things that they used to have before the rag came in."

"Why is it that the Tasaday—some seem to say one thing and some say another?" I asked. But I never received an answer. Amy Rara rushed in, breathless and smiling, and she and I made our apologies for missing each other at Quezon City Hall. Amy is a small woman but very self-possessed and garrulous, and she immediately took charge of the conversation.

Amy and I talked about visiting the Tasaday together, though I had little intention of doing so. I had made my plans. In any case, Amy said that because of the La Niña weather pattern, the rainy season had been extended and the area was pretty muddy. I had good hiking boots, I boasted. Amy thought sometime in February might be good. Or sometime in March.

"I'd love to get there," I said, a little disingenuously perhaps, because if all went well, I'd be there in a few days, accompanied by Joey Lozano. "I've read so much about the caves. I'd really like to see them."

Amy told me that a Korean group wanted to go in to do a film on the Tasaday, and maybe we could all go in together.

"Sure," I said. "Sure."

9

A Smoking Gun

What happened to you? Why haven't you visited for so long? What do you want this time?   —Carlos Fernandez quoting the Tasaday, *International Herald Tribune*, Thursday, May 5, 1986

On the heels of the Iten and *Stern* stories and the worldwide flurry of publicity the hoax charges brought, those who had known the Tasaday in the early seventies organized an expedition to look into the situation for themselves. Like some kind of authenticity swat team, they made it on the scene a mere two weeks after the kidnapping of the *Stern* reporters. The group included John Nance, Jack Reynolds with an NBC film crew, Carlos Fernandez, and Jesus Peralta. The first person they encountered was Belayem, sitting in a leaf G-string on a rock by a stream, as though he'd been waiting for them there for the past dozen years. When he saw his visitors, he shouted and laughed, but his laughter seemed strained, almost "mocking." Sindi' accompanied Belayem, as did two adolescents, Sius and Maman, who had been toddlers when Nance had visited last. Nance and the others had expected them to be wearing Western-style clothing, but all wore leaves, though up close one could see cloth poking through. Where had they been? Belayem wanted to know. And where was Momo' Dakel?

Nance and the others said they didn't know where he was. But would he be back? Belayem asked. They had waited a long time for him.

107

He might never return, they told Belayem, who stiffened and blinked.

The group trudged up the hill to the Tasaday caves, where they found "a considerable number of women and children" they didn't recognize, as well as Dul, now a woman of about forty. She and the others were dressed in a mishmash of styles, some with leaves over clothes, some bare-breasted, some wearing leaf brassieres. Several wore beads and brass. The wooden platforms and drying racks had been rebuilt since Iten's visit, but the caves seemed bare as ever. A credulous Nance reported that one of the caves showed evidence of having lately been swept clean with a leaf broom.

Dul too wanted to know where they had been. The visitors said they lived far away. They were just making excuses, she told them.

The Tasaday were wary of their visitors now. If times had changed in the outside world, if people behaved and believed differently from the way they had in 1971, if the world was more cynical, so, too, had the Tasaday changed. If they had loved Elizalde, had he reciprocated? No, he hadn't at all, though they'd waited. For twelve years. And when they heard a helicopter overhead, perhaps as in the old days they hurried to see if it might be he, but it never was. They'd been told by Oswald Iten that Momo' Dakel had "left the country." But what did that mean to them? What did they know of the country, of that concept? Then Walter and Jay had shown up and been taken away by bandits. Now, once again, Jambangan and his friends had returned. But was this something to be happy about? What did they want now?

In the old days the outsiders had asked her and the others many questions, Dul told Nance and the others. Now she and the Tasaday had some questions for them.

"We often thought of you," one of the visitors told them, trying to salve their feelings. "But we were unable to visit."

The Tasaday conferred and replied: "Yes? Well, we waited and waited. . . . We kept you inside of us all this time, but you never came."[1]

That evening the visitors presented the Tasaday with some gifts, ten steel bolos and five axes. The Tasaday passed them around, made some appreciative noises, and then Dul asked, "Is that all?"

The visitors were befuddled and asked Dul what she meant.

"Is that all you're giving us?" she asked. She said they hadn't seen the things that had been promised to them.

Who made promises? the visitors wanted to know.

Momo' Dakel. He had promised them salt and beads, cloth, and flashlights, and none of it had come.

Someone in the group had the temerity to ask them what they had given in return for these promised gifts.

"What we give you is that you click your cameras at us," Dul replied sternly. "That is what we give!"

Throughout that day and the next, more and more of the original Tasaday appeared, allegedly returning from food gathering. Several of the older members of the clan had died, but intermarriages with the people from Blit had swelled their numbers to sixty-one.

Peralta tried to make sense of their strange mixture of clothing styles: "The Tasaday were putting on the leaves for the benefit of outsiders who had come to see and photograph them, having been conditioned to this in the past. The less reticent among them even knew what was wanted of them in terms of action and poses. It appeared that they were conscious of the image that was wanted of them and, in fact, they were putting on a visual and even an auditive performance. There was no indication from any of the dialogue that they had been asked to attempt this seeming deception. It appeared rather to be a spontaneous attempt to maintain an appearance because of the economic benefits that it brought."[2]

When the visitors told the Tasaday they should live their own lives from now on without depending on Elizalde, they declared a *magtu kagi* (new word), a liberation from the past. But liberation from the past, especially when the past is disputed and others record it for you, is not as easily achieved as all that.

Consider Jack Reynolds's report on NBC's *Today Show* of May 30, 1986. In his introduction, Bryant Gumbel said: "Fourteen years ago NBC News correspondent Jack Reynolds lived for a month with a Stone Age tribe in a rain forest in the Philippines. The tribe was newly discovered and was called the Tasaday. Reynolds came back from the jungle with a fascinating look at mankind frozen in time for thousands of years."

Reynolds too kept the Tasaday frozen in time. In recapping his story, he used much the same hyperbolic language and overblown metaphors as he had in his original report for the *NBC Nightly News*. He explained how Dafal had introduced knives and brass earrings, and with those small gifts, the tiny group had moved immediately "through countless thousands of years from the Stone Age to the Iron Age." The Tasaday, he told the viewing audience, had only recently seen houses. "What kind of cave is this?" he reported one incredulous Tasaday asking as he climbed into a hut.

What of reports that the Tasaday were a hoax?

"Absolutely not true, Bryant. The anthropologists say that the Tasaday are the Tasaday. They are what they are." If Reynolds had been making an existential statement, that would be one thing, but claiming emphatically that the Tasaday are what they are was saying nothing at all.

Reynolds's reassessment of the Tasaday on the *Today* show and Nance's in *Asiaweek* satisfied virtually no one. As Oswald Iten later remarked, sending in Nance to uncover whether the Tasaday had been a hoax or not was like sending a "bulldog to guard [the] hamburger."[3]

S hortly before my trip down south with Joey Lozano, I took a cab to Intramuros, the old walled city of Manila, which had been bombed to near oblivion along with the rest of the city during World War II by the Americans as they recaptured Manila from the Japanese. Early for my appointment with Dr. Peralta at the National Commission for the Arts, I wandered up the busy narrow street of General Luna. A calesa, the old-fashioned horse and buggy used in colonial days, kept following me, the driver urging me to climb in his carriage for a spin around Intramuros, which has been reconstructed, though it looks "authentic." I have seen other cities like this: Frankfurt and its Old Town, another reconstruction of a place bombed to smithereens, like Manila, in World War II, and Charlotte, North Carolina, where I used to live, the victim not of war but of "urban renewal." After demolishing most of its historic buildings, Charlotte decided to truck in some more and create the "historic" Fourth Ward. We'll make the past even better than before, such constructions tell us.

I made my way back down the street crowded with jeepneys, taxis, and pedestrians, another calesa following me now. A rooster, someone's fighting cock, was tied outside the National Commission for the Arts. Inside the building I took the elevator to the sixth floor and was directed through a large office to a far corner where Dr. Peralta emerged to greet me. A small man, about seventy, with gray hair and a wispy mustache, he was dressed in a black jacket with a barong, a light-colored shirt that Filipino men wear untucked for business and formal occasions. He wore several beautiful silver rings, and on one wrist was a black bracelet from Indonesia of a type that's widely believed to cure rheumatism. He told me that when he'd first met Dul in 1971, she'd asked him for a piece of the bracelet and he'd given it to her. When he returned in 1986, she remembered him and his gift immediately.

Peralta seemed relaxed and unthreatened by my questions. Nor did he seem to have any discernable agenda. Right off the bat he deflated the Tasaday's Stone Age image.

One Manobo *datu* had explained to him that the Tasaday were a "poorer segment of the Manobo," he told me. "We have Tasaday in Luneta Park [the Central Park of Manila] . . . who forage in garbage cans. The Tasaday were garnished, but they don't need garnishing. They're wonderful as is."

The study of the Tasaday was incomplete at best, but when ethnic groups are studied in the Philippines, Peralta said, scientists are "wary of the first three months of data." They throw them out more often than not. Douglas Yen had told me much the same, and Nance had said as much in his book. What was problematic was the reason for the lack of anything but the most preliminary data. Elizalde was the one who controlled the gates to the Tasaday paradise. Had he barred entrance because there were no data worth gathering? Had he barred entrance because he wanted to control the Tasaday? Or had he simply wanted to protect them?

Peralta thought that Manda's machinations derived "probably out of ignorance. Elizalde was very well-meaning, but he did a lot of wrong things because he was ill-advised.* But he tried to do his best. For instance, he screened people going there with the common cold and stuff like . . . He didn't want people to bring in things like knives. He kept an inventory of what's being brought in."

"But at the same time, he did bring in all these people," I said. "I think if they were truly isolated, they would have had a little more illness."

*Primarily it seems by his attorney and executive director of PANAMIN, the late Oscar Trinidad.

"Let's face it," Peralta said. "He's not an anthropologist. He didn't know what to do. I think he kept public relations people around him, and they wanted publicity. They want to probably generate more funding," and he waved his hand, dismissing those people as if they had surrounded his desk.

Peralta had asked Dafal in 1986 what he was wearing when he met the Tasaday.

"Same as the Tasaday," Dafal told him. It wasn't until very late in the 1950s that cloth made it to the area. So Dafal too had worn curculigo leaves.

"They use a vine to tie it, and the way they tie the knot is to keep on twirling until it forms a knot," Peralta said. "Only an anthropologist could have faked that thing. No anthropologist would dare fake it. His career is—" He made a downward motion. "Of course," he continued, "they're making baskets and all of that and making sago. I didn't buy that, of course. You can't do that without metal tools. Some baskets were shown to us as made by the Tasaday, but they could have been taught that later on by Dafal. Dafal taught them a lot. . . . And language. It would take some orchestration to teach even the little kids to speak consistently. . . ."

What about the caves? I wondered.

"Frequentation stations. When they go out to hunt, they stay there for a while. We didn't really do archaeology, but even the surface to an archaeologist shows the signs of habitation, how long it was, how intense it was." This interpretation was consistent with Frank Lynch's initial assessment. "They are frequentation stations," he repeated with certainty.

Peralta's views had been middle of the road from the beginning, but no one in Manda's organization wanted middle of the road, least of all Manda. Middle of the road meant less funding and publicity. Middle of the road meant relinquishing one's fantasies.

"If you start with the aerial photograph of the area done around the fifties," Peralta continued, "upriver you will see . . . You know, a one-to-fifty-thousand-scale map is so fine that houses can be seen."

"Where?" I asked quietly. What was he telling me? *There was a photo? There was a map?* From the 1950s?

"In the map," he said. "In the aerial photograph. When the scale is one to fifty thousand."

"Whhh," I said, momentarily aphasic. "You can see houses?"

"In archaeology and anthropology we use a topographic map. The scale is usually one to fifty thousand because it is highly detailed. You can see the contours. . . . Since this was based on aerial photographs, some house structures are located."

"Where? Very close?"

"Upstream of the Tasaday area," he said, "are houses."

If this was true, then no one could argue that the Tasaday were "isolated."

"How . . . far?" I asked.

"A few kilometers," he said. "But what're a few kilometers to people there? Even kids in the rural areas walk two kilometers back and forth going to school."

"Where would I get this photo?" I asked.

"All you have to do," he said, "is buy a one to fifty thousand map. Of course . . . it's possible that [the structures] are not there now or possibly there are other houses there now. But I do not think they are that isolated."

I liked Peralta's idea that there were Tasaday in Luneta Park, that anyone poor and forgotten, the isolated bands of disenfranchised people roaming the fringes of so-called civilization could be considered Tasaday. The Tasaday, Mai Tuan had said, were simply poor Manobo (so poor it hurt his eyes), and I mentioned how I thought of the original Fox-Elizalde report as a kind of police blotter, with a lot of inaccuracies, but perhaps some reliable facts as well. Peralta thought that the exaggerations that were picked up by the press were understandable. They weren't anthropologists, he said, so you couldn't blame them. The Tasaday made good copy. We talked about how the Tasaday stayed near the caves when Elizalde was around. Undoubtedly the caves were not their only home—at best, a Tasaday time share. But neither, according to Peralta, were the Tasaday comfortable outside the forest.

"When we first went in [in 1971]," Peralta said, "they were at the edge of the forest. The group I talked with didn't want to go [beyond it]. . . . They had agoraphobia. They can't stand the open space. It's difficult to teach that."

"So they were forest people," I said.

"They're forest people," he said.

I wondered why the map had made its appearance only now. Obviously, people had known about it but had been either afraid or unwilling to mention its existence. Still, Peralta's nuance seemed reasonable: The Tasaday weren't Elizalde's fabrication; neither were they "isolated Stone Age cave dwellers." But his view of Manda as a well-meaning but misguided dilettante was almost more difficult for me to accept than the idea that the Tasaday were not a hoax. Obviously, Peralta had been intimidated by Manda and his goons. I had heard plenty of stories. Gossip, or *chismis*, as it's known, is as much a currency in the Philippines as the peso. Once a rumor goes around the block a few times it tends to be accepted as fact, especially among the elite *ilustrados* of Manila. But even if half of what I'd been told about Manda was true, that still made him one of the most scandalous people I'd ever heard of.

Early the next week I took a taxi to the headquarters of the National Mapping Institute (NAMRIA) at Fort Bonafacio. With me was Jim Brotherton, a former graduate student of mine who had offered to act as my research assistant, and I'd welcomed him. He was a seasoned hiker, climber, camper, and wilderness survival expert, and his experience would certainly be helpful.

In a large office crammed with filing cabinets and maps piled in disarray, we were met by a genial official who asked what my interest was in a 1:50,000 scale map of this particular area near Lake Sebu. I had been told not to tell anyone that my interest was in the Tasaday, but I'm an awkward liar at best, so I said craftily, "Well, actually, I'm researching the Tasaday."

"Oh, the Tasaday," the official said with interest.

I gave him and his assistant my business card, and then I took out a couple of packs of cigarettes and offered them clumsily. I am not much of a briber either, but the official seemed somehow charmed by what an idiot I was and happily took the cigarettes, telling the assistant to go look for the map in question.

After about an hour or so of searching they produced a map of the coordinates I had given them. The problem was, they said, that the series I wanted was out of stock, and all that was left was this military map, one with bombing grids, which they couldn't possibly give me. I bent over the map and studied it.

The official knew the map well and told me that it had not been revised since the early fifties, not where I was looking at any rate. The area around Lake Sebu proper had been updated somewhat, but the Tasaday land was on the opposite end of the map from Lake Sebu, in the far west. The official assured me that this was as it had been when the first aerial photos had been taken in the late forties and early fifties.*

I studied the coordinates. Sure enough, just as Dr. Peralta had indicated, there were little dots in fairly close proximity to the Tasaday caves. Those dots represented human structures. The structures had been there in the fifties.

I couldn't leave without the map. I started to tell the man how important this map was to my research and that I promise I promise I promise I won't tell anyone your name and I'm not planning on bombing anyone . . .

Well, the official said, maybe I could make a photocopy. But this made him visibly nervous. After many pathetic looks, he finally agreed I could copy the small portion of the map I was interested in. If I returned later, perhaps in a day or so, I could have a photocopy of the entire map. "Don't get caught with it," he told me. I offered my thanks and took my little copy of the Tasaday area, which was more or less worthless outside the context of the whole.

The next day, while I was off interviewing one of Manda's former friends, Jim went out to NAMRIA alone to retrieve the promised photocopy. But the official refused to give it to him. I called the man myself. He said it wasn't a good idea. He felt "apprehensive." He had spoken to the chief archivist. Once again I resorted to begging and wheedling, and he finally gave in. Or, more accurately, he said I could have the map tomorrow.

The next day Jim returned to Fort Bonafacio. He asked the cabbie who'd driven him there to wait while he went inside. The official was gone. Instead there was a woman Jim had not seen before and the official's assistant. The assistant spoke to the woman, who seemed apprehensive about giving the map to Jim. It lay on a table in full view

---

*"Lake Sebu, Sheet 3938 IV." The legend in the left-hand corner of the map reads: "Sources of information Bureau of Coast and Geodetic Survey, US Army Map Series 711. Compiled in 1956 from 1947–1953. Photographs, Department of Public Highways and others."

while the two spoke. The woman left to make a call, and while she was gone, the assistant hurriedly rolled up the map and handed it to Jim.

"Is your cab waiting?" the assistant asked Jim.

Taking this as his cue, Jim walked as quickly as possible out of the building, dashed into the cab, and told the cabbie to drive.

This episode added to my growing sense of paranoia. Everyone was telling me to keep my head low and lie as much as possible, and I started to think that the problem was not military grids but the sensitivity of the Tasaday story. Whatever the case, as soon as Jim gave me the map, I went to the front desk of the hotel and placed it in my safe-deposit box.

10

Quiet Understandings

Do you have friends who are journalists? Put your lips to their tracks. Because what is truth? Truth is that thing which makes what we want to happen happen. Truth is that thing which, when told, makes those on our team look good, and inspires them to greater efforts, and causes people not on our team to see things our way and feel sort of jealous. Truth is that thing which empowers us to do even better than we are already doing, which by the way is fine, we are doing fine, truth is the wind in our sails that blows only for us. So when a rumor makes you doubt us up here, it is therefore not true, since we have already defined truth as that thing which helps us win.   —George Saunders, *Pastoralia*

When the international edition of *Newsweek* appeared with a story on the hoax charges in 1986, Judith Moses was intrigued. Moses, primarily a health reporter, had come to Manila for a story on vitamin A deficiencies, an important issue, but not a headline grabber. She found herself, like Oswald Iten, in the middle of a revolution. But it was the story of the Tasaday that called to her, much as the story of a lost tribe had called to Nance fifteen years earlier.

She phoned Oswald Iten and tracked down Walter Unger of *Stern*. Soon she had secured ABC's interest in pursuing a story for the television news digest *20/20*. Of course, reporters in general, and television reporters in particular, are rarely, if ever, given the green light to do a story and come back with whatever truth they might uncover. That would cost a network too much money. Television journalists tend to approach a story with a particular angle and then try to prove their point. Confirmation bias (the tendency to see what one wants to see) is a given, even a virtue, rather than the occupational hazard it is to anthropologists.

Kristina Luz was eighteen at the time and just breaking into the business. Hired by Moses as a research assistant, she remembers that

Moses did *all* her own research and refused to share any sources with her staff in Manila. Her protectiveness stemmed in part from a desire to shield her sources from retaliation, but Luz and others had wanted to make sure that Moses's sources were not NPA or MNLF.

This time Joey Lozano led the ABC crew, which included reporter Tom Jarriel, Moses, Luz, and a number of porters from the north, on a ten-hour hike, ending up as before in Datu' Galang's settlement of Tubak. They had been assured safe passage by the NPA, for which Lozano told me that he had given provisions. Moses would have been furious if she had known, but Lozano did not tell her. She insisted, "Not only did I not have to [give provisions], but I would not have. . . . There was absolutely no money ever or even any talk of it, nor did they ask. That was not an issue. They [the NPA] wanted the story done, and they made sure that it was done, and I know that because our [second day] there was this savvy-looking gentleman who wandered in from God knows where. His name was Remy. And you know, one doesn't go up and shake hands and say, 'Hi. I'm Judith. Are you the N.P.A.?' There were quiet understandings."[1]

Perhaps the fact that the NPA wanted the story done should have given her pause. When Remy showed up, he informed them that there were indeed MNLF rebels in the area. Immediately guns started materializing from the huts in Tubak. People reached up into the thatch and pulled out Garand rifles, even AK-47s, to Moses's disbelief, but she figured they had probably come from the Muslims. People took up positions around the perimeter.

The guns in fact probably came from Manda. He was, after all, the candy man when it came to distributing weapons to the tribes, and Garands were standard PANAMIN issue. Despite Galang's noble denials to Iten, conveyed via Lozano, it seems unlikely the *datu* would have refused such an offer.

"What's going on here?" Moses wanted to know, as did Tom Jarriel.

"We heard there's a Lost Command," someone* told her. "We don't know. The air is, you know, it just feels a little funny."

The MNLF possessed Libyan rocket-propelled grenade launchers. Moses worried that they might have to take a helicopter out of the area and that they had not arranged safe passage from the Muslims.

---

*Probably Joey Lozano.

Given the circumstances, Moses decided to invite the Tasaday to visit them in Tubak. The resulting documentary, broadcast to millions of Americans that August, is in itself a wonderful, if guileless, study in cultural chauvinism. The handful of Tasaday who showed up, including Lobo, Lolo', and Gintuy, were questioned like wary Teamster officials. "Who made you wear leaves? Who taught you to climb trees and swing on vines?" "Elizalde, John Nance, Mai Tuan" were the answers.

Jarriel asked Lozano what people "around here" thought of the Tasaday. No one took them seriously, Lozano assured him. In fact, a woman at the market at Lake Sebu told Lozano he should just wait until market day, because the Tasaday showed up there often. Jarriel reported that *20/20* invited the Tasaday to a "typical" T'boli settlement "nearly a day's walk" from their home to see if "the former cavemen really do only hover close to [their] home base as reported on NBC." Actually Tubak *was* close to home base, not anywhere near a day's walk. At Datu' Galang's encampment, Moses says, they "were just one mountain over, at the base of the mountain that leads up to the base of Mount Tasaday. We were about an hour and a half from Mount Tasaday" and about three hours from the caves.

Why hadn't *20/20* simply asked the Tasaday to meet them on Saturday in the market in Lake Sebu? The Tasaday apparently knew their way there.

The report's highlight, Jarriel's interview with the Tasaday, showed the young men in a hut, all wearing T-shirts, a couple of them smoking cigarettes.

"Adug Tasaday," said Adug, introducing himself.

"You a Tasaday," Jarriel said merrily. "I see. Okay."

Lobo introduced himself in the same manner, using Tasaday as a kind of last name, and Jarriel told Lobo that he was "on the cover of a magazine, that he was famous." "Did you know that?"

Lobo looked down, smiling. Did he know what a magazine was? Did he know what "famous" was? The conversation seemed too rapid for Jarriel's words and concepts to be translated and understood quickly by someone who had never seen TV and probably not many magazines and had no idea what *20/20* was or that his face would be broadcast into millions of American homes. He had no concept of America, no concept of any of the ideas Jarriel took for granted.

"The cover of a magazine," Jarriel repeated.

Gintuy wore a brass and bead earring. Jarriel admired it, nearly touching it. The Tasaday were all smiles and laughter now.

Jarriel shook hands with Natek, who withdrew his hand, put it over his mouth, and giggled.

Sitting with the Tasaday, staring blankly ahead, was Datu' Galang, wearing a red kerchief on his head.

Jarriel interpreted this scene for viewers: the giggling of the Tasaday as this foreigner spoke to them in a language they didn't understand. The so-called Tasaday, he said, were "poking fun, we noticed, at the tribal name by which foreigners had known them." But how did Jarriel know they weren't simply laughing out of shyness or nervousness or even making fun of this goofy white guy babbling at them as though they had a clue to what he wanted, this silly guy trying to touch their earrings?

Jarriel asked Datu' Galang whether he had been induced to take off his clothes and wear a G-string or a "fig leaf"? A fig leaf? Surely, Galang had never seen a fig or a fig leaf, but of course the wording was meant for the American audience.

Galang said he had been offered money and even guns if he'd pose as a Tasaday, but he had refused.

The Tasaday were asked if they'd go naked and live in caves again.

"They all agreed," Jarriel said triumphantly. "If anyone else comes and orders us to go naked, we'll refuse to do it!"[2]

And so the journalists were satisfied, but they'd ignored the crucial problems of the Tasaday story: the fluidity of language, the impossibility of translation, the ways in which our imaginations combust with events to create fantasies and conspiracies, the ways in which we can be manipulated by our own expectations as much as by the machinations of others.

11

Heart of Grayness

People say, believe half of what you see, Son, and none of what you hear. But I can't help being confused. . . .

—Marvin Gaye, "I Heard It Through the Grapevine"

The timing for my trip down south was perhaps not ideal. Because of La Niña, what was supposed to be the dry season remained very much the rainy season. Moreover, fighting had broken out between the government and Moro Islamic Liberation Front (MILF) forces. The government shelled the rebel camps with howitzers, and the rebels returned fire with mortar and grenade attacks. Thousands were refugees, and casualties mounted every day. Jim and I flew to General Santos City (Gen San, as it's known locally) and booked ourselves into a hotel called the Phela Grande. While armed guards are a common sight in Manila, few people carry guns, but nearly everyone in the hotel lobby was armed, and not just with peashooters. A group of six guys with AK-47s sat at a table in the lobby café, staring at us and laughing. We were obviously Kano (as in "Americanos," but a generic term for all white foreigners), and they must have wondered what in the world tourists were doing there.

The next day we caught a bus to Marbel, setting our bulky backpacks in the aisle. A man sitting beside us chatted us up the entire trip. He wanted to know if we were mountaineers. Why didn't I just say yes? Instead I told him we were studying T'boli culture. The man said he did anthropology fieldwork and he worked for a mission group, but by the end of the trip he had changed his story. Now he worked for Dole in its lab and was home visiting family. In Marbel we rented a van that took us to Surallah, where we had arranged to meet Joey Lozano.

At the Municipal Hall, Joey came out to greet us and led us upstairs, where we met the mayor and vice mayor. When we headed into the hills, we were going to stay in radio contact with the mayor's office in case of trouble. After we made small talk over coffee and listened to the vice mayor's repertoire of Clinton jokes, Joey's brother-in-law Nonoy drove us to the mayor's rice mill, where we picked up one of our guides. We then started for the mayor's resort, Punta Isla, on Lake Sebu. The road there was deeply rutted, and signs every few hundred meters warned us to slow down. Jeepneys piled with passengers and sacks of grain strapped to the roof passed us. We crossed the Allah River and traveled into the hills past T'boli huts and a group of armed paramilitary men, past a sign welcoming travelers to the ancestral domain of the T'boli.

After we arrived, we had lunch by the water and watched a man net dozens of farmed tilapia while Joey plotted our trip. In addition to the fee I owed Joey, I handed him two thousand pesos (about fifty dollars) to give to the rebels in the area for food so that they wouldn't bother us.

We spent the next couple of days waiting for Joey and cooling our heels, feeling impatient and anxious to get on with our expedition. Joey had to attend a meeting at PAFID headquarters in Davao, and that was fine with me, but I started to wonder why we needed to be at Punta Isla at all. Lake Sebu was lovely, the fresh tilapia was delicious, and I enjoyed our hike to a waterfall one day, a boat ride around Lake Sebu on another, and a junket to buy T'boli trinkets, but they weren't why I was here. Joey's original timetable had me gladhanding all the locals: meeting Mayor Loko of Lake Sebu, and going to the Santa Cruz Mission spending two days visiting none other than Mai and Dad Tuan, then heading to the Tasaday area. But I wanted to get up into the mountains as soon as possible. I could meet these people afterward if needed. I started to suspect that I was here mostly to boost the local economy and Joey's friends and family.

After several days I shelled out another thousand pesos for a truck, and we bade a fond adieu to the mayor's resort. It was back again to

Marbel, over rutted roads, past curfew and army checkpoints, past a jeep full of more nasty-looking gun-toting guys. Most cars in the area had tinted windows that hid their occupants from view.

We spent the next couple of days at the beautiful Ramona Plaza Hotel while it rained and rained and we waited and waited. Joey was nowhere in sight, scouting, no doubt, and I even called up his wife in Davao to find out where he was. She wasn't sure. Most of my money, it seemed, had gone to the mayor of Surallah, various hotels and eateries, a rebel group or two, various rental vehicles, and God knows what else. I was now busted and had to wire a friend in Manila for another five hundred dollars.

One evening I was approached in the hotel lobby by a man who introduced himself as a former English teacher at Notre Dame University of Marbel who now worked in a bank. He invited me to join him and some others at a videoke bar. I declined, and he then asked how long I'd be staying. I told him a week. He asked me why I was here. I said I was a tourist. "Have you not heard the bad news?" he asked, shocked. He meant the fighting. He meant the kidnappings. He meant the shellings. I told him I wasn't worried. That morning the headline in the *Philippine Inquirer* had been MILF OCCUPIES HIGHWAY. That was less than ninety-three miles away. We were traveling in that direction the next day, and the MILF, on the move, was headed in ours.

There was more bad news, as it turned out. Our driver had backed out; his wife was worried and didn't want him to go. Joey secured another, though, and the next morning at dawn we made our way to the house of Joey's brother-in-law, where we waited for our new truck to take us to the mountains. Our party was growing. There were now five of us. Jim and I, Joey and Johnny (who'd gone along with Joey and Oswald Iten back in 1986), and a cheerful friend of Joey's named Mulong. The truck had an extended cab and a covered back; Jim and I sat in the back of the cab so we wouldn't call attention to ourselves. We drove for half an hour, past rice paddies, water buffalo, and palm trees until we arrived at the small Muslim enclave of tiny concrete houses called Ambalgan. There we picked up two more guides, a man named Pineda and another named Toks, both of whom had also been on the 1986 trip. Not only did Toks speak several local dialects, but he was connected to the various warring factions (he was in fact an

MNLF commander) and could offer some modicum of protection for us if we ran across the MILF. The hill people, Joey told us, wouldn't mess with us either because in order to get out of the hills, they have to go through Muslim territory and the Muslims can be vindictive. Toks sat by me rather stoically.

The road we traveled over for the next hour was the muddiest, most rutted road I had ever been on, far worse than the logging roads back on Mount Baker in Washington State, near where I lived. Jim and I were amazed by the driver's skill; we had assumed that we were in a four-wheel-drive vehicle, but it turned out not even to be front-wheel drive. The driver veered from left to right, stopped, and read the road before proceeding, nearly tipping us over into ditches. We passed a waterway where people were catching fish by shocking them with electric current, effective but devastating and nonselective.*

The end of the line was the Sepali River. There was a small settlement where motorcycles known as skylabs and their drivers waited for passengers and cargo. Skylabs have elongated seats and can be loaded down with as many as five people, including the driver, along with sacks of rice and chickens and whatever else can be balanced on their thin frames.† But we were packing in with horses and had to wait for them to arrive. A small boat ferried us across the river forty-five minutes later, and our hike began.

We passed cornfields and more water buffalo and small farms and huts. Joey told me about some of the other expeditions he had led, including one with Britain's Central TV. The producer, he said, was an arrogant British woman who viewed all the locals disdainfully and treated them like serfs. This was stupid because it only angered Joey, who made sure that she was charged hefty sums so she would at least help out some of the locals she so disdained. That must have been quite a sum, I figured. He seemed to like me and I was broke.

After a half hour of hiking across fields crisscrossed by rice paddies, we waded across a river. The water quickly rose to our waists,

---

*Two other effective methods used in the Philippines are dynamite (in recent years the government has had some success in cracking down on dynamiting) and poison. The fact that people also poisoned themselves with this latter method didn't impress the practitioners as much as their immediate hunger or the need to supply food for a wedding.
†In the town of Mongkayo skylabs are designed to hold as many as a dozen passengers.

and on the opposite bank Jim and I took off our gaiters and hiking boots, removed our socks, and wrung them out.

In the late morning we reached a small T'boli house ringed by a fence and flower beds. We decided to stop here for lunch. Jim and I removed our socks to dry and sat in a small shelter where a poster on the wall read, "Save Our Ancestral Domain."

As I wandered the small compound, the man who owned it cornered me and asked me what our purpose was.

"Oh, I'm just a tourist," I said, as devious as ever.

Almost from the beginning those caught up in the Tasaday story had operated in a kind of cloak-and-dagger atmosphere. Manda was gone, yet paranoia still hung heavily around many Tasaday devotees, even some of the stateside anthropologists I'd talked to. Both Joey and Judith Moses had told me to avoid letting strangers know my purpose or destination. Not only was the Tasaday story still potentially sensitive, but the area was dangerous, and the less outsiders knew the better.

"I ask you again," the man said, staring me down. "What is your purpose?"

I ran for Joey, who spoke to the man and seemed to allay his suspicions. But another man was there, a small, wiry *datu* in his late sixties, who lived in the mountains. Joey approached me and pointed to this man. "Robin," he said, "did you write to Mai Tuan? The *datu* says that they've been expecting you in T'boli."

Oh. Well, yes, I had written to Mai Tuan. I had written him simply telling him that I'd like to interview him when I arrived in Manila. But my original plan had been to visit in November. The fact that my presence was expected disconcerted me now that I was here. Was it possible that Amy Rara and Mai Tuan had guessed my plans and sent warning that I was heading to the Tasaday area?

After lunch the rain started, and we resumed our hike. We walked along the border of a cornfield until our trail turned into a river. Joey, who was walking ahead of me, at one point doubled back and said, "The *datu* is up there, and he's got a gun." This was the *datu* we had eaten lunch with, who had said that I was expected in T'boli. In retrospect, it was a slightly strange thing for Joey to announce, at least the way he announced it, as though the man were waiting in ambush. Nearly everyone in the area had a gun. But I didn't know that. I didn't say much, but I stopped dead in my tracks. I'm sure I looked terrified.

The *datu*, whose name was Kabo Bansawan, didn't seem threatening at all. He wasn't waving his gun around. It was true he held a rifle in one hand, but he also had a small bird, which was alive and unharmed, but bound by the feet, in his other hand. "Don't let anyone see you're afraid of guns," Joey had told me. "As long as you don't seem afraid, they won't have so much power over you."

Good advice, and I took it. Eventually another armed escort joined us. It was some kid with a homemade rifle. He started walking behind me, pointing the gun at my back, but not, it seemed, with any actual intention to harm me. Some timber poachers passed us by, all with rifles and horses with already milled boards strapped to their sides. Eventually a T'boli family, a man and a woman and their son, joined us as well. The man had a rifle, and the boy a machete.

We stopped for a snack of some crackers on the river's edge. My numerous companions threw the cracker wrappers everywhere, and I went around futilely trying to gather them all up. Then Joey delivered the bad news, pointing at the hill above us.

Jim and I looked at the path going straight up between sixty and seventy-five degrees, a solid mud trail, no switchbacks. We had already been hiking for six hours and thought we were almost done.

Scrambling on all fours, I kept sliding, trying to find a foothold in the mud. And it wasn't the only hill. We kept going from hill to hill to hill. Joey had made friends with the *datu* with the gun, who invited us to spend the night with him. Late in the afternoon, Joey pointed out the man's house to me, a tiny dot kilometers away, across numerous hills and valleys. Often one of my companions, wearing flip-flops, would gain a purchase ahead and then pull me up. My boots, caked now with mud, felt simply like concrete blocks. As often as not, I'd slip and grab on to the sharp cogon grass all around us, and my arms and hands became lacerated up and down.

With barely any light remaining, we straggled into the *datu*'s camp, called Lamsaging. We set up our tents on a hill, then went down to eat a supper of canned tuna, corned beef, and mounds of rice. The *datu*'s hut was filled with smoke, and people hacked out their tubercular and asthmatic coughs as we ate. Joey stayed up late with the *datu*; I could hear them talking as I fell asleep.

The next morning I awoke to a horse nuzzling my tent and a stunning view of the valleys and hills we had just traversed. In the near distance was heavy forest, but even the valleys of cogon grass and small farms looked as lovely as anything I'd seen. Joey was already up and taking photos of the *datu*, sitting on a ladder leading to a hut on stilts. Joey told me that I should interview the *datu* because he had worked for PANAMIN as a hired guard and had lived here since the 1960s. I hadn't been able to interview anyone but Joey since we'd left Punta Isla, so I was eager to talk to him. The *datu* and Joey spoke Ilonggo together, one of the languages of the Christian settlers. The interview was a godsend. I asked questions about the Tasaday, and Joey translated. The *datu*'s answers were revelatory and damning. Yet how did I know that what I was asking was what Joey conveyed to the man? And how did I know that what the *datu* answered was conveyed properly to me? I had to take it on faith because I was not a native speaker. Since ultimately I couldn't take anything on faith, I later had the tapes translated.[1]

"*Datu'*," Joey asked in Ilonggo, "*what were you saying . . . is it true what Elizalde was saying about the Tasaday? That they were naked?*"

"*They were naked,*" the *datu* answered.

"*Why were they naked?*" Joey asked.

"*They went naked so they would be given food. The women were told to unclothe themselves and stay in the caves.*"

"*But they were not living there in the caves?*" Joey asked.

"*No, they are not living there in the caves!*"

"He said," Joey told me in English, "what Elizalde did was to tell the women to unclothe themselves, to have themselves naked and for them to stay in the caves for promises of food. . . ."

Joey asked the *datu* who these people were who had been told to go naked, and the *datu* mentioned several names: "Yaokon from T'boli, Tinda, Mahayag. And Okon. Okon is the child of Yaokon."

Mahayag was one of the original Tasaday. Okon was the daughter of Dul and Udelen.* Tinda was Bilengan's real name according to the hoax proponents. And then there was this completely new character, Yaokon from T'boli.

---

*Okon was not yet born when the Tasaday first captured the attention of the media. If she was asked to go naked at the caves, it wasn't back then. If later, then someone other than Elizalde told her to do so, as Manda never returned to the area after the early seventies. If this is a different Okon entirely, then it's the first mention I've heard of her, as of Yaokon.

The *datu* said he'd known the Tasaday for a long time because their place was just on the other side of the mountain. He and Mahayag used to go around together when they were bachelors.

"He knew them prior to their being made [by Elizalde] to be Tasaday?" I asked.

Yes.

"Did he actually find these people living in the forest or were they living outside the forest?"

"So who really discovered them, Datu'?" Joey asked.

The *datu* said Dafal was the guide, as was Mai Tuan, and, remarkably, so was the *datu* himself. Suddenly he'd been elevated from being a PANAMIN guard to being one of the Tasaday "discoverers." He added that the Tasaday were really living in the forest but not in the caves.

"It was just made up," he said.

Joey's translation to me was: "It was through Dafal and Mai Tuan and through his help also that they were able to meet and gather these people and told them to go to the caves for promises of help."

"So that's what you're saying," Joey said, *"that Elizalde knew of Tinda and Yaokon through Dafal? And also you?"*

"Yes, through Dafal and also me."

Did they come out of the forest? I asked.

"Were they living in the forest? Tinda, Yaokon? Where were they living?"

"In the forest. And they were just being commanded to stay there. In the forest. In the caves."

"What part of the forest were they living in before?"

"In the Tasaday area."

"When Elizalde came, they were told to go to the caves," Joey said.

"How did the people feel here about Elizalde?" I asked.

"So what do you feel about Elizalde," Joey asked, *"about what he was doing?"*

"They were good!" the *datu* answered enthusiastically. This most likely was not an answer Joey cared to hear. *"Because he gives money to the people,"* the *datu* said. *"But,"* he added, *"some people were given, and some were not. In my area here we were not given."*

Joey translated, "He was good for one reason, that he gives some people some money. But not all are given money. He's selective in who he's giving the money."

"So who is he only giving the money?"

"Kabayo."

Although I didn't understand the conversation, I definitely recognized this name. The *datu* continued: "*Dudim. And Mefalu. Everyone.*"

"*Why were only they given?*" Joey asked. Hadn't the *datu* said "everyone"?

"*Because you know that the people have their place,* * and I was only an interpreter for them. It was the three of us, Dafal, me, and Mai Tuan.*"

"They were paid much better," Joey told me, "those people who played the Tasaday roles and those who actively participated. But for example, Dudim, Mefalu and Mai Tuan and Dafal. They were paid well. They served as interpreter although I also helped as interpreter."

"Is Kabayo the one who was shooting at them in the forest in John Nance's book?" I asked. "They said he was a bandit. Does he know anything about the time that they were shot at at the caves?

"*Do you remember the time when the people were still in the caves that Mefalu fired some shots? What's the reason why he fired the shots?*"

Again, I had no idea what Joey was saying, though I recognized Mefalu, the son of Datu' Dudim. There's a big difference between the idea of Mefalu's firing shots and Kabayo's firing shots. If Mefalu of Blit, a supposed friend of the Tasaday, was firing shots, then indeed it was a ruse to make the scientists leave. But the *datu* hadn't said Mefalu, nor had I. We had been talking of Kabayo, and Joey had substituted the name Mefalu for Kabayo.

"*The reason why Safalo fired some shots was because he didn't understand it yet,*" the *datu* said.

"*Kabayo?*" Joey asked.

"*Yes.*"

"*Didn't understand what?*" Joey asked.

"*He didn't understand about PANAMIN and the government. So he fired some shots because he didn't know yet if the government was straight or crooked.*" Here he made a snakelike motion with his hand.

This was an interesting answer, and I wish it had been translated for me, but it wasn't. It was interesting because it fitted what John Nance had reported in *The Gentle Tasaday.*

---

*Ilonggo: *lugar.* Joey translated this as "roles," but it's more like place or area, a much more ambiguous word.

"*Safalo,*" Joey asked. "*Kabayo?*"

"*Safalo,*" the *datu* said firmly.*

"*Mefalu?*" Joey asked. "*So it's not Kabayo?*"

"*Kabayo is someone else,*" the *datu* said. "*His area is there.*" And he pointed.

"*So it's Mefalu. Mefalu?*"

"*Yes.*"

"So it was Mefalu who fired the gun," Joey said to me. I should have checked to see if he had his hand up the back of the *datu*'s shirt, manipulating the old man's jaws: "Repeat after me: Mefalu Mefalu Mefalu!" But I was buying every word of this so-called interview. Joey's strategy was relentless and foolproof. Start off one's question with the assumption that Mefalu fired the shots, and even if the *datu* gets the name wrong, keep at it until he's said what you want to hear.

"And it's a way of having the people understand what the PANAMIN program is," Joey added, as though this had any bearing on the matter. "To believe what the PANAMIN program is. The government program is different from the PANAMIN. So the PANAMIN is the program."

The *datu* clearly *wasn't* speaking about Mefalu, and even if he were, his words would have made little sense. Mefalu, the son of Datu' Dudim in Blit, in cahoots with Elizalde supposedly, didn't trust the government and PANAMIN, so he fired shots at them? "But there were some anthropologists there in the caves," I said. "And they were scared. . . ."

"David Baradas?" Joey asked.

"*There were researchers who arrived [at the caves] to learn and [Manda's henchmen] didn't want to let them discover what Elizalde was doing,*" Joey told the *datu*. "*So someone fired shots. Who fired it?*" This barely qualified as a leading question because it was barely a question.

"*Mefalu,*" the *datu* said, and he smiled.

"*Do you know who he wanted to scare off?*"

---

*In Thomas Headland's book *The Tasaday Controversy: Assessing the Evidence*, Zeus Salazar calls him Fafalo, pages 81 and 84. Salazar identifies Mefalu as a nephew of Tinda/Bilengan's and apparently a nephew of Datu' Galang's as well, since Tinda/Bilengan and Datu' Galang were supposedly brothers.

"They scared them off because these supposedly Tasaday were fake. The Tasaday were called fake when Datu' Galang was caught on his way to Manila. Maybe on his way to a meeting."

"But that was before . . . that was before Datu' Galang went to Manila, when he fired the shots, right?" Joey asked.

"Yes, before that."

Joey didn't mention Datu' Galang in his translation to me, though Datu' Galang's settlement of Tubak was where we were headed. But what was this about Datu' Galang's getting caught on his way to Manila? Joey would have mentioned it if it could have bolstered the hoax arguments. He didn't.

"They were sensing," Joey told me, "that [the anthropologists] were beginning to doubt it was true, that it was fake. [The *datu*] used the word 'fake.' And Mefalu fired his guns to scare them."

"I think that's what David Baradas suspected," I said, "because the guns were fired over their heads." It sounded plausible to me at the time.

After my interview with the *datu*, we had breakfast and readied ourselves for the remainder of the hike to Tubak. I asked Joey how long the hike would take and why it was so roundabout. The guides, he told me, hadn't been here for quite some time. Joey himself hadn't been to the area since the eighties, and Toks and the others just wanted to make sure that we bypassed bandits, Lost Commands, and assorted rebels. After hiking ten hours on the previous day, I was fairly exhausted. I asked Joey how long the hike would take from here to Datu' Galang's. For the locals, he told me, an hour or so but for us, four hours.

The second day of hiking was more of the same: slipping, sliding, climbing, getting cut by cogon grass. Four hours after we set out, we were nowhere near Datu' Galang's, but another *datu's* house, Datu' Salik. Jim and I went down to the river and bathed, then had our lunch, rice and salty dried fish. We hadn't traveled much farther when my legs started cramping and my asthma acted up, and eventually I just couldn't go much farther. I had to stop and rest while Joey sent someone to find a horse for me. Eventually one was found. It was too small, though I'm sure the horse would say, if it could, that I was too big for it. For the next two miles I sat precariously on the horse as it gingerly negotiated muddy trails upon which it clearly did not want to go. A young man, the horse's owner, urged it forward with hisses and clucks.

Eventually we reached a little grove where we surprised a woman who, after talking briefly to my guide, ran off and started yelling loudly. This did not seem to be a good sign, and I dismounted. A man appeared from the direction in which the woman had fled, and after he and the guide talked, he motioned me forward to a small hut where a man sat on a porch, casually holding an M-16 on me. He stood up and ambled over, the gun pointed directly at my face. But for some reason I had lost my fear of his gun. Perhaps his T-shirt had something to do with it: a huge picture of Princess Diana smiling radiantly. I kept looking from Princess Diana to his gun, and eventually I understood that he was inviting me inside his house. I didn't want to go, and I managed to convey that I was expecting friends soon and we should wait for them.

Joey arrived within five minutes and chatted with the gunman, who turned out to be a commander of the local Citizens Armed Forces Geographical Unit (CAFGU), or paramilitary. We were soon on our way again. We had only another couple of miles to go, Joey told us. It was now three o'clock. I held on to a tiny wooden peg on the incredibly uncomfortable wooden saddle while we clambered down steep inclines. As we climbed up one particularly muddy slope, the horse collapsed under me. Or rather, it tilted sideways, leaning against the hill, and I stepped off. The horse was okay, but it wasn't carrying me a step farther. I had to climb the hill on my own. Then I climbed another hill.

We reached Datu' Galang's at twilight. The settlement was a thin line of T'boli huts set along ridges. In the near distance was virgin forest, the Tasaday area. According to Joey, we were a three-hour hike from the caves, but that could have meant nine hours for all I knew. A man cleared a spot with a machete for us to set up our tents on a hill a short distance from Datu' Galang's hut. I was dead tired and couldn't even walk down the hill for dinner that night. They had run out of rice in any case and had sent one of our porters to buy it somewhere.

Joey had offered to send a runner to call the Tasaday if we were too tired. They could come meet us here at Datu' Galang's. After some twenty hours of hiking over two days that sounded brilliant.

By the time Jim and I awoke the next morning the runner had already been sent. Jim and I relieved ourselves of our precious high-tech boots and walked barefoot down a muddy (what else?) path through fields down to the river. Datu' Galang had gone to church while we were gone so we sat around waiting to see if the Tasaday would show. Apparently I'd bought a chicken. There were lots of things I apparently bought, and this was one of them. Toks said a Muslim prayer and slit its throat, and Mulong happily plucked while I read *The Perfect Storm* under the thatch awning of Datu' Galang's hut. After lunch I decided to interview Toks because Joey told me that Muslims had been passing through this area for generations, that Tasaday Mountain was in fact well known to them. Joey did the talking at first, giving me the necessary background. He told me that large portions of land in this region had been claimed by the Muslims. But little by little some of it was sold to the Christians "without the knowledge of members of the clan." So some of the Muslims had armed themselves to fight the incursions of the Christian settlers. But the Christians also armed themselves and formed the Ilagas or Rats. The Muslim group was known as the Black Shirts.

Because of this war, Joey told me, the military was able to come in and appropriate the land for whomever they favored. "Was Elizalde involved?" I asked. "Or was this before his time, before martial law?"

"About the same time," Joey told me. "It was the height of the Ilaga–Black Shirt, Muslim-Ilonggo war."

We talked about how the Muslims had long ago seen the Tasaday. The Tasaday used to come into market all the time, at least some of them did, like Bilengan, who didn't live near the caves but in Blit, which Toks figured was two and a half miles from the caves.

I asked him if Blit had always been where it was now. Proponents of Tasaday authenticity claimed that Blit had not always been in its present location, that its inhabitants, slash-and-burn farmers, had migrated. Joey spoke to Toks and then laughed and told me, "Same old Blit." In fact, Joey told me, the Muslims had had coconut trees planted in Blit because they were fond of coconut milk. And an old Muslim woman had died in the Tasaday area in the early sixties and been buried there.

I wondered about the Tasaday caves. Had the Muslims been to the caves? I asked.

As Toks was answering, Joey exclaimed, "Oh, here comes Lolo'!"
"Lolo'?" I said.*

We stood up and saw an old man wearing shorts and a T-shirt, with a kerchief wrapped around his head, accompanied by a man in his thirties wearing an Adidas cap and a multicolored warm-up jacket and pants.

"Lolo'!" Joey shouted. "Tinda!" Joey approached them as though they were long-lost relatives. Tinda looked blankly at Joey, and Lolo' looked tense.

"I'm Robin," I said, and shook their hands.

The old man said, *"Fion. Niko,"* and then pointed to his son and said, "Tasaday Lolo' *ini*."†

"Very nice to meet you," I said. Lolo' stared at me without expression.

"Oho'," the old man said.

"Maybe I can take some pictures," I said.

Joey coughed. "Just take it easy, Robin," he said, then indicated something I hadn't noticed before: Several men with Garand rifles and carbines were standing near us. I can't say if there were three or six of them, though I want to say there were only three at that moment and later there were six. Unlike all the other armed men we had seen before, these did not seem friendly, and Joey's nervousness alarmed me, too. The men crouched down facing us, their guns at their side.

Joey told me that he wasn't sure who these men were or what was going on but that I should just cool it. So I put away my camera and cooled it.

"You've come a long way," I told the men, who obviously couldn't understand me. "Thank you for coming. Let me offer my chair to Lolo'." I extended my hand, and Lolo' sat. He lowered his head down between his knees and didn't say a thing. He didn't smile. The old man introduced himself to me as Bilengan.

---

*I didn't wonder then, but I wonder now why Joey called him Lolo' and not Bonga, the name hoax proponent Zeus Salazar identifies as Lolo''s real name. Then again, maybe Bonga wasn't his name either. In a letter to Judith Moses dated July 22, 1988, Lozano claimed that he had it on good authority that Lolo''s *real* real name was Agem.

†In a preliminary lexicon of Blit Manobo words, compiled by Lawrence Reid, I found that the word *niko* means "you." *Fion* seems to be a contraction of *mafion*, which means "good" or "beautiful." *Ini* means "this."

Joey told me he would straighten things out when Datu' Galang returned from church. We passed a tense hour. The armed men eventually stood up and wandered around; a couple seemed to go off altogether. There wasn't much to do, so Jim and I tried to be as lighthearted as possible. At one point I asked Joey if he thought it would be okay for me to retrieve something from my tent. He said he thought it would. As I walked up the hill, two of the armed men followed me, but they kept a respectful distance, and when I reached the tent, they laughed together and seemed less threatening than before.

Datu' Galang finally arrived, and everyone, it seemed, besides Jim and me crowded into his hut for a conference, which lasted an hour. In the meantime Jim and I played doctor, treating people mostly for toothaches, with Orajel. One of the armed men had a toothache, so I gave him some Orajel, too. There was an enormous need for medical attention, which we of course could not provide. A toddler whose head was covered in scabs was brought to us; we didn't know what was wrong and didn't want inadvertently to cause the child harm. Jim gently scrubbed the toddler's head with soap and water and applied some aloe.

Finally Joey emerged from Datu' Galang's hut and said, "The *datu* says they'll talk to the highest bidder." Joey must have seen how I balked. I wasn't paying any more. Immediately Joey modified the message and told me that they would speak to me after all, that I didn't have to pay them—all because of his heroic efforts. The way he recounted it to me later that day was that he hadn't been in on the meeting at first.* The people conferring had consisted of Datu' Galang, Bilengan, and Lolo' and some of the other Ubu tribesmen. Toks had been there, too. Eventually they asked Joey to join them. Joey explained to me that "the *datu* said something which Toks translated. Datu' Galang said that the Tasadays consider him as the father and the Tasadays are like a lady who is now being courted by several groups, and it is normal, in a tribe, for a father to look for whoever is courting who could give them the best price, the best dowry. So after having heard that, I told Datu' Galang that since we met in 1986 and in the succeeding years of our meetings I have always considered him a brother, if not a father . . . and he accepts that kind of relationship.

*Though he hadn't been with Jim or me.

So after he accepted that kind of relationship between us, I told him that I am not here to propose to the Tasadays, he being my father, or like a brother, the Tasadays are like my sisters and I could not marry my own sisters, and . . . my reason for coming here, I told him, is just to find out the problems, what the problems are, so that I could keep on telling the truth, the true stories, or the facts surrounding the Tasaday story."

This speech had apparently swayed them, and they were now ready to talk to me. Bilengan sat on a bench outside the *datu*'s hut, flanked by a still-somber and silent Lolo' and a smiling Datu' Galang, dressed in a black leather jacket, a kerchief, pants, and running shoes. About thirty-five people, including the armed men, gathered around curiously as Joey and Jim took videos for me and I prepared the questions I wanted to ask. A hungry pig squealed incessantly, and a parrot that Toks had been given cried. Toks and a local minister, Pastor Kuyan, served as translators for Datu' Galang and the Tasaday. Joey would translate what Toks and the pastor told him into English.

The first question I asked was where and when they had met Dafal. Joey relayed the question in Ilonggo to Toks and asked him to ask Datu' Galang.

This was a funny moment, though I didn't realize it at the time. Datu' Galang started to answer in Ilonggo, but instead of allowing him to do this, Toks interrupted him and asked the question in the language of the Muslims, Maguindanao. Datu' Galang politely waited. It was odd too that Datu' Galang was answering this question without conferring with Bilengan or the sullen Lolo'. I should say here that I don't blame Lolo' for being sullen. He was being exploited again, and this time I was one of the exploiters. His silence was the most eloquent statement of all, one that I did not understand for several months.

Much of the time Datu' Galang spoke for Bilengan and Lolo'.* Toks reported to Joey that Datu' Galang had said they had known Dafal but didn't know what year it was.

"So you've known Dafal for a long time?" Joey asked.

Toks translated, and Datu' Galang said yes.

"Even before PANAMIN came?" Joey asked.

*In August 2002 Lawrence Reid listened to copies of the tape I made of this interview and supplied me with translations of Bilengan's words.

Toks answered yes without bothering to ask Datu' Galang.

Joey said to me, "He's known Dafal even before the PANAMIN came."

"And Tinda, too?" I asked. I was polite, but I couldn't help noticing that Tinda hadn't spoken. Prior to the arrival of the Tasaday, Joey had called him Tinda exclusively, so that's what I called him now.

"Even"—here Joey paused—*"Bilengan. Does he know Dafal?"*

Toks seemed to slip up a bit. Instead of asking the question in Maguindanao he used Ilonggo. *"Can you ask Bilengan if he knows Dafal, even before?"* Datu' Galang said yes. The *datu* understood him perfectly. Toks was unnecessary. It seemed Joey could have spoken to the *datu* directly all along.

"Where did he meet Dafal?" I asked.

The question was relayed, and Toks told Joey, *"They've known Dafal a long time in the Tasaday area."*

"We've known Dafal a long, long time ago, and we used to meet him in the Tasaday area," Joey told me. He had added the "meet him," a small addition but an important one.

"I was wondering if—when and where Bilengan first met Elizalde?" I asked.

"In the caves," was Bilengan's answer. This didn't make much sense. Nance had reported that Bilengan had been with the group that had met Elizalde at the edge of the forest June 7, 1971.[2]

"They first met Elizalde when they were already in the caves," Joey said.

"When they were already in the caves?" I asked. "So how did they get to the—how was it they went to the caves?"

Joey asked Toks, who relayed the question to Datu' Galang in Magindanao, who relayed it to Bilengan.

"What is his answer?" Joey asked impatiently.

"They were there in the caves because Mai was going there," Toks said.

"So we went there in the caves because Mai was there," Joey told me. Then he added, "Mai told us to be there."

"And did he say why?" I asked.

"So they were saying that they met Mai because Mai visited them in the caves," Joey told me after the answer had been relayed. This was fairly ambiguous. Did Bilengan understand the questions? Was he saying that Mai told him to be in the caves or that they met Mai when he visited the caves?

"They were not the one who gave orders?" Joey asked Toks. *"Ask them why they were in the caves."*

"That has been their place ever since," Toks told Joey. *"They live there."*

"They say that they've been staying in that cave ever since," Joey told me.

"Ever since?" I asked, flabbergasted. "And were they living near Mount Tasaday before? Mai and Dafal and . . ." I could hardly form a question.

"They were living in the Tasaday area," he said.

"Where did they live?" Joey asked. *"There in the caves or is their house just there in the surrounding area?"*

The relaying back and forth took minutes, and I waited impatiently, studying the faces of the three men. Lolo' had still said nothing though Bilengan seemed to be talking freely now. Joey told me that Bilengan had "corrected himself," that they used to live around the cave but that when Elizalde and Mai Tuan came, they were told to go to the cave. This was essentially what Oswald Iten had reported, that they had used the caves for religious purposes but lived in the caves only because they were told to do so.*

I asked if they had known or interacted with any other people in the area besides Dafal.

"Did they know of other people aside from Dafal?" Joey asked Toks. *"Because, for example, you said before that they go down . . . to Sefaka?"*†

"Safalo, Carding, Dafal. Those are the only people they know," Toks told Joey. Joey and Toks weren't sure whether he had said Carding or Carling.

"Who is Carding?" Joey asked.

---

*What Bilengan said, according to Reid, was actually more ambiguous. "Bilengan . . . states, 'Mai Tuan told us that we should stay at the caves, it was necessary to stay there, he told us.' There is no mention of Elizalde. I interpret this, in the context of his previous statement, that they should stay at the caves when he (and Elizalde) were visiting— i.e., not go out food gathering. It does not imply that the caves were not their traditional 'home.' He does not say that they used to live in the vicinity of the caves."

†Sefaka is in Surallah.

"The son of Dafal," Toks said after asking Bilengan.

"So they know Dafal, Mefalu, and Carling, who is the son of Dafal," Joey translated to me. Here was this Safalo character again whom Joey "translated" as Mefalu.

"Carling?" I asked.

"Yes. So they knew three people."

Actually, Joey had inserted Safalo into the conversation again. What Bilengan really said was, "There weren't other people, just Dafal, who used to see us Tasaday, and Carding."[3]

I asked what foods they ate before they met Dafal.

Bilengan said they ate *biking*, *natek*, and *bunga' kayu* (fruit of trees). *Biking* was the wild yam, and *natek* was the starchy food made from the caryota palm. I understood that it was remotely possible but unlikely that *natek* could be made without the use of metal. One had to cut down the palm before one could make it into *natek*, and that would be difficult at best without metal tools.

"Biking, natek, and fruits," Toks translated to Joey.

"They were not eating rice then?" Joey asked. "If he was going to Sefaka before, what were they eating?"

"They've just eaten rice recently," Toks said. "Only when they came to Sefaka."

"They just tasted rice . . ." Joey seemed as flabbergasted as I was. As it stood now, Bilengan was saying that Mai Tuan had told them to go to the caves and that they had stayed there until now and that they had only recently tasted rice.

This was certainly untrue about the rice, but of course I was as ignorant and naïve as all those journalists before me. I had little choice at the moment but to listen to, if not trust, what was being relayed to me. Actually, Bilengan hadn't said that they had only recently tasted rice. When asked if they had eaten rice before, Bilengan had answered immediately: *"No! Not before, just biking, natek and bunga' kayu."* But I didn't know that was what he had said.

"Only recently?" Joey asked Toks. "Like when?"

Toks didn't ask. Instead he asked his own question of Datu' Galang. "Datu', ask him [Bilengan] if he knows the younger brother of Datu' Kapok of Blit that was killed there. Does he know him? Did he see it?"

"Datu' Kapok that was killed in Blit?" Bilengan asked. "No . . ."

"*Do you remember it, 19—1969?*" Toks persisted, asking the Datu.

"What was the question?" I asked. All this talk, and I could tell it wasn't all being translated.

"They eat only before," Joey told me. "They eat only *biking* and fruit trees." Clearly, Joey was not happy with much of what they were saying, and I had not expected such answers either.

"So if they ate *natek*, then they must have used a metal knife to make the *natek*, to cut down the tree."

"*So how did they cut down the natek, how did they make it before eating it? What were they using?*" Joey asked.

Toks told Joey: "*What they were using was stone and what they were saying about where they get the natek is masag, a masag tree. And then, once it falls down, they get the contents and then pound it with a stone. That's what they eat.*"

"They were using a stone implement," Joey said to me in a quiet, pained voice.

"A stone implement?" I said.*

"What—ask them if they call themselves Tasaday or someone else called them that?" I asked.

"*Who calls them . . . what do they really call themselves, their tribe?*" Joey asked.

Bilengan misunderstood the question. "Kakay," he said. "What do you call yourselves? We call each other friends." Really, if you think about it, why would they call each other anything but friend? Why would they need a label? What would the idea of tribe mean to them, especially if, as the original reports stated, they had no name for anyone else, knew of virtually no one else?

They asked him again over the coughs of children and the ever-present squeal of the pig.

"*Manubu' Tasaday,*" Bilengan answered this time. "*Etau Manubu' Tasaday.*"† "People who are Manobo, who are Tasaday." And then, as the words I heard him say were being relayed back to me like some kind of distant radio transmission, he said it again, more quietly this time. "*Manubu' Tasaday.*"

---

*Bilengan had answered that they used *fais batu* (stone ax), to cut down the tree.
†According to Reid, this is the best representation of Bilengan's words: "Manubu' " in Tasaday rather than "Manobo" as it is commonly spelled in English.

"They call themselves Manobo Tasaday," Joey said in that same quiet, reluctant voice.

"What kind of clothing did they wear?" I asked.

"What they were wearing is not clothes but leaves," Toks reported. "They were wearing leaves," Joey said almost inaudibly. Bilengan kept talking: *"Du'en kenami sia begay, duen begay aken si Dafal sadu ilib, egoh anay sadu ilib."* "He gave them to us, Dafal gave them to us in the caves, before when we lived in the caves." But he wasn't referring to leaves. It was the opposite of the question ABC and Central TV had asked the Tasaday. Instead of, "Who made you wear leaves?" the question apparently was "Who gave you cloth or Western clothes?" A good reason Joey didn't translate it for me. As Bilengan answered, he pulled at his pants leg, unmistakably indicating that what Dafal had given them in the caves were Western clothes (though they could be more accurately called rags), not leaves.*

Joey asked me if he could ask a question, and I said sure. Joey didn't want to go through interpreters anymore. He and the *datu* started conversing in fluent Ilonggo, which leads me once again to ask why he hadn't spoken to Datu' Galang in Ilonggo all along. Why did he need Toks as an intermediary? I should repeat here that Datu' Galang's Ilonggo was fluent. Why did Joey tell Toks, when Toks started speaking to the *datu* in Ilonggo, that he should speak in Maguindanao? Why had he told me that earlier, during their conference in the hut, the *datu* had "said something which Toks translated"? Why this elaborate subterfuge? It seems strange that he had not been the one talking to Datu' Galang the whole time. Of course, if he couldn't converse with Datu' Galang, it would be more difficult to accuse him of influencing the *datu*.

"Datu'," he said, *"you go to church, right? So you know that it's not good to lie. When we talked the last time in 1986 to 1987, what they were telling us, the three of us, what you were saying is different from what they're saying [now]. So what is the real truth?"*

It was a little strange too to attack the *datu*, who hadn't been the one speaking. Bilengan was the one talking, and if Joey had just shut up, he probably would have kept talking.

---

*Laurie Reid couldn't make out the question in its entirety after listening to a tape and viewing the video of the session, but he heard the term for Western clothes. Bilengan pulling his pants leg is clearly visible on the videotape.

"You just have to wait," the Datu answered. "I told you, you just have to wait. In any case"—here he paused—"it's up to you."

What did that mean? Was the datu implying that he wanted money to tell the truth, or was he really saying it was up to Joey to say the truth? Or that it was up to Joey to interpret the truth? And wait for what? What did Joey have to wait for? The way the two of them spoke, it seemed a continuation of a conversation I had not been privy to.

"But you know, you believe in God and you go to church, so is what they're saying true or not?"

If this had been a court case, Joey might have been accused of badgering the witness. But the datu remained calm. "If I said that this is the case, you know that I go to church. And you know I didn't say that. If I go there, and then I come back, then you'll know that what I'm saying is serious."

Didn't say what? This was another ambiguous statement. Was the gist of his statement that if he went to church, then one could assume he was telling the truth?

Joey, as always, turned ambiguity into certainty, like water into wine. He didn't report the datu's comment that "it" was up to Joey. He *did* report that he had reminded the datu that as a churchgoer the datu must know it was not good to say something untrue. He *did* report that he had reminded the datu of what he had said in the late eighties. He *did* report he had asked the datu if what they were saying now was a lie or not. But he also reported that the datu had said, "Can you just wait for the time when I have met Mai Tuan? And I'll tell you what I will say." Joey kept his voice low.

"After he meets—"

"Yes," Joey said, interrupting me.

"Won't the chances be worse if he meets Mai?" I asked weakly, my hopes sinking.

"I think they've been intimidated," Joey said. Here he told me to cut off the tape for a while.

Of course the problem with Joey's scenario was that the datu never mentioned Mai Tuan.* All he'd mentioned was church, going to church. But let's give Joey the benefit of the doubt and say Datu'

*In reviewing the tape, Laurie Reid heard no mention of Mai Tuan either and said that he was "suspicious of that response too."

Galang had mentioned Mai earlier in the hut, when he and Joey were conversing (through Toks). Then why hadn't Joey told me this? Why hadn't he told me during his "Tasadays are my sisters" speech, "The *datu* wanted to talk to Mai Tuan before he talks to you, but I convinced him otherwise"? Generally Joey didn't shy away from casting himself in a heroic or noble light. Also, this was not an omission he would have made. He never would have resisted casting Mai or Manda in the most sinister light possible. And hadn't the *datu* said, in any case, *"And you'll know what I'm saying is serious"*? "What I'm saying." As in "now."

Bilengan and Lolo' didn't hang around much longer. They went off in the direction from which they'd come. Joey told me there was no hope of getting them to open up, but he took me aside and said that Datu' Galang would meet us later, that he would come down to Ambalgan and Toks would bring him to see us in Marbel, where he would be freer to talk.* Joey said in a low voice not to tell anyone, but that he thought it was best we leave tomorrow at daybreak. He didn't know what the armed men, who were still hanging around after the Tasaday left, were planning for us. Maybe they'd ambush us. It was bewildering. Whom would I tell besides Jim? No one else could speak English. And why was Joey speaking to me as though others could overhear us and understand what we were saying? And if the armed men were planning an ambush, wouldn't they simply attack us there? Why wait? We were unarmed.

Of course the *datu* would need traveling expenses, which I gave to Joey. But already, Joey said, Datu' Galang was opening up to him.

"So, who were those men?" I asked.

"It could be that they're [the Tasaday] being followed or there might be an order to do a surveillance on these people," he told me, formulating his theory.

"You don't know who those guys were?"

"My first inkling would be Mai Tuan," he said, "knowing for a fact that there's a case against him right now.† That case states that he has been a part in the creation of the false tribe, and for him as a commissioner to remain as a commissioner of the NCIP, he has to main-

---

*Datu' Galang, in fact, never showed up.
†A case Joey had helped instigate.

tain that story. Because agreeing that it is fake is tantamount to admitting the crime already."

Sounded plausible, but I had some lingering doubts. I wondered why Bilengan had not responded to the name Tinda—not when Joey called him that and not when I called him that.

"I think it's obvious that if they want to maintain themselves as Tasaday, they should avoid mentioning their original identity," Joey told me.

"But it's interesting," I said. "They weren't exactly consistent because they said they knew not just Dafal but . . ."

"Carling and Mefalu," Joey finished.

"Which is interesting that they would say that because it's not exactly the original story."

"I think obviously they're exerting efforts to maintain the story that they had before," Joey said.

"Why didn't Lobo come?" I asked Joey.

"I think they came here just to scout, to find out what's going on. And as I said earlier, they seem to have gotten that attitude of let's talk to the highest bidder, having undergone those years of abuse."

"Well, that was disappointing," I said, "but it was still enlightening."

"But Datu' Galang said he would talk later," Joey assured me. "He just wanted to consult Mai Tuan, and again, that brings out the link."

"Seems like Mai Tuan would be the worst person to consult right now." I laughed, and so did Joey.

By the late afternoon Joey's theory about the armed men had become fact. He told me I should interview Toks, who had supposedly spoken with the armed men and had learned who they were. Joey called them the Bantay Tasaday, or Tasaday protectors. Toks told me through Joey that the Bantay Tasaday had been formed in 1994 to keep people, particularly foreigners, out of the area. It was a team of six men, he told me, and they answered to Igna. Well, that was a nice twist. Igna, the original translator for the Tasaday. But, he added, she in turn took her orders from Mai Tuan.

"What arms do they have?" Joey asked Toks, a strange question since he had plainly seen them.

"Garand. Carbine," Toks said.

"Ah," Joey said. "So they're armed normally with Garand rifles and carbine rifles." Standard PANAMIN issue, he pointed out knowingly.

"How'd they know we were here?" I asked.

Here Joey took matters into his own hands once again. He asked Toks in Ilonggo how they knew we were here, and Toks asked whom he meant. *"The Tasaday,"* Joey told Toks. *"How did they know we were here?"*

I didn't want to know that! Why would I want to know that? I already knew that! But I didn't know he'd distorted my question. We had been talking exclusively for the past several minutes about the armed men, not about the Tasaday, so it seems unlikely Joey misunderstood my question.

"Because Datu' Galang had them called this morning and they were informed that there are foreigners coming here," Joey said. Then, displaying his amazing skill as a manipulator, if not a translator, he added, "The way Datu' Galang told us the other day, they were told in T'boli they were expecting you there."*

I thought of course that he meant Datu' Galang had informed the Bantay Tasaday that there were foreigners here and that we'd been blocked because of my own naïveté, because I'd sent Mai Tuan a letter. My real question—how did the Bantay Tasaday know we were here?—went unanswered . . . at least, for several months.

"And there are six men?" I asked, feeling guilty that I'd drawn this attention to us.

"As far as he knows, there are six armed men regularly patrolling the area." He spoke again with Toks and then told me, "Two of those armed men who came here this morning and who stayed until the afternoon are members of the Bantay Tasaday."

I considered this. I had thought *all* the armed men were members of the Bantay Tasaday.

After the last of the armed men departed, we sent someone to fetch us some Tanduay. Not only is Tanduay the best rum in the Philippines, but it's pretty much the *only* rum, and most important, it was Manda's rum. His family had owned Tanduay for years, though he'd sold the company in 1988. When the rum arrived, a bunch of us, including Datu' Galang, Joey, Jim, Toks, and me, sat outside the hut,

*Either he meant the other *datu* I had interviewed or he had told me that Datu Galang had also been expecting me, but this latter possibility is not something I remember.

imbibing and trading songs. The locals made up their songs as they went—sometimes histories, sometimes humorous songs. The Tanduay loosened the vocal cords of the usually stoic Toks, who treated us to a passionate song in a minor key about PANAMIN, the Tasaday, Elizalde, and the Muslims. Joey told me he was doing it in part to shame Datu' Galang for not telling us all he knew. The only words I could make out were Tasaday, Mindanao, PANAMIN, and 1971, but I didn't need to understand the words to understand. Next, I sang. I couldn't make up a song, so I chose two of my favorite blues songs, Taj Mahal's "Cakewalk into Town" and Josh White's "Evil-Hearted Me," which I sang in honor of Manda.

I don't remember Datu' Galang's song. By that time the Tanduay was starting to have its effect, and anyway, the *datu* and I had no real means of understanding. But that didn't matter. I didn't need to understand because I knew what I had seen. At that moment I was convinced the Tasaday were a hoax. If the Tasaday denied something, that was proof. If they corroborated something, that was proof. Lolo"s not smiling was proof. What wasn't proof could be dismissed. I had little choice but to believe what I thought I'd been told. Above all, I had to believe Joey.

12

Tribal Warfare

[A] middle-aged Tasaday [lay] down in a trunk of a tree and the mouth of a cave at the background. He was posing like a movie star. All gusto. *Nakadikuwatro pa!* [Cross-legged yet!]. And you really can see that the face is really one who is a pro. Yes, so he is in G-strings and in the other [magazine], I have also read that these people have never been touched by civilization and that they have no contact with other people before. How come that he can act very well in front of a cameraman? So I began to doubt. . . .
> —Testimony of Mrs. Alabrilla Rivero, a former social studies coordinator from South Cotabato, at the 1986 University of the Philippines conference on the Tasaday

vents had come in quick succession to bring about the University of the Philippines conference on the Tasaday in August 1986. First, the Marcoses had flown to exile in Hawai'i in February that year, followed by Oswald Iten and *Stern*'s visits to the Tasaday area in March. Elizalde had also left the country, in 1983, and there seemed little the millionaire could do to impede such a gathering. A giddy sense of possibility came in the wake of Marcos's ouster, yet in the words of one participant, Christian Adler, a German adventurer and social critic, "shadows" remained. Such fears could not simply be chalked up to paranoia. Marcos and some of his cronies might have fled, but they still had loyal eyes and ears everywhere. During the years of martial law, plenty of people had been "salvaged" (murdered) by the regime and its supporters, maybe not in the numbers of the *desaparecidos* in Argentina, but in numbers great enough to promote fear and suspicion among many participants at the conference.*

---

*Without downplaying the depredations of martial law under Marcos, it's worth noting that political violence not only continued but intensified under Corazon Aquino's presidency. A report by FIND (Families of Victims of Involuntary Disappearances) from December 4, 1992, assessed that during Aquino's six-year rule, more activists disappeared than during Marcos's twenty-one-year tenure. For more on this, see James Hamilton-Paterson's *America's Boy,* particularly his chapter, "Edsa and After."

Armed guards were posted outside. The buzz had been that the Tasaday themselves were supposed to fly up to Manila—tickets had been purchased for them—but they had been afraid to leave their families. The Philippines was still a dangerous country.

In the Philippines in the months after the downfall of the Marcoses, there existed a simple binary. Everything associated with Marcos was bad. Everything post-Marcos was good. And the Tasaday in 1986 became, in no small measure, emblems of the corrupt Marcos regime. Of course they were fake. They had to be. The poor people (simple farmers apparently) who had been forced to play Tasaday by the Marcos regime (represented by Manda and PANAMIN) were stand-ins for all the exploited people of the Philippines, who had been made empty promises by the Marcoses. What's more, the Tasaday controversy presented an opportunity for old scores to be settled and for grudge matches to be waged on various fronts: the University of the Philippines against the National Museum, tribal power brokers against one another, and journalists from opposing networks and newspapers.

Jerome Bailen, a professor of anthropology at the University of the Philippines, cobbled together the International Anthropological Conference on the Tasaday Controversy and Other Urgent Anthropological Issues in two months' time with virtually no money, though it's not unlikely that some of Manda's old enemies had at least a nominal hand in the organization of the conference.

Bailen's invitation for the conference reads in part: "The import of this controversy is not only of national but of international concern as well. It should be of national concern as Filipinos were actually involved in the alleged fraud; a Philippine cultural group was a victim of this fraud and Filipino agencies, organizations and associations by their active endorsement, quiet acquiescence if not total unconcern helped 'foist' the 'Tasaday consciousness' [on the world]." The only word in the invitation that even hinted at impartiality was "alleged" before the word "fraud."

One after another, hoax proponents took to the podium and exhorted the crowd as though at a political rally. Christian Adler delivered a paper titled "The Tasaday Hoax, the Never-Ending Scandal" to a packed audience of four hundred people. Using slides of Nance's photographs without Nance's permission, Adler said that the Tasaday affair was not simply a harmless masquerade. The Tasaday, he said, were Ubus who had been horribly victimized and abused, made prisoners in their own territory, and all this "under the guise of benevolence and brotherly love."

"There is only one statement," Adler said, "in which I can agree with those on the pro-Tasaday side: Elizalde was not capable enough of carrying out this hoax all by himself.

"The native informers reported about a 'White' who was said to be much older than me and who had accompanied Elizalde during his second flight to Blit. The informants said: 'He observed the people and designed a new clothing. For G-strings he used *kasongi* leaves. The people's clothing was changed and they were taken to the caves. Pictures had been taken.' "[1]

A furious Nance tried to pull the plug on the projector as Adler spoke, but he was blocked. Flustered, he tried to explain that his photographs were being used without his permission and that the charges were baseless. He was told to sit down, that he'd have a chance to respond in due course.

"Who was this white man?" Adler continued. "I have no proof for the following assertions, but a lot of evidence points to the chief anthropologist of PANAMIN, the American anthropologist, Dr. Robert Fox."

Adler outlined the reasons for his suspicions. Dr. Fox, he said, had indeed been part of the second expedition. Fox had published a report with Elizalde early on but then "strangely enough" refused to investigate further and resigned from PANAMIN. The stone tools of the Tasaday were a dead giveaway. Fox had done excavations at the Tabon Caves in Palawan from 1962 to 1970, and the flake tools he had excavated reappeared with the Tasaday. Adler conjectured that Fox had loaned the Tasaday their tools. Fox wanted security for his old age, and PANAMIN had given him a "pension until his death in Baguio."

"It is surely more than just an unkind suspicion if I presume that Fox tried to re-create his Tabon people in the Tasaday. He made a deal for that purpose with Elizalde, to do the latter a favor."

Unlike Adler, Carlos Fernandez, sitting in the audience, had spent time with the Tasaday. Although he had survived the shooting at the caves and had his doubts about Elizalde, he still believed the Tasaday were no hoax as such. More important, Fernandez had been mentored by Fox and treated almost like a son. The man who had taught so many Philippine anthropologists and could no longer defend himself was being maligned in the most hateful manner, and Fernandez could bear no more.

"Son of a bitch!" he yelled, running toward the stage. Cornering Jerome Bailen, he warned that he'd better get ready for fireworks the next morning.

Bailen took Fernandez's threats literally. There had already been rumors that "certain parties" intended to disrupt the proceedings and harm or intimidate pro-hoax witnesses. Rumors of violence and other misdeeds had always surrounded Manda, and his absence did nothing to curtail them, perhaps even fed them. When journalist Arnold Azurin took the stage, he pointedly acknowledged Tony Cervantes, Elizalde's longtime associate, in the audience. The subtext of his greeting seemed to be: "You don't scare me."

In response to Fernandez's perceived threat, Bailen stationed six police officers outside the conference hall. He needn't have bothered, for hardly anyone showed up to hear what Fernandez and Nance had to say. Nance lamented the fact that there was no way to defend himself against such a "big lie." "And yet he [Adler] got this huge outpouring of applause. . . . How do we defend ourselves against somebody who's standing up here, staring me in the eye and lying about me?"[2]

The answer: You can't. The hoax proponents had the momentum. Azurin characterized Nance as someone who was "too gullible or had served as a willing tool of one of Manda's queer games." He also criticized Jesus Peralta for trying to "blow away the heat of the controversy." Peralta had mentioned to Azurin that he had found an "opaline quartz" tool during the second expedition to the Tasaday and pointed out that only a trained anthropologist could detect such a tool. In other words, only Fox or another anthropologist (certainly not Elizalde) would have had the expertise to fake such tools, and no respectable anthropologist would dare risk his reputation. Adler was the only hoax proponent who seriously suggested that Fox had helped perpetrate the "hoax." Now Azurin suggested that Peralta was the one who was lying. "The real problem," Azurin said, "with such a claim was that (Ret.) Colonel Jose Guerrero [one of PANAMIN's operations managers], disclaimed it repeatedly, saying, 'How could he do that?

He was never with us in Tasaday.' " Colonel Guerrero, if he indeed asserted that Peralta hadn't been to see the Tasaday, was mistaken. Apparently Azurin took Guerrero at his word.

Oswald Iten too went into the ring swinging, using slides from his field trip as illustration. "[H]ardly any scientists of repute" were given access by Elizalde to the Tasaday, he told the audience, and "second-rate researchers" cobbled together reports during "lightning visits" to support Elizalde's Stone Age claims. The Elizaldes, he noted, were a fabulously wealthy family. All they lacked was political office, "a shortcoming which Manuel was to fill in the fall 1971 elections." The Tasaday gave him the media attention he desired, but after Elizalde failed in his Senate bid, he didn't visit the Tasaday again for months. Then he'd evidently hit upon the idea of posing the Tasaday in caves, causing an even greater media sensation than before, which suited him as much as winning a seat in the Senate.

Besides "the unknown researchers" Elizalde brought to Tasaday land, Iten recounted that Lynch and Fox had resigned their posts with PANAMIN. Still others, he charged, "notably Irenäus Eibl-Eibesfeldt, felt qualified to publish after brief visits of only a few days."[3]

Carlos Fernandez's fireworks went off on the final day of the conference, when Zeus Salazar told the audience that he was going to "deliver the goods." He proceeded to diagram the genealogies of some Tasaday "relatives" he planned to present to the conference. These were Elizir, Joel, and Blessen Boone, and they were accompanied by George Tanedo, one of the T'boli who had dressed up for Gerald Ford's visit in 1975. The relatives had arrived, he explained, at midnight the previous evening, and he "had to interview them for about two hours. This is anthropological work, Mr. Nance, no?"

Well, actually no. It was at least a little odd to gather genealogical data in this manner, without fieldwork, and even more odd to present the data the next day at a supposedly scientific conference.

According to Salazar, Datu' Dudim, the leader of Blit, was the *real* father of Doloy, or Dul, as she was known to the Tasaday believers. Nance and others had wondered why Dul had such an "imperious character. It is normal. She is the daughter of a datu." Dul, he said, was married to Yong, alias Udelen. Yong's brother Saay was known as

Lefonok. A man named Yabes was known among the Tasaday as Adug. And the polygamous Gintuy was really named Fidlo. Igna, the original translator, was actually Belayem's sister. Bilengan was really known as Tinda.

"Anybody who knows the country can draw it in one minute." Salazar hastily drew for his audience a "map" of the area that showed a river, the caves, and Blit in close proximity. "And, if you are in the caves and you look down you would see cogon* country . . . at any rate according to George Tanedo." This was an important caveat— according to Tanedo. In truth, cogon grass isn't at *all* visible from the caves, but the hoax proponents couldn't be expected to know that, because none of them, with the exception of Lozano and Iten, had ever visited or would ever visit the area.

George Tanedo got up to speak next. "Organizers of this conference, anthropologists, especially John Nance, visitors, observers, Good Morning." Tanedo told his audience that it was hard for him to talk in a borrowed language, harder still because of the threats that he had received for exposing the truth. But he was going to do his best to ignore those threats. Before the coming of Elizalde, he said, the Tasaday forest had been split into several logging concessions. The companies had combed and surveyed the forest, and no such group had ever been reported. Tanedo, who lived in the coastal town of Maitum, had traveled to Blit two weeks before. "I talked with Udol, well-known in books as 'Lobo,' the son of Tinda, known as Bilengan of the Tasaday. For very great and serious reasons I cannot fully disclose here, it is not possible and advisable to bring with me the Tasadays in this conference. However, I have with me some relatives who happened to be the relatives of the so-called Tasadays. They will narrate briefly their lives with this maligned and exploited group of human beings."

With that, he sat down, and a T'boli man named Elizir Boone began his testimony, which was translated by Jerry Malayang, a reporter and T'boli who had written, along with just about everyone else in attendance, it seemed, a series of articles on the Tasaday exposé.

"The start of the story of the Tasaday," Boone said, "was when Elizalde came to South Cotabato because I was there and Mr. Jam-

*Cogon grass supplants the rain forest after it has been cut.

bangan, which is John Nance, knows me. Because when Elizalde first came to our place he sent Dafal through a helicopter. Now Dafal called all the people in Blit for a meeting. Now Dafal said our so-called God . . . has come to give us help. The one who will arrive as our demi-God is Elizalde, Jr. And then after that Elizalde arrived in Blit. Many people welcomed him. When Elizalde arrived, he said, 'Now I have arrived to give help to you.' When he arrived he stayed four days before he left. . . . When he left, he left two men behind. Those were Dafal and Fludi Tuan. Now Fludi Tuan and Dafal called for another meeting to explain to them how they can get help. Now they said this is what we will do. We will wear *bahag* or G-strings so that all the people in the world will know we are very poor." Elizir related how various people, including Dul, the daughter of Datu' Dudim, had been offered up to play Tasaday.

"They said, when this is all through this place will become like Manila," Boone said. "You won't be needing anything. The money would be delivered to you. But now we haven't seen any kind of that help. But the tribe known as Tasaday really do not exist. Plain T'bolis were made to wear G-strings. Thank you."

Next Blessen Boone spoke briefly and vaguely and didn't once mention the Tasaday. She was followed by Joel Boone, who related that his uncle Udol (Lobo) and his grandfather Tinda (Bilengan) were frequent visitors to the coastal town of Maitum.

"Udol went to see me," he said, "in Maitum to invite me to go to Blit and farm for rice production.* I went up with him to Blit and farmed but I was not able to wait for the harvest as something unexpected happened in Maitum." He didn't specify what this unexpected thing was, but later he returned with George Tanedo.

"When [Joel Boone and Tanedo] went up," he continued, "I tried to convince my uncle to come down with me but they cannot do so because of some happenings up . . . some arrangements."

Here Malayang paused in his translation. "Sorry," he said, "but he mentioned something about Mr. Iten, Oswald Iten. According to Udol, they were waiting the promises Mr. Oswald Iten made to Lobo or Udol. That's the reason why they can't bring him down [from Blit to the conference]."

---

*He didn't specify when, but presumably he meant the recent past.

This was a strange wrinkle. What did Iten have to do with this? They were here to talk about Elizalde's abuses. The scenario seemed to be that Boone and Tanedo had gone to Blit to bring Lobo to the conference, but Lobo wouldn't go because of some perceived promises from Iten. These were presumably *not* the "very great and serious reasons" Tanedo had spoken of.

Boone's remark created an odd moment at the conference. Someone might have at least asked him what he meant. But no one did; the statement was politely ignored.

At the open forum that followed, Christian Adler and Salazar tried to find out from Tanedo and the Boones who had participated in the "training" of the Tasaday. When Salazar asked Elizir Boone, "Who told Dafal to train the T'boli and Manobo?" Boone answered, "It was from the plan of Elizalde and Jambangan [Nance]."

Nance seemed flabbergasted. "Well, that's I . . . I quite understand that he's, what he's saying is that . . ."

"What's he's saying is that you and Elizalde told Dafal to teach the so-called Tasaday to make the tools."

There were several languages flying about the stage, and no one was certain what anyone else was saying. As Nance tried to figure out his role in "training" the Tasaday to make stone tools, Elizir said he didn't know exactly who taught Dafal to teach the Tasaday to make stone tools, so Nance asked if Elizir had seen Dafal teaching the Tasaday to make stone tools. No, he hadn't because it was forbidden to go into the area. How did he know then? It was only Dafal who had been sent by Elizalde; that was how he knew.

It was not an open forum exactly, but a cross-examination. Clearly, the "witness" was uncomfortable, and so was the audience. Finally, Salazar said he thought this was all just a matter of details. "Were there T'bolis who were recruited by Manda Elizalde and taken to the caves? That is all we want to know . . . Do not confuse us, John, because these are matters of detail."

The University of California, Berkeley, anthropologist Gerald Berreman had been invited to the conference as an impartial outside expert, along with John Bodley, an anthropologist from Washington State University. Neither was a Philippine specialist, but both were widely respected human rights advocates. Bodley thought the conference organizers weren't letting in people who could be seen as pro-

Elizalde. He also didn't think that Nance was given enough space or time to present his side.

But Berreman's sympathies lay with Elizir Boone. He had listened impassively throughout the proceedings. But now he decided to intervene. "[T]he nature of this interaction has bothered me. It has turned into a real circus. . . . What I want to say is that you cannot conduct an ethnographic inquisition before two hundred people and klieg lights and cameras and the television audience and expect them to respond adequately under pressure of time, when everybody's hungry, everybody wants out. And it certainly cannot substitute for the kind of systematic inquiry that should have been done in the past or should be done now in the future, to try to ascertain some of these facts at issue here. . . . And I think it's our responsibility to try to resolve those through more systematic inquiry . . . in the context of South Cotabato and in context of the area that's called 'Tasaday' and the people that have been called Tasaday, not in front of the audience. . . . I don't think we should make them answer questions in this kind of a context. . . . It's not fruitful and I think it's not ethical and certainly not polite."

This was a good point, although he neglected to note that the authenticity proponents, especially Nance, had been subjected themselves to an inquisition at this conference. But Nance was old news, and no one paid much attention to him. He had been duped at best, had perpetrated a hoax at worst. Really, who cared what he thought about the Tasaday? Certainly, virtually no one in the audience at UP as he almost pleaded: "I'm not a scientist. I'm a journalist. I think that's a very important distinction to make. We have two really different languages that people speak and I think the cultural language of the anthropologist and the cultural language of the journalist are often very much apart. [When] we have people moving back and forth from one profession to the other, we find that language loses its precision."

Nance threw away the twenty-page paper he had brought and spent most of his time at the podium trying to defend himself. The conference had become personal. He told the audience that he had gone down to see the Tasaday the first time believing them to be a hoax, but that he'd had a "revolution of thinking about that."

"If you read that book [*The Gentle Tasaday*] . . . you will find that I don't call them Stone Age people. But it was . . . what does that mean, if we get back to the business of language, between anthropologists and journalists of the layworld. I mean, how many of us would say, if I ask for a vote, that we live . . . in a space age? Commonly yes, we say we live in the Space Age. We hear it all the time from the media. How many of you have been to space? How many of us on this planet have been to outer space? A hundred? See! There are five billion of us. How could we possibly live in the space age. . . . So what is Stone Age. . . ? It's a term. It's a metaphor."

To many in his audience, he must have seemed as though he was trying to dodge the issue, losing himself, as Salazar had said, in mere matters of detail and excuses. He furthered this impression by saying that he had written in his book that the Tasaday had worn cloth at the first meetings, that their "isolation was always relative." He challenged the validity of the conference. He told the audience that he had not received a copy of the conference program. Nance was swimming upstream. The clincher came when he said, "See, to me as a journalist, once I get past the headlines, whether they've been there five years or fifty thousand is irrelevant."

Perhaps it was irrelevant to Nance personally, but to a journalist, whether the Tasaday had been in the forest five years or fifty thousand years should have made all the difference in the world.

"My original truth about the Tasaday [remains] that here are people no matter who they were, that lived in a rainforest, and through cooperation, they develop the strategy for survival. . . . We do need to realize that we are all connected. I think that's one of the most profound messages the Tasaday brought to me. That across whatever kind of technology, from the Stone Age to the Space Age across the years, from metal to wood or whatever you want to talk about, that there was a great bond between us."

Nance's bond with the Tasaday remained for many years reforged and even strengthened in some ways after he spoke at the UP conference, but his career as a journalist was over.

Writing in *Social Science Information* after the conclusion of the conference, Dr. Michael Tan of the University of the Philippines Department of Anthropology, summed up the proceedings. His tone was diplomatic but critical. Acknowledging that the conference was "highly emotional" and that it had lost "touch with its original objective of launching a scholarly investigation," he concluded that as "the conference ended, it became clear that the stakes were higher than expected. It was not just a question of professional reputations, or the authenticity of the Tasaday, but the whole issue of whether the sciences are indeed value-free and apolitical."[4]

Of course no discipline is value-free and apolitical. More to the point, language is neither apolitical nor value-free. "Without making any excuses, we were caught in the temper of the times," Doug Yen had told the conferees. "We get caught up in the whirlwind. . . . I suppose this is why we are so often accused of being blind, even when we don't realize it, when we talk to somebody from the press. . . . Actually, we have no idea what the translation is going to be."

The Tasaday whirlwind had spun in one direction in the seventies; now it spun in the opposite direction, and the audience had been caught up in it and carried away from Dr. Yen's words. Cultural whirlwinds, unlike the real thing, are largely unnoticed, and one doesn't even know one has touched down far away until many years later.

13

Return of the Native

How foolish it would be to suppose that one only needs to point out this origin and this misty shroud of delusion in order to destroy the world that counts for real, so-called "reality." We can only destroy as creators.
—Friedrich Nietzsche, *The Gay Science*

fter Judith Moses's *The Tribe That Never Was* aired in 1986 on ABC's 20/20, Jack Reynolds called John Nance and said, "God, they just shit on us. I mean, they just really did a nasty piece of work." It didn't get better from there for either veteran reporter. After RCA sold NBC to GE, the company had a "big cleaning out," and Reynolds was let go after twenty years of service. The scandal didn't help, though it wasn't named as a cause for his dismissal.

Nance fared just as poorly. Following publication of *The Gentle Tasaday* in 1975, he had published two other Tasaday books, a children's book, *Lobo of the Tasaday: A Stone Age Boy Meets the Modern World*, and *Discovery of the Tasaday, a Photo Novel*, prompting Judith Moses to say he had made a "cottage industry out of the Tasaday."

Nance claims he actually wanted to call his famous book *The Tasaday*. His editor was the one who added the "Gentle." As for the use of the term "Stone Age" in the book (not to mention in everything else he'd written since containing the term), well, he'd meant it as a metaphor, just as he'd told the audience at the UP conference. This kind of sidestepping only played into the hands of his detractors, like Oswald Iten, who had remarked at the UP conference that "some irresponsible editor must have smuggled [Stone Age] on his book cover." In fact, that was pretty much what Nance claimed.

"Metaphor," at any rate, isn't quite the right term. The Tasaday became an alternate reality for Nance; he'd become lost in them the way a moviegoer gets lost in the darkness of the theater. They were not metaphors strewn about *The Gentle Tasaday*; they were foraging cave dwellers with stone tools—no metal, no cloth, except what Dafal had given them.

Nance had shown his film *A Message from the Stone Age* around the Northwest in hundreds of classrooms. He says he didn't make much money from it, that he worked his tail off, charging at first one hundred dollars a visit, but later three hundred for the day, during which he'd visit six classrooms.

It was, he says, his "poem to the human race."

Then, when the hoax story came out, whole school districts threw out his film. They didn't want to be associated with it. Some of them called him back. He'd visit. The kids would be in tears.

"Let me come back," he told anyone who'd listen. He'd show them his film and he'd show them the *20/20* report—if they were old enough. He'd go to high schools and say, "I'm happy to talk about it. Take a look at this first film. I'm not ashamed of it. I'll show that again. And I'll show you *20/20*, and then I'll show you what I've seen now. And we'll talk about what's the truth. Could I be wrong? Sure I could be wrong. We could all be wrong."

But it did no good, really. Browse through a used bookstore these days, and you'll find plenty of copies of *The Gentle Tasaday* or *Lobo of the Tasaday*, some personally inscribed. No one wants to be associated with a hoax. None of the magazines Nance had worked for would take his writing, and both his photo agent and his literary agent dumped him. His editor at Harcourt, his former newspaper colleagues, virtually anyone he'd ever worked with heard from Judith Moses, who, now interested in writing a book on the scandal herself, had caught the Tasaday bug and become increasingly vested in her opinion. Nance's friends told him that she was writing and calling them, saying "some really undermining things."

The Associated Press told Nance it couldn't use his stories anymore, though he had an agreement with the bureau chief that he was going to write a story about his 1986 visit to see the Tasaday after the hoax allegations surfaced. The foreign editor refused it. Nance went to see him and was told, "John, I'm not saying you're—but we couldn't use your stuff; everyone knows you're in the wrong—you made that story up."

Even *Asiaweek*, for whom he'd written what turned out to be his last article, wouldn't touch him after 1986. It was getting too much heat. The editors told him, "Write about anything else but not the Tasaday. We can't use it." But Nance wasn't interested in anything else *but* the Tasaday.

Where were all his friends? Nance wondered. He'd stood up for others, but no one would stand up for him.

Joey Lozano's career meanwhile flourished, thanks to Oswald Iten and Judith Moses. Several months after the *20/20* report, another film crew, this one from Britain's Central TV, wanted to do a feature on the hoax, and Moses put them in touch with Joey Lozano. This time Lozano went ahead of the crew to Datu' Galang's encampment of Tubak, which was the launching point for the various expeditions led by Lozano. This was where he had led first Iten and then Moses, where Tom Jarriel had interviewed the Tasaday and Datu' Galang. Now it was to be home base for the British crew. But Lozano and the Brits got their signals crossed, and Lozano waited in vain in Tubak for the crew to show up. Meanwhile British journalist Adrian Wood chartered a light aircraft to hover around the area where he thought Lozano was, and he threw toilet paper on the ground as a sign for Joey that they were looking for him, though one wonders what message would really have been conveyed had Joey stumbled upon the rolls of toilet paper strewn across the hills.

Frustrated from two days of waiting for the film crew, Lozano made a twelve-hour trek from Tubak to the Muslim enclave of Ambalgan, the next scheduled rendezvous point. There he was supposed to meet the film crew for an interview with Mariano Mondragon, a Habaluyas logging official and "early critic of the so-called Tasaday." The next day, furious and limping, Lozano made his way to a predesignated restaurant in General Santos City and met the crew.

The crew had landed by mistake apparently in an encampment of the MILF, the Muslim rebel group. The curious rebels made their way to the helicopter. The Brits, terrified, ran back to the chopper, thinking they were about to be attacked.[1] The film leaves that part out. The narrator tells us that before the crew proceeds into the jungle, they have to make an "important rendezvous" with Muslim guerrillas, who have to make sure the Brits aren't spies. We see a shot of the helicopter landing and reporter Adrian Wood stepping out and shaking hands with a rebel leader. The men and women of the rebel camp stand around with their guns, looking as though this were the fiftieth take.

The narrator tells us that now they can resume their journey deep into the forest to find the place where the Tasaday live. They find it but only "after hours of searching." Under nearly the same conditions as Iten and Moses's trip (Datu' Galang and Joey Lozano translating), the Central TV group then interviews the Tasaday.

The most famous and photogenic of the Tasaday are gathered: Lobo, who graced the cover of the August 1971 issue of *National Geographic* in silhouette, climbing a vine in the rain forest; Natek, whom we saw as a toddler in NBC's *Cave People of Mindanao* sliding down a rock face by the caves; Dul, the Tasaday matriarch who is yet to secure a place in the 100th anniversary issue of *National Geographic* in 1988; Belayem, one of the stars of John Nance's *Gentle Tasaday*. These four people and the others with them have become considerably famous, but what has the renown brought them?

For now it has brought them a British TV crew. Unlike the rebels, the Tasaday do not look bored. They smile; they laugh. They are used to the camera. They will sit through as many takes as necessary to get it right. They are your consummate Stone Age professionals.

What's telling is not so much *what's* said but *how* the information is being elicited. Wood's questions are leading. "Who taught you to climb trees?" he asks Lobo. Elizalde.

He wants to know who told them they should call themselves Tasaday and pretend to live in caves. When he doesn't get an immediate response, he asks who "*first* suggested it." And then he asks again.

"Elizalde," Datu' Galang answers, though he's not a Tasaday. Someone has to take some initiative here.

We're told that whenever Elizalde visited, a messenger came running to tell them to strip naked and dash off to the caves. Only after Elizalde's companions snapped all the photos their romantic hearts desired were the Tasaday allowed to clock out and return to their homes.

The film largely focuses on how awful Elizalde is, trotting out assorted Elizalde enemies. A Father Gerald Nagle claims that Elizalde would dock his yacht off the coast and have young women brought to him and certified virgins by a doctor. Mariano Mondragon, the Habaluyas logging official (an important fact that the filmmakers somehow forget to tell us), asserts: "Tasaday is not a tribe. . . . They are T'bolis, Manobos. In fact, some of them are my in-laws!"

Manda's brother, Freddy, calls him "paranoid." The Tasaday occasionally demonstrated to visitors how they made stone tools. Zeus Salazar displays one and claims it will fall apart with one good whack. And this proves . . . that tools the Tasaday made in a hurry weren't well constructed. David Baradas recounts the Kabayo saga and then says research was shut down forever after that. Pretty damning—but it's not true. Yen, Elkins, Molony, et al. followed on his heels. The narrator informs us that the Tasaday supposedly spoke a unique language, but on recordings only words that other groups use are heard. What does this prove? Nothing because it's not true.

We're told that PANAMIN is simply a cover for "stripping the wealth from the land." We're shown footage of a vast mining wasteland, pits and scarred land and bulldozers. A cello or something like it sounds one plaintive note. This is a copper mine, the narrator informs us, owned by the North Davao Mining Company. In the 1960s this was tribal homeland, but the area was cleared on the orders of the company. The chairman of the company was . . . Manda Elizalde!

What does this prove? Nothing because it's not true. Whatever one thinks of Elizalde's resettlement tactics, this tribal homeland was *not* tribal land (except in the sense that *all* land had been tribal land at one time), certainly not PANAMIN-controlled as implied, but a barrio called New Leyte, squatted on by "Christian" settlers who had previously worked for Samar Mining, the forerunner of North Davao.

The resulting 1986 film, *Scandal, the Lost Tribe*, makes Judith Moses' *The Tribe That Never Was* look about as sensational as a farm report.

Five months after the UP conference, Elizir Boone, the man who had testified dramatically that he was a "Tasaday relative," was killed in a paramilitary raid in South Cotabato. The police reports conflicted. A report from the police station in Maitum said his death was suspicious. His brother Rodrigo claimed that Elizir was shot after he had surrendered and that the bullet had entered his skull from behind and exited the top. A second report justified the shooting. According to this report, Elizir and several others had kidnapped a sixteen-year-old T'boli girl and brought her to a "hideout" on a logging road. The local Civilian Home Defense Forces conducted a raid on the hideout and killed him.

Who killed him and why remain a mystery. But Iten, Moses, and Berreman were appalled. They were sure that he had been killed in retribution for his testimony at the conference. Berreman dedicated an article to the slain young man. Moses launched a letter-writing campaign to various Philippine government officials in protest, demanding an investigation and protection for other Tasaday whistle-blowers. For Moses, this was what the Tasaday controversy amounted to: It wasn't a polite disagreement among academics about the primitiveness of a group of forest dwellers, but a human rights issue. The Tasaday and other ordinary Filipinos such as Elizir Boone were simply victims of greedy and ruthless men, the Marcoses and Mandas and their various henchmen who didn't care whom they killed to maintain their positions of power and wealth. In that context, whether the Tasaday used stone tools or not hardly mattered. To her, Elizalde was a kind of war criminal, and the Tasaday were his hapless victims.

Where had Manda been all this time? In 1983, unnerved by Aquino's assassination, he'd fled without a word to Hong Kong. Marcos's chief of staff, General Ver, called to find out why he'd left. But Manda didn't speak to him and soon departed for London. From there he traveled to southern Spain and then to New York, where he had an eye operation. He settled for a while in Miami and even assumed the identity of a Cuban national while retaining his real name, an odd strategy if he was trying to hide. But never mind; Imelda caught up with him anyway. When he was in Miami, he was "ordered" to report to her in New York. "She said I should return with them to the country. . . . She also said I should make Tanduay Distillery . . . available to them [for] purchase. I don't know at what price, but she said they would like to take over Tanduay. After this, we went to dinner with the 'Philippine government'—George Hamilton, Mama Hamilton, Van Cliburn, all of them—to an Italian restaurant. I excused myself during dinner to get my bags. I took my son and . . . drove twenty-six hours non-stop to Miami."[2]

From there Elizalde flew to Belize, a "nice place to get lost," and after a few months settled in Costa Rica, bought a hundred-acre hacienda, and started to develop it, creating an artificial lake and beach. He still had the money to create a fair facsimile of paradise.

By this time Judith Moses had become as obsessed with the Tasaday as John Nance. At every opportunity she screened her 20/20 report. She had supplied the documentary to Jerome Bailen as scientific evidence, and it was shown to the assembled conferees at the UP gathering a bare twelve hours after it showed in millions of homes in the United States. She gave it to the Costa Rican government, which used it, in her words, as an "excuse to throw Manda out of Costa Rica on the prostitution/racketeering charge. They had been trying to get rid of Manda for a very long time." Costa Rica had developed a reputation as a haven for millionaire fugitives like Robert Vesco, and people like him and Manda were bad for its image. But neither did it help that Manda had backed the wrong candidate for the presidential election, his former Harvard roommate Jaime Gutierrez.

At one point Moses traveled to Costa Rica and showed up at Manda's hacienda, where she was told by the manager of the estate, Walter Chaverri, that Elizalde was in Panama. According to Moses, "There are only two things you do in Panama. You do arms or you do banking." Then she tracked him through a transit form from the INS to Miami, where there was an "inquiry made about drug use in Costa Rica." To her, there was no question that there had been drug use at his home in Costa Rica.

Not surprisingly, Chaverri painted an entirely different portrait of his boss from that of Moses for the Costa Rican paper *La Nación*:

Rich . . . but plain in his attitude when dealing with people . . . enemy of drink and drugs, and passionate to help the poor; this was the description of the Filipino Manuel Elizalde given by one of his employees. . . . Some alleged irregular acts with children on his property have been investigated, as well as the possession of arms . . . [But] according to Chaverri, Elizalde has helped hundreds of people, families and institutions in need in this country. From sewing machines for clothing factories, undertaker's cars for the slums, dental services, wheel chairs, houses, land, Christmas donations for poor children, contributions for football teams . . . and even the payment of water and electricity bills of the Nuns of Guadalupe; all these are part of a list of activities that Chaverri associated with his boss.[3]

Within Manda, both extremes existed. He probably *was* involved with young girls on his estate, and he certainly had guns around. Money, to him, solved everything, and while he used it to exploit people, he also tended to throw huge sums, whether his own or others, at various social ills, major and minor. When he was hauled into court in Costa Rica to respond to charges against him, he admitted to having women (he denied any of them were underage) brought to him weekly like so many goods by a woman named Ivonne. He showered these women with gifts whether they accepted his advances or not:

> At this point the witness revealed two lists of names, A and B. List A, titled "Cariari," had 9 women's names; list B was titled "Dentist" and had 29 names which included 9 from list A.
>
> JUDGE: Could you please explain the meaning of these lists?
>
> MANDA: List A consists of girls who were brought to the Hotel by Ivonne. List B are the people who went to the dentist Ronal de Paz . . . The bills for services rendered to these people by the dentists were paid by me, and this I did of my own free will with pleasure. Ivonne never asked me to send these people to the dentist as part of the payment; I helped them out because I wanted to.[4]

After being told to leave Costa Rica or face deportation, Manda slipped back into the Philippines sometime between the end of 1986 and March 1987 (accounts vary) with the help of Freddy's wife, Josine, who was close to President Aquino. He most likely paid something to get back in—standard procedure. His reappearance outraged many.

Now that Manda had returned, he started to throw his considerable resources around, and this involved more than trips to the dentist. "Their [Manda's enemies'] mistake was attacking the Tasaday," says Manda's associate Tony Cervantes. "He loved the Tasaday." But Elizalde sometimes had an odd way of showing his love.

14

Video Tribe

I yam what I yam.
—Popeye the sailor man

For a short period Manda became a born-again Christian. This flabbergasted his longtime friend and sometime business associate John Hicks. "Manda, you've got to be kidding," he said.

"Well, you do what you got to do," Manda replied.

How far Manda took that simple but powerful philosophy is one of the central questions here. His newfound faith didn't last, but it may have influenced his strange decision to send Roger "Bomba" Arienda, a popular televangelist, down to the Tasaday Reserve in October 1987 with a camera crew to help "authenticate" the Tasaday. And authenticate he did: Standing in the middle of about thirty or so leaf-clad Tasaday, with Mai Tuan and Igna serving as translators, Bomba asked if the Tasaday still lived at the caves.[1] Mai replied, "The one that they learned is the second home."

"The one that they learned," Arienda repeated, "this is the hut, is the second home." Apparently, the caves had become too crowded because the Tasaday had been steadily intermarrying with their neighbors from Blit, so they had built huts nearby. "Have they abandoned the caves?"

"They still love the caves," Mai said.

"They still live in . . ." said Arienda.

"Love, love!" Mai said.

"And love the caves," Arienda finished.

Thank you, Bomba. Case closed. What more proof was needed that the Tasaday were authentic?

Between October and December 1987 the Philippine Congress conducted a series of hearings on the Tasaday, largely at the urging of Professors Bailen, Salazar, and Ernesto Constantino. That the Tasaday had landed in Congress shows how political the issue had become. If the UP conference had been a circus, the machinations surrounding the congressional hearings were a grand puppet show. Both sides manipulated witnesses and marshaled their forces. Before the hearings, Judith Moses had wired Salazar some damning news from New York: "Encyclopaedia Britannica has expunged the Tasaday and all references to the Tasaday from their forthcoming edition. They have concluded the story was a hoax."[2]

Bailen parroted this fact at the National Press Club, and Roy de Guzman, the hoax proponents' main news ally, reported it as gospel in the *Philippine Daily Inquirer*. The only problem was that it wasn't true. The *Britannica* had revised its 1987 entry on the Tasaday to include the hoax allegations but took no position on the controversy.[3]

Arnold Azurin got in on the act, too, writing that the *Britannica*'s reversal of its position on the Tasaday had reduced Elizalde's "sensational find . . . to the ethnological hoax of the century."[4]

The substance of the allegations didn't seem to matter. The hoax proponents simply made them and hoped they'd influence the congressional hearings. Next, the *Philippine Star* reported that *National Geographic* had "excluded" all references to the Tasaday in its 100th anniversary issue. Bailen was quoted as saying, "This is a telling development."[5] Indeed, it would have been had it been true. When the 100th anniversary issue of *National Geographic* appeared, it featured a portrait of Dul breast-feeding one of her children. "Recent stories that the Tasaday were a hoax," the caption writer intoned, "have largely been discredited."[6] Wishful thinking, perhaps, but it put the lie to Bailen's allegations.

Father Sean McDonagh, a Santa Cruz Mission priest trained as an anthropologist, made an impassioned plea at the time of the hearings under the imprimatur of the diocese of Marbel.[7] The Tasaday, he wrote, had told church workers that they had once thought they were the only people in the world. The presidential reserve set aside for them had largely been a good thing, but that didn't mean that Father McDonagh endorsed the policies of PANAMIN or Elizalde. The diocese of Marbel had long been in conflict with Elizalde. Manda had always viewed the church as so much Western garb hiding the "true" native within, while the church regarded him and PANAMIN as interlopers and rivals as much as exploiters. Throughout the 1970s the two groups had battled, complaining about each other to the Marcoses. The church saw PANAMIN as simply the first of a long line of exploiters, but the current investigation had forced the diocese to make a stand reluctantly because the Tasaday's dignity as human beings had been offended:

This does not mean that we agree with the way PANAMIN handled the early contacts between outsiders and the Tasaday. It is our belief that PANAMIN exploited the Tasaday by an extensive public relations effort to gain international notoriety. One apparent objective of this effort was to improve their credibility and thus to generate funds.

Other individuals, including journalists, and media people have exploited the Tasadays for their career advancement and financial gain.

Academicians and politicians have also rode [sic] on the Tasaday issue to enhance their positions. The national controversy raging in the newspapers and hall of the academe have not, in our opinion, served the best interest of the Tasaday but have frequently been self-serving.[8]

But the diocese's plea went unheeded, and the hearings continued. Some congressional members charged with investigating the hoax allegations had similar misgivings about the legitimacy of the hearings, in particular concerning Bailen's character and motives. In a letter to the chair of the hearings, William Claver, eight members of the committee complained about Bailen: "Time and again, it has been pointed out that Congress is not the proper forum to resolve the Tasaday question. The scientific community possesses adequate forums where the issue can be threshed out to their full satisfaction. We therefore request that Bailen and his group, none of whom have first-hand knowledge of the inquiry's subject matter, the Tasaday, be disqualified from testifying before the Committee and that the investigation initiated by the Bailen group be terminated."[9]

The request was ignored, and Bailen, Salazar, and Constantino testified before the committee, screening Judith Moses's ever-helpful *The Tribe That Never Was* before the group.

Meanwhile outside the chambers of Congress the propaganda wars heated up. The hoax proponents' main source was once again George Tanedo. Identified as a "T'boli spokesman," Tanedo told the *Inquirer* that Mai Tuan was bribing people scheduled to appear at the hearings and furthermore that eight tribesmen with Garand and Armalite rifles were guarding the caves, on Mai's orders. The "lives of anthropologists and Congressmen [would be] in danger if they insist [as planned] on visiting the supposed Stone-Age caves," the newspaper warned. But was it Mai Tuan who guarded the caves and bribed people or Tanedo, his rival as a leader of the T'boli, who had something to lose if his own claims were independently verified? He evidently knew nothing about the caves or the area surrounding them, as his remarks at the UP conference about cogon grass indicated. It's one thing to manipulate testimony at a conference or a hearing, but another to try to do so in the field.

The truth was that the motives of which people accused Manda—greed and megalomania—were just as applicable to many of his critics. The forty-five-thousand-acre reserve that he had pushed Marcos to create in 1971 had not been undesired. Logging roads had been pushing into the forest at the time of the discovery of the Tasaday, and a number of people, loggers and miners and those in their employ, now stood to gain if they were proved to be fake and the reserve were invalidated. There were also political motives for declaring the Tasaday a hoax: Manda had enemies, and the Tasaday themselves had been showpieces of the Marcos regime. Many of Manda's detractors were lining up to discredit him, if not Marcos, and perhaps use the scandal as a means of wresting away his valuable business interests. Finally, there were the academics, some of whom had felt snubbed by not having been invited in the early days to be part of the Tasaday glory.

In mid-November, de Guzman reported in the *Inquirer* that Joel and Blessen Boone had been "abducted" by "armed followers of South Cotabato tribal Warlord, Mai Tuan."[10] The source once again was

Bailen, this time quoting George Tanedo's brother, Franklin. Bailen claimed that "twelve of the original twenty-eight [sic] Tasaday poseurs" were being held at the Admiral Hotel "for unknown purposes."[11] All that could be learned from the front desk was that three rooms had been rented and that Mai Tuan's wife, Amy, was out . . . grocery shopping! The number of Tasaday "poseurs," it turned out, had been *somewhat* exaggerated by Professor Bailen. The next day the "unknown purposes" became known when Joel and Blessen Boone showed up at the office of pro-Elizalde Congressman Gualberto Lumauig, accompanied by Amy Tuan. There, in front of TV cameras and reporters, they "recanted," charging that the Tanedo brothers had threatened them at gunpoint to testify at the UP conference. In return for their testimony, George had promised them "money, [a] logging concession, rattan, and land."[12] No, they hadn't been kidnapped. In fact, they had requested that Amy Tuan and an interpreter accompany them to Manila so they could, according to the newspaper *Malaya*, "collect" [sic] their previous testimony.[13] Indeed, to judge from the new tennis shoes they sported, they *had* collected.*

On the heels of this bout of conscience clearing, Datu' Galang showed up in the Manila office of South Cotabato Congressman James Chiongbian to recant *his* previous statements to 20/20. Joey Lozano, he claimed, had bribed him with five hundred pesos, and Iten had told him that "Manda is no more."[14] Galang's motive for coming forward now? "I only want to apologize for lying about the Tasadays," he said. That was good enough for Congressman Chiongbian, who declared the controversy settled: "Datu' Galang came to Manila to clear up this mess and confirm the authenticity of the Tasaday. I hope his recantation will put the case to rest."[15]

An outraged Judith Moses began a new letter-writing campaign protesting the obvious intimidation and coercion of the Boones and Galang. A bemused Zeus Salazar later noted: "All this retracting proves precisely the truth that is being denied. They are overdoing it. . . . It is clear that the PANAMIN people are ready (and able) to distort everything."[16]

---

*I should note that I had read none of these recantings before my trip with Joey to see the Tasaday in 1999. By that time I already had a mountain of Tasaday documents to sift through. When I did read all the various recantings, I took them with a grain of salt, anyway, preferring to trust my own instincts and conclusions. I tried to give everyone the benefit of the doubt until those benefits produced diminishing returns.

While Manda didn't have a monopoly on manipulation, his brand of damage control usually involved creating more damage. The hoax proponents were about to bring out a smoking gun as big as a cannon.

On November 20 and 21 the Tasaday woman Dula testified at a special hearing of Congress at the Santa Cruz Mission that she was a T'boli who had been coerced by Elizalde to pretend to be a Tasaday. What's more, she gave her testimony in the T'boli language. Dula seemed irreproachable as a witness, an actual Tasaday testifying that she was in fact a T'boli and not a Tasaday. But the fact that Dula and Lobo could speak the T'boli language in 1986 said nothing of what they could speak in 1971. One of Lobo's two wives was T'boli.

So much, as we should know by now, depends on translation. Among Dula's revelations, she accused Elizalde of sleeping with Igna, the translator of early Tasaday speech and making the Tasaday "go naked." Or maybe not. Dula's testimony before the committee seems to have been coached and distorted, often outrageously. When shown pictures of Belayem, Mahayag, and others, she identified them by their Tasaday names and was asked by the translator if she was "related" to any of them.

"Wen ke deme hu be ne." "I am related with them."[17]

Wrong answer. The translator neglected to translate this and coached, *"La na."* "None at all." *"Ne be ni de ge, be ne be tau fat ne-e . . . sotu, luwe, telu, fat . . .? Wen ke demehem be ni fat?"* "Are you related with these four persons here . . . one, two, three, four . . . ? Are you related with these four?"

"La, la wenen ke deme buddu." "None, I am no longer related with them," Dula answered. This was indeed correct. By 1986 Mahayag and Dula had been divorced, and she had remarried a T'boli man, Banas.

Throughout the interrogation, Dula's words were changed or were often simply not translated at all when she didn't give the desired response. Always, lurking in the background, sat the Tanedos, apparently her siblings. When asked to name her brothers, she identified someone named Bungot, and then the "translator" urged her to name another.

"Buye . . . buye, Franklin." "It's Franklin," she said hesitantly. Dula looked behind her, and a helpful soul from the audience said, "Tanedo."

"Tanedo," Dula said.

"Tanedo," the translator affirmed.

Igna didn't react well to the news that she had slept with the boss. "Yes, I slept one time in the Tasaday cave," she complained bitterly during a TV interview.[18] "But I was with my husband. We slept with many others—Tasaday and their visitors who included Sir Manda Elizalde. There is nothing wrong with that." Dula had said as much at the hearing ("They slept with us at the caves"), but the translator again distorted her words. Igna threatened to sue to clear her good name, but whom was she going to sue, Dula?

The Santa Cruz Mission was as close as the congressmen came to the Tasaday Reserve. After hearing the testimonies of Dula, Mai Tuan, and George Tanedo, the subcommittee of six congressmen returned to Manila.

Now it was Manda's turn.

On December 1 Franklin Tanedo did an about-face, declaring that he had been "hoodwinked" into testifying against Elizalde by a syndicate of former Tanduay officials, who were trying to wrest control of the company from Manda, and that several of the committee members, including the chairman, William Claver, and the most outspoken Elizalde critic, Gregorio Andolana, had "conspired with the syndicate in waging a smear campaign against Elizalde."[19]

The next day Manda filed a two-hundred-million-peso libel suit (approximately eight million dollars) against Roy de Guzman, Arnold Azurin, Jerome Bailen, and a number of others, associated mainly with the *Inquirer*.

Fighting video with video, Elizalde produced two responses to the hoax proponents: *Reply to 20/20*, aired during the congressional hearings, and *Twilight of the Tasaday*, a more professionally done film for a wider audience in which, remarkably, we see an assembled group of Tasaday watching themselves on TV. Someone—Nance thinks it was Amy Rara—had the idea to show the Tasaday *The Tribe That Never Was* and record their reactions. With Elizalde's blessing, they mounted an expedition, bringing TV and a generator to the Tasaday. The TV, like some altar, sits in the middle of a clearing as the Tasaday, seated facing it, are shown their likenesses and asked for their responses.

Lobo stands in a clearing dressed in a green shirt and pants, a red kerchief on his forehead. Adug stands beside him, dressed similarly. Nine other Tasaday sit near Lobo facing the TV. On TV, Lobo/Udol is saying that his mother is a Manobo and his father is a T'boli. Amy asks the Lobo in the clearing if what Video Lobo says is true.

Lobo speaks emphatically, a cigarette in his hand. His voice is forceful as he says, *"Butbut!"* "It's a lie!" The translator says, "That's a big lie. All that I'm saying there is being told to me!"

"Who keeps telling you all these lies in the film?" Amy asks.

"Datu' Galang."

"Why does he have to tell these lies about himself?" Amy asks the translator.

"We will give you money," the translator says, "clothes, whatever you want."

"Did they receive it?" Nance asks softly, off camera.

"Were you given what you were promised?"

"They did not give us. They just left."

Relaxing on a balcony in Manila, Nance explains that the Tasaday were told that Momo' Dakel was dead, and they thought this new man, Iten, was their friend. Nance says it wasn't Iten and the other journalists who were making these claims, but their translator, Joey Lozano, and that "this will come out in due course." Nance, recalling what the Tasaday told him, says, "And then we learned they went out and called us *fék . . . fék* [fake, fake]." They said, "Now we must correct that. We want to talk straight to correct that crooked story."

Again we see the clearing, the TV and the Tasaday's visitors no longer visible, only the eleven Tasaday sitting and standing, listening to Lobo speak.

"We are real Tasaday," says the translator's voice. "Yes, there are many people who have been disturbing us, telling us we are not Tasaday so they will help us. But now we affirm that we are still Tasaday. We are Tasaday!"

His hand strikes the air for emphasis. He takes a quick drag on his cigarette and falls silent, the smoke from his cigarette trailing off and fading into the mists of the rain forest.

What's not shown on film is Nance, believing that he is in part responsible for their troubles, weeping.

On December 3 Joel and Blessen Boone testified that their UP testimony had been coerced by George Tanedo. The following day Peralta and Fernandez gave their proauthenticity testimony, and Manda screened *Reply to 20/20*, narrated by Tony Cervantes.

Manda continued to turn up the heat. As one by one his critics suddenly saw the light and changed their stories, the climate of fear became palpable. Representative Oscar Rodriguez asked Congress to protect the Tanedos. "I understand their lives are in danger," he said.[20] The brothers were reported in the company of Elizalde aides. Congressman Claver reported to the *Inquirer* that he was being tailed by men he believed to be armed and that his relatives had been contacted by Elizalde emissaries who wanted him to meet with Manda. "I myself am convinced that there exists a Tasaday tribe," he said, "but that is not the subject of this investigation. What is insulting to the members of the cultural communities is that there are people here trying to manipulate us here." Claver said that "certain people," whom he refused to identify, were forcing witnesses to alter statements or keep silent. Asked to elaborate, he refused to name names but said, "I am laying the blame for this manipulation on the doors of whoever will be affected by the results of this probe."

The remarks raised de Guzman's eyebrows. He reported them, but he was not pleased by Claver's statement that the Tasaday existed. The statements were made, he noted, at the end of a tense three-hour session to a "disbelieving audience."[21]

Elizalde was scheduled to appear before the committee on the fourth to respond to allegations about his misappropriation of PANAMIN funds and his exploitation of cultural minorities. That would have been an explosive session, but Manda begged off through a lawyer, claiming he was ill and would appear the following week.

He didn't have to.

On December 10 Dula returned. Manda's emissaries had brought her to Manila.

This time she testified in "Tasaday"* that she was in fact a Tasaday and that she had been coached by George Tanedo to claim she was a T'boli. In her first appearance she had become agitated, at one point asking, "What is going on? What is going on? This is what the others said. What is going on?" The translator had tried to calm her: "You wait, you wait. Don't be too emotional. Wait." But they hadn't waited or cared what she was going through. Now, here she was in Manila,

---

*As I have not been able to obtain a tape of this testimony, I can't be sure what's meant by "Tasaday." I assume the language is that of their Manobo Blit neighbors.

being cross-examined once again. "On cross-examination by Congressman Lagman, the witness claimed she is, *in fact* and *in truth*, a Tasaday, but that she was instructed by one George Tanedo to speak in T'boli and not in Tasaday during the hearing in Lake Sebu. She claimed being married to one Mahayag, a Tasaday man, and had two (2) offspring with him, Ti'il and Biking. At present, she said she has a new husband, Banas, a T'boli native."[22]

After Dula's testimony, a motion was made to call off the hearings. Although three members of the committee opposed this, the majority, led by Chairman Claver, decided that there was no point in continuing the investigation. Of Tanedo's testimony, they found: "In an attempt to show that the Tasaday is a hoax, George Tanedo, a T'boli-Pampangueno mestizo and a former PANAMIN employee, testified. However, the Committee doubts his credibility and suspects his motives. The hoax story appears to be a calculated move to open the 19,000 hectares of rich agricultural and timber ancestral lands for exploitation."[23]

After two months of disruptive hearings in which both sides engaged in coercion, distortions, and manipulations, Congress finally came to the foregone conclusion that the questions regarding the Tasaday's "authenticity" were better suited to a scientific than a political forum.

Although Manda sometimes was able to undo the damage done to others, he could never undo the damage to his own reputation. He had won this round, but his reputation had come out worse for the wear, if that was possible. When he learned that Kristina Luz, Judith Moses's onetime research assistant, had been involved with the hoax story, he called her. He knew her family. She went over to his house and said, "I'm willing to talk to you, but you're not going to change the story, because the story already ran." Then, to her "shock and dismay," Datu' Galang showed up speaking Tagalog.[24] She had been made to believe that he couldn't speak a word of Tagalog, and this was the reason they'd had to bring in Lozano.*

---

*I was not able to talk to Kristina Luz until 2001, two years after my expedition to see the Tasaday with Joey, so I didn't know about her experiences with him, just as I didn't know about the various documents asserting he had bribed Datu' Galang and others. Nor had I yet secured a copy of *Reply to 20/20* when I traveled with Joey. In retrospect, I'm delighted this was the case, as I accompanied Lozano without bias, if a bit naïvely.

Galang told her that Lozano had used money and provisions as an incentive, but they'd had a falling-out because Joey hadn't given him everything he'd promised.

Manda, she thought, was a "crackpot." But even so . . .

"My feeling," Luz says, "was that when we got down there [during the 20/20 shoot], these people were not as Stone Age as Manda made everyone believe. But what I didn't like was that Joey Lozano and these guys were concocting [the idea] that in fact he had pulled a big hoax on everybody."

Seth Mydans, in a cheery little report in the New York Times, turned this battle royal into a human interest story, focusing on Dula's visit to the big city. Interviewing her in Elizalde's living room, Mydans noted that the "skeptics appeared to be in retreat." Asked how she liked the city, Dula, accompanied by Banas, said through an Elizalde-provided translator, that she thought it was "nice," but that she wanted to go home, where it was quieter. "I do not feel very happy inside myself," she said. "It is very painful in the head. It is very painful in the heart." Did she want to bring back anything with her from Manila? she was asked.

"I want to take Momo' Dakel."[25]

15

Loaded Words

For the record, please be informed that the OSCC has not herded [the Tasaday] back to the caves wearing leaves for selected Western camera crews; we have more to do than such "puting tabing palabas" [screen productions].
—Letter from the Office of Southern Cultural Communities to Judith Moses, April 5, 1993

PANAMIN collapsed in 1983 in the wake of charges that Manda had disappeared with a good portion of its coffers. But PANAMIN, in some ways, had never been dismantled; it had merely morphed into the Office of Southern Cultural Communities. By 1988 the OSCC had declared war on the Santa Cruz Mission. The charge against the missionaries was that they had defied the order barring entry into the reserve and had cleared twenty hectares of land and that they were also friendly with the NPA operating in the area. An article in the *Philippine Daily Globe* explained: "President Corazon Aquino has directed the Office for Southern Cultural Communities (OSCC) to look into the alleged illegal entry of an American charity mission into the Tasaday Reservation in South Cotabato."[1]

Had the war between the OSCC and Santa Cruz been instigated by Manda now that he was back in the country? It seemed entirely possible, and Father Rex Mansmann suspected Manda's motives for keeping others out of the Tasaday forest. In the late eighties, Mansmann suggested to Central TV and newspapers that Manda was after gold or uranium in the reserve. He alleged that "the reported abundance of gold deposits and precious metals like uranium in the area [is] the reason that the mission is being evicted from the reservation."[2]

179

He also claimed that the Tasaday had asked for the mission's help. In response, he'd sent eight teachers and community workers to Blit to help the Tasaday and the inhabitants of Blit.

Despite his suspicions, Father Rex, as he's known, didn't doubt the Tasaday's "authenticity." Hoax proponents latched on to his mistrust of Elizalde while deriding or dismissing his views on the Tasaday. Some even went as far as to distort his position. Others figured he'd cut some sort of deal or variously, that he and Father McDonagh had been intimidated by Elizalde and his associates.

I visited Mansmann after my interview with Bilengan, Datu' Galang, and Lolo' in Tubak. He was living on an asparagus farm in the town of Tupi, head of an all-female cooperative of T'bolis. He had been tried and ultimately acquitted of charges that he'd raped a fifteen-year-old T'boli schoolgirl. Still, he had been defrocked. He hastened to tell me that he'd given up working with T'boli men, who by and large he found lazy and oppressive in their treatment of the opposite sex.

Undoubtedly, Mansmann's brush with scandal and the subsequent destruction of his career had humbled him and given him a perspective of someone who no longer believed in absolutes. He was surprisingly generous when it came to Manda. He told me that Manda was quite charming and that the two got along personally. "Actually, I enjoyed being with him." But Mansmann was also well acquainted with Manda's explosive side.

Mansmann admitted he felt threatened by the arrival of Manda and PANAMIN. After all, he had been working with the T'boli since 1963, and PANAMIN tried in many ways to diminish his influence. "Right from the beginning," he said, "there was some kind of animosity there. As time went on, they really tried to undermine the mission. The guy [Manda] was sincere about trying to help, but he had his own ideas about what kind of help there would be. And he had a strong prejudice about any kind of religious involvement there, which I would say at this point in my life was not unjustified entirely. Religion, of course, is a great destroyer of culture." In the years since his feud with Elizalde, Father Rex had, it seems, come around to Manda's way of thinking.

Manda sworn in by Marcos as Presidential Adviser on National Minorities, August 10, 1967. (Lopez Memorial Museum Collection)

Surallah Mayor Jose (Joe) Sison takes a short break from attempting to ambush and kill Manda to make Charles Lindbergh an Honorary Police Chief, August 1970. Manda seated at left. (Lopez Memorial Museum Collection)

In April 1972, a helicopter from Clark Air Base was sent to "rescue" Lindbergh and Manda and his staff from the Tasaday jungle. This made news around the world, much to the publicity-shy Lindbergh's chagrin and Manda's embarrassment. (Lopez Memorial Museum Collection)

The clearing at the edge of the forest as it appeared in 1971. (Nance)

One of the first photos taken of the Tasaday. Photography was forbidden by Manda at the first meeting, but Helen Mabandos disobeyed and smuggled in a camera. Note Dula's cloth skirt. (Mabandos)

Tasaday in main habitation cave looking at helicopter flying over forest, 1972. (Nance)

Jack Reynolds and NBC camera crew filming at the caves. Jack Reynolds, cameraman, Igna (seated), Lobo (seated), Manda (seated), Belayem (standing), Gintuy (crouching in cave). (Nance)

Manda and the Tasaday in front of the cave complex. (Nance)

Manda and Lobo. (Nance)

(below) Lobo with pet bird
(note vine thread leash),
1972. (Nance)

One of Mai Tuan's wives, pilot Ching Rivero, and Helen Mabandos in front of Manda's helicopter. (Mabandos)

John Nance and Zeus Salazar (on stage) at the 1986 University of the Philippines Conference on the Tasaday. (Berreman)

Joey Lozano and Oswald Iten at the 1986 University of the Philippines Conference on the Tasaday. (Berreman)

Joey Lozano shaking hands with local paramilitary in the mountains on the author's first trip, 1999. (Hemley)

Lolo, Bilengan, and Datu' Galang being interviewed by the author in Tubak, South Cotabato, January 1999. (Hemley)

Bilengan greeting Amy Rara at Magtu Inilingan, August 1999. (Hemley)

The caves as they appeared in 1999. Note rotted platforms in back. (Hemley)

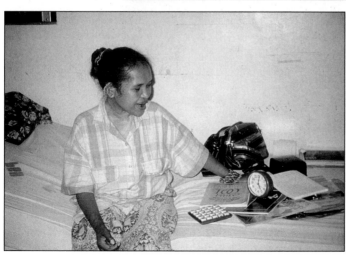

Dul in hospital room at University of the Philippines— Philippines General Hospital. After being stabbed months before, Dul was given treatment with the financial support of John Nance. Beside her on the bed are literacy tools provided by Nance. (Hemley)

Adug in a leaf G-string smoking
a Marlboro, August 1999.
(Hemley)

(below) Bilengan and Lobo
pausing in the cave before the
hike back to Magtu Inilingan,
1999. (Hemley)

Mansmann bristled at the suggestion that Manda might have intimidated him into supporting authenticity claims. "No way," he said. "I mean, that's not my style. Not intimidated. Definitely not. Maybe the opposite. Maybe more inclined to be strongly against rather than to be intimidated."

He recounted Manda's stationing himself in a room with piles and piles of money on a table. As the tribal people filed in, he sat there like a king and asked what they wanted. He gave away ten thousand, thirty thousand pesos at a time.

"That's a lot of big bucks," Mansmann said. "And they would say something about God, and he would say, 'Don't talk to me about God. This is my God.'"

He told me about a time in the 1970s when Manda beat Mai Tuan with his pistol.* I had heard this one before, and I've heard much worse. Lou Goduco, the head of Dole Philippines, said that Manda tortured people; he roasted at least one person alive in an oil drum.† Goduco claimed to have met one of Manda's bodyguards who'd admitted to participating in the torture.

"Oh, yeah, that was a thing they used to do," Mansmann confirmed as if he were talking about some kids breaking windows with baseballs. "Yeah, they did that. I don't think he did it personally. He had all these goons with him, you know. What they would do is they would take a steel drum and put water in it, and then they would take banana leaves and tie it around the steel drum, you know? And this guy that was giving them a hard time, whatever reason it was, they'd put him in the drum and then light these banana leaves. So you really weren't going to hurt the guy. Apparently, you'd scare the heck out of [him]. . . ."

"Did they kill them?" I asked.

---

*In a 1977 letter to President Marcos, Mai Tuan complained for several pages about Manda's physical abuse of him. Apparently, Elizalde had accused Mai of disloyalty, of being in the employ of a logging company, and of sleeping with Manda's sponsored students (scholars). Mai denied the accusations, which triggered the beating. Mai, in his letter to Marcos, accused Manda, among other things, of having sex with one of Mai's wives. He urged Marcos to appoint a director of PANAMIN from among the tribes rather than the egomaniacal millionaire. After the beating, Mai was imprisoned in Manda's White Plains mansion, but soon managed to escape and flee to his home territory in Mindanao where he kept a wary distance from Manda for a number of years.
†This same account was related by Christian Adler at the 1986 UP conference.

"No, I don't think so. I'm quite sure they didn't. They would do things like that. It was kind of one of their little persuaders, shall we say?"

This version of the story surprised me a bit. Not that it redeemed Manda, but it did bring him down a few notches from Vlad the Impaler to maybe the level of, say, Manuel Noriega, former kingpin of Panama.

"So Manda and PANAMIN were bad," I said. "But the Tasaday were 'genuine.'"

"That would be our position, and especially as time went on, there's no doubt that [Manda and PANAMIN] tried to hoax people."

This apparent contradiction surprised me at first, but it soon became clear that he was referring to the time George Tanedo and Sam Ganguso had been brought to Manila to dress up as Tasaday for Gerald Ford's visit. This wasn't exactly news. When I asked if there'd been any dressing up at the caves, it was Rex's turn to be perplexed. No, he told me. No T'boli had pretended to be Tasaday at the caves. "I slept in the cave myself," he said. "To my mind, there's no doubt that this is a separate group of people."

"How were they dressed when you visited them at the caves?" I asked.

"Well, they were already then using other kinds of clothing, but they showed me where they got the cloth. They did dress up in the original stuff, and they showed me where they would get these leaves and how they would do it and how they would put them on."

The idea that the priests might have changed their minds based on their own experiences and discussions seemed simply implausible to Iten and Moses. Iten's scenario had the cynical priests deciding that the Tasaday myth would be a useful fund-raising tool. The fact that they had refused to help him with his 1986 expedition flummoxed Iten, and he needed to find an explanation that fitted his model of human behavior. He writes: "Was it sheer coincidence that after Elizalde had fled the country the mission had used the Tasaday in a successful 1984 grant application for USAID funding (USAID 1984)? Had the Tasaday become a convenient bit of Panamin's legacy that might now be used to trigger the imagination of American donors? USAID did come up with $750,000 for the Santa Cruz Mission, and the mission, in fact, became the most potent political and economic institution in the area, filling the power vacuum left when Elizalde fled the Philippines in 1983."[3]

Perhaps, as Iten suggested, the fathers were testy simply because he was threatening their gravy train, but maybe he annoyed them just because he was annoying. Perhaps their profound opposition stemmed not from self-interest but because they were profoundly opposed to an outsider's coming in again and upsetting the Tasaday.

Mansmann received an awful lot of taxpayer money for the area during a period that was intense, in terms of both military activity around the Tasaday area and the scrutiny of the Tasaday controversy. But the grants to Santa Cruz (for projects to teach local people methods of sustainable agriculture) began in 1984, a full two years before Iten first deemed a hoax had been perpetrated and also at a time when Manda was in Costa Rica. In many ways, Father Rex's agricultural activities made sense. In the vacuum of Manda's departure and PANAMIN's demise, Mansmann naturally started a project that took over the ostensible functions of PANAMIN, providing economic assistance to the area.

If anything, Rex wanted to be the new Momo' Dakel. But the Tasaday did not particularly care for him. In 1988 the mission invited the Tasaday to participate in the annual cultural festival at Lake Sebu. As part of their cultural demonstration, an imitation cave was constructed by the mission staff, and the Tasaday, among them Lobo, Dul, and Belayem sat in their caves as visitors gawked. It was "corny," Mansmann admitted, but well intentioned. The Tasaday enjoyed themselves, and their visitors, mostly their tribal and Christian neighbors, visited in droves. Clayton Jones, a reporter for the *Christian Science Monitor*, stumbled upon them posed in their papier-mâché cave. He was properly horrified and went home and filed a properly horrified report (with underlying ironic glee at his journalistic good fortune) about the exploitation of the Tasaday: "They appeared right at home, like the bears in the San Diego Zoo, although my first stunned impression was that of wax mannequins in a museum. Was this another abominable display of tribal Filipinos, like the one at the 1904 exhibition in St. Louis . . . ? On the front of their mock grotto was a small placard proclaiming it, 'Our Home.'"[4]

Though unnamed by Jones, it's clearly Mansmann to whom he refers when he reports a missionary's visit to the caves soon after the

Iten exposé. "Now I know the Tasaday are true," Rex reportedly told Dul when he visited the caves. "Before I had doubts. When Elizalde falls down, I will control you."

"We don't want your control," Dul responded. "We want to be what we are."

"But I come from the true God while Elizalde is a god with a tail."

"Why do you want to remove our feelings toward Elizalde?" Dul asked. "Even if he is a god with a tail, he is our god. He really loves us. Others love us in words."

Later, according to Jones, the Tasaday were visited by fifteen Communist guerrillas, who, "not quite understanding that a utopian communist society in its purest form might be standing right in front of them," told the Tasaday that the guerrillas were "fighting for the poor" and that if the Tasaday didn't join them, they would be killed. "Why do people hurt us with words?" Dul asked Jones. "So many people call us fake, fake, fake. When we meet people, we don't call them fake."[5]

16

Trial in the Jungle

In the beginning, before I saw the Tasaday, I had felt it was wrong to simply keep them as they were found, deprived of what we have. But they have something far better than what we have. Seeing them was like going back to reality, after the illusion of civilization.   —Gina Lollobrigida*

ance hadn't known about the 1988 International Congress on Anthropological and Ethnological Sciences in Zagreb until Bettina Lerner from the BBC called him up and told him that his "friends" were going to be gathering in a few days to discuss the Tasaday.† "My friends?" Nance said.

"Yes, your friends, Mr. Nance. Gerald Berreman, Zeus Salazar, and Judith Moses. It's a shame you won't be attending. We'll be there, of course." The BBC was going to be filming, and obviously it would be much more interesting to have representatives of the authenticity argument in addition to the hoax proponents.

The organizers of the Tasaday session had stacked the deck in such a way that little would be heard from those who disagreed with advocates of the hoax theory. Berreman, an impartial observer at the UP conference, now championed the hoax position among anthropol-

---

*From Lollobrigida's coffee-table book on the Philippines, bankrolled and later suppressed (after feuding with Lollobrigida) by First Lady Imelda Marcos. The quote was taken from one of the few surviving copies of the book, found in a room of Malacañang Palace by American expatriate Jim Turner after the Marcoses fled and the palace was opened to the public.
†The ICAES was held on July 24–31, 1988.

185

ogists, anointing his group the "hoax busters." He was to chair the session. Douglas Yen, the scientist who had spent the most time with the Tasaday in the early seventies, hadn't been invited. Nor were the linguists Carol Molony or Richard Elkins. The speakers included Jerome Bailen, Judith Moses, Zeus Salazar, and Berreman himself.

Nance had been taken by surprise by the force of the allegations made by his "friends" two years earlier at the UP conference, but he, along with others in Elizalde's camp, had regrouped during the congressional hearings and fought off what they considered an attempt to invalidate the Tasaday Reserve. The stakes in Zagreb might not have been as high for the Tasaday themselves, but Nance's reputation had been ruined by the charges. People far and wide thought he was either a fool or a fraud. He still thought his experience with the Tasaday the most meaningful of his life, and he still believed the Tasaday had something important to teach.

Nance called Elizalde to see if he was sending anyone. Manda hadn't known about the conference but soon persuaded Tony Cervantes and Amy Rara to attend. Nance flew from Chicago to New York to London to Frankfurt to Zagreb and made it just in time for the conference with virtually no sleep. If not for Lerner's call, no one from the opposing camp would have been represented in Zagreb at all.

Lerner had become interested in the Tasaday story when she'd read of Iten's hoax allegations in 1986. She assumed the Tasaday *were* a hoax and wanted to find out how the scientists had been duped. Instead she found herself questioning the journalists in the story, the "ones who were so sure that the Tasaday were fakes," and their methods.

When Lerner first called Judith Moses, she hadn't known about Adrian Wood's Central TV production. "Well, we're a science program," she told Moses, "and our focus is very different. It will be purely scientific."

"Bettina," Moses said, "this is an investigative report, and it's only marginally about science. Once you get beyond the tools and the clothes and a few other things . . . it took place in the middle of a civil war, smack in the middle of a civil war where people were killing each other. You're going to really miss the point."

"We're going to focus on the science," Lerner insisted, "because that's the kind of program we are."

"Well, fine," Moses said. "There isn't very much of it. It gives you a very thin read, a very small hook to hang your coat on."

Whether the Tasaday story is purely scientific or purely journalistic is debatable. It tends to be a disconcerting mix of the two. From the beginning, journalists rather than anthropologists dominated the story of the Tasaday, and Zagreb was no different. So it was unsurprising that Judith Moses had become an expert witness.

She hadn't originally been invited, though. One of her closest friends was the president of the College of William and Mary. Their daughters were best friends, and on a visit to the college she met Mario Zamora, the organizer of the Zagreb forum. They had breakfast together, and after hearing her views, he told her he wanted her to make a presentation.

Bailen, Moses, and Salazar had no idea that Cervantes, Nance, and Rara were on their way. In preparation Cervantes and Rara had photocopied packets of materials that bolstered their views, the various early papers written by Yen, Fernandez, Lynch, et al.

In the meantime Judith Moses was alarmed to hear a rumor that Cervantes was "following" Bailen and Salazar from Manila to intimidate and keep tabs on them. She and Berreman went to meet Bailen at the airport. As they were walking out, another plane landed. They noticed a man holding up a sign that read "Antonio Cervantes." Berreman went over to the man, who told them, "I'm supposed to pick this guy up."

Bailen stayed in his room that night. The feelings of paranoia increased among the hoax proponents, though Cervantes *hadn't* been sent by Elizalde as an enforcer but as someone who would help present another side to the story.

Lerner and Moses had planned to meet to discuss the BBC film, and that night they went to the dining room to have coffee with Berreman. As they were talking, Lerner referred to "my friends Doug Yen and Carol Molony," and Moses sensed an agenda that differed from her own. "All of a sudden it came into my mind," she says, "that she was doing this with John and Carol and Doug Yen as an antidote to my piece."

Moses's suspicions about Lerner were later confirmed when Lerner interviewed her for the BBC documentary. She felt she was being written off. Lerner asked Moses how she found the Tasaday. "I started describing the route we took, and she said, 'No, no, how did you *find* them . . . how did you like them?' I was stunned. I said, 'I found them very moving and very credible, and I didn't meet all of them. But the ones I met I felt told me what was in their hearts and minds. I didn't sense any second agenda.' And then she said, 'What did they tell you?' That's actually in the cut piece. They told me they were promised material goods in exchange for their cooperation, and what shocked me most was that they were promised their own helicopter, which they told me again and again. They really wanted a helicopter. Big time."

As Berreman, Moses, and Lerner chatted over coffee, someone came up behind them.

"Antonio Cervantes is my name."

Judith Moses took his hand and then dropped it when looking up at his dark glasses, she realized who he was.

After that Cervantes was always nearby. Salazar suggested they invite him for a drink. Berreman didn't think that was a good idea. "He's a coward," Salazar said. "All these people are cowards. They're trying to intimidate me. They want me to know I'm being watched."

In truth Cervantes had more to fear from them.

The registration for the conference was $175. Nance, who had caught up with Cervantes after chatting with Lerner, figured they'd just walk in and sit down since they were attending only one session. But they were asked for tickets, and Nance didn't want to be thrown out of the conference on a technicality. On their way to get tickets, Nance ran into Judith Moses, who said, "Oh, John! I thought I'd see you here."

While he and Cervantes were waiting in line to buy their tickets, two brawny men and a woman from Yugoslavian security demanded to look into Cervantes's briefcase. Moses had approached Zamora and accused Cervantes of being a "hitman" for Elizalde, come to terrorize the Filipino scholars in attendance. There was a perception, spawned by Moses's paranoia, that Cervantes had a gun in the briefcase. The security people made him open the briefcase, but all they found were the papers he had brought with him to distribute, which they confiscated.

Eventually Rara and Cervantes were allowed in, and Cervantes, deeply offended, declared to the gathering that he'd been mistreated. He was a businessman and a scholar, not a thug. He had even been to the United States on a Fulbright. Moses didn't buy that. Later she spread the story that he'd actually been trained in the United States by the CIA. In fact, Moses was again spreading false information.

Cervantes had been not a Fulbright Fellow, but a Hubert Humphrey Fellow.*

Lerner approached Moses after this showdown. "You don't believe in free speech," she said.

"I don't believe in speech with guns," Moses said. "I don't believe in speech with threats. We're not talking about speech here. We're talking about people who have been in mortal danger. This is not a free speech issue. They can talk all they want. We're talking about life and limb here, my dear."

All Moses wanted, she claimed, were safety precautions: for all of them, but particularly for Bailen and Salazar, because she knew what they had been through, the threats and intimidation they'd received. She also knew what was coming. Bailen was going to be reading a statement from Lozano that he'd written "underground," while Salazar was going to be talking about the threats to himself.

Indeed, both Salazar and Bailen had faced intimidation by either Manda or his associates. Mai Tuan, for one, had initiated a libel suit against Bailen and others. One of the differences between U.S. and Philippine law is that libel, a civil offense in the United States, is a criminal offense in the Philippines, where a wronged party can ask for an arrest warrant. A pair of Criminal Investigation Service officers from South Cotabato arrived in Manila to arrest Bailen, who went into hiding.[1] "I don't want to be brought to South Cotabato," he told reporters. "I'll die there."[2] To forestall any action taken by Mai Tuan, Bailen had himself arrested and kept in custody at the UP police station, after which he paid his bail and went into hiding. Salazar, whose phone Manda bugged,† went into hiding, too, for a while, in Germany, where his wife is from. No doubt Manda was thoroughly capable of violence, but his image preceded him, and it's unclear just how much he might have encouraged some of the more exaggerated stories. In certain circumstances, he might have found such stories useful. That's not to say they're all untrue, but tales such as the one that had him roasting a man alive in the oil drum or that he brought virgins

---

*Cervantes had been a Hubert Humphrey Fellow in 1984. The program is administered by the Fulbright Commission to bring foreign professionals to the United States, where they attend workshops (but not on hand-to-hand combat or poisons), and are assigned to host universities.

†According to a trustworthy source who heard a portion of one of the tapes.

to his yacht to be examined by doctors made the rounds in Manila and elsewhere, gathered energy and scraps like whirlwinds as they passed from one person to another. In a sense, Manda had become his own urban legend.

His ex-wife contributed significantly to the trove of Manda lore. After viewing *The Tribe That Never Was* in 1986, she wrote to ABC News saying that she had left Manda when she learned that he was fabricating the Tasaday hoax with Lindbergh. Later she confided to Moses that Manda had group sex with children and beat up adopted and blind kids and that Nance and Manda had done a hoax rehearsal on the island of Palawan, as a kind of "joke" that later turned serious.

The history between Manda and her was bitter. He'd had her committed to a sanitarium in the United States and had gained custody of their children. Her later charges against him, Lindbergh, and Nance were the most fantastic of anyone's save perhaps Christian Adler. But no one (including the author) was able to get her to repeat her charges. Some said that she feared for her life while Manda was alive, but even after his death she avoided saying anything more publicly about her ex-husband.

When asked about the violence Moses so often referred to, Bailen and the others invariably evaded specifics or told vague stories of relatives approached by intermediaries or of someone they didn't know asking about them. The exceptions were the questionable death of Elizir Boone and an incident on a dark road in Mindanao when Lozano was shot at by a pair on a motorcycle. Mai Tuan's brother Dad was apparently one of his assailants.[3] Clearly, the Tuans weren't above violence, and they surely saw Lozano as a threat. But Mai Tuan wasn't simply Manda's puppet. In the 1980s he had his own agenda to serve. When Aquino took over, many, if not most, Marcos-era officials, including Mai Tuan, temporarily lost their positions. In response, Mai and his men retreated to the hills and ignited a new war against the government, Christian settlers, and other perceived enemies.

Manda's preferred methods of intimidation were lawsuits, affidavits, bribes, and wire taps. Baradas and Fernandez had gone into hiding, too, for a brief time, but what they were afraid of, more than physical violence, was the rumor that Manda was going to sue them for breach of contract. Manda, like Mai, also sued Salazar, Bailen, and others in a libel lawsuit, after which de Guzman was arrested and then released on a bail of five hundred pesos. Certainly, Manda would have liked to have the "hoax professors" arrested, too. He gravitated toward such maneuvers, no matter how heavy-handed or unethical.

The Zagreb conference was not entirely devoted to the Tasaday issue, as the UP conference had been. It was a small part of the conference, where two thousand anthropologists, linguists, and others were in attendance. Among them were Lawrence Reid and Thomas Headland. Headland is both a missionary and an anthropologist, a fact that doesn't sit well with some anthropologists, many of whom are ambivalent at best toward missionaries. His home institution, the Summer Institute of Linguistics, was founded in 1934 by American missionary-linguist William Cameron Townsend, based on the "realist humanitarian philosophy" that Christianity, introduced through native languages, is the best way to help "the needy and oppressed" tribal peoples of the world.[4] The SIL's translation of the New Testament into various tribal languages has also produced numerous lexicons in the most obscure tongues, an invaluable resource for future researchers, especially as speakers of the smaller languages die out.

Headland's main role at the ICAES in Zagreb was as the chair of a symposium he'd put together, titled "Deculturation and Survival Among Southeast Asian Negritos: What Can Be Done?" He was also presenting three papers, including one on the Tasaday, "What Did the Tasaday Eat?"

He roomed with his longtime friend Lawrence Reid, a former member of the SIL and a professor of linguistics at the University of Hawai'i. Headland considered Reid "the leading expert on Philippine Austronesian linguistics," and the two were working together on several papers.

The night before the Tasaday session Reid found himself seated next to Judith Moses at a dinner hosted by Mario Zamora. The Tasaday came up in conversation, and Moses whispered into his ear, "It's really terrible the way these people have been exploited. It's all a hoax, you know." She proceeded to tell her side of the story in whispered tones. This piqued Reid's interest, and he decided to attend the Tasaday session.

It began at eight-thirty the next morning. The BBC presence didn't help. The participants played to the camera with less ease and certainly less goodwill than the Tasaday. In the BBC production we see Berreman telling the roomful of anthropologists that the people who went down to see the Tasaday tended to go down there with an "idée fixe as to what they were going to see, and they tended to see it."

"Berreman had gone on for oh, about an hour," Headland says, "on and on trying to read this whole long thing." People, Nance in particular, tried to interrupt him, but Berreman forged ahead, simply holding up his hand as if someone were going to hit him.

Finally Headland stood and said, "I beg your pardon. Sir, I just have one question, Jerry. Are the rest of the people going to be allowed to speak today? Is this a filibuster? Are the people on the other side even going to be allowed to say anything today? I've come several thousand miles to hear this. This is an important symposium to me, and I would like to hear the other speakers."

Berreman stopped not long after that, and Judith Moses got up to speak. "I'm going to tell you what I really want to tell you, and it's going to be no holds barred, but you have to understand that I don't have to go back to the Philippines and live, and that's the difference between me and my colleagues."

As she spoke, she noticed Cervantes sitting with an implacable expression. The only time he registered anything was when she was talking about the documents she had obtained through the Freedom of Information Act that had some names crossed out to protect the identities of intelligence operatives. Cervantes nodded to her, and she looked away quickly. In her mind, this was some kind of tacit acknowledgment from a CIA operative that the government was doing right by its spies.

"John," she said, addressing Nance, who was taking notes on the proceedings for a book of his own, "if you did know about the hoax, then shame on you. And if you didn't know, double shame on you. Because nobody had access like you had. Nobody could have had their questions answered."

Afterward Nance addressed the assembled scholars and told them he felt he was being libeled. But even years later Moses remained intractable. "Nance, of all people, was capable of getting answers and getting answers from the right people and confronting them, or else joining forces with us and saying, 'Come on, let's put an end to this thing.' But this defensive, adversarial posture from the very beginning was totally uncalled for." Berreman, Iten, Azurin, Bailen, Salazar, and

Moses had each taken turns gnawing on Nance at one time or another like a chew toy. Hard to see why he didn't simply join in.

Passing around a photo of a corpse on a slab with its head sewn back on, Moses claimed that Mai Tuan himself had killed this man. But waving around the gruesome photo (undoubtedly supplied by Lozano) proved nothing about the Tasaday. Violence was part of the everyday landscape of South Cotabato.

Lawrence Reid was intrigued by all the politics in the room in Zagreb:

> It seemed to me that there was one line of evidence that had not been explored. If a hoax was involved, surely it would be apparent in the linguistic data that was gathered by the linguists and anthropologists during the initial contacts that had been made with them in the early 70's. T'boli is not a Manobo language, in fact it is as different from Manobo languages as perhaps English is from Russian. . . . It would be interesting, I thought, to critically examine the responses that were recorded to questions posed by the first investigators, for signs of linguistic hanky-panky, or at least for evidence that there was an educated T'boli masquerading as a primitive stone-age cave dweller.[5]

Reid also wondered why if the Tasaday were a hoax, Manda would have recruited a deaf-mute couple and a sickly albino child for the original group. It couldn't have been easy to send them running to the caves in advance of his helicopter.

After Moses had finished her admonishments, someone suggested that they gather again that afternoon so that the other side could respond. Headland was tapped to lead the afternoon session since both sides seemed willing to listen to him. He was reluctant at first but finally agreed. A consummate organizer, he gave everyone a set amount of time for his or her remarks. Everything ran smoothly after that. No one interrupted, and no one shouted. Most important of all, TV cameras were banned.

It's fitting perhaps that the BBC filming in Zagreb had turned the proceedings into a circus. Never before have images been so crucial to a supposedly scientific inquiry.

In February 1990, in the pages of *Anthropology Today*, Judith

Moses ridiculed Bettina Lerner's methods for coming to a conclusion different from her own. Moses writes: "[She] is the *only* reporter who traveled to the Philippines and never bothered to go to Mindanao. . . . Of what use is an armchair report? I find such an attitude somewhat arrogant at the very least."[6]

Lerner responded with her own broadside in the June issue: "Although she sees me as an armchair journalist, I deliberately chose *not* to go down to Mindanao to interview the Tasaday . . . journalists, as opposed to anthropologists, will never find out the truth about the Tasaday from the Tasaday themselves. The Tasaday have changed their story for every journalist who has been down to see them. . . . If there is any 'arrogance' in this issue it is shown by journalists like Ms. Moses, who pop down to Mindanao for a couple of days and triumphantly return with the definitive 'truth.' . . . Rather than attacking me, it might be more pertinent to question the many 'armchair' *anthropologists* involved in this story."[7]

Lerner's choice not to disturb the Tasaday might have been derided by Moses, but it was lauded by Father McDonagh of the Santa Cruz Mission, who cooperated with the BBC *only* because of this agreement. The most important consideration for the mission was to protect the Tasaday and their forest.[8]

Even so, Lerner's film ends with exactly that which she says we cannot trust, an affirmation of authenticity by one of the Tasaday. The words that conclude this film are from *Twilight of the Tasaday*. An interpreter speaks for Lobo: "Lobo says we are real Tasaday. Yes, there are many people who are disturbing us, telling us we are not Tasaday. We come here to affirm ourselves as real Tasaday, real Tasaday."

Perhaps, as Lerner asserts, we shall never learn the truth from the Tasaday themselves. But this is what we're left with, the voice of an interpreter, his voice raised in anger as he shouts those last words, "real Tasaday," as though he were speaking not about someone else but for and about himself.

For the most part, Bettina Lerner's *Trial in the Jungle* is a sober and balanced piece of journalism, though it goes a bit off course in its determined presentation of Manda as Tau Bong ("Good Man"). The film portrays him righteously indignant, declaring that his detractors have been saying for seventeen years that he cordoned off the Tasaday Reserve for personal gain, yet in that time, he has "still gotten nothing from this land whatsoever." True enough, but then the narrator informs us that Manda "continues to champion the Tasaday. In 1988, he brought the Tasaday to Manila in hopes of proving their authenticity in court."

Indeed the Tasaday *were* the first "Stone Age" tribe to sue for libel. The plaintiffs—namely, Belayem, Mahayag, Dul, and Lobo, as Tasaday representatives, and Manda, ad litem as their guardian—filed suit against the "hoax professors" for thirty-two thousand pesos (or two months' combined wages for the professors), declaring that Bailen and Salazar's statements that the Tasaday were "nonexistent or frauds deprived [the Tasaday] of their peace of mind and defiled the Tasaday's 'dignity and personality.' " The Tasaday also deserved a "judgment declaring them a distinct ethnic community qualified to receive the benefits of Presidential Proclamation No. 995."[9]

Nearly a year earlier Seth Mydans of the *New York Times* had interviewed Dula in Manda's living room after Elizalde had flown her up to Manila for the congressional hearings. Now he interviewed several other Tasaday in Manda's living room with an interpreter provided by Elizalde.

"We are the forest," he reported Dul saying as she "gravely affixed her thumbprint to the complaint. 'We are the Tasaday. We are as real as the forest and the flowers and the trees and the stream. We are as strong as the stone of the cave of the Tasaday.' "[10]

The Tasaday, dressed in shirts and pants, some of them wearing baseball caps, didn't look much like the forest as they inspected the gadgets of modern living: an electric chandelier Mahayag said he wanted to take back to the Tasaday forest and a music box that played *Swan Lake* while others picked through their companions' hair in what Mydans oddly referred to as "ritual grooming."

While in Manila, the Tasaday rode a Ferris wheel and drove golf carts around Manda's jungle lawn, laughing as they careened into bushes. In their hotel room they watched *The Gods Must Be Crazy* over and over again.

Whatever can be said about Manda's intentions, the Tasaday's libel suit only guaranteed more spectacle, not proof of "authenticity" or protection of the Tasaday forest. Bailen and Salazar refused to show up in court and claimed, rightly, that they were only exercising their academic freedom.

In her opening address to the First International Festival and Conference on Indigenous and Traditional Cultures in Manila soon after the libel trial had begun, Cory Aquino made special mention of the Tasaday, confirming "that the Tasaday tribe is indeed a genuine and separate tribal group."

Why was the president of the Philippines weighing in on the issue? Given its timing on the heels of the new lawsuit filed by Manda on the Tasaday's behalf, given the fact that Manda had powerful friends close to the President, given the fact that the speech was written for Mrs. Aquino, it seems likely this was another political gambit of Elizalde's. The previous year's congressional hearings had ended with the reasonable conclusion that a political forum was not the proper body to decide on the "authenticity" of an ethnic group, but now the country's top leader had stepped in and done just that, in effect making it difficult for anyone to say otherwise.

On the last day of the festival the proceedings were, in the words of the *Manila Standard*, "pleasantly disrupted" by the well-timed entrance of three Tasaday, led by Dul and accompanied by Mai Tuan.[11] After being ushered to the front, Dul, carrying her baby, told the audience through interpreters that the "Tasaday merely wanted to survive and exercise their personal rights and their right to their land."[12] She then thanked President Aquino for recognizing the Tasaday "as a separate, authentic tribe." After her remarks the delegates adopted a resolution recognizing the Tasaday's "fundamental rights . . . and dignity as human beings."[13]

At virtually the same moment Dul was telling her audience that the Tasaday simply wanted to survive and exercise their property rights, the military had invaded their reserve and the gentle Tasaday had become temporary war refugees. On November 21, five helicopters, one a Sikorsky gunship, appeared over Blit, fired rockets, then landed, with a contingent of fully armed troops. Later in the day forty-five more soldiers entered the Tasaday area and occupied the houses "left vacant by the Manobos and Tasadays who evacuated two days earlier, upon receiving reports that the military will 'operate' in the place."[14]

The day before Dul's remarks of gratitude toward the president, Colonel Orlando Soriano and Mai Tuan (who had since won back his good offices as mayor of T'boli) had arrived in Blit by helicopter, accompanied by reporters with cameras and videos. Colonel Soriano was on an NPA hunt; he summoned three of the Santa Cruz staff members in Blit and asked them if any NPAs or other rebels operated in the area. They said no, but the colonel was dissatisfied with their answers and warned that there were "suspicions" that they had NPA connections.

On December 3 the Tasaday Dul, Udelen, Natek, Okon (Dul's daughter, a teenager at the time), and Lobo returned to the caves—in helicopters—escorted by Mai Tuan and other provincial officials and a bevy of reporters, just like the old days. The Santa Cruz Mission teachers were summoned and shown petitions, supposedly signed by the Tasaday and various residents of Blit, demanding their removal as well as that of the schools. Clearly this was a battle over resources, over hearts and minds, and the Tasaday had the misfortune of living in the middle of a war zone.

Occam's razor suggests the best reason for the military action at Blit. Military personnel, who tend not to be subtle creatures anyway, thought the mission was sympathetic to the Communist rebels (not an outlandish supposition) and wanted to root them out, "them" meaning both the missionaries and the rebels, one and the same to many in the military.

But whether it was over alleged gold or hearts and minds, the Tasaday as usual were the losers all the way around. The ironies are almost too grotesque to imagine. The Tasaday, once noted, rightly or wrongly, for their gentle ways, now fled the area in panic or arrived in gunships with military escorts. In their place, as a photo of the time documents, one can see Colonel Soriano, his soldiers, and a number of reporters crouched in one of the caves, smiles on their faces, pretending to be something other than themselves.

17

Your Own Private Tasaday

Circumstantial evidence is a very tricky thing; . . . it may seem to point very straight to one thing, but if you shift your own point of view a little, you may find it pointing in an equally uncompromising manner to something entirely different. . . . There is nothing more deceptive than an obvious fact.
—Arthur Conan Doyle, "The Boscombe Valley Mystery,"
The Complete Sherlock Holmes

When the hoax story broke, anthropology was on the cusp of an identity crisis that has divided the discipline with feuds and jealousies. The neofunctionalists (who believe in the ecologically noble savage) disdain the postmodernists ("navel gazers" who only want to discuss "signs" and "signifiers" and personal narratives). Groups that are ostensibly on the same side hate one another, too. The British group Survival International champions the rights of indigenous peoples. It believes in the self-determination of tribes, as does its American counterpart, Cultural Survival, but the two organizations have historically loathed each other because of their differing approaches. The Brits believe that tribal lands should be off limits and that there should be no interaction with the larger world. The Americans believe this is impossible and want the tribes to have a little nest egg for those rainy rain forest days.

Meanwhile we're learning that many of our treasured beliefs about anthropology are make-believe. Perhaps Margaret Mead was duped by some Samoan teenagers who didn't want to answer her embarrassing questions about sexuality. Napoleon Chagnon exaggerated the "fierceness" of the Yanomamo and even, according to the sensational charges of journalist Patrick Tierney, purposely injected them with a measles vaccine to test his theories of their genetic superiority (a charge that turns out to be false, but people tend to remember a smear rather than a retraction). And the Kalahari !Kung, whom Richard Lee made famous (and who were the subject of *The Gods Must Be Crazy* films), are not as isolated as we thought. To our great dismay, no one is isolated as we once thought, and that's a shame because we're pretty bad company as it turns out. To paraphrase Groucho Marx, we don't want to be members of a human race that would have us as members.

But it's natural to romanticize, isn't it? Anthropologists, adventurers, and missionaries alike all had reasons to pursue "isolated" tribes. In 1976 ethnographer Anton Lukesch wrote, "It is the fondest dream of every ethnologist to make contact with one of the world's few remaining unacculturated tribes." In the late 1960s missionaries in Surinam ran across a group, the Akuriyo, which fled farther into the Amazon. The missionaries doggedly pursued the Akuriyo, despite some fairly obvious hints that they didn't want to be followed: arrows in paths, abandoned villages. When the missionaries finally caught up with the exhausted Akuriyo, they convinced them to abandon the forest and live in a missionized village. Within a couple of years a quarter of them had died of disease. In the early 1900s, Dean Worcester, Secretary of the Interior of the Philippines, went in search of the Agta of northern Luzon and seemed befuddled when they ran in advance of his steamship despite his attempts to convince them he was friendly. The *National Geographic* photos published after his expedition cropped out a clay pot to make the Agta appear more primitive.[1]

Anthropologists usually like to claim the moral high ground here; of the three groups, they believe they're the least intrusive, most respectful. But for years a good number of them played doctor, dress-up, and house (or hut) in the name of science. While many anthropologists and missionaries have championed the rights of native peoples, often heroically standing in the way of bulldozers or men with machetes and guns or greedy government officials, there's inevitably in them a bit of the colonizer.

But is it wrong in all circumstances to romanticize the few small-scale cultures that exist in the world, to project our hopeless yearnings upon them? It depends perhaps on how we define romanticism.

It seems too easy to say that our yearning is simply a veil to hide our true feelings of superiority, though perhaps such feelings coexist. Ten thousand years ago there really did exist such a world as we have reimagined and idealized, but the small-scale cultures of our distant ancestors were viable and sustainable, and ours are not. Perhaps such idealizing would not be all bad if we could just figure out some lesson, anything at all, that would change for the better our relationship to the natural world. I'm betraying myself, am I not? Obviously I'm subscribing to that silly notion of the ecologically noble savage. Such clever terms we come up with. But remember, every time you read such a term, it plays to distance us from some disgraced paradigm. Moreover, every new term you read represents some anthropologist's career.

In 1971, Edith Terry, a twenty-one-year-old Yale anthropology student, had the good fortune to be one of the earliest outside observers of the Tasaday. Her professor, Harold Conklin (who in coming years wisely chose to avoid both Elizalde and the Tasaday), had arranged for her to meet Robert Fox on a visit to the Philippines, where her family lived. Fox, who had just returned from his first visit with the Tasaday, invited her to join him at an organizational meeting with Manda. The men discussed the danger the Tasaday were in and their stone tools. Manda invited Terry to go along as Fox's assistant. She and Manda took a private train down to Legazpi and from there flew by helicopter to T'boli, where Fox was to meet them. She was with Fox, Elizalde, and PANAMIN staffers from July 8 to August 1971 and spent July 13 to 19 with the Tasaday, ahead of John Nance and other invited reporters, sleeping in Blit, adjacent to the clearing in the forest.

The group spent two long days at the clearing in the forest with the Tasaday, and on that first day, Terry remembers Manda's asking them if the rags they wore were what they had always worn. They said no.

"Show me how you used to dress," Manda said.

"He had a rhetoric of tribal pride," Terry recalls. "He was trying to say, 'Don't be ashamed of yourselves. You don't have to look like us.' The Tasaday went upstream and came back wearing leaves. Manda said something to the effect of 'That's lovely. Why don't you get rid of these other things?' I didn't think at the time this was manipulative. I think that when the journalists came in, some of the Tasaday were still wearing bits of clothing and earrings, so there wasn't elaborate staging."

Besides Elizalde and Terry, the only other people who witnessed this transformation were Manda's staff, the T'boli, including Mai Tuan, and some of the Manobo from Blit. What stuck with Terry was the fact that the leaves they wore seemed complex and they wove them quickly. The women pulled out the leaves to form something like a skirt, which didn't mean necessarily that they were emulating twentieth-century miniskirts. Terry was reminded of the ancient Polynesian tradition of dangling leaves in women's clothing.

She didn't think anyone in Manda's group could have come up with the clothes they were wearing. If it was being staged, it was being staged for Manda's staff and her. "There was not a lot in that first encounter to generate skepticism," she says. "Later on, the next year, when the journalists came in, then you started to get into a manipulative zone. At that point, frankly, it was a zoo."[2]

When the Tasaday hoax story broke, Terry thought it would be discredited quickly and was surprised when it wasn't. She has a hundred pages of unpublished and well-guarded field notes she wrote in 1971, as well as the original telexes between Elizalde and Fox. She considered participating in a 1989 session on the Tasaday at the American Anthropological Association's annual conference in Washington, D.C. but withdrew her offer after she and conference organizer Thomas Headland clashed in correspondence and by phone.[3] She thought that Headland was too closely aligned with the hoax proponents.

In a letter from the late eighties to Eugene Sterud, editor of the American Anthropological Association's newsletter, she reproduced in its entirety Manda's telex to Fox that Nance quotes in part in *The Gentle Tasaday*. Nance's excerpt reads as follows: "In extremely isolated region about 25 minutes by chopper from Ma Falen's area have found extremely primitive people who can in fact be called a 'lost tribe.' By comparison much more primitive than Batangan Taong Buid or interior Agta although by appearance much healthier."[4] After this, Nance writes: "He [Elizalde] then listed various aspects of the visit. . . ."

Those "aspects" are quite telling, and it's hard to understand why he left them out. The telex continues:

They have absolutely no trade with outside *except for the Manobo Blit* who have begged this group for wild palm meal in exchange for rags and bolos in periods of extreme food shortage but this is not a regular or even yearly occurrence. *This group which does not seem to agree on what their group name is** also not sure of their number and in fact estimate their number between 15 and 30 people. They are not familiar with any form of planting and live strictly from hunting and food gathering. They do not know salt or rice and in fact ate rice given them in raw form and did not like it. They never come out of thick unbroken jungle where they roam and have no houses.

Nance continues quoting from a different part of the telex: "No Tboli or Ubu from Ma Falen, Lake Sebu side down to Tboli settlement, have ever heard of this group except for one Ma Falen hunter [Dafal]. People closest to them, the Blit, are a pretty wild bunch themselves, 95 percent of whom have never even seen a motor vehicle except for high-flying airplanes and now a helicopter. Biggest problem with this group—which we should refer to as Tasaday [Manda spelled it T'saday], which is high mountain around where they are from—is communication as even Manubo Blit [*sic*] can hardly communicate."

Nance, in leaving out a couple of crucial details, makes the Tasaday seem more isolated then they were, and by naming them he gives them a unity they did not necessarily possess. Essentially, according to this first telex, the people of Blit knew of the Tasaday. The Tasaday knew of the Blit. Manda named them. In hindsight these seem pretty huge things to omit. So what are we to make of all this? Evidence of Nance's complicity in the "hoax"? A cover-up? A conspiracy? Delusion? Wishful thinking? Take your pick from this lazy Susan of labels, but what you choose might say as much about you as about John Nance.

Even in the original Elizalde-Fox report, the Tasaday said they were aware of other people living around them (besides their never-located forest neighbors, the Tasafeng and Sanduka). The report supposes that the Tasaday had previous, limited contacts with other

---

*Italics the author's.

hunters; these they termed "rare." The report also states that their musical instrument was a "jew's harp," made of bamboo, an instrument that has to be cut with metal. Their brass earrings came from Dafal and their ancestors, and the report notes that their ancestors probably had greater contact in the past with outsiders. The report reads:

> The Tasaday have no formal trade or recurring contacts with the outside world living in almost total social and geographical isolation, an incredible fact in this day when man has walked on the moon. *They know there are different people who live around them, people who terrify them, they say.* * *They have sometimes glimpsed and heard the voices of balatic hunters in the forest. They speak of seeing fields and houses of people who live at lower elevations towards where the sun sets,* but we were unable to record any word in their language for another people. They do not use or have ever heard the terms Filipino, Moro, Tboli, Ubu, Bilaan [sic], or Tiruray. Their world view is encompassed by the forest in which they are born, live and die. They have no term in their language for the "sea," least of all for a "boat."

In *The Gentle Tasaday*, their "almost total" isolation became total:

> No Tasaday words could be found for Philippines, Filipino, Mindanao, Manubo [sic], Ubu, Blit, Tboli, or any other islands or peoples; no words for boat, ocean, sea, or lake—although the Celebes Sea was less than forty miles south of where they were sitting, and Lake Sebu was some thirty miles east; no words for many common local foods; none for clearing, plain, or flatland—although apparently new phrases were noted for the land beyond the clearing: "the place without up and down" and "where the eye looks too far." *Every Tasaday interviewed said he had not known such a place existed, had never been out-*

---

*This would be in line with John Bodley's idea of "active avoidance." Bodley notes that sometimes small-scale groups such as the Tasaday isolate themselves on purpose. They know other people exist but do their best to stay out of their way, a wise idea in most cases.

side the forest, and never met anyone from outside except Dafal, and none of them knew where he had come from. . . . The Tasaday said they lived in the forest, and that was all they knew.[5]

Nearly every event surrounding the Tasaday is ambiguous and open to interpretation. What do we mean when we use such terms as "Stone Age" and even "isolation" and "tribe"? What do we mean by the words "hoax" and "authentic"? Whether you mention the word "hoax" or not, it hangs in the air above you, and people clank each other on the head with it as if it were some cartoon mallet. But the words "hoax" and "authentic" are essentially ways of falsely simplifying and bringing closure to something that is actually much more complex. Imagine the headlines: POOR MANOBOS LOCATED IN SOUTH COTABATO RAIN FOREST or TASADAY FOUND TO BE SOMEWHAT EXAGGERATED. Would these have attracted anyone's attention?

Prior to the convening of the D.C. symposium in November 1989, both sides did what they could to win over the scientific community. Judith Moses wrote letters to everyone involved and spent hours on the phone with Headland and others, influencing the tenor of the entire debate with an incessant barrage of accusations. Lawrence Reid received "a whole screed of stuff about Elizalde and his misfortunes" from her. She wrote repeatedly to Richard Elkins, the linguist who had taken ill after only a few days with the Tasaday in the early seventies, hoping he would concur with her conclusions. He told her, "Look, you're talking to the wrong man. I'm convinced that this is no hoax at all."

Moses collared Yen at the conference and tried to persuade him to take sides. No one knew exactly where he stood on the issue. "She seemed to be trying to get me to say there was room to say it was a fake," he recalls.

Elizalde too wanted all his ducks in a row. One afternoon, while Elkins was in residence in Nasuli in central Mindanao at SIL headquarters, the director and his wife sent for him. There was a man interested in the Tasaday. When Elkins went down to see the visitor, the man asked him, "What is SIL's official position on the Tasaday?"

"We don't have an official position," Elkins said. The SIL was trying to stay out of the controversy. "I personally feel that they were absolutely genuine and that a lot of this is political, but we don't have an official position. I didn't know that he was one of Elizalde's people, sent there to sort of feel me out."

One day Elizalde's attorney, Oscar Trinidad, visited Jesus Peralta and began to "sweet talk" him into a "better relationship with them." Peralta wasn't sure what Trinidad wanted, but he knew he wanted something. Then he was visited by another Elizalde emissary, Colonel Jose Guerrero. They were building a foundation, Guerrero told him. They wanted Peralta to be there, and they wanted to offer him a job after he retired from the National Museum. In fact, two jobs. "I didn't say yes, and I didn't say no," says Peralta, curious what this was about.

Finally, Manda summoned Peralta to his house. He wanted Peralta to write up the data that Amy Rara had gathered. He said Peralta had credibility.

"If I'm going to write a paper," Peralta told him, "I will gather my own data. In any case, Amy Rara is an anthropologist, so she should write her own paper. Besides, with your . . . credibility, it's really down and out. If I go and write for you I will lose my own credibility."

Elkins had a similar experience. Manda invited Elkins to his house right before the D.C. conference. "We're going to have a meeting tonight of all of us," Elizalde said, "and get together and program our strategy."

"No, Mr. Elizalde," Elkins said. "I'm not going to be there. That's a mistake. If we all get together then somebody will say 'collusion.' I'll be glad to come and talk to you after it's all over. But I don't think it's very wise for us to talk now together because it'll look like we all got together and worked on our story."

"Okay, okay, fine," Manda responded.

Manda was doing a little sweet-talking in the United States, too. After Headland had been turned down by the National Science Foundation for a grant to help with expenses for the conference (the NSF apparently wanted nothing to do with the Tasaday), he received a call from Dwight Chapin, formerly the appointments secretary for Richard Nixon and an indicted and convicted coconspirator in the Watergate scandal, who was now working with Preston Brown, Manda's lawyer in the United States. Chapin told Headland he was representing Manda. He said that Elizalde had learned that Headland had been turned down by the NSF for a grant, and Elizalde, understanding that Headland needed money, wanted to supply it. Chapin told Headland he could use the money for whatever he wanted, no strings attached. Politely Headland declined, then hung up.*

Unlike previous conferences, this one invited to Washington advocates of both sides of the controversy, people who could discuss all aspects of the issue: linguistics, archaeology, anthropology, and journalism.

Amy Rara and Emmanuel "Manny" Nabayra, in response to the genealogies George Tanedo had assisted Zeus Salazar with at the UP conference, spent months in the field (with Manda's blessing and his bankroll), between August 1988 and May 1989, collecting data. They interviewed Tasaday and non-Tasaday alike, including fourteen "Tasaday poseurs," who said they had been bribed by George Tanedo to participate in a kind of Stone Age identity theft, substituting their family trees for those of the actual Tasaday.

To bolster their genealogical evidence, the pair photographed the poseurs as well. The resulting genealogies were impressive. Headland later remarked: "If we can accept, as I do, the detailed genealogical data described by Rogel-Rara [the name Amy Rara went by for a time] and Nabayra . . . then we may be forced to conclude that George Tanedo pulled off one of the biggest hoaxes of all: that his brief genealogical data given to Salazar . . . is nothing less than faked. If Salazar's genealogies collected from Tanedo are correct, then the Tasaday story was indeed a complete and outrageous hoax. But if Rogel-Rara and Nabayra's genealogies are correct, then the Tasaday were, though not Paleolithic and isolated, at least not intermarrying with outsiders."[6]

But Rara and Nabayra weren't alone in collecting genealogies. An anthropology doctoral student, Levita Duhaylungsod, and her dissertation adviser, David Hyndman of the Australian National University, conducted their own investigation into the Tasaday affair prior to the D.C. symposium. Duhaylungsod had been in attendance at the UP conference, where she had gone backstage afterward to meet

*Both sides heavily lobbied the American Anthropological Association, Judith Moses representing the "hoax busters," Chapin representing Manda. Chapin, however, offered the association's director of information and programs, David Givens, a trip to see the Tasaday for himself, which Givens refused.

the Tanedos. Her family hailed from Maitum, and the Tanedos were relatives by marriage. In February 1989 she and Hyndman teamed up for a thirteen-day visit to Maitum. There they encountered plenty of people who claimed the Tasaday were frauds, including the Tanedos, the Boones, Joey Lozano, and even Duhaylungsod's father-in-law, who taught at Edenton College in Maitum and declared that some of the Tasaday had been his school chums while growing up. They met none of the Tasaday, nor did they travel to the Tasaday area. The result of their expedition was another Tanedo-inspired genealogy.

A number of the people interviewed by the pair were likely lying. Maitum was Tanedo's stronghold, just as Surallah had been the stronghold of Mayor Sison, Manda's old rival, in the early seventies. Some in the area had their eyes on the reserve, some held grudges against Manda and PANAMIN, and some certainly felt what Filipinos call *utang na loob* (profound inner debt) to Tanedo, a prominent businessman. It is difficult to underestimate the force of *chismis* (gossip) in shaping public opinion in the provinces as well as in metro Manila, perhaps in part as a result of living for a decade under martial law, when reliable information was shared in whispers. Rumor often carries the weight of fact. Those who weren't lying or gossiping about the Tasaday almost certainly were referring to the Tasaday poseurs, not to the Tasaday themselves. In any case, the meat of their argument was that everyone in the area knew the Tasaday are fake: "The continuing contention that the 'Tasaday' are authentic finds no credence among any of the interest groups in Maitum. The notion of 'primitive' Tasaday is laughable to them, for one of the 26 Tasaday 'discovered' in 1971, Saay (Udelen), was a well-known Tboli man once resident in their community!"[7]

The cloak-and-dagger tone of Hyndman and Duhaylungsod's research reached its zenith at this bit of tantalizing gossip: "A radio announcer, who claimed he was a National Intelligence Coordinating Agency (NICA) agent deployed as a deep penetration agent (DPA) in the MNLF, promised us a videotape interview with Saay (alias Udelen) produced by Radio Philippines Network (RPN) in General Santos City. We paid him P160 ($7 U.S.) in exchange for a copy to be sent through RPN in Manila. It never reached us despite several follow-ups."[8] The implication was that Saay/Udelen had spilled the beans, and even though Hyndman and Duhaylungsod hadn't viewed the tape, or even verified its existence, they still used it to support their contentions.

In the BBC film on the Tasaday and the subsequent PBS *Nova* special (which used much of the same footage) we see Doug Yen collecting plants. The narrator of the *Nova* special describes Yen's methods for collecting plants and cataloging them; we're shown a simulation of his methods as he asks an informant what a particular plant is used for. In this way, Yen creates a kind of portrait of the culture through its uses of various plants. Yen found that the Tasaday diet lacked sufficient protein and carbohydrates, and here the narrator surmises that "Life in the Garden of Eden" may not have been the happy idyll it was depicted as; it might have been tough.

Another distinct possibility, not mentioned by the narrator, is that the Tasaday's diet, insufficient in proteins and carbohydrates, proved not that life was tough in the Garden of Eden but that the Tasaday had been kicked out of that garden and had started their own gardens long ago. In other words, perhaps they weren't purely foragers, not even purely hunter-gatherers. Headland in fact hypothesized that the staple food of their diet, the wild yam, was incapable of sustaining them over time. They had to have "recourse to at least some cultivated foods."[9] At least as damning, on the surface, is the fact that David Baradas and Carlos Fernandez, and later Yen, discovered that Elizalde's men were giving (or "smuggling," if one prefers) rice to the Tasaday at the caves. It was damning because it seemed to prove that the Tasaday couldn't or wouldn't survive on their own purely by foraging (or even hunting) as originally described. To some, the rice doling proved a PANAMIN cover-up, while others questioned the likelihood that any group, unaccustomed to a new staple, such as rice, would quickly develop an appetite for it.

But in the *Nova* film, much is made of Yen's fieldwork. In the film, he says he was "skeptical" at first about the isolation of the Tasaday. One day he went to Blit, and he brought back a stalk of rice and showed it to "two or three or four kids. I just pulled this out of the pack and I said, 'What is this?' My usual question . . . Their expressions were of absolute surprise. They didn't know what it was. They didn't associate it with anything. Keep in mind they were children. . . . This—this one couldn't have been fake. So I—it's not conclusive evidence for isolation, but gosh, it's—it's pretty persuasive, don't you think?"

Headland, not terribly impressed by Yen's reasoning, didn't think so. He wondered why Yen hadn't shown the plant to any Tasaday adults: "It is amazing to me that he failed to ask his usual question to any adult about the rice plant he had picked from a Blit Manobo field just four kilometers away; children are not normally reliable informants, not only because they are shy before strangers, but because they do not know the plant world near as well as their elders do."[10]

Yen disagreed sharply and acrimoniously with Headland's wild yam hypothesis to the point of withdrawing the paper he delivered at the D.C. conference from Headland's 1992 edited volume on the controversy. While Yen himself had at first been skeptical concerning the likelihood of wild yams supporting the Tasaday to the extent reported, that did not mean that his "conclusions" were final or that it was impossible for the wild yam to have been a substantial part of the Tasaday diet. Furthermore, Yen thought Headland was out of line to attack him for something he'd said in passing in an interview. They were adolescents, not children. And "if they didn't know their major crop, there's something wrong."

Tasaday life, whatever it had been twenty years earlier, had changed since the coming of Dafal and certainly since the coming of PANAMIN. It was entirely possible that the lack of wild yams noted around the caves was a recent development, that this small band was depleting what had once been able to sustain them.

Yen also noted that the wild yam hypothesis does not take into account the variability of rain forests, "the fact that there are 30 to 40 rain forest subvarieties." The idea that rain forests couldn't possibly sustain pure foragers he found insupportable. Yen resented Headland's interpretation of his data. He had called the Tasaday's diet low-level, but Headland had construed this to mean their diet was "marginal." In Headland's construction of the Tasaday lifestyle, PANAMIN's doles of rice (as well as an inferred reliance on small agricultural plots) made up the deficit in the Tasaday's paltry calorie intake. Yen bristled at Headland's theory.

Neither Yen nor any other observers had seen such small gardens, nor had the Tasaday ever admitted cultivating any crops. If Yen agreed with anything that Headland wrote, it was merely that the Tasaday had not *always* been foragers, that their ancestors had been agriculturists and that over time they had lost the knowledge of farming. And so "in the remoter past and the immediate future, Headland's hypothesis is correct."[11] The Tasaday were, in other words, what Claude Lévi-Strauss terms pseudo-archaics.

Largely thanks to Headland's ability as an organizer, the D.C. conference lacked the sideshow quality of the previous conferences. Headland tightly regulated the proceedings, giving everyone precisely fifteen minutes to speak, assistants flanking him, writing the amount of time remaining for each speaker. He also restricted who spoke. Although Bailen wanted to be part of the conference, Headland, who'd met him in Zagreb, didn't think he had much to offer. He didn't want Nance onstage either, at first claiming that only Ph.D.'s would be allowed to speak. Nance pointed out that others who were part of the conference, such as Headland's SIL colleague linguist Clay Johnston, didn't have Ph.D.'s. Finally Headland admitted that he wasn't allowing him to speak because he had been rude at Zagreb. But Nance had felt he was being libeled in Zagreb by some of the speakers. Nance went to D.C., anyway, and Headland did allow him five minutes. Nance took seven and divided up the pro and con this way: All the pro Tasaday had been to see the Tasaday, but the con hadn't. This was the crucial distinction for him.

While it's not an ironclad argument for "authenticity," it's an interesting distinction nonetheless. In the absence of experience, speculation often became certainty for no better reason than careerism, paranoia, or some other ego-driven neurosis. When he first brought Amy Rara down to see the Tasaday, Elizalde bemoaned the fact that everyone had to see for himself before he was satisfied the Tasaday were no hoax. There seemed to be truth in that, though some interpreted the conversion of skeptics somewhat more nefariously.

Most of the Filipino scientists Headland invited did not attend the D.C. conference. They were afraid to come, he thought. Peralta was going to attend but then didn't, and Headland had to read his paper for him. It wasn't simply fear of Elizalde that made Filipinos in 1989 afraid of attending the AAA conference, Headland thought. Aquino's proauthenticity statement hadn't helped. "They couldn't contradict Cory Aquino," Headland says.

But the real reason was that Peralta couldn't afford to attend, and his office couldn't afford to send him. The National Museum didn't have funding to send scholars to the United States for academic presentations. Elizalde offered to send him, but Peralta refused because he believed he would lose credibility if he accepted Manda's help. Although Headland had secured funds for him, the problem was that the arrangement necessitated Peralta's first paying for the expensive international ticket and then being reimbursed, an arrangement that was well beyond the means of a modestly paid Filipino scholar. So he did "the next best thing. I sent him the paper and asked him to read it."

Even in the United States the long arm of Manda seemed a part of every turn of events save earthquakes and other natural disasters, but Manda in fact seemed curiously ineffective in influencing anyone. Peralta was a no show in D.C. for financial, not political, reasons.

The American Anthropological Association, concurrent with Headland's 1989 session in Washington, set up an independent investigative commission to "put its house in order," headed by eminent University of Chicago anthropologist and Philippine specialist Fred Eggan, along with the respected anthropologists and Philippine specialist Charles Frake, Renato Rosaldo, Karl Hutterer, and Harold Conklin.

Berreman's view, like that of most of the hoax proponents, was that the Tasaday were "a group of local swidden farmer folk," a kind of prefab tribe (just add leaves and stone tools!), organized by Elizalde to rush up to the caves whenever the arrival of visitors was heralded by radio. If true, it would have to be called a hoax. He even calculated his scenario's likelihood variously at "perhaps a 66% probability"[12] and at a "66 to 75% probability,"[13] though he neglected to mention how he arrived at these statistics.

Of the other possibilities, he writes: "[The] variant . . . that the Tasaday were swidden farmers unusually close to, involved with, and adapted to the forests—is less likely, but not implausible, with a probability of something like 25 to 33 percent. The . . . explanation—that the Tasaday were hunter-gatherer recruits to Tasaydom—is very, but not entirely, improbable, at a level of no more than one percent. The first two scenarios—the authentic stone-age Tasaday, of disparate histories—are so improbable in my view as to be totally implausible."[14]

In the evening Berreman ran into Eggan and decided to talk to him. He figured Nance was "indoctrinating" him. He talked to Eggan about the Tasaday, how implausible the group was.

Eggan snapped at him. "Fox and Lynch were my grad students, and they wouldn't be fooled."

Berreman said nothing, but he was thinking, "No, they weren't fooled. That's why they quit." This is one of the sacred pillars of belief among the hoax busters. Oswald Iten writes: "It is untrue that all anthropologists who visited the Tasaday remain firm on their authenticity. . . . Lynch and Fox split over the nature of the Tasaday but both recoiled in disgust."[15]

Cheering him on, Berreman states: "And haven't others claimed or implied that everyone who has actually seen the Tasaday has affirmed their authenticity? The answer is, of course, that most have not been fooled, at least not for long. Robert Fox, Frank Lynch, and David Baradas . . . were enthusiastic about them to begin with but soon had second thoughts, and each soon resigned from PANAMIN."[16]

But if Fox and Lynch "recoiled in disgust" over the "hoax," what were they doing having dinner with Elizalde to help plan Yen's period of fieldwork, which followed their own?

Actually, Fox had revealed his reasons for quitting to Headland in the late seventies, when Headland visited the National Museum. He'd quit PANAMIN because "he was so absolutely disgusted with Elizalde that he found it intolerable to try to work with him. He said Elizalde was the most arrogant person he had ever met, and an egomaniac."[17] Fox never mentioned to Headland or to anyone else that he suspected the Tasaday were a hoax.

And Lynch? Judith Moses, during the D.C. conference and afterward, circulated the story in anthropology circles that anthropologist Karl Hutterer had a letter from Frank Lynch saying he believed the Tasaday to be a hoax. Hutterer, she said, had told her about the letter but refused to give it up out of deference to Lynch's memory.

In fact, Hutterer says that Moses "misstated the case of Frank Lynch," a distressingly frequent habit of hers. In 1976 he published an article in the journal *Current Anthropology* under the title "An Evolutionary Approach to the Southeast Asian Cultural Sequence." In it, he made reference to the Tasaday. After the article appeared, he received a letter from Father Lynch, who had been a friend since 1966 and was upset by and "deeply disappointed" in what Hutterer had written. He thought it "called into question his personal integrity as well as his professional judgment as an anthropologist. The implications of the letter were clearly that Frank Lynch believed strongly in what he had seen and what he had reported," says Hutterer, who continues:

> I wrote to Lynch to apologize for the misunderstanding and assured him that it had not been my intention to cast doubt on the reliability and veracity of his Tasaday report. Rather, what my footnote referred to were the atrocious circumstances of first contact with the Tasaday who were, supposedly, brought out of their jungle isolation into a clearing to be assaulted by helicopters and a horde of journalists outnumbering the Tasaday. This was a terribly inhumane thing to do. Scientifically speaking, it was terrible because it contaminated forever whatever information we might have learned from a small community that had, supposedly, lived in the tropical forest under isolated conditions for a long time. . . . As to Ms. Moses, I will say that, when I encountered her at the AAA conference, she struck me as somebody with a very large axe to grind. Why, I never bothered to find out.

The Eggan commission never filed its report because Eggan died before the report could be completed, and no one else took over the reins.

One seemingly incontrovertible solution to the controversy was proposed by archaeologist William Longacre at the D.C. conference. He claimed that a group of trained archaeologists could settle the matter in "a matter of hours," that no matter how carefully the Tasaday might have swept their caves, the archaeological evidence would have accumulated over generations. It would be impossible to fool a team of qualified archaeologists, if it were possible to get them into and out of the site safely over a period of a couple of days. But the last "if" was a big hurdle. Anthropologist Daniel Stiles later reported that his planned visit to the Tasaday in 1991 was "blocked at the last minute by military operations and threats of kidnappings."[18] There was also the standing presidential decree of Ferdinand Marcos, threatening imprisonment or deportation for anyone entering the Tasaday Reserve without government permission.

But would such a visit really solve the controversy? If it found a substantial midden, then yes, the hoax proponents would clearly be proved wrong. But if the pickings were slim, that would prove they hadn't lived in the caves for generations, something authenticity proponents had already backed away from. That wouldn't make them "fake," merely exaggerated, not in itself the rarest transgression among anthropologists and laypeople alike.

Headland writes in his introduction to his edited volume on the controversy that no one in the book would dispute the fact that the Tasaday exist. In fact, Salazar, Duhaylungsod, and Hyndman said just that, and to a slightly lesser degree, so did Berreman and Iten, not to mention Moses and the many people who believed her journalistic accounts. Yet Berreman, who cast the controversy as one between "hoax busters" and "true believers," balks at the suggestion that his view relegates the Tasaday to a kind of identity limbo:

> These believers would have it that the argument has become simply:
> 1. whether the Tasaday exist(ed)—as individuals and/or as a collectivity or group worthy of public respect and deserving of social justice, and
> 2. whether there are or have been people in the world living in relatively peaceful, nonviolent, egalitarian, self-sufficient bands, in harmony with their environments, making their living largely by foraging.[19]

Berreman didn't say who or when Tasaday proponents have argued this fuzzy second point, which of course would make the debate so general as to become meaningless. But in regard to his first point, this is exactly what the argument, or part of it at any rate, was reduced to by the hoax busters themselves. There *is* a difference, and not a subtle one, between saying the Tasaday were a band of tribal people misrepresented by media exaggeration and even by Manda's exploitation and saying that they were a group *actively recruited* to play the role of cavemen. "In my view," Berreman writes, ". . . the 'Tasaday' comprised a group of the local swidden-farming folk recruited to act as cave men in the nearby forest."[20]

The controversy once again wasn't just a matter of deciding the degree of isolation and "primitivity" of the Tasaday, as put forth in some of the original reports. If so, that would have entailed the kind of normal backpedaling associated with any anthropological find. As Yen and others had noted, anthropologists usually throw away the first three months' notes, but with the Tasaday, that was all that existed. Since so much had been made of the Tasaday in the first place, the hoax proponents would *allow* no revision of the original assertions. Any backpedaling was further evidence of a hoax.

18

Missing Links

If these . . . inanities are not enough to exceed one's tolerance for conversational implausibility, note that in the 1001 lines . . . of alleged translation of natural conversation . . . the four word honorific referring to Elizalde . . . appears 439 times, an average of nearly *every second line*, comprising therefore about one eighth (12.5%) of the total number of words in the entire transcript!
—Gerald Berreman, "The Tasaday: Stone Age Survivors or Space Age Fakes?"

awrence Reid invited me to his condo to listen to the original surreptitiously recorded cave tapes over a couple of Steinlager beers (as a New Zealander, he's loyal to the home product and will keep no other brand in his refrigerator). Laurie also had agreed to show me a stone tool Belayem had given him—*if* he could find it. It might be packed away, he said, in preparation for forthcoming scholarly appointments and conferences in France and Japan that would keep him out of the country for the next sixteen months. The tool turned up after a quick search, and he brought it over for me to inspect.

My initial feelings about the Tasaday stone tool were merely acquisitive. I simply wished I had one. Only later, after I returned home, did it occur to me that I should have taken a picture of it. Laurie was amenable to the idea of having the tool photographed, but it would have to wait for at least sixteen months and his return to Hawai'i. Typical of Manda, he had sent all three of the Tasaday tools that were found and examined by National Museum staff in those first days (the scraper Peralta found, a hafted stone hammer, and another hafted tool) to Imelda as a political gesture.[1] The tools had not been seen since. The Tasaday hastily crafted other tools for their frequent visitors. Some of these tools had been displayed at PANAMIN's museum. Mai Tuan had even made a tool for an insistent visitor (unbeknownst to the visitor), as John Nance describes in *The Gentle Tasaday*. Judith Moses had sent photographs of the existing stone tools to Robert Carniero, curator of South American ethnology at the American Museum of Natural History in New York, who had pronounced them fake, a statement that irked Doug Yen, who wondered why such an eminent authority would risk his reputation on the basis of a photograph. The supporters of authenticity saw such tools as demonstration tools. The other tools, the ones the Tasaday said were used by their ancestors, which were of better quality, were referred to as heirloom tools.

In Reid's apartment were two of the very objects whose loss the hoax supporters had bemoaned, even ridiculed: the tapes *and* a stone tool, apparently one that had actually been used before Elizalde's arrival. Laurie fetched a small boom box and popped in a copy of one of the Tasaday cave tapes; the rise-and-fall chirping of thousands of insects blanketed the small living room. He remarked that he had to have higher frequencies eliminated to reduce the noise, but the insects still dominated the tape. He expressed his doubts that such a recording could have been concocted. This felt as close as I could get to time travel—if not to the Stone Age, at least to 1972. Shouts and exclamations, long pauses, then bursts of language, and, over it all, incessantly, the sound of bugs.

The transcriptions of the tapes that Nance included in *The Gentle Tasaday* were made in the jungle, translated in large part by Mai Tuan. But like the stone tools, they were lost, or, rather, misplaced, and Elizalde's laissez-faire attitude only deepened suspicions against him. As of 1992, and Berreman's article in Thomas Headland's AAA volume on the controversy, the tapes had not been located. "The loss of the tapes," Berreman crowed, "especially combined with the loss of irreplaceable evidence for other exciting discoveries in various of Elizalde's enterprises, suggests a pattern amounting to a rain forest 'Watergate.'"

Elizalde dominated their discussions so much that in Nance's transcriptions in *The Gentle Tasaday*, he abbreviated Momo' Dakel Diwata' Tasaday to MDDT, a fact that Berreman considers a "knee-slapper." Berreman thought it absurd when Belayem, in Nance's tape transcriptions in *The Gentle Tasaday*, tells his fellow Tasaday, "We'll always be happy now that we have Momo' Dakel Diwata' Tasaday with us—not like before when he was not with us. Have you heard what I said?" Belayem asked everyone by name, and each answered that yes, he had heard. Berreman counted the number of times the abbreviation MDDT appeared in Nance's "alleged translation" (439 times). "The Tasaday," he pronounced, "must have been hard up for conversational fare."[2]

Manda handed over three of the cave tapes to Laurie in 1993, a mere twenty years after Frank Lynch asked for them. Reid's expertise in Austronesian languages qualified him to analyze the tapes in a way that few others could, and Manda recognized this. By this time, Reid says, Elizalde was probably convinced that Laurie wouldn't add to the hoax stories by manipulating the data on the tapes. Perhaps Manda had indeed misplaced the tapes all those years, as he claimed, or maybe he had simply not wanted to bother with the people asking for them, some of whom doubted the tapes' existence. Regardless, Reid had succeeded where others hadn't, and he had since transcribed and translated the tapes. He read me several passages: *"The words of Big Uncle Master of the Tasaday* [Elizalde], *the words of Brother Short-One* [Mai Tuan]. *Your rattan. Don't give them away. Your rattan. Don't deplete it. Your yams, don't deplete them. Your palm starch, don't deplete it. Don't distribute your palm starch to other people."*

"This is Belayem," Reid told me. "He's reporting on things that cannot be shared with other people. And he says, *'Everything is for Big Uncle Master of the Tasaday, the palm starch, the tadpoles, the frogs, the crabs, the monkeys. . . .'* "

"Not the gold," Laurie added, and we laughed. "This is their [the hoax proponents'] interpretation."

"All of the fish, all of the little fish of the Tasaday. The little things that are eaten here . . . yams . . . especially the palm starch. There is none that can be given away."

"You read this stuff through, and this was spontaneous," said Reid. "It wasn't set up."

Elizalde constantly admonished the Tasaday to protect their forest, not to give any of it away. This seems to be the most eloquent argument against the hoax, and it is buttressed by the fact that so long as he was alive, the reserve stayed more or less intact and protected. If

Elizalde had had designs on it, he could have exploited its resources quite easily during the decade or so that the Tasaday vanished from the public consciousness.* It was always outsiders, loggers, miners, and settlers, who wanted the reserve opened up. "Had Elizalde or Marcos not declared it a reserve . . ." I said.

"Oh, it would have gone," Reid declared. "I think that Elizalde's heart was in the right place, but sometimes he made moves which were not in the best interests of the people he was trying to protect. He was trying to establish areas which were tribal areas where people would be able to maintain their traditional ways of life. He really was convinced that it would be good for people to maintain the original ways they had and not to be engulfed with the lowland cultures which were moving in. And this was part of the reason why he told them to continue to wear your old clothes. This comes out of course on the tapes, where Elizalde supposedly tells them, 'Don't let people come in there and take your things.' "

At the D.C. conference Reid presented his initial findings, based largely on the word lists made by Fox, Peralta, Llamzon, Molony, and Elkins, as well as a tape that Carol Molony had made at the caves in 1972 (but before the reappearance of the tapes Nance mentioned). A year later, in 1990, he was in the Philippines conducting five months' research with several of the Negrito groups of northern Luzon. Responding to pleas for assistance from the tribes, Reid called the undersecretary for agriculture in charge of special projects, none other than Carlos Fernandez, to see if any aid could be made available. In discussing Reid's request, Fernandez surprised him by asking if he'd like to see the Tasaday.

Fernandez had just returned from the Tasaday area; some of the Tasaday had ventured into T'boli to complain of incursions by loggers

---

*The Gentle Tasaday was published in 1975. Between 1976 and 1986, virtually nothing was heard about the Tasaday or their reserve. But if Manda and Marcos had wanted the reserve's resources, neither would have had to resort to creating a fake tribe to protect. There were much easier ways during the Marcos regime to grab land. Elizalde, who was rich, powerful, and influential with the Marcoses, could have found a way to get what he wanted. The Marcoses bought a number of businesses via offers that couldn't be refused.

into the Tasaday Reserve, and he had gone to investigate. Fernandez told Reid that if he wanted to conduct some research, this would be an excellent opportunity for him to do so in the relative comfort of T'boli township, as opposed to the arduous hike into the Tasaday area. "He said all expenses would be taken care of. A hasty meeting was arranged with Elizalde, whom I had never met before."[3]

When he met Elizalde, Reid told him he would be "completely objective" about his findings and warned him not to expect that he would say the Tasaday were not a hoax if he found them to be so. Manda told him he had no trouble with that. Reid found Elizalde friendly and nonconfrontational. In fact, Manda welcomed his research.

Reid had applied for outside funding from the National Geographic Society to support a three-year research project on the Tasaday, and he asked if Elizalde would be interested in funding the project if the society turned down the proposal. Elizalde said he would. Reid talked to a couple of the committee members from the National Geographic, and they were enthusiastic about the project, but then he received a letter of rejection. "Apparently they decided not to continue getting involved in this ongoing controversy, just to disassociate themselves from it," says Reid.

Reid doubts he could have done any research without Elizalde's backing, so he went in telling Elizalde that he would brook no interference. Manda in turn asked Reid to sign a form saying he wouldn't disclose in print where his funding came from. "He just didn't want to be involved with anything to do with the Tasaday at that point. He wanted to be disassociated with the Tasaday, from the Tasaday problems. He was still interested in it and continued to keep Amy Rara in his office. She was supposed to be organizing the Tasaday stuff."[4]

After an initial ten-day foray Reid did three more periods of extensive fieldwork with the Tasaday: two months between February and July 1994, a second trip during the summer of 1995, and a third trip during the summer of 1996.

The first trip was "hellish." He didn't realize how difficult it was going to be. It took him two days of hiking twelve hours a day, starting at Lake Sebu. The trails were muddy and overgrown, and the hiking was over steep hillsides. He wore only tennis shoes, and they became so slippery he couldn't keep them on his feet. He wound up walking barefoot even though his feet weren't accustomed to such hiking. The hike became even more torturous when he struck his foot against a rotten log and splinters lodged in a nail. By the beginning of the second day he was getting stiff. At nightfall they were still hiking across the final ridge, in the darkness, down a rock-studded river, a gorge leading into the Tasaday area. Laurie had to be supported by two of his guides as he staggered along. He wasn't able to walk for four days afterward.

When he arrived, he stayed in the house of Dul and her husband, Udelen. This was on a ridge in the little settlement the Tasaday call Magtu Inilingan (New Learning). There, to Reid's surprise, he found another Westerner living among the Tasaday, a Belgian in his late twenties or early thirties named Pascal Lays, a member of the London-based organization Survival International. Lays, for his part, was not happy to see another foreigner and acted coolly toward Reid, though he agreed to help him with his initial research. Lays, who had been living with the Tasaday for a couple of years, was fluent in the language, so for a time he acted as an interpreter for Laurie. Lays told Reid that the lingua franca the Tasaday used these days among themselves and to outsiders was Blit Manobo. The Tasaday had been finding wives in Blit since 1972, when Belayem married Sindi'. Lays, trained as a pharmacologist, was gathering an extensive number of plants from the rain forest, and Reid describes him as a "self-educated academic" who hoped to use his research to earn a Ph.D.

One day Reid discovered that Lays was excavating large shards of pottery from one of the hillsides.* The presence of pottery implies that people had been in the area for quite a long time, but the fragments could also have been from people who passed through centuries ago. Lays, who jealously guarded his notes and materials, kept the discovery to himself at first, and by the time Reid found out about the fragments, Lays had collected the best examples for himself.

"He's of course completely convinced about the authenticity [of the Tasaday]," Reid says of Lays. "He thinks they came from the Kulaman Valley area [and] he is strongly pro-Tasaday as a group."

---

*The pottery was discovered by one of the Tasaday while farming a field. Dul was convinced the shards were magical and didn't want them taken away.

Reid agrees with Lays. "The last time I was there one of the things I did was to spend some time in Blit with Belayem and his family, and then I went up to Cotabato City, took a boat along the southern coast to a place called Lebak. I went up into the Kulaman area. I got an informant, brought him back down to Lebak with me, and worked with him for about ten days or so going through materials I had collected with the Tasaday to see if he recognized stuff." The theory, which had been espoused even in the earliest days, was that the Tasaday had escaped into the forest to avoid a *fugu*, or smallpox plague. Apparently they had come from the Kulaman Valley and migrated to their present location.

Reid asked his Kulaman Valley informant specifically about some of the forms unique to the Tasaday that are not known at all by the Blit, common words like *kumundom* (to eat).

Reid asked, "Do you know what the word *dumuntot* means?"

"Oh, yeah, *dumuntot*," the man replied. "I think that means 'drink.' "

"Do you use this term?"

"I don't know where I heard that word," the man said. "I don't know. . . . There's a dialect that uses *dumondot* for drink."

But he *knew* the word. The same was true for the term for "to eat." The man recognized the word and others like it used only by the Tasaday, not by the Blit from whom they had supposedly been recruited, according to the hoax busters. However, they weren't his normal words, and there were many words that he didn't recognize or didn't know.

Eventually Reid asked about numerals. When the Tasaday were first "discovered," they had several different ways of counting. Lobo counted by giving each number the name of a bird. When Reid first met Lobo, he asked about the bird names. Yes, Lobo told him, he could still count that way. Reid asked him to demonstrate, and Lobo recited the ten bird names in the correct order. The other Tasaday said, "Oh, that's Lobo's way of counting. It's his unique system." There was another method that looked like "funny numerals," with some similarity to numbers, but like "play numbers." The Blit didn't use any of these. Reid's informant from the Kulaman Valley, when asked if he knew of any special ways to count, apart from the normal one, two, three, said no at first. Reid told him the Tasaday had a special way of counting and gave the man the first two numbers.

"Oh!" the man told him. "When I was young, I used to use those words."

"Do you know the rest of them?" Reid asked.

The man started counting, and he gave Reid the same ten numbers, not exactly the way the Tasaday used them, but so close that it was obviously the same sequence, with one or two numbers reversed.

Before long Reid concluded that the period of the Tasaday's separation was not in the order of hundreds of years, but no more than five or six generations, maybe 100 to 150 years.[5] The original estimations of the Tasaday's "separation" had been wrong, but did this constitute a hoax? Reid writes: "The result of this examination of the data was that I became pretty much convinced that the hoax proponents were themselves the hoax makers. There seemed to be no evidence whatsoever that there had been any linguistic shenanigans going on. In fact, the types of responses given and the differences apparent in the lists of different investigators, seemed to me to be clear evidence of the linguistically unsophisticated nature of the Tasaday."[6]

Of course, linguistic evidence, while at times as convincing as archaeological artifacts, is not foolproof, hence the downward revision of the Tasaday's relative "isolation." Sometimes the evidence is inconclusive and even contradictory. Of Carol Molony's* assertion that Tasaday had no Spanish borrowings, Reid found at first several possible borrowings, though at least one he believed to have been picked up by Belayem relatively recently.† He also thought he found some T'boli influences.[7] Perhaps most damning of all, he caught Belayem coining new Tasaday words. Of all this he writes:

> The data . . . appear to be of two different kinds and lead to two different conclusions. A person who is skeptical of the authenticity of the Tasaday would focus on one set and surely jump to the conclusion that here is the evidence that is needed to settle the case. . . . Such a conclusion would have to disregard the other set. . . .
>
> What then is the explanation for the first set? There is no

---

*Linguist Carol Molony was Richard Elkins's replacement after he became ill.
†Reid now believes there was only one possible borrowing of a Spanish term, the widespread term from the Spanish *jepe*, but that may be a coincidental similarity.

doubt that much of the data that Belayem gave me were indeed made up for the occasion. . . .

At the root of the apparent obfuscation is the obviously deep-rooted sense of identity that the Tasaday (not only Belayem) have of themselves. In the twenty-three years since their first publicized meeting with outsiders, not a single member of the original Tasaday group has "recanted," even though the supposed motivation for their formation as a group, the all-powerful influence of Elizalde, has long since faded. The group lives in poverty, and has no reason to continue the charade, if indeed there was one. Time and again, Belayem and other members of the group expressed frustration and anger over the questions that have been raised about their authenticity.[8]

Actually, several of them *had* recanted, at various times: Lobo, Bilengan, and most famously Dula. It's also true that the ones who had said they weren't Tasaday later claimed they had been coerced and bribed into saying so by Joey Lozano and George Tanedo.

Still, Reid was essentially correct. The Tasaday had not benefited at all from the "charade" if there was one. Why would they continue if they had nothing to gain?

Seated at his kitchen counter, Laurie started to translate a transcript from his interviews with Belayem. I have always been a sucker for origin stories—they carry a kind of cultural force more imaginatively potent than any other kind—and this was a good one. I was quickly mesmerized as Laurie did his spot translation:

This has always been the origin of the caves. I have already told this story to Momo' Dakel in the tape recorder before. Exactly the same. There were no other people here except Bibang. He came from there carrying his place . . . on his back . . . that place . . . he was holding under his arm. There was an ax, a stone ax he was holding under his arm. . . . He went walking along the trail . . . suddenly he arrived here, the place of the Tasaday. He said, "This is my cave. I will leave it here. I will follow the barking of my dog." . . .

From a far place, this dog could be heard far away. Following the trail of Bibang. Suddenly, he saw Bibang crossing the stream on the other side. He had a huge head, a wide chest. The size of his chest was the length of his arm. So Bibang wanted to pass over this river. The spirit wouldn't let him pass.

It was a nice tale, but like everything else, it was full of contradictions. In the story the Tasaday's ancestor Bibang is out hunting with his dog, and the dog is baying after his quarry, a wild pig. The only problem is that the Tasaday supposedly didn't have dogs before they were "discovered"; they wouldn't be able to survive in the rain forest. So how could a dog be following Bibang around?

Laurie asked Belayem about this. "I thought you didn't have any dogs."

"It wasn't a dog," Belayem said. "We call it a dog today; it was a wildcat."* It seemed to Laurie a convenient explanation, but not a very good one since cats don't bay after wild pigs.

Laurie mentioned this one day to Elizalde, who said, "Do you really believe that these stories remain unchanged, that they aren't adapted to modern things that they know, that they introduce to their stories, aspects of modern life, assuming that they were part of old life?"

Of course that was true. It was something Laurie hadn't thought of; he had similar tales from the mountain province of ancient times into which customs and objects from the Spanish times had been incorporated. Still, it was a puzzle.

"Well, this is the way the story goes," Laurie told me. "But the point is, he dropped the caves from under his arm, this guy Bibang."†

On one of Reid's visits to the Tasaday, he found Belayem gravely ill with tuberculosis. He reported back to Elizalde, who released funds through Amy Rara for a helicopter to be sent in to bring

---

*Belayem told this story to Reid in the 1990s. By that time the Tasaday had presumably seen many dogs. Nance even reports in *The Gentle Tasaday* that Dafal had given them a dog, but it had died. The word they used for dog was almost certainly the word the Monobo Blit use.

†Pascal Lays, in his hometown newspaper in Belgium, recounted the same story, more or less, that Laurie Reid elicited from Belayem about the origins of the caves.

Belayem to the hospital. The helicopter from Davao flew into Blit. Belayem was so sick (a gallon of fluid was removed from his lungs) that he had to be carried to the nearest settlement with a road in a chair constructed for him. He was flown to the clinic in T'boli and from there to another hospital in the town of Marbel. Both Amy and Laurie joined him.

"When he was so sick," Reid recalls, "I would sit by him for hours and ask him about words. He wanted to help. I thought he was going to die. He was in the hospital for two months."

At that time Mai Tuan's younger brother Dad Tuan, who had since inherited the mantle of mayor from Mai, decided to take a little unscheduled side trip in the chopper, along with his vice mayor Salvador Ramos. Where they went is anybody's guess, but a pretty good one would be Mount Parker and Lake Maughan. To understand what happened next, one has to understand a little about the gold fever that infects the Philippines. For years it has been rumored that the Japanese hid billions of dollars of war booty in the Philippines ahead of the advancing Americans; it's come to be known as Yamashita's Treasure. Thousands of holes have been dug around the Philippines and thousands of lives lost in mostly futile attempts to locate the treasure, while Marcos is rumored to have found it. The story has several mutations; in some ways the persistent rumors that the Tasaday Reserve is laden with gold is one of them.

The rumor of the day had it that billions of dollars in lost gold were hidden in underwater caves in Lake Maughan, so Dad Tuan and Ramos, in collusion with the army, decided to lower the water table of Lake Maughan by breaching the lake's banks with dynamite to gain access to the caves. It's likely their jaunt with the helicopter was a scouting mission.

Unfortunately they eventually were able to put their plan into action. The ensuing explosion sent a flash flood racing down into the valley. According to some estimates, the flood killed at least two thousand people, but it's impossible to know for sure how many perished.*
At first the flood was blamed on an earthquake, but it was soon learned that explosives had been used. The army pretended it knew

*This information is based on news reports and personal communication with several sources, including one of the investigators in the crime laboratory, who, for obvious reasons, wishes to remain anonymous.

nothing, and Tuan and Ramos were left as the fall guys. Dad Tuan, for his part, spent a day in jail. Ramos went into hiding, and the issue has dogged both men since, but everyone so far has managed to avoid any real blame. In the Philippines, as elsewhere, when culpability likely rests with the rich and powerful, crimes are rarely solved. However, the body count in the Philippines tends to be high. When thousands of people die in a ferryboat sinking, the captain goes missing. When a landslide buries hundreds in a subdivision, no one can find the official who signed the building authorization.

Ramos, a reporter turned politician, wrote about the evacuation of Belayem (though not about his subsequent expedition to Lake Maughan, of course) for a Manila newspaper. When he saw it, the story infuriated Elizalde, who didn't want the publicity, especially if it had anything to do with the Tasaday. He "blew his lid," in Reid's words, and railed at both Dad Tuan and Amy Rara. Humiliated and angered by this dressing down, Rara quit Manda's employ.

One of Reid's colleagues at the University of Hawai'i is Rebecca Cann, a renowned pioneer in DNA research. Cann was working on an NSF project for research on Pacific peoples and their relationship to Asian mainland populations when Reid approached her and asked if she could include some Tasaday samples in the study. "You go get the hair," she told him. "I'll get the DNA analysis done." He wanted to do this because of the claim that some of the Tasaday are genealogically related to people in the Blit area. With Elizalde's blessing Reid traveled to the Tasaday area in November 1996. He spent five days getting forty or so hair samples. People would come to meet him, and he would try to persuade them to let him pull out three or four hairs from their head, which he sealed in envelopes along with data about whom he got them from and genealogical data. Some, like Lobo, refused.

In his office, Laurie showed me Cann's preliminary report with the names of the subjects and the initial analysis. "These are the names of the people from whom I got hair," he said. "A lot of them are Tasadays; a lot of them are Blits."

He pointed to his own name. "Lawrence Reid, New Zealander. I put my name; they suggested I do that so they would be able to make sure there was no contamination. 'Place of birth. Paternal kin group. Approximate date of birth.' They were able to extract DNA from some of this stuff, but not from all of it. Here's Lef, the daughter of Mefalu who gave me hair. They got DNA from her. But not apparently from Mefalu himself . . ."

According to Zeus Salazar's data, Mefalu, the son of Datu' Dudim, the chief of Blit, is the half brother of Dul, another of Datu' Dudim's progeny. If this is so, that makes Dul the aunt of Mefalu's daughter, Lef.

If Manda had set up the Tasaday with the knowledge that the Tasaday and the Blit were relatives, he would have been crazy to authorize a study that would once and for all uncover this bald hoax. The DNA analysis would be at least as elucidating as examining the midden outside the caves to see if the Tasaday had indeed lived in them. On the other hand, it's hard not to be uncomfortable with all this. The Tasaday have suffered so much already. Maybe it's best to leave them alone and let everyone think whatever he or she chooses.

19

Good Men

He was always talking about helping the little people, and I'd say it's your Abraham Lincoln routine you're going through. But he would espouse that back when we were teenagers. In that respect, he wasn't all bad. He wasn't a hundred percent bad. I think there was some effort to help, but in helping them he was also helping himself. I mean, that's kind of the way he did things.
                                                    —A childhood friend of Manda's[1]

When Manda died in May 1997 after "a long illness," the *Manila Bulletin* reported that he had been "responsible for the discovery of the much-publicized Tasadays in Palawan." It's fitting that there would be factual errors in Manda's various obits; throughout his life, people filled in the blanks with inaccuracy, innuendo, and falsehood. His enemies vilified him, claiming he was the devious mastermind of a sensational fraud, responsible for the invention of a Stone Age tribe and for the intimidation, kidnapping, even the murder of those who got in his way. On the other hand, his cronies lauded him, saying he should be nominated for the Nobel Peace Prize. Manda had many enemies and was the patron of others. People didn't necessarily talk about him truthfully, but they talked about him. Reporters didn't necessarily write truthfully about him, but they wrote about him because he had always made good copy.

The Tasaday, living in the jungles of Mindanao, were his most infamous claim to fame in his obituaries, and they took up most of the space. The *Economist* of London wrote: "When Manuel Elizalde announced the discovery of a tribe in the Philippines uncorrupted by civilisation, he touched a sympathetic chord among the ordinary corrupted millions who sometimes allow themselves to muse on the appeal of the simple life. Here, it seemed was the modern version of Rousseau's noble savage, a people who lived in harmony, had no word for war, and whose modest needs were provided by the rain forest which had sheltered them from contact with the outside world."

Obituaries tend to be favorable, but the *Economist* painted Elizalde as a saint, "protector of minority children," noting that his wife and he had adopted fifty orphaned children and that he was the founder of the humanitarian organization PANAMIN, dedicated to the preservation of tribal peoples and lands throughout the Philippines. It mentioned the scandal only in a muted fashion. "Whatever controversy may surround the Tasaday," the paper wrote, "Mr. Elizalde did not invent the tribe."

The AP, less laudatory than the *Economist*, noted that "some anthropologists say the Tasaday are simply people from nearby tribes who were forced by the Marcos government to abandon the vestiges of modern life and live together in a primitive lifestyle with a manufactured language."[2]

The *Seattle Times* and other papers in their obits of Manda noted that in 1988 the president of the Philippines, Corazon Aquino, had declared that the Tasaday were "a legitimate Stone Age tribe."[3]

The *Economist* didn't see fit to mention Manda's last legal legacy, a warrant against him in Spain. According to newspapers in that country and the Philippines, he was importing beauty queens from Spain with the lure of lucrative modeling and acting contracts in Manila, but he neglected to tell the women that part of the contract involved sleeping with him. There were also the usual fantastic charges, this time that he enlisted these Spanish beauty queens in a jewel-smuggling scam, transporting diamonds and emeralds inside dolls back to Spain and laundering the proceeds. It was known as the *peluche* scandal, *peluche* being the word for a stuffed doll in Spanish. Sounds fanciful, and at least one beauty queen denied this, saying it was all on the up-and-up, but *everything* about Manda's life was fanciful.

When one reads such stories, it is difficult to believe that anything Elizalde touched could be legitimate. Could so much trouble follow someone who was the innocent victim of his enemies, of rumor-mongers, as he always claimed? Elizalde said the charges against him were "very insulting, unfair, and foul." But as the *Philippine Daily In-*

quirer said in an editorial when he was chosen as his country's ambassador to Mexico (and then rejected after his appointment caused a general outcry), "If only half of what has been charged or suspected of Elizalde is true, then he comes close to embodying the worst of the Marcos regime."[4]

Manda described charges that he misspent PANAMIN funds as "lies peddled by members of the mental institution," and said he'd undergo a lie detector test if his critics would do the same.[5]

Even in death, Manda inspired rumors. The story around Manila and among some anthropologists was that he had died of AIDS. He died of cancer, a growth he knew about but waited too long to check out. Amy Rara, at his side when he died, had nursed him in his last days. In a letter she wrote shortly after Manda's death to his son, Miguel, she recounted Manda's hopes for the future as he battled his cancer. Like so many others facing their mortality, he sought refuge in faith, hoping that God might come down from on high and save him. Rara writes: "One night in March, with rosary in hand, he asked: 'How many years do you think will I live? Do you think after the chemo I will still have the strength to go back to the mountains of Mindoro or the shoreline of Palawan? Let's do those medical missions again, with Doctor Villaroza organizing it. She's the best there is, or, why not build a hospital in Mindoro?' These plans were inspiring for him then. He also thought about [the] Tasaday, but it was so distant and his strength might not carry him through. Here, God is closest to the people and the forest."[6]

Perhaps the best assessment of Manda comes from Carlos Fernandez: "Manda took a public trust and he bungled it. That is the biggest sin he committed. He used the people he was supposed to serve. In the final analysis, it made him such a dwarf instead of the giant he could have been." To Nance and others, Manda always maintained that the Tasaday were the "most honest thing" he ever did.

John Nance attended his funeral as a pallbearer. When the Tasaday heard Manda was dead, they didn't believe it at first, and then they cried. What would happen to them now that he was gone? In the last years of his life Elizalde had distanced himself from the Tasaday, but he had created the Tasaday Community Care Foundation, run out of his White Plains mansion. Soon after Manda's death, Miguel closed the foundation and locked away all its files.

Nance now became their benefactor, but more misfortune awaited the Tasaday, borne, as it often had been, of a desire to help. Dul told me the following story.[7]

When Nance traveled to tell the Tasaday of Manda's death, he went with Dul and her husband, Udelen, to Isulan, where Nance cashed a check, and then to Mai Tuan's place in Kematu. There Nance met Raul, a friendly young man who spoke English well and offered to write to Nance about Dul's requests or problems. After Nance returned to the United States, he sent money to Pascal Lays, in T'boli, who gave Dul six thousand pesos. Raul suggested to Dul that they take this money and open a bank account at the bank where his brother worked. She affixed her thumbprint to the documents Raul filled out for her.

Afterward Raul stayed in Kematu while Dul traveled to Tasaday. With the money she had been given she bought a horse from a man named Turingan, invested in a fishpond with Datu' Dudim's son Toto', and also received a shotgun from him for her son, Maman. On her return from the mountains, Turingan took his horse back. Still, she was pleased with her purchases and delighted that she had opened a bank account, though she couldn't add or write her name.

Another check arrived from Nance, and Lays helped her cash this one. Then Dul received word from Mai asking her to come down to T'boli. He wanted her help in collecting various materials from the rain forest that could be fashioned into beads for necklaces and wristbands to be presented to visitors to his office at the National Commission for Indigenous Peoples. He asked her to await his return from conducting some business in Manila.

While she was waiting, Raul came to visit her. He told her another notice had arrived from the Land Bank. "Jambangan has sent you money," he told her, and asked her to go to the bank with him.

For some reason, she wasn't able to cash the check at the bank, and the teller asked her to leave it there and come back at the end of the month to cash it. So she left, but now Raul shadowed her and wouldn't leave her alone. He told her not to tell Mai that she had been to the bank.

When Mai returned from Manila, he paid Dul for the beads and asked her to stay a bit longer so that they could talk about problems she was having in Tasaday. Manda had asked Mai to take care of the

Tasaday, and Mai took this responsibility seriously. But he had to return to Manila yet again and stay another eight days.

Raul went to see Dul in T'boli and wanted to know whether she had told Mai that she had received money.

"Yes, I did," she told him. She wanted to buy more useful things with the money, and Mai would certainly wonder how she could afford these things if she kept her money a secret from him.

The next afternoon Dul spent stringing beads for Mai, surrounded by friends and family. Her baby Suk was in a T'boli hammock, and Bingas, a friend of Datu' Galang's, was trying to keep the child pacified by singing to him. Udelen teased Bingas: "Since you know so many songs, why don't you sing one to Dul?"

Galang asked for some betel chew from Udelen, but Udelen said the bag was with Dul. She brought the bag to Udelen, who seemed suddenly depressed. But soon he was talking and laughing again, exchanging jokes. In the midst of this, Galang said, "Why don't you put one of those necklaces on Raul?" And to Raul he said, "You should have yourself photographed with the necklace on."

Udelen, in high spirits, teased Bingas some more and then fell into a laughing fit. Then his laughter suddenly stopped, and he fell backward. Dul, Galang, and Raul rushed to him. They tried to sit him up, but he was limp. Galang quickly fetched Mai Tuan, who placed his hand over Udelen's heart, then hurried to get a jeep to bring a doctor. The doctor could do nothing for him, and Mai suggested that they wait and see if the warmth would return to Udelen. Dul knew better. His body was already cold, and she knew it wouldn't get warm again.

"What are you thinking now?" Mai asked.

She told him that she wanted to send Adug, who was there with his wife, Gili, back to Tasaday to tell her children the news. The next morning Adug left.

Toward the late afternoon they held a wake with mouth harp playing, dancing, and singing. Raul, however, was deep in thought. Mai noticed that he was acting strangely and wanted to know why. "What are you worrying about?" he asked. "Don't get disturbed by what has happened. You should watch over Dul. What's happened is not your fault. You're not the source of Udelen's death."

Raul said he was fine, and the two left it at that.

But Raul was still agitated, and he confronted Dul. Suk was in his hammock, being watched over by Gili, who was cutting some betel chew with her knife. Galang was asleep. Raul wanted her to go with him to Mai's house to talk to him, apparently to explain about his role as caretaker for Dul's money.

"Let's do it tomorrow," Dul said.

But Raul insisted that they go to Mai and wake him. Raul wanted Dul to wake up Galang, too.

"Why do you have to wake up Galang?" Dul asked.

Raul pulled Dul to her feet. Frightened, she asked Gili to take care of her child, and then she tried to wake Galang. Raul grabbed Dul by her hair and pulled her head back. She tried to back away. He took Gili's knife and tried to slash Dul's neck, but she ducked. Raul still held her arm, and instead of striking her neck, he slashed her wrist. Blood gushed from her wound. The room was packed with other people, and now they all awakened. Everyone but Gili, Bingas, and Galang rushed outside. Dul told Gili to get her child while Galang and Bingas restrained Raul. They got him out of the house and tied him to the tree with his hands behind his back. It took three people to restrain Raul.

Dul felt blood draining from her head, and she collapsed.

"What has caused Raul to hurt you?" Mai asked Dul in the ambulance that took her to the hospital.

"I told Raul," she said, "that I told you about the money I had in the bank—after I had made a promise to him that I was to keep this secret from you."

While Dul languished in the hospital—she'd lost a lot of blood and nearly died—Udelen remained unburied for three days.

Eventually Mai brought Dul back to T'boli, and Raul was jailed.

As Dul lay in the house, Dafal, Adug, Maman, Fakol, and many others arrived, about thirty in all. Mai asked about her burial plans for Udelen. She said it was the Tasaday's custom to bury their dead where they died. It was senseless to bring him back to Tasaday since he would not live. "Go ahead and bury Udelen," she told Dafal.

She was not able to attend the burial. When the mourners returned, they had to go through a cleansing ritual. Each one was asked to get a bundle of different grasses and rub it over his or her body. They helped Dul to the river and gave her a bundle of grasses, then threw it in the river so the spirit of Udelen would leave her.

A couple of days later Pascal Lays arrived. "What's happened to you?"

"Raul hurt my hand."

"That's your fault then," he said. "Why do you deal with evil people? They're not even of your own tribe."

"We're trusting," she said. "We don't know what it means to be bad against others. We don't know how to kill another person. We put faith in other people."

But the Tasaday weren't alone in putting their trust in people who betrayed them. Nance too had put his trust in Raul, and in fact, much of the story of the Tasaday involved misplaced trust. But Lays was unsympathetic. He told Dul that she should only talk to people from her own tribe (Manobo) from now on. He told her this in "Tasaday" and said that he didn't want her to deal with Muslims and especially not Ilonggo. Dul didn't see the irony in the fact that Lays, an outsider, was advising her not to deal with outsiders. To Dul, Lays was like a son, while he told others that he felt he had finally found a home. But of course he hadn't. Even in his speech to her he betrayed the fact that he was anything but a Tasaday. By one definition at least, a Tasaday is anyone without power (i.e., Peralta's Tasaday in Luneta Park) whose existence society works hard to extinguish while simultaneously expressing a desire to help.

I'm reminded of an enigmatic comment I read in the guest book at John Nance's photography exhibit in Portland: "Believers have become the takers corrupted by the takers." At the time the remark seemed self-righteous and rather harsh. But to some degree it seems true to me now. The violence done to the Tasaday had been done by everyone, even those sympathetic to them. They had things the rest of us wanted to take, both tangible and intangible. Some wanted their gold. Some wanted their trees. Some wanted images. Some wanted what they represented. And the transaction was always and inevitably hopelessly uneven.

20

Postcard from the Stone Age

I can understand the mad passion for travel books and their deceptiveness. They create an illusion of something that no longer exists, but still should exist, if we were to have any hope of avoiding the overwhelming conclusion that the history of the last twenty thousand years is irrevocable.
—Claude Lévi-Strauss, *Tristes Tropíques*

I didn't know why I was sneaking into the hospital. I just trusted that it was what we had to do, maybe because I wasn't family. Amy Rara said she looked like a doctor anyway, and if we acted as if we knew what we were doing, no one would bother us. I walked with her past the guard, no questions asked, then through a labyrinth of streets and dilapidated buildings, halls and overcrowded corridors, dimly lit, in need of paint, radiating heat and humidity, until we came to the charity ward. One large room was crammed with beds and patients with arms and legs missing or in bandages, most of them with a designated "watcher" beside them. The hospital allows only one watcher per patient, and everyone needs a watcher, a kind of volunteer nurse in an otherwise stressed and difficult environment. The watcher stays with the patient day and night until the patient recovers or dies. The watcher is usually a family member, but Dul's watcher was a middle-aged woman from the Mandaya tribe named Helen Mabandos. Helen is an Elizalde loyalist who, at the age of twenty-one, was one of the few outsiders present when Manda's chopper landed at the edge of the forest in June 1971.

On the way to the room, Amy complained that Helen had been too possessive of Dul. She wouldn't let Dul out of her sight, and that was a problem because Helen snored loudly, and Dul could hardly sleep. It was also a problem for one of Dul's companions from the Tasaday area, a wispy man named Joe Igid, who seemed to be courting Dul now that she was a widow. Igid had been a caretaker for some of Dul's children and also a conduit for much of the money John Nance had been sending to help Dul and other Tasaday. I had met him earlier, at the Shalom Center, a Christian pension a couple of blocks away from the College of Medicine, where he and Amy had been sharing a room. He seemed harmless enough, if a little obsequious, but Helen didn't seem to trust him at all. She didn't approve of Joe and Dul's budding relationship. Joe was already married, but that wasn't it. Even though he was a Christian, a pastor, he was also T'boli, so he could take as many wives as he could afford. Helen seemed to think Joe was after Dul's money (Dul was rich in the sense that she had an outside benefactor, John Nance, sending her money, and no one else had such an arrangement), and she took every opportunity to warn him that he was treading in dangerous territory, even lecturing him on the penalties for sexual assault in Manila. Amy was amused by Helen's interference.

I had brought an offering, some grapes. According to Amy, that was about the only food in Manila that Dul liked. Amy had been "foraging" for Dul in Manila for the last week, trying to find anything that Dul, a picky eater, would find acceptable to her palate. At Robinson's department store in a nearby mall she'd located some rattan fruit, which look like tan golf balls, but the fruit was dry. The closest thing to rattan fruit, according to Dul, were grapes.

Dul was getting treatment only now, fourteen months after Raul stabbed her. Nance was paying for her physical rehabilitation. She had her own private room, donated by the hospital, though it was pressuring her to move to more crowded quarters. The room was small and bare with a high ceiling and a noisy fan attached to it. Dul sat on the bed wearing a pair of flowery pants and a T-shirt with the caption "Mini-Olympics." Many of the tribal peoples in the area of South Cotabato borrow freely from one another, and in one of her ears she wore the multiple earrings of the Ubu. Her teeth were stained yellow and black from chewing betel nut. The hospital wouldn't allow her to chew betel nut, nor could she smoke more than one or two cigarettes out on a deck, so she'd taken to a substitute for betel nut, Bazooka bubble gum. She chewed bags of it and sometimes stuck the gum on the wall beside her bed.

"Kakay Dul," Amy said, smiling, when we walked in, "Kakay Robin has brought you some grapes."

I handed over my grapes. She took one, put it in her mouth, and shot a hand to her cheek, making a pained face. Dul spit out the grape into her hand. It was too cold for her sensitive teeth.

I had spent two years talking to various experts on the subject of the Tasaday and gathering armloads of documents. I had also visited the Tasaday with Joey Lozano in January 1999. Now, eight months later, if all went well, I would soon visit the same area with the "other side," including one of the original Tasaday. This was something no one had done before, and I thought it might shed some light on the conflicting perspectives. Early on I had become intrigued with the fact that I could have written two books, each with supporting "evidence," one showing that the Tasaday were a hoax and the other showing that they weren't. On a personal level, I had long known that memories are fallible, that two people often see the same event differently, but I'd never before seen the phenomenon on such a dramatic scale.

A small stand in the corner had a hot-water thermos on it and a metal tray with some leftover institutional food, a piece of desiccated chicken foremost among the morsels. Dul had a small alarm clock with big numbers on her bed and a stack of magazines and books, a calendar, an old PANAMIN brochure, and a notebook. This was all part of John Nance's "literacy program." He wanted her and the other Tasaday to be able to tell time, to read a calendar, to learn to sign their names. For Dul, this was important so that no one could withdraw money in her name. Right now she could only make a thumbprint as a signature. I recognized on the bed the *National Geographic* from 1972 that had made her and her small band so famous. As we chatted, she flipped through the magazines, unmistakably nostalgic. Sometimes she'd smile and point and say the name of one of the other Tasaday or Manda Elizalde, whom she called Momo' Dakel. The lights in the room stayed on all night, and Amy said that Helen had awakened that morning at two to find Dul sitting on the bed flipping through a copy of *The Gentle Tasaday*. Momo"s spirit was in the cave, she told Helen.

We talked for a little over two hours as nurses popped in and out of the room, checking in and taking Dul's temperature. Amy said the nurses and doctors thought Dul was remarkably healthy. She also said the nurses and doctors had been skeptical at first about Dul's presence. The doctor had said to Amy, "I thought the Tasaday were a hoax," but Amy, unflappable, simply treated the doctor's skepticism by presenting her with the physical evidence of Dul—not the most indisputable scientific evidence, but it seemed to satisfy the doctors and nurses at UP. Some had taken their pictures with Dul, and she was being treated a little like a star. It seemed to suit her just fine.

Her hand was much better now. Proudly she wiggled a couple of her fingers. Now she could pinch her thumb and forefinger together, and that was all she needed. She'd been in Manila long enough. The last time she'd been here had been ten years before, when Manda sued Professors Bailen, Salazar, and others for libel. When she'd arrived in late July, her hand had been atrophied, and she couldn't move any of her fingers. She told me that Momo' Dakel had come to her in a dream the night before her rehabilitation started and asked what was she doing here. "You don't need to be here," he told her. He flexed her fingers and massaged her feet. "You'll be cured, but then you have to go back to the caves because I have something there for you." There was a place in the caves where he was pointing. Inside there were many different colored stones. This was his gift for her. When she returned to the caves, she said, she was confident she'd see it there.

She hadn't seen Momo' Dakel in person since the libel trial, but he still seemed to be the primary figure in her thoughts. Even in death he exerted a great influence on her.

She needed to return home for another reason. There was something on her mind. According to her, and as strange as it sounded, she had heard that ex-Father Rex was planning to go to Tasafeng in search of platinum. She didn't know what platinum was, but she knew the rocks in some of the caves were special, and she wanted to keep outsiders away.

I asked her if she could take me to Tasafeng. She said, "I know how to go there. There's only one way to Tasafeng."

Pascal Lays, the Belgian chemist who had lived with the Tasaday on and off for the past seven years, was the only outsider I knew of who had gone to Tasafeng. Having become so ill with hepatitis he'd had to be evacuated, he was now back in Belgium, writing a treatise on the Tasaday. Dul adored Lays, but Amy was more than a little annoyed with him. He had sent more than two hundred plants from the Tasaday rain forest to Belgium in diplomatic pouches. He said he didn't trust the National Museum to identify the specimens properly, understandably infuriating the Botanical Department when it got back to them. In the Philippines and other postcolonial nations, the issue of biopiracy is serious, and Amy worried that Lays might turn out to be another exploiter.

But in an article in his hometown newspaper in Liège, Belgium, Lays seemed as ardent a supporter of the Tasaday as Nance was. He had stumbled upon the 1972 issue of *National Geographic*, and it was "love at first sight!"[1] Even after he had trekked in to see the Tasaday, through torrential rains and encounters with scorpions, snakes, and leeches, his romantic image had not dissipated: "As early as my first contact with the Tasadays, I found everything I saw in the *National Geographic*: the sweetness, the complete absence of aggression, their innocence-filled gaze. The Tasadays immediately welcomed me, asking me to stay with them. I brought them some gifts, especially in the form of medicine."[2]

Lays reported that the Tasaday were now eighty-six in number, but that as many as thirty-five hundred Manobo and T'boli shared their reserve. The Tasaday, though they lived now in small huts, had not abandoned the caves; they still brought children there to be cured when they were sick. What further intrigued me about Lays's report was that he recounted the same story, more or less, that Reid had elicited from Belayem about the origins of the caves. The first man, Bibang, had carried the caves on his back to the place they now stood. They had started off as small stones but had grown into large rocks in the story Lays had been told.

The young Belgian, who had lived with the Tasaday longer than any other outsider, sounded rhapsodic in his admiration for the Tasaday and their fabled gentleness: "What is extraordinary is their joviality, their good humor. There is never any frowning, or shouting, or expressions of anger. When they witness disputes among the T'bolis, they are shocked. In the heart of the Tasadays, there are never any conflicts. . . . It was truly an enriching experience. I believe we have a lot to learn from them."[3]

He sounded like Nance. Perhaps the only thing that made the

Tasaday unique, what Professor Berreman had sneered at, was the unquantifiable impression of those who met them that they were indeed wonderful people. In light of all the violence that surrounded them, perhaps this made them the most unusual people on earth after all.

Dul, if not frowning, at least seemed tense as she talked about the caves and returning home. Helen and Amy translated for her. She relaxed as she flipped through the magazines in front of her. She pointed to a picture of a camera. "Jambangan," she said, smiling, the Tasaday's name for John Nance.

I asked Dul what she liked and disliked about Manila. She told me that she missed the forest, of course. She awoke every morning at four, had a sponge bath, and went with Helen to a porch where she had a cigarette. According to Helen, Dul watched the sunrise and she spoke about it and the tall trees in front of the porch. Helen often could not keep up with what she was saying.

I asked what language Dul was speaking right now, and I was told that it was a combination of Manobo Blit and Tasaday. I wanted a little language lesson, so I asked how to say hello or good morning in Tasaday. *Sit, kakay, mafion.* I remembered all three words from the various documentaries I'd seen on the Tasaday, pro and con, as well as John Nance's book. *Kakay* was the word for "friend," and I remembered hearing the word *sit* in Jack Reynolds's 1972 NBC documentary and later in the footage that Walter Unger and Jay Ullal from *Stern* had shot at the caves in 1986, right before they were kidnapped and held for ransom. In his documentary, Reynolds had delightedly repeated the words *sit* and *kakay* to the camera for the viewers at home. Years later, viewing the *Stern* tape in the private screening room at her home in Connecticut, Judith Moses laughed as Belayem approached Unger at the caves, hugged him, and shouted "*Sit kakay*," sounding eerily like Walt Disney's Goofy. In that context, when one knew that Walter and Jay were about to be kidnapped, the words and situation had seemed utterly ludicrous.

"Is *mafion* a word that other groups use," I asked, "or is it only Tasaday?"

"*Tigtu mafion Tasaday kagi?*" Amy asked Dul. *Tigtu*, Amy explained, means "true," and *kagi* is the word for "word" or "language."

"*Metolol,*" Dul said, then repeated it a number of times.

"The real Tasaday word for *mafion* is *metolol*,"* Amy said.

I was puzzled because Nance always used *mafion* in his book.†

Amy explained that the truth of the linguistic picture is muddled. The Manobo language is very large, and Reid had had to double-check the words that were really Tasaday against words that had been borrowed by their neighbors and elsewhere in the region. Manobo is a family consisting of a number of closely related languages. The Tasaday had learned a lot of words from their neighbors in Blit very quickly, and sometimes words that had been borrowed were recorded by early chroniclers and researchers as the Tasaday's own words. So one always had to ask about the *tigtu* Tasaday, the real word for something in their language.

"We [Dul and Amy] are conversing now in a language where we can communicate," Amy told me.

"How many languages does Dul know?" I asked.

Dul said she could understand many. She said she picked up words from people she met. She even knew German.

"German?" I asked.

Yes, she'd learned a little from the *Stern* reporters and some French from Lays.

I asked her what she thought of all these visitors over the years.

The ones who came with John Nance or Mafoko' (their nickname for Mai Tuan, meaning "short one") were okay. The others they didn't like. Whom specifically didn't they like? They didn't like Father Rex, and they didn't like Oswald Iten.

As she was speaking, I thought I heard the word "marijuana" and something about Father Rex. The story of the Tasaday was wild

---

*In Reid's "Preliminary Tasaday Lexicon," of June 1994, gathered primarily from Belayem and containing words Belayem claimed the Tasaday used before 1971, the word *metolol* appears with the word *enda'* preceding it. *Enda'*, according to the lexicon, means "not," so *enda' metolol* means "not good" or "ugly." If *enda' metolol* means not good, then *metolol* obviously means "good" or "beautiful," which is what *mafion* means. On September 24, 1999, Laurie Reid added in an e-mail: "*Mefi'on* (good) is found in most dialects of Cotabato Manobo, including that spoken in Blit, but not in other Manobo languages. It also has the meaning of 'pretty' or 'handsome' in these dialects. However, in South Cotabato Manobo (but not in Blit), *metolol* is used for 'pretty/ handsome.' In Tasaday, *metolol* (sometimes in Tasaday the final *l* is not pronounced) has been generalized to cover the meanings of 'good,' as well as 'pretty/handsome,' and is also used in such phrases as 'good smell' to mean 'fragrant.' " In other words, Dul was telling me the truth.
†In *The Gentle Tasaday*, it's spelled *mafeon*.

enough without marijuana. In fact, drugs and rock and roll were the only things it lacked. But there it was clearly again, the word spoken by Dul: "marijuana."

I asked Amy what Dul was talking about.

"Okay," she said. "First of all, they started discriminating between those with good intentions and those with bad intentions if they had an endorsement from Mafoko' or Jambangan or Momo'. Why did Father Rex have bad intentions? Because he introduced three crops: mongo beans, string beans, and marijuana."

"Marijuana?" I asked.

"The teachers of Father Rex," she clarified. "When Father Rex brought his teachers into Magtu Inilingan in the late eighties. So these teachers taught them to plant these crops because they said they're good. If you mix them together as food, they're good. String beans, mongo," Amy said.

"Were they harvesting it and selling it?" I asked.

"According to Dul, the teacher said if you mix the marijuana and the mongo, it would brighten your eyesight. So they tried it and became dizzy. They felt crazy," she said. Amy said she'd never heard this story before, and it explained some things. She said that some of Dul's children were hooked on pot, and she had long wanted to know who had introduced the Tasaday to marijuana.

"Why don't you like Iten?" I asked.

Dul didn't want to move on. She kept talking about the marijuana story. She said that when the military heard that the Tasaday were planting marijuana, soldiers came up to check on them. Dul was asked to report, and she went to the judge in Banga with Mai Tuan's brother Dad Tuan, Mefalu, and Emilio Fado, who used to be an official for the Office of Southern Cultural Communities. Dul asked the judge, "Why do you have to run after my people? We believed what they told us, that if you planted this crop, it would be good for us, for our food. Why don't you go after Father Rex? It was his teachers who taught us. You should forgive me."

In mid-August, Dul, Joe, Amy, and I flew from Manila to General Santos City, where we were met by an ambulance donated to Mai Tuan by the Japanese. As I told my friends, better to be picked up in an ambulance than a hearse.

Oscar, one of Mai's henchmen as far back as the early seventies, drove the ambulance, and I sat up front with him while Dul, Joe, and Amy sat in the back. He was nothing if not a jolly driver. He happily pointed out the spot in the road where Mayor Sison's men had tried to ambush Manda one night in the early seventies. I kept him supplied with Marlboros.

The road between General Santos and Mai Tuan's home in the T'boli town of Kematu was much better than most in the rural Philippines. It took us nearly five hours, including stops for lunch to buy some rice and other provisions at a market so we wouldn't arrive empty-handed. Eventually we had to turn off the highway and take a dirt road that led to a creek for a couple of miles. Oscar studied the current and the rocks on which to balance the tires, drove across, and we were at Mai's house. At first glance, it looked more impressive than most in the area. It was the kind of stucco two-story one might see in a middle-class neighborhood in Miami. Then I noticed that the second story was open to the elements, with walls and rooms that were incomplete, giving it the look of an inhabited ruin. The house had no electricity.

Mai met us in the large parking area in front of his house, with his twenty-sixth wife, Amy. (The others, it was explained to me, did not live with Mai. He had bought them all off with nice pieces of property, perhaps explaining why his own home was unfinished.) Mai had suffered a stroke since we'd met, and his English was slurred. I could hardly understand him. His eldest son, Mai Tuan, Jr., also known as Dibu, was there as well. Dibu was being groomed as the next mayor. Mai's brother Dad, presently the mayor, had a luxury car, a motorcycle, and a house that would not look out of place in most well-to-do suburbs in the United States. Understandably, Mayor Dad wanted to get the term limit he was saddled with rescinded so that he could keep serving his people, as he had when he dynamited Mount Parker and killed hundreds in the ensuing floods.

My visit was well timed. The next day was the twenty-fifth anniversary of the founding of Kematu. There would be a feast, with traditional T'boli dances and music and the favorite T'boli sport of horse fighting.

Back in the seventies, before Manda had fled the country, Kematu had been a showcase town, with row after row of neat houses, paved roads, a clinic. Set on a hill above it all had been Manda's house, where he received his guests. Even President and Mrs. Marcos had made the trek to Kematu in the old days. There was a picture of them standing on a hill near the helicopter pad wearing traditional tribal dress. In the background on a hill, a topiary sculpture the size of the famous Hollywood sign read "Imelda." Movie stars and journalists and other important visitors had trekked through the town in the heady days of the early seventies, when the Tasaday were in the news all the time and Manda was at the height of his power. Now his house was an overgrown ruin, the roads were potholed muddy tracks, the clinic abandoned.

The town had invested in an enormous PA system, and for the next two days the sound of disco music permeated every conversation. As I sat in the darkening foyer of Mai Tuan's unfinished house on that first day, I asked Amy Rara questions about the founding of Kematu, but I could barely hear what she had to say as music shook the walls. Dul went right to sleep, and I stayed up until it grew dark, about seven o'clock. Wearing my headlamp, I trudged into my room, rolled out my sleeping mat, and listened to the music until dawn. That morning I drove into the town of Koronadal with Oscar and Joe to buy more provisions for our trip. I had already purchased a lot of asthma medicine, antibiotic ointments, burn creams, and vitamins for the people in the mountains because, as I'd seen on my last trip, they had virtually no access to doctors. But they also needed food, so we purchased sacks of rice and canned goods before returning to Mai's place.

Despite the maniacally drunk MC who shouted incessantly over the blaring music, no one really seemed to be celebrating. Person after person told me I should have seen Kematu back in the old days. The celebrations culminated the following night at around three in the morning with the MC conducting a beauty contest. Apparently, there were only three contestants, and they took turns winning. Every once in a while I'd hear the MC scream in English: "Miss Friendship! Contestant number one! Best in swimsuit! Contestant number two! Miss Darling of the Crowd! Contestant number three!"

We headed into the mountains the next day and stopped in the town of Isulan, where we hired three skylab drivers to carry us as far as the muddy mountain roads would allow. We waited for three hours while the drivers lashed our sacks of rice and backpacks onto the sides of the skylabs.

While we were waiting, we met a Department of Agrarian Reform engineer who had just come from Kibang, where we were headed. Amy asked him a lot of questions, trying to find out if he was working on any projects in the Tasaday area, but he seemed reserved, even a bit guarded.

Storm clouds gathered over the mountains in the distance. The worst of them passed, and only then did we buzz out of town on our motorbikes. I was on a skylab that carried Melel (one of the Tasaday literacy teachers John Nance had hired, who rode on the handlebars), the driver, Philip, and sacks of rice and backpacks. The roads were fine for the first couple of hours as we rode past water buffalo, pigs, and chickens that darted ahead of us. The people we passed shouted, "Hey, Joe!" when they saw me, the universal greeting for foreign white men. We passed schoolchildren dressed in their clean and pressed uniforms. The bike inevitably broke down at almost the same instant the sky opened and it began pouring. After an hour we were able to get under way again and traveled up roads that became increasingly muddy and impassable. We had to get off the cycles several times and trudge through shin-deep mud while our drivers spun the motorcycles through the muck. We stopped at a little roadside shack where we were served soft drinks and sweet rice cakes, while a radio screeching "GIVE IT TO ME, BABY, UH HUH UH HUH . . . PRETTY FLY FOR A WHITE GUY" competed with the insect noise.

After five hours we reached the little village of Kibang. The people here almost never encounter white guys (no matter how fly), and I was immediately surrounded by a crowd, including one woman who boldly walked up to me and asked me if I was married. I took out the portable Global Positioning System (GPS) unit I'd brought with me to get a satellite reading of Kibang's position. I wanted to take readings at every stop. Primarily I wanted to find out the exact location of the caves, if I ever reached them; no one had ever fixed them precisely.

I noticed a decrepit sign down the road that called the settlement Sungan rather than Kibang. Amy told me that this had originally been a PANAMIN settlement, and the sign was left over from those days. In 1971, PANAMIN had resettled T'boli here. This had been their land before they had been displaced by Christian lowland settlers.

The land was briefly returned to them under PANAMIN, but ownership had shifted once again. Christian settlers had again been resettled here by the Department of Agrarian Reform. The T'boli had been pushed out and were now moving into the Tasaday/Manobo Reserve. The Department of the Environment and Natural Resources was building a road into the area, opening it up to settlers and more agribusiness.

The Department of Agrarian Reform had built a rather nice guesthouse nearby, and this was where we would spend the next several nights. Mary Beth Oliver was both caretaker and cook at the guesthouse, as well as a government community health care worker. Her husband suffered from asthma, so I gave her one of the inhalers I'd brought along and showed her how to use it. Dul told us that raw bamboo shoots were a good cure for asthma. The people in the area had little access to medical attention, and even if they had, there was no money to pay for it.

The guesthouse had a large meeting room in front, a kitchen to the side, and two hallways of dorm-style rooms with bunk beds covered by thin straw mats. There was a boom box in the front room that I regarded uneasily when I entered the building, but it was silent. There was also a CB radio that was used for one hour a day to communicate with Blit and Lake Sebu.

Word of our arrival reached the Tasaday pretty quickly. Early the next morning Belayem showed up with family and several friends. I recognized him at once, his curly head of hair, his delicate, almost feminine features, made more so by the red on his lips from chewing betel nut.

"*Sit kakay,*" Belayem told me. I felt as though I were in a movie. How many times had I seen and heard him say those words in someone's film? When we sat down with Belayem, he turned to Amy and asked where Momo' Dakel was.

"Kakay," she explained to him, "he's dead." She told him that he was buried in Manila. Both Amy and I were a little shocked. John Nance had told the Tasaday of Manda's death, so Belayem knew that he was dead. Maybe he just wanted to hear it again to make sure.

People drifted in and out of the hall all morning. Belayem excused himself after a couple of hours and headed back toward Blit. I gave away a lot of Marlboros while problems that did not really involve me were discussed. Joe's wife showed up and teased Dul about sparing her husband for a moment. But this wasn't a joke. As the morning wore on, it became clear that people were pretty unhappy with Joe. Mai had told Joe to take care of the Tasaday, and some of Dul's children were living in his house, but Amy thought he was spending money meant for them on his wife and his own family. He had once been a PANAMIN official, and apparently a pretty corrupt one at that, and he wasn't well liked. Even his nephew Melel seemed a little suspicious of his motives.

A T'boli *datu* named Huaning Asu Labi sat next to me at the table. He told us he had been displaced from his land in the seventies and wanted to be able to move back. He seemed to think that I could help, that I, as a visitor, as a white man, had Manda's power. All I could do was listen sympathetically. When he left the hall, he grasped my hands, put them to his forehead, and gave me a traditional blessing. I would not have wanted to be Manda, but I imagined how this same scene would have gone almost thirty years earlier: instead of one displaced *datu* seeking redress, hundreds of T'boli and others coming to Manda for help. I tried to visualize what it would be like to have even a modicum of Manda's power.

One of the things Dul revealed to me that morning was that a couple of Americans had been brought to the caves the previous month, not by her but by her son Talihin and one of the teachers from Blit, a man named Roling Abig. Americans? I wondered who they could be and what they wanted. But Amy told me they might not be Americans. They could be Italians or mestizos. Practically anyone with light skin was referred to as an American. They had given Adug and Belayem medicine and a hundred pesos each. They said they were here to bring medicine and a water system, but they had also recorded examples of Tasaday speech to study and had said they'd be back in a couple of months. This time they wanted to go to Tasafeng. Amy was upset that they had not gone through Mai; they could be anyone, and who knew what they were really after?

Dul wasn't happy with this incursion either; she hadn't okayed it and had heard about it after the fact while she was in Kematu. The Tasaday man Mahayag had been sent to the headwaters of Tasafeng to protect the caves there. Supposedly, he had built a little shelter and was waiting with a quiver of poison arrows. Dul was the gatekeeper.

Amy had told me before the trip to write an e-mail saying why I wanted to go to the caves. And if Dul didn't like me, I wasn't going anywhere. This seemed fair enough to me. It wasn't my land. I told Amy that I had been reading about the caves and seeing them in videos for two years, and I wanted to see them for myself now.

Amy reminded me now how lucky I was that I was getting a chance to visit the caves. Laurie had never made it. He hadn't even been invited to the caves until his third visit, but he'd had to leave without seeing them. Dul told us the reason she hadn't allowed him to visit the caves earlier was that he was stingy with his provisions. He wouldn't share his coffee with her.* This seemed like an object lesson to me; I offered Dul another cigarette and let her tell me more.

A chicken and a couple of feral-looking dogs wandered in during my talk with Dul. The dogs reminded me of the story that Belayem had told Laurie Reid about the origin of the caves. I didn't tell Dul that I had already heard a version of this story. Dul told me they had an ancestor named Bibang who was powerful and had supernatural powers. He had with him some small stones and also carried with him the teeth of a black dog, a native dog called a *tuyang*. With his powers, Bibang turned the tooth into a real dog. There were some small boars in the areas. The dog ran after the boars, and Bibang followed the dog in pursuit. Along the way they met an evil spirit. Amy interrupted the story at this point to tell me that in *The Gentle Tasaday* Nance had called this a *busaw*. The real term, she said, the Tasaday term, the *tigtu kagi*, was *ngotngot*. "That's not a word I can pronounce right now," I said. Still, I spent the next few minutes making a fool of myself trying to do so.

"Anyway, it's not *busaw. Busaw* would be Manobo," Amy said. Berreman had picked up on this word, *busaw*, noting it was a Manobo word that ethnographer John Garvan had written about in the thirties. Had I had my wits about me, I might have asked Belayem and others separately what a *ngotngot* was. If they had shrugged and said they didn't know, that might have suggested that the word was made up on the spot to counter Berreman. If they had told me that *ngotngot* meant "witch" or "spirit," that would have suggested that Dul was

---

*This was news to Laurie, who remarked in an e-mail that his provisions were "quickly demolished by Dul and others in the neighborhood."

telling the truth. In any case, since Berreman had not actually met the Tasaday or done fieldwork on his own, he'd had to rely on the fieldwork of others—namely, John Nance—and Nance had even noted, when he mentioned the word in *The Gentle Tasaday*, that *busaw* was a word the Ubu used.

Dul continued her story and said (through Amy) that the *ngotngot* told Bibang he could not pass unless he could chop a stone with his hatchet. The *ngotngot* had a very long knife. And Bibang had a knife, too, as fine as a cogon blade. The *ngotngot* tried to chop the rock but couldn't. But Bibang did chop it, and Dul said you could still see the place where the cut was made. Bibang pursued his boars. He pursued them so long that they grew big and fat. He had another contest with the *ngotngot* and won that one, too. Finally he decided to go back and check on the stones he'd left behind. Like the boars, they had grown up and had become big rocks, the rocks of the Tasaday caves.

Dul's story includes the usual discrepancies that don't jibe with the original notions of the Tasaday's "primitiveness," "gentleness," or "isolation" in the rain forest: knives, cogon grass, dogs, the hunting of wild boars. But these concern me as much as Dul's Mini-Olympics T-shirt. Elizalde was right when Laurie Reid mentioned the problem of the dog in Belayem's Bibang story. Stories change over time, especially in oral cultures. What Dul told me is essentially the same story Belayem told Reid and that Pascal Lays recounted to the Belgian newspaper. Laurie had elicited the story of the caves' origins from Belayem many years after the controversy, and now I was asking Dul for her version several years after Laurie had heard his.

I asked what a *tuyang* was.

"It's a dog," Amy answered.

"But they didn't have dogs," I said.

So she asked Dul, who said it was just the tooth of a dog, that Bibang was the only one who had a dog.

"But they had a word for dog," I said, pressing the point.

There were two kinds of dogs in the forest, Dul said. One, called a *klifas* by the Tasaday, was not exactly a *tuyang*. The *klifas* is black, she said. It's actually a wildcat, but larger than common wildcats. This was what Bibang had with him. I remembered that Belayem had told Laurie that it was really a wildcat, but Laurie had noted that cats don't bay (in Belayem's version, it had been baying). So I asked what sound the *klifas* was making, and Dul used the same word as Belayem had: *gumabu*. She even demonstrated the sound for me, a kind of hooting. She told me of another remarkable animal, this one called a *tinggalung*. She said the *tinggalung* was spotted with seven colors. It wasn't a dog either. It was bigger than the *klifas* and looked more like a fox than a dog. Among its odd behaviors, the *tinggalung* always defecated in the same spot, and it jumped on the backs of deer and boars, bit their necks, and ate only their brains.

"It's rare," Amy noted.

Tinggalung were around the forest, Dul told me, but *ngotngot* you needed supernatural powers to see. She could see them, she said.

It rained most of the day, so we sat around the table and talked. A typhoon was due to hit the coast near Maitum, and while there was no danger this far up in the mountains, Mrs. Oliver was concerned about her parents and waited nervously to use the CB radio. That evening, as we sat in the precious electric light around the table, we ate cassava cakes and drank a little *tuba* (coconut wine), from what looked like an old Clorox bottle. Dul didn't drink, preferring her Marlboros and her *mama'* (betel nut chew).

We talked a little about whom I wanted to meet in the Tasaday area. When I said I wanted to see Datu' Galang again, Dul reacted negatively. She didn't like him, she said. She didn't trust him, and furthermore, he wanted to court her. She said that Galang was the one who convinced the younger Tasaday to say they were not Tasaday, that he had promised them things. He had told them they would tap the resources inside the forest and they would log the forest and in helping him the Tasaday would be helped. Oswald Iten, Datu' Galang had said, would be the one who would make things good for them.

I asked if others had told her to say things that weren't true. She mentioned a certain NPA commander named Ting, who had pointed a gun at her and threatened her.* She had been threatened many times before. She was told not to follow Momo' Dakel and Mai Tuan because they were bad people. But she said she'd stood her ground and been unafraid because she knew what was true and what was not.

---

*Presumably, this was the same NPA commander of whom she had spoken in 1988 to Clayton Jones of the *Christian Science Monitor*.

I asked Dul why she thought the Tasaday had received so much attention over the years.

"Because we have the forest," Amy translated. I thought that was a lovely, simple answer. She was right, of course, in both a metaphorical and physical sense. "Others have taken an interest because they have rocks that glitter."

Dul also told me that when she came from Tasafeng (one of the other forest groups, along with the Sanduka with whom the Tasaday intermarried), the first of the Tasaday she met was Belayem's father, Salibuko, and that before she met Dafal, she met Dafal's father, Mindal.* Mindal gave Salibuko a small knife.† After Mindal's visit it was a long time before anyone came back, and then it was only Dafal. He and the Tasaday had told a number of people, including Doug Yen, Carlos Fernandez, Jesus Peralta, and John Nance, that his father, Mindal had first met the Tasaday. Even Joey Lozano had learned this. According to a letter Lozano had written in 1986, he'd intercepted Dafal on his trip to get supplies for the *Stern* team the day before their abduction.[4] He'd interviewed Dafal, who had told him that he first met the Tasaday with his father, a fact Lozano never uttered in public, of course, as it bolstered the claims of the authenticity proponents.

Apparently, Mindal had not made frequent contacts with the Tasaday, but he knew them, and at least one of them knew him. Belayem's father, Salibuko, had met Mindal, but Belayem had not. That could mean Belayem wasn't born yet or was very young when *this* first encounter happened. This in turn means that the Tasaday had known of someone who lived outside the forest much earlier than first reported, though contacts with outsiders still might have been rare.

I had a number of gadgets and accoutrements with me that amused Dul: a water filter, tent, headlamp, and giant backpack. Amy

---

*Before 1971 all the Tasaday women came from either the Sanduka or Tasafeng. When Richard Elkins asked each of the women, in turn, where they had come from, each said that they were from Sanduka or Tasafeng. He remarked to me in conversation that this perfectly fitted the model of a "patrilocal exogamous band"—that is, the women joining their husbands' groups—and that this was yet another reason he believed they weren't a hoax. A trained anthropologist would have had to coach their answers.

†Belayem told Laurie Reid that Mindal had to teach Salibuko how to use the knife without cutting himself. Personal communication.

suggested I put on my bug shirt for Dul; it had a hood with mosquito netting, as well as netting around the armpits. Dul couldn't stop laughing. She told Amy that I looked like a big handsome flying lemur, certainly one of the nicest compliments I'd received in a long time.

The guesthouse got three hours a night of electricity from a gas-powered generator, and while we were talking, the lights went off. I turned on my little headlamp so we could talk a little longer. I grew tired and left the others talking by candlelight. As I lay in bed, I thought about something Amy had told me. In the eighties at the Edenton School in Maitum, copies of *The Gentle Tasaday* had been burned in a bonfire. I wondered if so few people, purportedly gentle at that, had ever before aroused such violent passions in others. Now the lingering image of the Tasaday I had was of Mahayag, waiting with a quiver of poison arrows, somewhere in a place called Tasafeng, where a people had once lived that no one but the Tasaday had ever met.

The next morning I was awakened by love songs coming from the boom box in the DAR hall. It was raining again, but we were going to try to head for Blit. We just needed to secure some horses for our packs.

A small contingent from Blit arrived that morning. It included Toto', one of Datu' Dudim's sons. Amy told me that Toto', a lanky man with big eyes, a deformed chin, and a smile with a lot of gaps, had helped build the helicopter platform the first visitors had jumped onto. Toto' was our security; he had a friendly, harmless look, but he'd been a PANAMIN stalwart in the old days. He'd waited in ambush along the route to the caves, and now he carried a shotgun. Apparently, there was a need for protection. Mary Beth Oliver was worried about Commander Ting, who would certainly kidnap me and hold me for ransom if he found me. In the five years Oliver had lived in Kibang, she had not yet ventured to Blit, nor had most of the people who lived in the area, in part for fear of Commander Ting and others.

We waited for our horses for several hours under a shelter across from an abandoned truck in the center of the village. The animals never arrived. The rain was fierce, but I was determined to press on, impatient and unhappy about this delay that was no one's fault but the gods. We ate lunch in the back of a small bakery; I fed about four-teen people for two dollars.

Rarely do Filipinos ever say the word "no," but I started to understand after lunch that we weren't going to make it to Blit that day. Amy explained that the rivers would be flooded, and Toto' and the others were cold and tired from their hike in the rain. We headed back to the DAR guesthouse.

That night, as we were going to sleep in our bunk beds, we got on the subject of the secret language that the Tasaday had supposedly spoken when they didn't want outsiders to overhear. I asked Dul for samples of this language, which she called *nafnaf*, and she obliged, laughing as she did so, much as Nance had reported nearly three decades earlier. It was a strange thing to hear. Dul said that they used this language when they spoke in front of children and they didn't want them to understand. I asked Dul to say, "I am going to Kibang," first in Tasaday, then in Manobo, and finally in *nafnaf*. She obliged, laughing again when she spoke *nafnaf*.

The next morning we left as soon as we got our horses and our packs had been lashed to their sides. We had a caravan of ten or so, including Toto', who discreetly carried a shotgun. We walked along a muddy track, surrounded by Christian farms. Many of the T'boli had lost their farms to debt.

In Tafal, Dul had to take a break, so we sat on a bench under a shed beside a skylab. In the distance, past scores of denuded hills, one could spot the still-forested hills where Tasaday Mountain was. Amy told me that the area from Tafal to Tasaday, several miles over mountainous terrain, all had been rain forest in 1971. The rest of the way was impassable by most any kind of vehicle; deep, muddy inclines were the rule from here. At Tafal, I purchased two hundred pesos' worth of nails (about five dollars' worth) for the people around Tasaday and Blit. Nails were a precious commodity, all the dearer for the long trek to Tafal. As we sat there waiting for Dul to catch her breath, I thought about how the whole area had been transformed from a tribal culture to a peasant culture. I wrote in my journal, hearing the buzz of the skylabs, that we had lost something important.

Iten had noted that his hike into the Tasaday area would have taken him a mere thirteen hours if he'd done it all at once. Perhaps, but the landscape had already changed quite dramatically from 1971 to 1986; logging and farming had combined to decimate the rain forest. In 1999 one could see for miles over the rolling hills and farmlands between Blit and the little settlement of Tafal, where the road ended. In 1971 this had been solid rain forest, some trees soaring to two hundred feet.

Also, that five-minute helicopter flight from T'boli that Nance had written about was misleading. In 1971, from the air, no trails had been visible, the hills overgrown, and no one knew how circuitous the hike out might be. Elizalde too had been concerned about the seventy-something Lindbergh's health. He didn't want the famous old man dying on his watch, he'd told Nance.

Amy told me as we waited that Mahayag had built a makeshift hut on the route to Sanduka. I said that I'd like to see Sanduka if there was time. Dul told me with a mischievous look that the river here was full of leeches, poisonous plants, and little bugs that attached themselves to one's privates and had to be pulled off one by one. I asked about those little bugs. Dul laughed and said they were very painful, and with men, they attached themselves to the scrotum. I said I wasn't too worried, and Dul said she wanted to take a picture of me after one of the bugs had attached itself.

Pascal Lays, Amy told me, had gone around in a G-string. He had wanted to do and eat everything like the Tasaday, and that was what eventually made him sick with hepatitis. Amy told me that in addition, he had been stung by a poisonous plant; his leg and arm had swelled. This was not Club Med, or a theme park, at least not now. Gone were the days when Manda could chopper in visitors for a more or less painless excursion to the Land That Time Forgot. Now only the stubborn, the crazed, and the hopelessly curious bothered to make the trek. I felt I belonged to all three categories. At least this route to the caves was supposed to be fastest and the easiest.

There was nothing easy about it, of course. When I'd come in January, I'd made the mistake of wearing hiking boots, which of course filled with water the first time I stepped into a river, despite the rubber gaiters I wore above them. The boots simply weighed down my legs. Now I wore fifty-dollar Nike sandals, ever the slave to jungle fashion. The trail was so muddy and steep and the sandals so wet that when I walked, my feet slipped far forward and they were half on the sandal and half off and the only thing holding my foot in place at all was a thin strap.

We hiked for a couple of hours, the sun bearing down. I arranged my pack towel so that it fell behind my neck in the fashion of Japanese soldiers during World War II. Dul had to rest often; we stopped on mountain ridges where her teenage daughter Lahonen held a big umbrella from 7-Eleven over her mother to keep the sun off.

Shortly after noon we reached the boundaries of the reservation. On top of a particularly steep hill was the little Christian settlement of Kusog Fled. I was out of breath as I trudged up to the shelter. The fact that I was out of water and needed to filter some more kept me focused enough to keep climbing. Somewhere in the background I heard a radio, the Animals singing "There is a house in New Orleans/ They call the Rising Sun/And it's been the ruin of many a poor boy/ And God I know I'm one." At the top of the hill stood a small Catholic church. The two miles we'd hiked, once-forested T'boli land, were now farmland.

By midafternoon, when we were well within the boundaries of the reservation, we stopped at a small Baptist church with a cogon grass roof. There we met a Manobo named Turingan and his wife, Bol (who Zeus Salazar claimed was the "common-law wife of Mai Tuan"), a daughter of Datu' Dudim, the acknowledged leader of Blit.[5] Both Bol and Turingan had reputations as schemers. One of our companions, a young pastor named Nellis, another of the Tasaday literacy teachers, confided in me that Bol was his true mother but had not shown him "a mother's love," and Dul had adopted him. He considered Dul his mother now. The horse that Dul had bought from Turingan with Nance's money had been taken back again by Turingan, and never returned. Amy had a certain cachet in the area, and Dul, strengthened by Amy's presence, figured she could finally reclaim her horse.

Amy learned that the DAR engineer we'd met in Isulan had changed the boundaries of the Tasaday-Manobo Reserve to allow more Christians in. Dul said that Pascal Lays had brought her to meet with the DAR engineer in 1996. The first time she heard the boundaries had been reduced she went to Lake Sebu to speak with Mayor Sam Loko and the DAR resettlement engineer, Selso Caro. The first thing Mayor Loko asked Dul was, "Do you owe any of the Ilonggo settlers?"

"We don't owe anyone anything." Dul said. "That's why we don't want to get into the habit of debt."

Then she turned to the engineer and said, "You're the one in charge. Why were these people allowed to encroach on the boundaries?"

"We're paid by the government," the engineer said. "Whatever we're told to do we implement."

"Please forgive him," the mayor told Dul. "The next time he commits such a mistake he can be imprisoned."

"I'll let it pass for now," Dul told him, "but the next time I won't be forgiving."

This at least was Dul's version of events.[6] Perhaps the mayor had threatened the engineer in part to appease her. After all, a government engineer would seem to have more power than Dul, but if the saying "All politics is local" is true in most parts of the world, it's no truer than in provinces of Mindanao. The area is run by an amalgam of interest groups, all held together by the highly prized trait of *pakikisama*, Filipino for keeping relationships running smoothly. In any case, the engineer's authority to redraw the boundaries of the Tasaday Reserve was questionable, and Dul's claim to it was as credible as anyone else's.

D ul has her horse back," Amy informed me wryly after we left the church. Sure enough, I glanced back, and there was Dul riding atop it. We crossed a small river where Amy said the Blit settlement had been located prior to 1971. Helen Mabandos, who had a master's degree in anthropology, had conducted interviews in the area and had written a short paper in which she claimed the slash-and-burn farmers of Blit had migrated to their present location, within several kilometers of the caves.[7] There was no way to prove or disprove the assertion; the supposed old location was about an hour's walk from present-day Blit.

By the late afternoon we had arrived in Blit. Tasaday Mountain, in the near distance, was a clear demarcation of the forest. There was Belayem, crossing a peanut field with a bow and arrow in his hand. He walked with me past the government school and into the little village. We stopped at the Barangay* captain's hut, where I set up my

---

*"Barangay" is a Filipino term resurrected by Ferdinand Marcos to replace the Spanish "barrio." Barangays were the large ancestral boats that brought whole villages led by their *datus* to the Philippines during the early settlement of the islands. A barangay, like a barrio, is a neighborhood or village.

tent in an old sweet potato field in the front yard, surrounded by children who were curious about me and my tent. Here I met Mefalu Dudim, the son of the old and venerable Datu' Dudim. Zeus Salazar claimed Dudim was a key figure in the hoax; it was he who persuaded Tinda to become Bilengan at Elizalde's urging.

According to Dr. Salazar, all these people were related; the Tasaday were intimately connected with the people of Blit. His genealogy in Headland's book claimed that the Tasaday man Bilengan was the brother-in-law of Datu' Dudim, that Datu' Galang was a brother-in-law of Bilengan's, and that Mefalu was a nephew of Bilengan's and a cousin of Lobo and Lolo"s.[8] By contrast, Amy Rara and Manny Nabayra's genealogies in the same volume called the connection between Bilengan and Dudim "a complete fabrication."[9]

I had with me Headland's 1992 edited volume on the controversy, which was an object of curiosity among the people who clustered around Amy and me. Pastor Nellis flipped through the book, showing the pictures to the various children gathered. Mefalu looked at it, and then Belayem, who stopped at Nabayra and Amy's chapter, the only one in the book with pictures. Salazar, in his genealogies, had listed seventeen people by their true names as well as by their "Tasaday" aliases.[10] Rara and Nabayra had supposedly located fourteen of these seventeen and placed the pictures of the poseurs next to the "real" Tasaday.[11] Belayem effortlessly started rattling off the names of the people he saw in the pictures. The first picture was of a man named Bonga Mantang, also known as Kumander Machinegun (a local bandit who'd been gunned down several years earlier). According to Salazar, this was Lolo"s true name, but Belayem, who obviously couldn't read the English captions under the photos, knew him by the names Rara and Nabayra called him. Belayem had no trouble identifying the photos of the Tasaday by their Tasaday names, and he knew most of the poseurs as well, identifying nearly everyone by the names Salazar had offered as Tasaday aliases. Certainly no one in the area (and very few in the Philippines) had ever seen Headland's book, so it was unlikely that anyone could have coached Belayem beforehand. These people were of the area, and Belayem would have run across most of them. Salazar can't have been correct about these aliases. Nor was Amy coaching Belayem in the way Joey Lozano had coached the *datu* we met in the mountains.

I spoke with Mefalu as well. I read from Iten's account, which

Amy translated, and asked him for his reaction: "Datu' Mafalu [*sic*], a son of Datu' Dudim of the Manobo farming village of Blit . . . now joined our group and detailed how he had sometimes maintained a radio transmitter in Blit for Elizalde. He also described how he was in charge of transporting rice and other foodstuffs to the Tasaday. He said he was fully aware, from the beginning, that the whole thing was a swindle."[12]

Mefalu denied this last point. He remembers Joey Lozano telling Datu' Galang to tell the Tasaday to say they were fake. "So I asked them," Mefalu told me through Amy, " 'Why do you have to say the Tasadays are fake?' " He was told that if they went along, they would be helped. Mefalu said he didn't agree to the plan. He didn't deny operating the radio; everyone knew how to operate it, according to Amy. Nor did he deny giving the Tasaday rice. He said he shared with them, *konti lang* (only a little). This seemed to jibe with what Doug Yen had told me about the doling out of rice. "Filipinos look upon people like the Tasaday as poor," he said, "so they give them stuff. That's how the rice business probably started."

On our way out of Blit the next morning we stopped at Datu' Dudim's hut. A number of people from the village were gathered outside. The old man, I was told, was ill, and I'd be lucky to get an interview. When Amy and I entered the cramped hut, the *datu* was asleep, lying on a platform in a fetal position. His arms and legs were incredibly thin, and he looked brittle, wasted away. His back was to us. Gently Amy touched him and said, "Datu' Dudim, we've come to see you." She said her name, and slowly he uncurled and looked uncertainly up at both of us.

He looked at me and said, distinctly, "Momo' Dakel."

"No, Datu', this is Robin," Amy said.

Amy and I exchanged looks. I hadn't shaved in several days, and now I had a dark stubble. Elizalde had never shaved in the field either, so perhaps in some ways I resembled the young Manda. Amy told me later that when she looked at me unshaved, she was reminded of Manda, and perhaps this was why Belayem had asked about Momo' Dakel when he first met me at the DAR guesthouse in Kibang. This line of discussion gave me the creeps.

We asked the *datu* what was wrong, and he told Amy in a whisper that he had swallowed something wrong, and it had stuck in his throat—three months earlier. Now it was difficult for him to swallow, he said. But he told her that if he could eat, he'd be back to his old self again. It was apparent to me that this was not true, that he was dying. Anyone could see this, and I thought that he needed to see a doctor right away. I left money for this purpose, and several days later he was brought down from the mountains, accompanied by eighteen people, all of whom I became responsible for feeding. When we learned about this later, Amy asked Mai Tuan's son Dibu to send most of the eighteen home and conserve the money for Datu' Dudim's care. This was a concrete lesson in how easily money earmarked for one purpose can be frittered away. The care of one person soon becomes the care of eighteen; the care of eighteen soon becomes the care of two hundred. Datu' Dudim did not have a blockage in his throat. What he had was advanced tuberculosis, and he died two weeks later.

From the *datu*'s hut, we started our hike to Magtu Inilingan and the caves. Pastor Nellis wanted to carry my backpack. He wanted to do it as a service to me because he thought that I must "love the Tasaday" to have traveled so far to see them. He also had the motive, albeit a fine one, of wanting to go to school and continue his education. He wanted me to be his sponsor. I tried to tell him frankly that I just couldn't promise anything, as much as I'd like to help everyone in the area. Tasaday Mountain loomed in front of us—always near in view but still distant. I was eager to get inside the rain forest, partly to escape the heat and rain and partly because the sight of all those farm plots was sad and disconcerting. After half an hour we were still hiking through someone's farm, through fields of corn. Here Belayem pointed to a little hut in the distance, well below Tasaday Mountain, in the middle of some fields. Amy told me that this was Belayem's house, that he had built it at the edge of the clearing where Momo' Dakel and he had first met in 1971. Some of Belayem's children were going to school in Blit, and the explanation I received was that he wanted to be close by. But what a remarkable choice he had made— the spot where he first met Elizalde, where he had cowered beneath the blades of the helicopter, the spot where the eye sees too far. Now he lived in its nexus. Whatever the reason he'd chosen that location, Belayem's house was perched between the forest, where he could still hunt, and Blit, where he could trade.

We walked over steep ridges of cogon grass, and I drank prodigious amounts of water from my flasks. Dul proudly refused to drink any water along the way. "Water is for chickens," she told me. When I stopped to fill my flasks in a stream, I heard crackling behind me, and then I saw smoke. Mefalu had set the field behind us on fire to burn away the cogon grass. Amy explained to me that once the invasive grass takes hold, it is difficult to uproot.

Toto' showed us the remains of a foxhole. Toto', who'd been a PANAMIN bodyguard, had sat in the foxhole to ward off intruders. Now he clambered into the ditch, on top of a ridge with a commanding view of the valley, and posed, pretending to pick off imaginary enemies with his shotgun.

I asked Dul, through Amy, what she and the other Tasaday had thought when they'd seen smoke in the distance, prior to meeting Momo' Dakel. "We thought they were clouds," she said, and sure enough, wispy clouds like columns of smoke hung in the air over mountains, distant and close at hand. On a ridge, Dul pointed to one distant forested mountain and told me this was where the *ngotngot* lived.

As we entered the forest, Dul, who'd left her horse in Blit, visibly relaxed. Her pace quickened, and she started pointing out various fruits to me and allowing me to sample them. I tasted the petals of an edible orchid. We ate berries and the sap of a tree that Amy said was the Tasaday version of candy. I ate a chambered fruit Dul called *sayal*.* It had two skins; a hard skin was peeled off, and inside, the second skin was a sectioned green fruit that tasted like a sour apple. I was so impressed with this fruit that I wrote down its name, and later, when I returned to the United States, I looked to see if Doug Yen had noted it thirty years earlier. Indeed, he had: *syal dakel*.[13] That was what the Tasaday called it. In Blit, it was known as *klambug dakal*. The T'boli called it *doloy* or *klambug*. If Dul was faking, she must have had an excellent memory to recall the imaginary Tasaday word given to an ethnobotanist in 1972.

Anthropologist John Bodley told me that he and some colleagues at a conference in Australia had paid for a foraging tour that had been arranged by a group of Aborigines who wanted to earn enough money

---

*That was how I recorded it, at least, in my notebook. Reid says it's more properly represented as *seyal*.

to buy a truck. The fact that they wanted a truck, the fact that they were being paid for a tour, did not fundamentally change who they were, nor did it make the foraging tour a fraud. It just meant they had embraced, at least for the duration of their tour, the worldwide market economy, and if that strikes us as something to mourn, as a further loss of innocence, perhaps we need to examine our own notions of innocence vis-à-vis tribal cultures, and our own nostalgia for something we never knew. Not that I hadn't experienced this nostalgia myself. I experienced it with every step I took. I felt privileged in any event to be given my own private foraging tour by Dul. I was her guest here, and she was showing her hospitality.

In the forest we had to clamber up steep slopes by grabbing hold of roots and hoisting ourselves up. We had to make our way down slippery paths at forty-five-degree angles, but I tumbled only twice along the way, and I had learned a little from my last trip to the area. This time I'd purchased a pair of garden gloves so that if I grabbed on to the wrong plant, at least I'd stand a better chance of staying whole.

Dul also showed me a wild bamboo she called *nafnaf*, like her secret language. This bamboo, which grew in the forest, was large enough to make into cooking tubes. Whether or not the Tasaday had used cultivated bamboo before they were discovered was another point of contention. Mefalu, when asked, said that this bamboo could not be cultivated, that it grew only in the forest. Perhaps this was true; perhaps it wasn't. But it seemed worth looking into.

We arrived in Magtu Inilingan four hours after we had set off. Amy and Dul and I were the slowpokes. We climbed up a large hill and came to several huts. There we met Lolo', whom I had last seen with Joey in January. There was no mistaking his look; he was astonished to see me again, especially with someone from the Other Side. He studied me with suspicion and a little fear. I felt bad for this, but it couldn't be helped. I asked Amy to ask him if he recognized me, and he told her that yes, he did.

My punishment for shocking Lolo' was that I learned that I was not yet in Magtu Inilingan, but only in its suburb. This seemed unreasonably cruel to me, to make me stand up again and walk to yet another ridge, but I had to do it, so I did. I climbed a last slippery denuded hill, on the top of which stood the not so proud enclave of

Magtu Inilingan. There was a large hut where the literacy classes were held, a few huts nearby, and trails snaking off from the community hall. We were met by Belayem and Pastor Nellis and Lolo''s father, Bilengan.

Lolo' reappeared with some *natek* for me. He unwrapped it from a leaf, and I took some of the sticky substance. It had nearly no taste at all, but for me, this was an important moment, and I savored it. The original Elizalde-Fox report to the Center for Short-Lived Phenomena had mentioned that Dafal originally found the Tasaday preparing a deer at the river and that they had the ability to make *natek*, a complicated process that involved leaching the poisons from the caryota palm and that almost certainly required metal tools. Later the Tasaday supposedly said that they'd learned to make *natek* from Dafal.

The community house stood on sturdy posts so that the floor was well aboveground, no doubt to discourage rats and other creatures from entering. My back was hurting, so I sat on the platform on my pack chair while Tom Headland's book once again made the rounds. A fire was built just outside the house, and I watched Amy as she greeted the various Tasaday she hadn't seen for several years. Bilengan approached us and asked if we had any medicine for his eyes, which were bloodshot and bothering him. Unfortunately I had nothing for him. I asked him if he'd like to have a seat, and he sat in the chair I'd brought.

Lobo showed up and greeted Amy. I recognized him immediately, though of course he wasn't the young boy of John Nance's photos. His hair was long, as it had been then, but his hairline was receding. He was my age, and I remembered what Carlos Fernandez had told me about the differences between the radiant young Lobo and the broken man he'd become. Amy had told me that two of his children had died of illness and that he also seemed to feel guilty and bitter about the hoax controversy. He had had a breakdown of sorts; supposedly he'd been fed some pot brownies or something of the sort by some lowlanders and had run off into the woods. Now he fled when approached by outsiders.

When he saw me, he visibly shrank back, looking at me with terror. Amy reassured him that I was a friend, but he would not talk with me directly on that first day. He kept glancing over at me, with what seemed equal parts suspicion and curiosity.

We ate dinner in the community house: freshwater crabs wrapped in banana leaves and cassava with deer meat. About thirty people crowded into the house. We had bought plenty of provisions in Kibang, including biscuits for the children and plenty of rice, but apparently all our provisions had not made the trip. Joe Igid's wife had siphoned off some of our provisions, so I had less to offer than I had wished.

After dinner, two women asked me if I could help them. Both were suffering terribly from skin diseases. Their legs and arms were scabbed and reddened and infected. Amy thought that one of the women suffered from an advanced case of ringworm and that the other had been burned. I squirted generous amounts of antibiotic ointments and aloe vera on their skin and instructed them to rub it in. Within a day their lesions started healing. It seemed that really so little was needed in the area—merely something other than neglect.

The next morning, Sunday, Pastor Nellis led a church service for the Tasaday in the community house. I stayed outside with Amy, chatting softly, and watched Lobo and his toddler son playing joyfully with Headland's book, stealing it from each other and laughing quietly. Much of the book, had Lobo been able to read it, undoubtedly would have upset him greatly.

After the service I treated more people for sores and skin diseases.

That afternoon we hiked from Magtu Inilingan to the Tasaday caves, through a stream where I stepped gingerly from rock to rock to avoid leeches. Despite my best efforts—I must have looked like someone walking on hot coals rather than through a stream—a leech managed to attach itself to me. Along the way Lobo and Lolo', who now seemed almost fond of me, kept feeding me. Lobo picked up some small freshwater crabs, and Lolo' gave me *ubud*, large palm hearts, and more *seyal*. The trip from Magtu Inilingan to the caves took about half an hour. Again the rains came.

Finally we started up a long slope, thick with vegetation, including nasty-looking stickers on vines that Lobo held aside for me as I struggled up the slippery hill. Along the way he pointed out the sights, or the ghosts of sights. Here was where Fernandez and Baradas had pitched their tents. Here was Kakay Sharls's (Lindbergh's) tent. Here was Momo' Dakel's tent. If the Tasaday struck the world at first as our living ancestors, the past seemed just as alive to the Tasaday, a past less remote than the one we had imagined them living in, but nonetheless a time, the early 1970s, that was as irretrievable to them as the Pleistocene to us.

Then we reached the caves.

My reaction to the caves was like that of someone who spies his favorite movie star and whose only comment is, "He looks so much smaller in person." I felt exhilarated to be there, but it wasn't possible for me to be bowled over in the same way that early visitors had been. That wasn't even what I really wanted. The Tasaday children played around the caves as if they were at some familiar playground, climbing the trees in front of the caves, clambering over the rocks. The forest around the caves was thick with vegetation, and there was a constant buzzing of insects and birdcalls, much as it had always been, with or without the Tasaday. The first thing I did was try to take a GPS reading, but I had no luck. The forest canopy was too thick. Lobo helped me up the rain-slicked rocks into the caves, where the others had gathered. By way of small talk, I had told Belayem earlier that I had seen the tool he had given Laurie Reid; no sooner had I said this than he told me he'd give one to me, too. I had told him that wasn't necessary, but now he appeared from the direction of one of the upper caves with a stone tool, which he gave to me. I thanked him and asked when it had been made; he said he had made it around the time his father had died. In 1971 Belayem was already an orphan, so this tool supposedly dated from before the Tasaday met Elizalde. The stone was hafted securely, and it was dark in color. His gift delighted me, of course. He had shown such a tool to the *Stern* magazine team, and when they were kidnapped, they told him to hide it deep in the cave so it wouldn't be taken.

A fire was built in the cave using a resin that the Tasaday said came from the *sanduka* tree. Pastor Nellis had told me in Magtu Inilingan earlier that *sanduka* resin was "our gas." I had never heard of *sanduka*'s being a tree, and Amy acted as though she had not heard this either. She speculated that the place Sanduka, where the Sanduka band had once lived, most likely had an abundance of such trees.

I looked around the caves, noting right off the sleeping platforms, dating most likely from 1986. Iten had found them rotting, as they were now, but new ones miraculously appeared as soon as NBC made its expedition shortly thereafter. Supposedly, there were sixty-one or so Tasaday living in the caves at that time (a veritable population explosion, as Iten noted; just five years earlier there'd been only thirty-nine!),[14] but with living conditions so crowded, they moved to Magtu Inilingan. But I didn't believe that the Tasaday had ever lived at the caves, at least not in the sense of a permanent address. I went along with the theory that they were a frequentation site, one of many resting places for the Tasaday. Even Amy thought this was so.

It's likely the Tasaday sometimes stayed in this *Ilib Fusaka*.* At the DAR guesthouse, Dul told me that they used to spend time in many caves: *Sanduka. Ilib Nafnaf. Ilib Dendet.* But they always returned to *Ilib Fusaka*. They stayed at *Ilib Fusaka* when they had visitors, but neither Mai Tuan nor Manda ever told them to stay there, she said.

Iten's explanation for the rebuilding of the rotting platforms during the 1986 expedition was that the Tasaday "were preparing for a long new siege at the caves and did not want to wait too long for a minimum standard of comfort."[15] He was certainly right, but he was also right when he'd sarcastically suggested that the Tasaday had become by 1986 the equivalent of a Swiss yodeling society. Their memories were long, and why shouldn't they remember how to dress, how to act, even where to live when they had visitors? They had enjoyed their celebrity as much as any Westerner starring in a "reality" TV show. The crudeness of the "ruse" in 1986, men wearing leaf bras, underwear poking out from beneath their leaves, speaks sadly of false expectations, not of cynical conspiracy.

I tried again to get a GPS reading, this time from the cave's ledge, but the unit still couldn't lock on a satellite. Pastor Nellis wanted to give it a try, so I showed him how to use it, and he scrambled outside with it. Now there appeared before me a kind of apparition: Adug had changed from Western clothes into a leaf G-string. He stood calmly in the cave, the only one dressed in this manner, smoking one of the Marlboros I'd given him. I had to admit he looked pretty cool, but I asked Amy why he was dressed like this. Adug replied that when he was at the caves, he felt comfortable dressed this way. I took what he said at face value. He obviously wasn't trying to fool me; I'd seen him

---

Ilib is the term for cave. *Ilib Fusaka* is the name of their ancestral cave, the main cave complex.

in Western clothes. I couldn't blame him for changing. My clothes were soaked, and they weren't going to dry anytime soon.

Lest anyone think I consider myself less benighted than previous Tasaday tourists, I offer up the following account: I wanted to know for myself how the G-string of *bangi'* leaves felt, how it was constructed, if I'd be warm enough. So I asked Adug and Lobo if they could make me a *bangi'* leaf G-string. The only non-Tasaday I know who wore a G-string of *bangi'* leaves was Pascal Lays.

No problem, they said, or its equivalent. They set about weaving one right away. I stepped down from the ledge for a little privacy and stripped. Quickly Lobo and Adug fitted me. I knew what I looked like. I looked like a giant white baby in a leaf diaper. But that didn't seem to matter to the Tasaday. The *bangi'* leaves felt dry and snug, and with the fire in the cave, I didn't feel even slightly cold. I posed for a picture with Adug. Dul, usually the cynic of the bunch, wanted to be included (the photos of me of course will never see the light of day). She told Amy she was upset she didn't have time to make her leaf skirt. But she threw off her blouse and posed slightly behind me so that she looked mostly naked. It seemed I could not have done a better thing as far as they were concerned. Belayem said that he felt as if Momo' Dakel himself had returned. But no, Momo' Dakel, Jr., was not a title to which I aspired.

Soon, I changed back to my normal clothes, wet as they were, and we all sat down for an interview while the kids who had accompanied us ran around the caves screaming and shouting. Mefalu and Toto' and Joe Igid were there, as well as Natek, Lobo, Lolo', Adug, Belayem, Gintuy, and Dul. Mefalu and Amy served as translators for me. Amy spoke to Mefalu in Tagalog, and he spoke to the Tasaday in Manobo Blit.*

We talked about their first meeting with Manda at the clearing.

Belayem said that Momo' Dakel asked Mafoko' (Mai Tuan) to ask them (the Tasaday), "Are they good people or are they bad?"

Amy wanted to see if he meant Dafal, but no, he said Mafoko'. I remembered what Mai Tuan had told me when I asked him if they'd really had such trouble understanding the Tasaday. Not so much trou-

---

*Laurie Reid listened to this tape and remarked that Amy did a largely accurate job of translating and, unlike Lozano, wasn't manipulating the words of the Tasaday.

ble, he'd said. What all this means it's hard to say because the slippery "facts" keep slipping further away. It depends how you view this conversation, as a snapshot or something set in stone. It's the same as the dogs in their stories of Bibang, the knives, the blades of cogon grass. Stories change.

In *this* story, Belayem said they told Manda, "If you think we are good, we also treat other people good. If you think about us that we're bad, we can also be bad."

In this recounting, Belayem didn't cast the Tasaday as pure innocents. He cast them as human beings. Treat us well, and we'll treat you well.

"We are good people," Manda told them. "I have concern for people, and since I am your father, I would like to help you. Since you have a thicket of forest, I'm concerned for your well-being. I am going to help you."

I asked whether any of the Tasaday who met Momo' Dakel had any doubts or concerns about him or if they all immediately liked him. Belayem said it took time before they really trusted him.

"Of the early visitors," I asked Amy, "besides Momo' Dakel, who else did they like?"

They told me they liked Carlos Fernandez, Robert Fox, Jack Reynolds, whom they called Kakay Bian, David Baradas, Jambangan, Amy, Doc Rebong, a security guard named Felix, Ching, the pilot, and Doug Yen, whom they called Kakay Ning.

Did they remember Lindbergh? Oh, yes. Kakay Sharls. Everyone laughed.

"What do they remember about Kakay Sharls?"

Dul said Kakay Sharls had promised that he would give them a helicopter. A helicopter? Here it was again, the most basic example of how "facts" are changed to suit our own goals and expectations. First, Nance reported Lindbergh's casually asking them if they would like a helicopter. They took this as an offer, and when they repeated it to Judith Moses, she took it as proof of coercion, that they'd been promised a helicopter in *exchange* for their complicity in the hoax. Everyone laughed at the thought of having a helicopter, everyone but Lobo, whose voice was deeply resonant and forceful, bordering on angry. They'd been promised food, metal tools, a helicopter, clothes, rice, medicine, money. Charles had promised them many things.

"Do they remember Gina Lollobrigida?"* I asked.

Sure. Kakay Gina. Belayem said they liked her. She was good. She was going to help them. Dul said it was always words, just words. Kakay Gina promised clothes, plenty of rice, and help to solve their problems.

"The road to hell is paved with good intentions," I told them, which I immediately realized was untranslatable as such. "People sometimes have good intentions but don't follow through," I said.

Amy asked Mefalu to translate, and Belayem laughed as though this were the funniest thing he'd heard since the Dawn of Man.

"Who else has made them promises?" I asked.

Lobo and Dul said a lot of the foreigners who had come with Momo' had plenty of promises, but only Jambangan had really kept such promises. Their feelings for Nance and Elizalde seemed genuine to me. They treated Amy like an old friend as well. Lolo' and Bilengan seemed to have had no feeling for Joey Lozano when I'd been to the area months before, though he had acted as if they were long-lost buddies.

Eventually I had no more questions to ask. I thought it would be only fair to turn it around. "I've been asking them a lot of questions," I told Amy. "I was just wondering if they have any questions they wanted to ask me."

As a matter of fact, they did, and this surprised me. Everyone started talking excitedly at once. Nance, along with Lindbergh and Manda, had been baffled thirty years earlier by "their seeming lack of adventure, curiosity, competitiveness"[16] (though their trip to the edge

---

*Critics of Elizalde often use Gina Lollobrigida as an example of how the millionaire brought his "jetsetter friends" to see the Tasaday. In the early 1970s, the Italian film star was producing a couple of coffee table books on the Philippines, lavishly bankrolled with government funds by her friend, Imelda Marcos. Jim Turner, a longtime American expatriate in the Philippines, worked for Manda's brother Freddy back then. Mrs. Marcos asked Freddy to take care of Lollobrigida, and Freddy passed on the responsibility to Turner. Lollobrigida "asked repeatedly" to see the Tasaday. Manda apparently opposed the visit but couldn't long resist the pressure of Mrs. Marcos. Finally, Lollobrigida was allowed to make a foray of only a few hours. Her book was later suppressed by the First Lady out of jealousy; Imelda didn't appreciate a newspaper photo showing the president and Lollobrigida jogging alone on the beach in Boracay. Regarding the Tasaday, Lollobrigida complained in her book that PANAMIN "guarded them jealously from unnecessary intrusion." Turner remembers her as "a pain in the ass."

of the forest seemed pretty adventurous to me). But if this had ever been so, and I doubted it very much, they had learned all three attributes quite well in the intervening years.

Dul wanted to know how I felt now that I was here in the caves.

Her question startled me. I had to assess my feelings? Right now? I didn't know how I felt. "Tell her that I've been waiting three years to get here and I feel very privileged and it's one of the highlights of my life," I said. That sounded insincere because it was. In a sense it was true, but it was stated so badly; "privileged" is the only word that comes close to a feeling, and it's not a very meaningful one.

Dul wasn't satisfied with my answer. "What is your feeling right now, now that you're here?" she wanted to know.

I paused. "Well, I guess it's a feeling of peacefulness." I wasn't trying to be calculating or secretive in my response. What did I feel? I felt . . . that there were things that I would never know, that no one would ever know. I felt that these people had been abused in a way that no one could ever fully fathom. I felt that they had a right to call themselves whatever they wanted.

"Will you also add that I feel very respectful, too," I told Amy as they discussed what I meant by "peaceful."

"Since you showed respect for this place," Dul told me, "it would be most likely that whatever you would ask, we would say yes."

Lobo's turn was next. He was more direct, stronger in his discourse. "He's asking what your commitment is," Amy said, "if it's selfless."

"Tell them I don't want to be another person who makes empty promises," I said.

"Since I was small up to now," Lobo said, "I've heard many promises, and still no improvement has been made in this place."

"What kind of improvements do they want?" Amy asked.

Lobo said if there was any improvement, they'd want it at Magtu Inilingan. They wanted to see something like what was at T'boli. "At T'boli they have a school. They have clinics. They have services. And there are electric lights."

I told them that part of the problem was that as they knew, there had been a great deal of fighting in the past, and it was difficult to bring services here; that if there were services, they had to be for the region, for the people in Blit and others, not just for the Tasaday; that

I was a foreigner and the real solutions had to come from people who weren't foreigners.

"Those who have come here," Lobo said, "especially the foreigners who have come here, said that this is our reservation and the other Manobo"s, and that no one else will come in."

"But people have," I said.

"Now that the boundaries are clearly ours, within our forest, what help will come next?" Lobo wanted to know.

"I wish I could answer that," I said. "I'm not Momo' Dakel. I don't have his wealth or his power."

Amy clearly had a good rapport with them. She lectured them, and they listened. She explained to them the ancestral domain law, that with the change of presidents, there had been new laws that had come about, and now there was a new law whereby they had to have their territory mapped and titled. Barrio Ned, she told them, not many kilometers away, used to be a T'boli settlement, but another government with another law had made it a resettlement area. "So, as much as possible, we don't want that to happen here. . . . The reason this became a reservation was that it had many trees. If they keep reducing the trees, the boundaries will become smaller. The land will become resettlement."

The Tasaday listened intently.

Unable to get a reading anywhere, Pastor Nellis had returned in the meantime with my GPS. He'd even climbed a tree. Amy told me she thought the spirits of the cave didn't want me to get a reading. I didn't rule it out, but I tended to believe other possibilities. "This GPS won't work well here," I said to the Tasaday. "It works fine in Magtu Inilingan, and the reason is that there's open space. The reason it doesn't work here is that there are trees, and in a way that's good because I think it means that there are still enough trees here."

We left the caves a little after four that afternoon. On the way down the slope, Lobo paused by the rock face, bent down, and pried away a small piece of the cave. He smiled and gave it to me. There was no translator around, so I couldn't be sure of his intentions. He could have been recognizing me for what I was, perhaps nothing more than another tourist who wanted a piece of the Tasaday, a souvenir. Perhaps it was simply a gift. Or it could have meant more. It certainly wasn't a cynical gesture. Or maybe he meant it as a reminder. Lobo had wanted a commitment from me, and I wanted to believe I could help them. I wanted to believe I'd be back. But what could I give them that would mean something, anything to them?

As I gingerly stepped from stone to stone in the stream on our hike back to Magtu Inilingan, I felt flushed with success at having made it to the caves. I remarked to Amy that I felt part of an elite group now that I'd been to the caves.

"You and the rich and famous of the world," she said dryly, diverging from her usual chamber of commerce approach to the subject.

Slightly chastened, I sped ahead to catch up with Lobo and Pastor Nellis. As we climbed a muddy bare hill that signaled the approach to Magtu Inilingan, Nellis told me he thought I must love the Tasaday a lot to have made such a trip. I wished my motives were that pure, but they weren't, of course. It wasn't love that brought me here, but it wasn't entirely selfish curiosity either. At least I hoped not. As I brooded over my motives, Lobo told me through Nellis that those who used the Tasaday name for the wrong reasons were *butbut* (liars). I asked whom he meant, and he said he meant Oswald Iten. He said he wanted to learn how to write so he could compose a letter to Iten. As we climbed a slippery denuded hill directly below Magtu Inilingan, he said he felt good now that the Tasaday were strong once again. I wasn't so sure. I wasn't sure the Tasaday had ever been strong.

That night we sat in the Tasaday community house while it poured outside and a man from Blit played a flute with his nose. I recognized the sound from Jack Reynolds's film, "Cave People of the Philippines," a plaintive and simple song that seemed as lovely in its simplicity as any world-weary traveler might want. Even as I sat in such leaky quarters, it seemed easy to romanticize, to tune out the children coughing, the crying, the open sores.

In the morning before we left for Blit again, I again sat in the community house talking with Lobo, Lolo', Dul, and Belayem while Amy and Mefalu translated. The other night someone had brought in some monkey meat and wildcat; they'd cooked the hell out of them, and now they offered me some, which I ate, not because I was being polite but because I was hungry. I decided to talk to Lolo' about my last visit. I asked what he and Bilengan were told about me when I last came.

Amy relayed the question to Mefalu and then to Lolo' and then back again. "The son of Galang," she told me presently, "Bai, went to see them, and told them that Jambangan is there at Kasab,* so they went to Kasab and saw *you*." Everyone laughed. In other words, I was a disappointment.

"Who were the armed men with them?" I asked.

"All those who were there are with Galang," Amy said. "These are the CVOs of Galang, meaning like the Civilian Volunteers' Force."

"Really?" I said. "Because we were told . . . that they were Bantay Tasaday, that they were actually sent by Mai to prevent people from going into the area."

She asked Lolo' about this, and then she told me that they'd never heard of anything like that. I hadn't told Amy anything about my trip, except the fact of it.

"They were Galang's people?" I asked again, unsure what to make of this.

"CVO of Galang," Amy said.

"Because they seemed a little intimidating or threatening to us and we were staying with Galang."

I asked Lolo' when the armed men had joined him and his father.

"When they went out, this group was not with them," Amy told me.

"But when?" I asked.

"They saw this gang near the place where Galang had his farming plot being cultivated."

"And then those people joined them?"

"They followed them to Galang's house," Amy told me.

"Did they talk?" I asked. "Did they say anything?"

"They told them, him and Bilengan, that they were CVOs."

I was baffled. Joey had told me they were Bantay Tasaday, that they were Mai's men. Datu' Galang obviously had weapons. Even Judith Moses had told me that. But if these were his men, then we hadn't really been in any danger at all. Much as David Baradas and Carlos Fernandez had wondered if the whole Kabayo incident had been a charade, I too started to wonder. Different time. Different charade?

"He seemed kind of nervous when he was there, and I was wondering why he felt nervous."

*Everything, it seems, has more than one name. Kasab was another name for Tubak.

"He said he felt a little nervous because there were a lot of people around them," Amy translated.

"Joey Lozano was there," I said.

"Oh," said Amy, surprised. I hadn't told her even this much.

"Did he recognize Joey?" I asked.

Yes, he had, Lolo' said, but they didn't talk. They most likely couldn't understand each other.

"Did Datu' Galang tell him anything?" I asked.

"Datu' Galang talked to Bilengan," Amy said, "but Bilengan said they were going back because the faces they saw were not of Jambangan."

I mentioned the meeting in Datu' Galang's house and asked what they talked about. Lolo' said he didn't know what they were talking about. They were speaking in T'boli. One would think Lolo' would have known T'boli since according to Iten, they were half T'boli and half Manobo.[17]

"Did the CVOs leave with them or separately?" I asked.

"They left ahead," Amy said, "and the CVOs stayed." That was what I remembered, too. I remembered now Joey making a bit of a deal when the so-called Bantay Tasaday left Tubak. With my camera he filmed them heading off. "I always like to take pictures of men with guns leaving," he had told me. But the Tasaday had left long before, and I didn't question at the time why the Tasaday might have left ahead of their protectors.

I asked Lolo' if he was sure they were Datu' Galang's men, not Mai's.

Datu' Galang, he affirmed.

"If that's the case," I said, "then that whole thing was staged."

He told me again that when they didn't recognize me, when they saw that it wasn't Jambangan, they simply decided to go back.

I told them I was sorry for that inconvenience I'd caused them and that I was friends with Jambangan.

They all laughed, Belayem the loudest. Lolo', laughing, said they thought I was going to be another Oswald, because I was in the place of Galang.

Soon Bilengan arrived, and I asked him the same questions I asked his son. He told me virtually the same thing, that he had gone to the place of Galang because he thought that Jambangan was there. He hadn't recognized Lozano, nor had he realized that anyone (I at first) had called him Tinda. "All I know is my name, that I am Bilengan," he said. Nor had he known the armed men who accompanied him and Lolo'.

The hike from Magtu Inilingan back to Blit took me three hours. I hiked with Pastor Nellis and the other literacy teacher, Melel. On the way Nellis told me of a dream he'd had, a nightmare in which he'd seen the Tasaday forest burning and a huge cross in the sky in the direction of Blit. It hardly seemed a dream to me; it seemed more real than *tinggalung*. The forest was indeed burning, but slowly, invisibly, and the people coming in, the Christian settlers, filled the horizon.

I reached Blit ahead of Amy and Dul and was served hot *kamote* (sweet potato). I sat now with Belayem and the literacy teachers. I asked Melel to find out how long it took Belayem to walk from Magtu Inilingan to Blit. Half an hour or so, I was told, though I'm not quite sure how he measured time. In any event, it didn't take long. Food gatherers of course can walk enormous distances and hardly break a sweat. Even without the map Peralta had told me about, the idea that they had been unaware of their neighbors seemed a stretch.

We planned to stay overnight in Blit and head back to Kibang the next day. In the afternoon, after Amy and the others arrived, we met the teachers Father Rex had hired, who now taught in a government school in Blit. Among them was the husband of Maria Tudi-Wanan, the head of a T'boli dance troupe, who lived in Sebu and whom John Nance sent money to help implement programs for the Tasaday. Amy seemed distrustful of Maria and somewhat hurt that John hadn't gone through her to help the Tasaday.

One of the teachers spoke fluent Tasaday but said he'd never stayed there. I asked him about the marijuana charges and claims that he and the other teachers had NPA connections. He denied both accusations. No sooner had the teachers left than another son of Datu' Dudim's, Klil, also a pastor like Nellis, said that he'd worked at the teachers' staff house and that the men were lying. They'd grown marijuana right there and often passed through Tasaday.

The monsoon rains broke upon us half an hour into our trip and clobbered us for the rest of the hike, which took twice as long as it had on the way. Cold, wet, and hungry, we stopped after several hours at a little shelter in a Christian community within the reserve's boundaries. Nearby was a tiny *sari sari* store, where I purchased stale crackers, Happy brand salted peanuts, chocolate with bugs in it, and instant coffee for the group.* Dul's children were shivering. I sat by myself sipping coffee and saw Dul and Amy conversing in Manobo. After traveling with Dul and the others so many days, I had picked up some of the words, and as Dul and Amy chatted in a corner, I eavesdropped. I heard them talking about the caves. Amy asked whether it had been cold when the Tasaday lived in the caves. I wrote down the words *ilib nda magumgum*, which I took to mean that the caves weren't cold.† I wondered, if this were a hoax, why they would maintain this ruse in a language that the designated chronicler supposedly couldn't understand? Back in the United States I wrote to Laurie Reid and asked him if what I'd heard was correct. He wrote back: "The word for 'cold' in Tasaday is *megemgem*, where the letter *e* represents what is referred to as the schwa vowel, and is similar in pronunciation to that found in the English word 'gum.' I think the term *megemgem* is also used in Blit, while the term most commonly found in Manobo languages for cold is *megenaw*. The latter term is the one that is reconstructed for Proto-Manobo by Elkins."[18]

Toward the end of the hike we reached a flood-swollen river that could be crossed only by a slippery log stretched from bank to bank. I shimmied across on my derriere, much to the amusement of my fellow travelers, who walked across. I didn't care. This big handsome flying lemur wanted to live to tell the story and fly another day. We walked for another couple of hours from Tafal back to Kibang.

The skylab ride to Isulan took three and half hours over roads with potholes deeper, if not wider, than an Olympic-size swimming pool. When we reached Isulan, Mai's driver, Oscar, picked us up and we drove to Marbel, to the same barbecue place where I had eaten with Joey and his gang after my trip in January. The restaurant was large and airy, with a couple of dozen picnic tables and mangy cats begging for food. Amy somehow picked the same table I'd sat at with Joey. I told her this, but she didn't seem as charmed and delighted as I was. She just gave me a look. Dul had decided to travel with us back to Lake Sebu, and she sat a table alone, looking intently at a stunningly

---

Sari sari stores are the Filipino versions of convenience stores; often tiny and makeshift, they sell sundry goods.
†It's actually correctly represented as *ilib enda' megemgem*.

violent show blaring from the TV in the front of the restaurant. The show took place in a schoolyard and featured several heavily armed men mowing down row after row of schoolchildren dressed in neatly pressed uniforms. The dialogue required no translator.

The shots of children being blown apart went on for minutes, all in slow motion. Dul seemed to find this hilarious. She laughed and laughed as if she'd never seen anything so enchanting.

As it happened, the wife of Mayor Sam Loko of Lake Sebu was eating lunch here with friends. She had been one of Manda's scholars, a favorite of his whom he had called for as he was dying. She was a well-dressed woman with a confident bearing but a pinched look as she approached our table. She and Amy started to talk in Tagalog, and Amy explained what we were doing there. The mayor's wife switched to English for my benefit. "We don't need people coming in here investigating the controversy," she told me. "We don't need controversy."

When Amy mentioned that I was bringing in medicine, she told Amy that all aid should go through the local government. The two went back and forth for a while. If Mayor Loko was so concerned, why had he never been up to the Tasaday area? Why had they not received any aid? If they were under his jurisdiction, why were they neglected? I turned away from the argument. Dul had now turned around and seemed hypnotized by the fish swimming in a tank against the wall.

That night, as we feasted modestly by the dimmest of lights in Mai Tuan's kitchen, I listened to Mai Tuan and Amy and Dul tell stories while I kept my recorder running. Dul said there were thirty kinds of snakes in the forest. Mai, in a particularly garrulous mood, told me of one fantastic thing after another: When I returned, he said, he would take me up into the mountains to meet some truly isolated T'boli tribes. And he would show me the place where he had seen a snake that had to be the longest in the world. Dul looked my way and laughed, and I asked Amy why. Dul thought I was like a *manok dakel* (big bird, but also what the Tasaday called a helicopter), hovering over everything. She was right. This was exactly where I had hoped to be, hovering with a clear view that showed the forest and the denuded hillsides and the people in between.

21

Confirmation Bias

You ask me to accept your letter "in the collegial spirit in which it was intended." I regret that I find nothing of a collegial nature in your letter. It is a masterpiece of innuendo, and it is characteristic of your whole approach to the Tasaday question. I certainly do not categorize someone who is unable to be objective in their research as a colleague.

—Letter from Lawrence Reid to Judith Moses, May 25, 1992

n August 2000 I again flew to the Philippines, and my timing verged on the terrible. The government had attacked and overrun the main MILF stronghold, Camp Abubakar, as well as other MILF camps. In response, the MILF had declared a jihad, and had fanned out for major guerrilla action right where I wanted to be, near Maitum, where George Tanedo lived. Joey Lozano was going to the United States in September to be a human rights fellow at the University of Chicago; the previous year he had applied for a fellowship at Columbia University, and I had written a recommendation for him, but he had not been accepted there. He had almost been rejected again; according to Judith Moses, there had been some "misunderstanding" in his application. Instead of listing his degrees (he had none), he had listed courses taken and where he'd taken them. But the misunderstanding had been straightened out.

After my second trip to see the Tasaday, I wasn't sure I could trust Joey anymore, and he obviously had misgivings about me. The previous December he'd told me on the phone that "some people" were worried about what I was going to write. Anyway, he said, he'd told his wife that whatever I wrote was just my opinion. Of all the people I'd spent time with, Joey seemed most concerned. He tended to jump to his own defense when I didn't even know what he was talking about. He'd told me it was true that he'd given Datu' Galang money as a humanitarian gesture, but not as a bribe. I didn't know why he was telling me this until months later, when I read various affidavits claiming he'd bribed and coached the Tasaday and Datu' Galang. When I told him I wanted to listen to both sides, he said that some people, like Kristina Luz, weren't trustworthy. I didn't know why he singled her out. Luz was the young woman who had been Judith Moses's researcher during the filming of *The Tribe That Never Was*. Then I read a copy of a letter Luz had sent Judith Moses claiming that Joey and Datu' Galang had pulled the wool over their eyes.

With this in mind, I called Amy Rara upon my arrival in Manila and asked if she'd be willing to accompany Joey and me to talk with George Tanedo. She said she'd be willing, but she didn't think Joey would want her there. I agreed but thought it was worth a try.

I called Joey and floated my idea. I told him that I thought George Tanedo was a dubious character and that even Judith Moses had questioned his honesty (she had written me an e-mail saying she hoped he'd tell the truth "for once in his squalid life"), so I thought it would be good to have both Joey and Amy along. Joey gently suggested that maybe Judith said that because she had not worked with George. And Tanedo might feel he was being confronted.

"Amy Rara is an academic," he said, growing more agitated. "She might confuse George with her theories. But I don't care for her academic theories. I care for reality. If you want to bring Amy Rara along, then you had better count me out. To hell with Amy Rara and her theories!"

I told Joey I didn't mean to upset him.

"I'm not upset," he told me. "I'm passionate about this. I live in the area, and I know the reality."

Okay, I told him. We could count Amy Rara out if he didn't want her along.

"If she wants to go the real route with me," he said, "then yes. And talk to the real people, then yes, she can come."

"I don't understand," I said.

"She has taken the fantasy route," he said.

I told Joey I was a little concerned about security, that Tom Headland had told me that the SIL people in the area were saying it was very dangerous right now.

"They are more inland," he said.

"And how are the roads?"

"The roads are fine." He told me that if I was not open-minded about George Tanedo and if I was so worried about my security, maybe it would be for the best if we forgot about it.

I told him that I *was* open-minded, that I'd been open-minded all along, and that whatever fears I had had I had overcome in the past. I reminded him that I'd been to the area twice before. Somehow, I managed to salvage the conversation, and we decided to try to do the trip in one day.

Everyone besides Joey warned me not to go. The MILF reportedly was on the lookout for foreigners, especially Americans, to kidnap. Still, people in Manila tended to exaggerate the dangers of the south, and I decided to fly down to Mindanao and hole up with friends in Kidapawan in Cotabato, a largely Christian city, somewhat removed from the conflict. From there I'd monitor the situation and decide whether a trip to Maitum was advisable or even possible.

I arrived in Kidapawan just ahead of a nationwide transportation strike. Before I reached Kidapawan by bus, I had to get off in Maki-lala, where a group of strikers blocked the way. I was crammed along with thirty other people into a military truck with a few courteous soldiers dressed in full battle gear. I kept my head down because I felt exposed and in more danger in a military truck than on the bus, and I'd been told that Makilala was an NPA stronghold. The "troubles" with the MILF were only about nineteen miles away, and sixteen civilians had been massacred in the nearby village of Carmen the week before. In Kidapawan a bomb had been found in the public market, but it turned out to be fake.

Amy Rara had given me the name of a Canadian, Bob Heins, a converted Muslim who had been in the Philippines since 1968 and was the president of the Metro Kidapawan Chamber of Commerce. I met him and his wife, Taj Mahal Hassan, at their house. Heins, a plainspoken man who was connected to pretty much every group in the area, called someone to find out about the security situation in Maitum. He told me that as of 1:00 p.m., the *población* (the center of Maitum) was safe, but getting there might be a problem. Taj told me, "The timing is not so good right now."

I asked Heins if he knew Lozano, and he told me that he knew who he was, that he drank with the governor and knew some of the people Heins knew, but that the MILF and MNLF people didn't like him. He said a very well-connected friend was arriving tomorrow, and he might be able to accompany me there and assure my safety without Joey Lozano along. Heins told me it wouldn't be advisable to go with someone who wasn't well liked.

That night, by coincidence, a woman I was introduced to said that her husband, a local judge, knew something about the Tasaday. The judge's father was the late Mariano Mondragon, the man who, in Central TV's *Scandal*, asserted that the Tasaday were fake, that he knew the Tasaday personally. Mondragon had also been a witness at the UP conference but had later recanted, saying that as an official with the Habaluyas logging company he and others "launched a campaign to discredit the discovery."[1] In light of Habaluyas's heavy logging activity in the area, this seems almost certainly true.*

Mondragon's daughter-in-law told me that he had talked to her about the Tasaday and that he had believed the Tasaday were a hoax. She confirmed that he had been an official at the Habaluyas logging company and that he had been good friends with Joe Sison, Elizalde's great enemy. I mentioned his retraction, and she told me that her husband had been quite angry about it.

Meanwhile Joey and I exchanged e-mails about my trip to Maitum. He was now exerting a fair amount of pressure on me to let him accompany me. I had suggested that maybe George and Franklin Tanedo could come visit me in Kidapawan or Davao (at my expense, of course). It seemed less dangerous for them to come to me than for me to go through prime kidnapping territory. Joey said this would be culturally insensitive, something I'm mindful of, but in this case, it seemed a ploy. After all, he hadn't seemed concerned at all when he fetched Bilengan and Lolo' to see me in January 1999. Joey said that the situations weren't the same at all: Bilengan and Lolo' had been within their own ancestral domain. True, but they'd also been lied to in order to get them to Datu' Galang's, and they hadn't been happy to be there—not because of the so-called Bantay Tasaday but because I

*The Habaluyas and Sarmiento logging companies have long competed for logging rights in the area. In 1974, Habaluyas began cutting trees in the Lake Sebu watershed until a protest to the secretary of agriculture stopped it. But it wasn't clear whether this was due to concern for the environment or the fact that Sarmiento also claimed the trees. The conflict between the logging companies continued into the 1980s.

wasn't Jambangan, as they'd been told, presumably at Joey's instigation. Besides, the Tanedos were half T'boli; their father had been Pampangan, and they'd traveled widely outside their domain, including Australia. But I didn't mention any of this.

The next day I returned to Bob Heins's house and met his friend. This man, who was in the MILF, claimed to have been a member of Marcos's assassination squad before joining the rebels. He told me he could make some phone calls and give me clearance through MILF lines to get to Maitum, and he gave me the cell phone number of the MILF supply officer under Kumander Tigre.

The man proceeded to tell me his own wild stories about Elizalde. He said the Tasaday were a hoax, that they were a cover for Manda's marijuana plantation, which he had seen in the area when he was on special assignment with the army in the 1970s. The Tasaday were supposed to divert attention away from Manda's pot-growing operation. He also told me about some twelve-foot Vikings that a fisherman had found in a cave under the sea. He claimed to have seen the huge big toe of one of these Vikings. What the hell, I decided to ask him about the seven-colored *tinggalung*. It's very rare, he told me. He called it a *sigbin* and said that it's supposed to be the pet of the devil.*
It looks like a kangaroo, he said. He had seen one while in the military and had dropped his gun and run the other way when he saw it.

I decided to beg off. Even if I got through the lines, the military was on the move, and I could easily get stuck in the middle of an encounter between the two sides. It didn't seem worth it just to go see George Tanedo, who, though a swing figure in the controversy, had told different things to different people and wasn't likely to tell me the unvarnished truth in any case, especially not with only Joey along.

When Joey learned I had decided against going to Maitum after all, he sent me an e-mail brimming with anger and hostility, while

---

*I'm happy to report that the mystery of the *tinggalung* has been virtually solved, thanks once again, to Laurie Reid, who reports that Ross Errington's *Dictionary of Cotabato Manobo* lists it as a "raccoon." But the description given by Toto' Dudim of Blit "makes it sound like Viverricula indica pallida (Gray) or 'small chinese civet cat' described as 'a small buff and colored mammal with weasel-like face, long ringed tail, and a strong musky odor.'" The animal can be viewed at: http://www.tesri.gov.tw/content6/11.htm. In Cebuano, one kind of civet cat is called a *singgawong*. The Tasaday word and the Cebuano word are clearly cognate.

maintaining a weird patina of geniality. The gist was that some people were obviously more willing than others to put their lives on the line to find the truth.* And to him, it didn't matter that he was associated with one side because the truth, he thought, stood alone, indepen- dent of sides.

I wasn't sure I agreed with that completely, but I kept it to myself. In any case, if the truth stood alone, I no longer thought it stood any- where near him. If the truth stood alone, perhaps it stood alone some- where in the mountains, amid endless hectares of cogon grass in what had once been endless hectares of forest.

At the end of the e-mail, Joey included a quote for my edification, from the book *Dateline Earth: Journalism As If the Planet Mattered*: "Balanced reporting is a euphemism for status-quo journalism. If the scale is already tilted, balanced reporting just favors those who are al- ready rich and powerful." Duly noted, but did tipping the balance of power justify the manufacture of news?

I had been asked the night before to give a speech at the local Ro- tary Club, and I went there at six and sat down with about thirty Ro- tarians. The meeting began with a prayer, then the national anthem, then the singing of a song, kind of a communal karaoke, the Bee Gees' "Massachusetts." Then they swapped jokes. Judge Mondragon, a cheerful-looking man with large glasses and an impish smile, was there. His wife had told me that the judge had played with the Tasa- day when he was boy, so of course I was eager to talk to him about his experiences.

When it came time for my speech, I talked a little about my back- ground and then went into the Tasaday controversy. I said that I had traveled twice to the area and that my feelings on the issue were complex. People assumed the Tasaday were a hoax. They *wanted* the Tasaday to be a hoax.

When it came time for questions, a man told me that the Tasaday were a hoax. This was the regional director for the NCIP, one of PANAMIN's successor organizations. He explained the funding situa- tion to me. He said the Tasaday had been created as a funnel for

---

*Shortly after my return from the Philippines, an American was indeed kidnapped by a faction of the MILF, though far from where I had been, in the northern part of Min- danao. He was threatened with beheading and spent seven months in captivity before being rescued by the military.

foreign money, that PANAMIN had received 50 percent of its funding from the government and 50 percent as a private foundation. They were just a money-making scheme for the foundation. I told him that I knew that Elizalde had been corrupt, that this indeed was the funding structure, and that the publicity surrounding the Tasaday certainly added to the coffers of PANAMIN and probably Elizalde too. An old man, clearly upset, said he hoped I wasn't going to write a biased book. He told me that the Tasaday were a hoax and that the proof was that no one in the area believed they were real. I told him it depended on whom you spoke with. I had met a number of people around Lake Sebu who quietly took the Tasaday's existence for granted.

Another man asked if I had heard anything about gold. I told him I had, but it was mostly *chismis* (gossip) and that if Manda and Marcos had wanted to exploit the reserve for gold or logging or some other nefarious scheme, it would have happened a long time ago.

After that, I chatted with a jovial man who seemed very interested in the project. He had been born in 1947 in Mindanao. I told him I wanted to speak to Judge Mondragon about his father's recanting. He apparently knew about it. The elder Mondragon, he said, was very anti-Marcos. He agreed with me that the Tasaday had been a scapegoat for anti-Marcos feeling, and he suggested that maybe I could approach the judge by asking him to forget politics and Elizalde and just tell what he knew. I agreed that would be a good approach, but it seemed like an impossibility to me. You could forget everything. You could even forget the Tasaday, but you couldn't forget Manda, and you couldn't forget Marcos. The scars seemed too deep.

When I met with Judge Mondragon the next day, I confirmed some of the information I had heard about his father. He had indeed been a logging official and a close associate of Joe Sison's. Translation: anti-Marcos, definitely anti-Manda, definitely prologging. Had Central TV known this when it featured Mondragon proclaiming that the Tasaday were T'boli and Manobo and that some of them were even his in-laws? Had Central TV simply ignored the obvious conflict of interest behind such a statement? Had it not cared? Merely casting this as an academic debate about the degree of "primitiveness" of the Tasaday ignores the *real* story about resource exploitation, some hoax proponents stressed. But the argument of resource exploitation cuts both ways. If there had not been a reserve, the area would have been decimated by loggers.

Curiously, Mariano Mondragon had the T'boli-Manobo ratio reversed. By his reckoning, most were Manobo, but there were also four T'boli he knew quite well from Lake Sebu. Oswald Iten had told me that what had made him investigate the Tasaday were the many contradictions in the story. I too thought there were contradictions, but there seemed to be many more contradictions among the various hoax stories flying around than among the proponents of authenticity. Give me status quo journalism if the alternative is simply to prove a point at all costs.

I asked Judge Mondragon if he had played with the Tasaday as a child; he said he hadn't though he knew who they were and he knew their names. There was Landayong, Ampong, Flek, and Bibing. Manda had made them wear G-strings, and these were the people pictured in the photos. I asked him if he'd recognize any of them. Maybe. I showed him the pictures in Headland's book. None of them looked familiar. Here was yet a completely new set of Tasaday names, of which there seemed an almost endless number.

The judge told me that Jerome Bailen had sent his father money to go to the UP conference, where he'd been a key witness along with the Boones and Tanedo. The judge's wife had said that he'd been quite angered by his father's reversal, but the judge told me that this was the first he'd ever heard of it.

The Tasaday were T'boli, Judge Mondragon told me. When I mentioned something about their discovery, he interjected "their alleged discovery."

Then a fascinating thing happened. The judge became intrigued with Headland's book. No one in the area had seen it before. He also wanted to know more about my project; he wanted to know what I found out. "You let us know the results," he said, "and then we'll find out who's telling the truth." He wanted to take me to Lake Sebu to see if any of the people he had mentioned were still living; he thought they were. And he wanted to go with me next time to see the Tanedos in Maitum. His family had known them too.

"Their language, it was different from T'boli?" he asked, and I directed him to Laurie Reid's chapter. He wanted to know how long Reid had spent with the Tasaday.

I told him.

"Six months?" he said. "I think that's long enough to discover if they were really not Tasadays."

In 2000 Laurie Reid put portions of the long-lost 1972 cave tapes on the Internet, allowing others to analyze the linguistic evidence. Tom Headland asked several linguists, all speakers of Cotabato Manobo, independently of one another, to do just that. None of the four scholars (Clay Johnston, Ross Errington, Douglas Fraiser, and Meg Fraiser) collaborated with one another.[2] They all agreed that what they heard was a close dialect of Cotabato Manobo. Errington thought that "our Cotabato Manobo neighbors would . . . understand most of the oral text, although they would probably say that it has variations and is not 'pure' or 'good' Manobo." Douglas Fraiser, a "community development specialist" with SIL, seemed to think that while some word usage and definitions differed slightly from Cotabato dialects he knew, the majority of Tasaday words were either "identical or closely related" to Cotabato Manobo words. He added that in 1990 "some of the Manobo [people] we know visited the Tasaday people and got to talk with them for a short while. Some felt they had a hard time communicating. My impression from the Manobo men's reactions to meeting the Tasaday, and from what I have seen of the Tasaday language, is that they were having no more trouble understanding Tasaday than I once had understanding certain British dialects."[3]

When Elkins reviewed the transcripts posted on the Internet, he wrote, "Virtually none of the inflections of the verbs look anything at all like T'boli," and he too believed that the language reflected in the transcripts was "virtually identical to Cotabato Manobo."

"Case closed," Tom wrote in an e-mail to me after Elkins's comments.

Not quite, I thought. While this testimony demolished the notion that these were people whose first language was T'boli, but who pretended to be Manobo (one should note Reid's contention that such speakers, even if fluent in Manobo, would invariably borrow from T'boli, their first language, not to mention the fact that their inflections would be different), there was still the notion of *tigtu kagi*, or the Tasaday's true language, to be considered. By 1972, the time of the tape recordings, the Tasaday had been in frequent contact with their Blit neighbors. For instance, the widely reported word for "good" or "beautiful," *mafion*, was *metelol* in *tigtu kagi*, as I had been told on my second visit and then had corroborated with Laurie Reid. Likewise, botanical names like *dalikan* (a kind of fruit) and *seyal* had matched the names unique to the Tasaday recorded by Yen thirty years earlier. This suggests that the Tasaday rapidly learned many words from their neighbors in Blit, much as Carlos Fernandez and David Baradas quickly learned Tasaday words within only a week of contact. As Reid suggests in Headland's book, the dialect of their neighbors would have had a higher status to the Tasaday than their own,[4] but regardless of why or how long they had been speaking the dialect of their neighbors, one couldn't assume that the speech of the Tasaday recorded in 1972 was what they would have spoken prior to 1971.

I needed to make one more trip—to Hawai'i. I e-mailed Laurie Reid to ask him if he'd seen results from Rebecca Cann's DNA research. He hadn't heard anything in quite a while, so he called and made an appointment for us to meet her. I was experiencing a new feeling about my research; let's call it dread. I had come pretty certainly to the conclusion by now that the Tasaday were no hoax as such and that the real hoax had been perpetrated by some of the very same people who decried the Tasaday as fake. But DNA, that was incontrovertible, wasn't it? I felt confident it would show that Mefalu and Dul were not related, but what if they were? Why should I care one way or the other? Still, I did. What could I do about my biases at this point besides admit them?

Laurie and I met with Cann in her office. The news was disappointing, not because the DNA proved Salazar correct, but because, as Dr. Cann patiently explained to us, to prove the relationship of two people, one would need a much larger sampling of DNA from the population of Blit. Laurie had collected upward of fifty samples from the Tasaday and the people of Blit, but that wasn't enough to be conclusive.

When we returned to Laurie's office, I told him about my map, the one from the early fifties showing human structures of some kind relatively near the Tasaday caves. We spread the map on his desk, and he studied it. I expressed some regret that I had even found it.

"You can't hold anything back," Laurie said, looking up at me.

"No, of course not," I said.

Like Tom Headland, with whom I'd previously shared the discovery, Laurie thought the map indeed had significance. He wondered if it would be possible to match the arrival of Dafal's father, Mindal, to the approximate date of the maps.

He popped one of the cave tapes from 1972 in his tape deck and turned it on. The small office filled with the echoing sound of the caves and the ever-present cacophony of bugs. For ten minutes at least we listened to that tape, neither of us saying a word.

The next day I brought Belayem's stone tool to archaeologist Bion Griffin's office. Griffin was the director of the Center for Southeast Asian Studies and a Philippine specialist. While he wasn't directly involved with the Tasaday, he knew most of the players and had written a review of Headland's book that had been critical of the hoax proponents.

As I sat in his office, Bion silently studied the tool for maybe five minutes, turning it over in his hands like an appraiser. I felt as if I were on *Antiques Roadshow*. Did I have something valuable or not? In some sense, I had nothing to worry about. Even if it was fake, a step up from a rubber prop on the set of *The Clan of the Cave Bear*, it would still be an "authentic" Tasaday stone tool.

He examined the hafting. "Well, the rattan was cut with a steel knife," he said. "The way it's split. Nicely split. The same can't be said for the stone tool. It's not much good for cutting. Clearly, some flakes have been removed, but whether that was done by a human or not is anybody's guess. Could have been done by a rockfall. Doesn't do much for a cutting edge. The cutting edge seems worn and rounded, but it doesn't look worn down from cutting. Quite worn and rounded. You see something like this in a lot of riverbeds, where the rock is worn down. If I picked this stone up without the handle, I wouldn't be able to say for sure whether or not this was a human tool. It couldn't be used for real pounding, but it could be used to bash open nuts and things like that. You could clunk an animal on the head." He laughed. "It's got some edge on it. It's got some smoking on it. Unless someone went to real pains to fabricate it, there's no reason to think it's a fake, but the rattan part was cut with a steel knife. I suppose if it was kept in a dry, smoky environment, it could have stayed in this shape. The stone had been blackened by smoke from a fire. At the same time, wood-boring bugs eat this kind of thing. It had to be curated in some way. If it's old, it had to be purposefully kept because otherwise the rattan would be eaten up. At best, it's a crushing edge. Funny it hasn't deteriorated more."

Belayem had told me that he used it to break open *dalikan*, and I'd seen him retrieve the tool from one of the upper caves. He said that he'd had it since the death of his father. That accorded with Bion's appraisal, though there was the matter of the rattan's being cut with a knife and the fact that the stone could have been worn down from a rockfall.

Bion handed the tool back to me and went to his phone. He wanted to call in the university's archaeology lab manager, Jo Lynn Guiness. He wondered what she would say about the tool if we showed it to her and asked for her opinion without telling her a thing about it.

She joined us in Bion's office. Bion introduced me, and I asked her if she'd give me her impressions of the tool. Understandably, she seemed a little perplexed by the lack of any context. "What is it you'd like to know about this?" she asked cautiously.

"Your opinion of the crafting of it, what it could have been used for . . ."

She said it was typical of a lot of stone tools that have been taken out of a stream or riverbed. "They've taken some flakes off the edge to make a sharp edge, for either cutting or scraping tools. The way it's been hafted it looks like it would have been used as sort of like a cleaver . . . or a small ax or hatchet. The sharp edge that was created on it has been worn away, and it looks like it's been ground along one edge. It's probably, very possibly, used as a scraper. If you look at it, you can see sort of striations in there that get worn into the stone when it's used like that. If that's not the case, then at some point somebody probably tried to sharpen it on something like a grindstone to make this edge sharp again. But my guess is it's been used as a cleaver-ax and doubled as a scraper." She added that she didn't think it came from Hawai'i, that it could have been used to chop up meat. "Or possibly plant stuff."

"Why is it black like that?" I asked.

"My first guess would be that it's just dirty and greasy, and if it was used as a cleaver, that would explain it; it's grease and ash and stuff like that. You know, charcoal and stuff like that makes it black and a lot of hand stuff . . . This is really typical of what would happen to something over time if it's been used for that kind of a purpose."

"A rock wouldn't naturally be like that without use?"

"You mean, the damage along the edge."

"The damage and the blackness."

"Not without being handled or something like that. It would have dirt on it if it was in the ground, but it would have to be somewhere where there was some charcoal or ashy, greasy stuff to adhere to it like that probably. Unless somebody deliberately made it that way to make it look like something."

I laughed. She *would* have to add that. I should have kept a straight face. "That's entirely possible, too," she said, looking at me and smiling. "You could have made this yesterday and brought it in, too. But it's what happens over time when something gets used."

I didn't want her to think that I was trying to fool her or make her the butt of some practical joke, so I told her its origin.

Yes, she'd heard of the Tasaday, but she was still concentrating on the tool. "The one other thing I was going to tell you about this," she said, "is that there's a very strong possibility that this was probably used first for a while before it was hafted."

"Oh, that's interesting," Bion said. "Because I was worrying about the hafting's being in too good a condition."

"Well, it may have been rehafted," she said.

"That's a good point."

"But my guess is that this was used simply as a cobble tool first and was hafted later."

"Held by hand, you mean," Bion said. "That's an excellent point."

"It would be entirely possible," she continued, "and it would make a lot of sense if they had some particular reason for wanting to keep it; say it was Grandfather's or something like that, then it would have been rehafted any number of times over the course of time. However, that kind of thing shouldn't be that hard to replace, and so it would be more likely that it would be something that they were wanting to hang on to for some particular reason."

"Sentimental reason?"

"You could just go down to the stream and pick up another cobble and whack off a couple of flakes and have a better sharper tool again."

I met Doug Yen for lunch the next day. He'd recently had heart surgery, but he seemed in good spirits, and he was interested in my research. I told him the *bangi'* leaf story that Edith Terry had told me, about Manda's telling the Tasaday that they looked better in leaves than rags. Doug laughed. "It's natural to want to accentuate those things that make someone seem 'primitive.'" He told me the story of a famous anthropologist he didn't want to embarrass by naming, someone he respected tremendously, who used to bring out the cameras whenever the people he was studying stripped off their clothes. But when they put them back on to go to town, the cameras were stowed. "It's natural," he said.

Inevitably, we once again discussed his fieldwork with the Tasaday. What disconcerted Yen, even now, was that he had not been informed of Baradas and Fernandez's experience at the caves before he went in. He believed that Manda and the others had been afraid to tell him, that they were worried the shooting at the caves would scare him off. If Yen's hunch was correct, then it flew in the face of the idea that PANAMIN *wanted* to scare off anthropologists. Why would they bring Yen in and not tell him about the very ploy that they had supposedly used to frighten off Baradas and Fernandez? I was starting to believe more in Kabayo every day.

Manda was disorganized, disdainful, and impatient about field research, but to say that he tried to block research seems questionable. From the beginning he had tried to bring in the most qualified specialists, not "second-rate researchers," as Iten deemed them. Many of the scientists he brought in stayed for a short time because of prior commitments elsewhere, not because he wanted them out of the area. Yen, whose specialty was not Philippine botany, had insisted that a top-notch Philippine botanist as well as a top-notch linguist accompany him. He received both. That Richard Elkins took ill soon after he arrived and had to leave because his special diet had not been delivered seems evidence once more of Manda's rich kid indifference, not of a nefarious scheme to drive scientists away.

None of this rules out Elizalde's exploitation of the Tasaday. Yen and I talked about Nance too in this regard. They'd had a falling-out in the early nineties. Yen had told Nance that if he were asked whether Nance had exploited the Tasaday with his books and lectures and films, he wouldn't be able to say he hadn't.

I mentioned to Yen that since Elizalde's death, Nance had set up all kinds of aid programs for the Tasaday. I said I wanted to be sensitive to the exploitation issue, but I hoped that someday a clinic could be set up in Blit, not just for the Tasaday but for the T'boli and others in the area; the Tasaday weren't the only ones who needed medical attention.

Yen wasn't impressed by my well-meaning and admittedly empty words. He said he wasn't much for charity, in any case. "Once they get healthy, then what?" he asked. "It's not just health, you know. There's a lot that comes with it. Maybe next they want a TV. Over the years, throughout my so-called career, I've touched a lot of people. I've had a great time, and I hope they had a good time, too. Some of my colleagues say I'm generous. When I went into a place, I left everything behind. I sent some of them to school. But I can't support them cradle to the grave. After they're done with school, what have I given them? Dissatisfaction. They want the things I have, this shirt even. I called up the son of one of my main informants in the Solomons. He's been in jail several times, and when I called, I got demands. They wanted a house built in Honiara. I can't do that."

Chastened a bit, I told him that I wasn't trying to be sentimental or patronizing.

"I know that," he said.

I suggested that maybe in the same way it was natural for someone to want to accentuate those things that made someone seem "primitive," it was also natural to want to help people who seemed to be struggling. "When you go in there," I said, "you want to do something."

"You know what this conversation reminds me of?" he said, smiling. "This reminds me of talking to Manda. He used to say these things. Inside, he had a tender spot."

There's little doubt that the Tasaday, as "discovered" by Elizalde in 1971, had become a media construction by 1972. They were not the anthropological find of the century, nor had they been isolated for a thousand years or more. But this transformation was not all

Elizalde's doing; it fed a hungry public's imagination. The Tasaday were pseudo-archaics in Claude Lévi-Strauss's terminology, a small group that had fled into the forest to escape an epidemic of some sort. By 1986 they had become what anthropologist Richard Fox calls professional primitives.

When Manda told the Tasaday they should wear leaf G-strings, was this evidence of a hoax, the rhetoric of tribal pride, or enforced primitivism? When the Tasaday were given rice by the T'boli, was this a cover-up, a means of keeping them at the caves or simply a case of the T'boli's wanting to share with the poor, as is customary?

There is another unanswered question. What happened to the "missing boy" David Baradas had found in a photograph? Writes Nance: "[I]t became increasingly intriguing to consider where this information might lead. What had happened to the boy?"[5] Berreman scoffs at Nance's bewilderment over the boy's fate: "An obvious answer did not occur to him: I would guess that in dispatching people into the forest to pose as cave men for the occasional batch of visitors one boy chanced to be unavailable or disinclined, and another of similar age and description seemed to whomever [sic] rounded up the cast to be a suitable substitute. Little boys, they probably reasoned, look pretty much alike to strangers. But when one is perpetrating a charade, one must pay attention to detail—otherwise, one might give it away, and it seems to me that this was a slip that did exactly that."[6]

In order to believe this, you have to ignore the consistent behavior of the Tasaday themselves and the testimony of Elkins, Nance, Yen, and Fernandez regarding the Tasaday, not to mention their testimony on Elizalde and his motives. An equally plausible explanation about the missing boy is that the Tasaday's privacy was constantly being invaded, and they didn't feel obligated to offer information they deemed private. Nance described Lobo's reaction when he was shown the photograph: "[He] looked, frowned, jumped up, and dashed to the caves. Mai followed . . . and met Dul, who already had heard a report from Lobo. She said they would tell what happened to the boy when everyone was present."[7] But when the boy was mentioned later at the caves, Dul and Belayem switched into a "strange language," a kind of pig Latin. Nance writes: "It was almost like a code and sounded similar to children's pig Latin in that each word had a similar ending. The Tasaday's ending was *uff*. Mai and Igna puzzled over this; they could not understand a single word. Soon, other Tasaday joined in the secret conversation."[8]

Belayem later told Mai that the boy's name was Ukan and that he was the older brother of Odo'. Later still they were told the boy had been variously "lost" in a storm, or had simply become sick and died. Since he was dead, the Tasaday did not want to speak of him. It saddened them to talk of the dead.[9]

If we look at the moment they started to use this secret language (*nafnaf*) around their visitors, we might remember that Baradas and Fernandez had gained some fluency on their visit. Then Elkins had shocked the Tasaday by suddenly asking them questions in Manobo though he had hardly uttered a word in their presence prior to this.

Manda observed that they obviously didn't want to talk about the boy. Berreman's scenario would have us believe the Tasaday, panicked at being found out, had to stall until they came up with a plausible explanation, or one was supplied to them by the boss.

Berreman's view is supported in some ways by Baradas, but Fernandez disagrees. He says: "I think the embarrassment there was not being able to account for somebody who they claimed had died. That death is a major event."

Time and again the Tasaday had said they didn't like being asked so many questions. They said so on the tapes. They said so to their visitors. Naturally, they couldn't answer some questions; they didn't want to answer others. Imagine someone you barely know asking you about all your relatives, where you live, where you go to be alone, what your eating habits are, what you believe and why, and how your son died. You might tell him to mind his own business. You might tell him to go to hell.

"They just sent the word that he died," Baradas says. "And there [was] . . . no warning, no nothing—before I discovered the boy was missing."

"I still contend," Fernandez says, "that there is a group that call themselves the Tasaday, that they are not T'boli. The point of contention that we have may be you know, the interpretation of field data and all that and the use of descriptive labels like Stone Age. As far as I'm concerned, those items can be debated, but my concern now is that, having written them off as a hoax, what's going to happen to the people?"

Conceding that the Tasaday might not have been completely fabricated, Baradas says, "It's just that the way they then describe them as having had no contact with the outside world—it's probably stretching the point, and that's what they were trying to hide, trying to make them appear to have gone back in time. It's a very devastating thing, because that one factor alone will totally negate all the romanticizing that the whole world had surrounded them with."

On this point it's hard to disagree.

We'll never know who the Tasaday were in 1971, but the original reports, though certainly exaggerated, were not outrageous. In South America in 1971, for instance, there were groups that used primarily stone tools. Elsewhere people lived part of the time in rock shelters. The caves of the Tasaday certainly seemed warmer and drier to me than the leaky huts in Magtu Inilingan and elsewhere. Oswald Iten wondered why women from Blit would choose to leave their comfortable huts and live in the caves with their Tasaday husbands. Carlos Fernandez suggested to me that the Tasaday were celebrities in the area; they received not only attention but material goods as well, and this would be reason enough to follow them. Perhaps. If the Tasaday took shelter in caves around the forest, they certainly didn't stay in one place. Yet I strongly doubt the Tasaday were ever captive at the caves. Elizalde didn't need to order them to stay at the caves. For the Tasaday, it was not so much an order as a tacit expectation or, perhaps the simplest explanation, that they had guests.

Bilengan told me that before Dafal the Tasaday ate *biking*, *natek*, and fruits. Yen found *biking* scarce near the caves on his visit, contrary to Fernandez and Lynch's earlier report that it had been abundant: "Fernandez counted eight recently-dug *bikin* [sic] holes in an area 50 meters square."[10] Yen, Fernandez, and others observed no agricultural plots.

The Tasaday wore whatever was available to them; sometimes they wore *bangi'* leaves, and when they were given cloth, they wore that, too. They had some metal technology, with which they cut trees to make *natek*. They sometimes used stone tools for small tasks, such as opening nuts and fruits. They did not call themselves the Tasaday, but that's what they call themselves now.

The Tasaday were not residents of Maitum, frequenters of the market in Lake Sebu, or even longtime residents of Blit. Mindanao might be relatively small (though the second-largest island in the

Philippines), but the area of the Tasaday is rugged and mountainous and was covered in large swaths of rain forest in 1971 and before. While South Cotabato is not the Amazon, neither is it Central Park. One need only to think back on the World War II Japanese stragglers who avoided detection for thirty years or more on the Philippine island of Mindoro and on Guam.

To me, Belayam summed it up best: *If you think we are good, we also treat other people good. If you think about us that we're bad, we can also be bad.*

The journalists who followed Joey Lozano to see the Tasaday in the mid-eighties were clearly duped. As I was, initially. The true hoax was perpetrated by a confederation of sympathetic interests. There were those who wanted the reserve's resources, those who hated Elizalde and Marcos and wanted to discredit them, those who were jealous of the scientists and journalists who were allowed to visit the Tasaday, those who wanted to advance their academic careers, those who wanted fame. Nearly every evil motive ascribed to Manda, in fact, better fits many of those who called the Tasaday a hoax. At the center of it all was Joey Lozano.

Iten wrote of Nance that he either "knew about the fraud or else was simply not capable of grasping it. Neither conclusion is flattering."[11] But the sentiment seems to apply more to Moses and him than to Nance.

Iten and Moses in fact became Lozano's unabashed patrons, highlighted perhaps by Lozano's naming his child, born in the late eighties, Moses Oswaldo Lozano, a child whose schooling the pair paid for. Moses especially never budged an inch from the contention that the Tasaday are mostly T'boli because to do so would necessitate the painful admission that Lozano had set them up. Lozano had insisted to me that Mai Tuan wanted to "maintain the original story" at all costs (utilizing his so-called Bantay Tasaday and such), but Mai hadn't seemed interested in doing that at all when I'd visited him the first time at his office in Manila. He'd acted almost completely unguarded, admitting to me that the original stories about the Tasaday had been exaggerated. Lozano was the one, it seemed, who wanted to maintain his own hoax story at all costs.

The tantalizing question is not whether Dafal or Mai Tuan

arranged to have the *Stern* team kidnapped but whether Lozano had anything to do with it. On March 31, 1986, as Dafal was returning with provisions for the *Stern* reporters, Lozano stopped Dafal and interviewed him—before Iten had filed his hoax story. The hunter seems not to have acted especially tight-lipped or guarded, telling Lozano what he wanted to know, intent, it seems, simply on getting supplies for the *Stern* group. Lozano and Iten initially considered *Stern* their competitors, not friends, and neither had an idea exactly what the angle of the *Stern* story would be. Perhaps, led as they were by Dafal, they'd corroborate the original story. Most likely for this reason, Lozano asserted in his communications at the time that the *Stern* group's visit to the caves must have been arranged for payment, the intent obviously to belittle any alternate conclusion the *Stern* team might reach (i.e., the Tasaday are the Real Thing). He was sure it was all a hoax orchestrated by Mai, Elizalde, Igna, and Dafal, and he wanted to reassure Iten, who apparently was a little worried as of April 17, 1986, that what he had seen was the "truth." The day after Dafal ran into Lozano on his way to get supplies, the *Stern* team was kidnapped by people Lozano initially identified as Muslim rebels under Kumander Tigre and later as a "Lost Command."[12]

If the Tasaday story teaches us anything, it's that what seems cut-and-dry to one person is a magic show to someone else. Perhaps this explains how, if not why, Bishop Gutierrez, the man who first led Iten to the hoax story in 1986, could later do an about-face and say the Tasaday were no hoax after all.*

Iten, unaware of the history of conflict between Elizalde and the people of Surallah in particular, either didn't have the time or saw no reason to investigate the myriad motives of the people telling him the Tasaday were a hoax. The region brimmed with anti-Elizalde and anti-Marcos feelings, especially among the Christians, who still felt deep resentment over Elizalde's meddling in their battles over tribal lands. Iten was crossing a minefield: the many interest groups, the logging, the history of violence.

In September 1988 Datu' Galang swore a second statement for Manda's lawyers in Manila. The translation reads in part as follows: "[I swear that] on November 11, 1987, I executed a sworn statement admitting that the statements I made before the camera to Tom Jar-

---

*In conversation with Oswald Iten.

riel of 20/20 were false and were taught to me by Joey Lozano. That upon my return home after making my sworn statement, I noticed that the New People's Army leaders in my area as well as the Muslim Datu' Datun became hostile to me and my men."*

According to Joey Lozano, in late August or September 1988, Datu' Galang's brother was killed by the Bangsa Moro Army of the MILF because of a "misunderstanding."[13] To borrow Iten's rhetoric, is it purely a coincidence that Datu' Galang's brother was killed by Muslim guerrillas the same month he made his statement?

"In the mountains of South Cotabato," Iten later pronounced, "armed men convinced everybody who had made a 'wrong' statement to recant. One of Datu' Galang's brothers was shot dead."[14]

Unless Datu' Galang's brothers were used frequently for target practice, then Iten failed to mention who these armed men were and what exactly constituted a "wrong" statement. Maybe the "wrong" statement was that the Tasaday weren't a hoax. Iten conveniently declined to specify, but the implication was that these were Mai Tuan's men, though clearly they were not.

Iten saw what he wanted to see. What first started as a somewhat remote connection to the Tasaday on Datu' Galang's part—yes, there were some people who lived near the caves, but he hadn't seen them as described—soon transformed to an insider's knowledge. People had been asked to stay in the caves many times, Datu' Galang asserted. Iten, who by this time "firmly believed" the Tasaday to be a hoax, took confirmation where he could find it.

I tend to be skeptical of conspiracies, preferring to believe that most of us are too busy bumbling through life to do something as time-consuming as to conspire. But I'm as susceptible as anyone to paranoia and delusion if someone with an authoritative voice and an armload of insinuations works on me long enough. Such a person was Judith Moses, who perhaps more than anyone influenced the course of the controversy after the first charges were made. She made sensational charges that were patently false.

She was even bolder in her assertions than Iten, suggesting that

*As for the affidavits, which were collected for various lawsuits and the congressional hearings, they have to be viewed with some suspicion, tainted as they are by Manda's methods of obtaining them. Still, they contain enough telling details and places of convergence between the documents and various other testimonies I've gathered, as well as my own experience, that I don't think they can be discounted entirely either.

the Santa Cruz Mission turned into some kind of CIA front, that the agency gave it money through USAID grants to become a "listening post." When I gently pointed out the quaintness of her CIA theory, given the fact that the USAID grants made to Santa Cruz in the mid-eighties were contingent on matching funds, she seemed unfazed. "If it was an intelligence operation," I wondered, "would they do something like that, say it was contingent on matching funds? If they wanted the intelligence . . . if they wanted it to be a listening post."

"Why not?" she asked.

"I just think that it would be in their interest to promote it, and so they would just dump the money on it," I said.

There's something charming in the idea of the CIA's requiring matching funds before authorizing money for covert operations.

"I think it's a great idea," she insisted. "I mean, if I was running an intelligence operation, I think it would be a great idea." So wedded was she to this vision that she failed to see its inherent absurdity.

I felt Moses's influence most strongly around the time of my first expedition to see the Tasaday and in my quest for the map that I had such difficulty obtaining. I was sure someone was blocking me. One day, after my return to Manila from Mindanao, I walked into the office of a friend, Patrick Parsons. I had told him previously of my difficulties in securing the map I wanted from NAMRIA. He told me he didn't think he'd have a problem getting the map at all, that he could send his driver to buy one; he'd bought such maps quite often. And that was what happened. Patrick easily obtained several maps I asked for, including the one of the Tasaday area, minus bombing grids of course, and in color. The saga of the map was my own psycho drama all along, fueled by the suggestions of others, delusion, and paranoia.

Even in circumstances favorable to the hoax proponents, such as the UP conference, the truth had a nasty habit of slipping out. One need only recall Joel Boone's statement that Udol (Lobo) wouldn't leave the mountains with George Tanedo. "Sorry," Jerry Malayang, the translator, had told the audience, "but he mentioned something about Mr. Iten, Oswald Iten. According to Udol, they were waiting the promises Mr. Oswald Iten made to Lobo or Udol. That's the reason why they can't bring him down." Iten didn't promise Lobo anything, but Lozano certainly did. Joey was able to control the situation because he understood English and Ilonggo. Iten had no idea what Joey was telling the Tasaday (such as his remark to Bilengan that Elizalde had left the country. Joey, according to various testimonies, told Bilengan and others that Elizalde had died and that Iten would be their new benefactor). Consequently, George Tanedo entered the picture and added his influence and coercion. Without a doubt, others aided Tanedo and Lozano. Christian Adler had claimed that an anthropologist was needed to aid Elizalde in creating *his* hoax, but the same charge is more readily leveled at Tanedo and his group. At least one anthropologist who knew something about genealogy likely aided Tanedo. Amy Rara and Emmanuel Nabayra had written in Headland's book:

> Kafal said he was offered incentives by George Tanedo to impersonate Tasaday Mahayag. Two of his neighbors, the half-brothers Fidlo Swing and Yabis Baham, are also identified in the Poseur charts as "Gintuy" and "Adug" respectively. Yabis said that Fidlo accepted George Tanedo's offer of land in Tasaday in return for Fidlo's impersonating Gintuy. Then Fidlo persuaded Yabis to impersonate Adug. . . . Tinda Dayaw and Udol Lambayen, father-in-law and son-in-law, both farmers, . . . said they were approached by Lobong Badang, a T'boli security guard from a Maitum logging firm, who offered both of them permanent jobs as forest guards in return for playing "Bilangan" [*sic*] and "Lobo."[15]

These all were real people, but not the same people as the Tasaday. On my second visit Lobo, Gintuy, and Adug told me, as they had told others, that Datu' Galang had come up with the fake names for the Tasaday: Udol, Tinda, Fidlo. Again, this was certainly at Joey's urging. Galang went along with Joey because he too was made promises by Lozano, of money, goods, possibly a share of the reserve. Tanedo had his own interests to serve, primarily logging and mining. When Gintuy recalled his name, Fidlo, he laughed, and I asked him why he was laughing. He said he was laughing "because it's not his name."*

The reason I trusted Belayem when he confirmed the names and

---

*This was recorded in Kibang in the DAR guesthouse on a rainy day preceding our hike to Blit. The translators were Amy Rara and Joe Igid's nephew, Melel. The Tasaday all seemed relaxed, and the questions were asked and answered in a relaxed manner, quite a contrast with Bilengan and Lolo''s manner in Tubak when I visited with Joey.

faces of the Tasaday and the poseurs in Headland's book was that he didn't know English and hadn't known I was going to show him the book. The reason I trusted Bilengan and Lolo' when they told me that they'd been tricked to come see me in January 1999 was that neither knew the questions I was going to ask, and both independently told me the same thing.

Identities all around are a puzzle. Who, for instance, was Elizir Boone, the man who had been killed in a police raid some months after dramatically testifying at the UP conference? He was a T'boli for certain, but was he a relative of the Tasaday, and were they really T'boli, as he had claimed? If so, then the Tasaday were indeed an unqualified hoax, and Manda's agents had undoubtedly murdered him to stop him from speaking out further. But if the Tasaday were truly Manobo and not T'boli, and Elizir Boone had no relation to them at all, then someone had obviously coerced *him*. The likely candidate, in this case, would be his relative and traveling companion Uncle George Tanedo, for whom he had worked previously as a chain saw operator. His death in a police shoot-out some months later, which so outraged Iten, Berreman, and Moses, might have had nothing to do with the Tasaday. Boone had a long criminal record, and lying about his identity, it seems, was the least of his offenses.

Lobo was first introduced as Udol (or Odol) on Oswald Iten's expedition. Joey and Datu' Galang of course provided the translations. Udol existed and was most likely even present at Tubak. Asking Galang to provide new names for the Tasaday was a bold and inventive move on Joey's part, but one that eventually had to backfire. By giving the Tasaday new names and calling them the so-called Tasaday, Lozano boxed himself into a pretty tight corner. Perhaps he didn't realize he'd be riding the Tasaday train for so long.

Besides his lucrative business of leading in various gullible Western journalists to Tubak, Lozano soon found his entire career hinging on his initial deception. Not only did Iten and Moses support his child's education, but Moses championed him among Western journalists and Filipinos alike. Lozano went from struggling as a writer for Father Rex's diocesan newspaper *Concern* to writing articles for national newspapers and gaining an international reputation as a human rights activist. But initially his motives were most likely ideological. Levita Duhaylungsod and David Hyndman write that the "label of communist or communist sympathizer is conveniently used to discredit those who have attempted to expose the hoax. Joey Lozano, the local journalist who broke the hoax story, was so accused during the Philippine Congressional proceedings on the scandal." But the label in this case fits. Galang and Joey apparently first met at an NPA rally in which Joey exhorted the crowd to support their "brothers in the mountains." The local church, which was heavily anti-Marcos, set up Iten's expedition in the first place. Joey was the assigned guide and translator. One must also remember NPA Commander Remy hanging around the 20/20 shoot.

I should add that in my opinion, John Nance has taken far too many hits for his involvement with the Tasaday. Nearly every kernel of the hoax busters' most reasonable arguments—from the fact that the Tasaday wore cloth when first contacted, to the shooting at the caves and the missing boy—all were reported faithfully by Nance. Yes, he believed, and still believes, that the Tasaday have something valuable to teach. So do I, though I suspect we disagree somewhat on the lesson. Nance's loyalty to the Tasaday has come at great personal and professional sacrifice. John, as the Tasaday told me, is the only one who hasn't broken his promises to them.

In his provocative book *Thinking Through Cultures*, anthropologist Richard A. Shweder defends romanticism as a worthy view for the social scientist, not as something antithetical to science:

> Romanticism shares with skeptical empiricism the view that the senses and logic alone cannot bridge that gap between existence and pure being. Left to their own devices, all that the senses and logic can see is a mindless nature, "fallen and dead." Transcendental things are beyond their scope. To make contact with the really real, the inspired (= divinelike) imagination of human beings must be projected out to reality; or, alternatively, the gods must descend to earth.
>
> It is the doctrine of romanticism that existence is best appreciated (that is, understood *and* experienced) as a sensual manifestation of the transcendent, and that time and space, history and local variation in color (and culture), deserve to be

examined inspirationally, and artfully for diverse signs of our di-
vinity.[16]

There's a proper time for irony and a proper time for romanticism,
and the story of the Tasaday leaves room for both. The romantic pro-
jection that the early visitors imposed on the Tasaday are similar to
those imposed on small-scale cultures by anthropologists since anthropology began. When, in 1968, the organizers of the Man the
Hunter Conference, Irvin DeVore and Richard Lee, warned participants not to see the conference as anything but an "exercise in logic,"
they were more or less ignored like the disclaimer in the front of an
autobiographical novel warning that any similarity between characters
and the actual people, living or dead, is purely coincidental. The conference excited its participants in large part because it allowed them
to project romantically backward in time, using as models the hunter-
gatherer societies that still peppered the fringes of the earth. More
than one of these anthropologists exaggerated the link between the
groups they had studied and a past they imagined. How many anthropologists photographed their informants dressed in traditional garb
and quickly stowed their camera gear when those same people
changed into Western dress to go to town? How many ignored or
fudged data that would have shown the hunter-gatherers they thought
so isolated had been in contact for years with their agriculturalist
neighbors and beyond?
The gods have not descended to earth, it seems, in many years. No
deus ex machina, no helicopter at the edge of a clearing. What's
called for sometimes is for humans to transcend their humanness, to
come to the edge of a place they've never been and take a look. But
most of the hoax proponents could not see beyond their own petty designs, their own pieties.
And so a fair number of respected anthropologists were eager to
jump on the hoax bandwagon with a gusto that seemed to go beyond
the Tasaday. Perhaps the scientists imagined that the Angel of Illegit-
imacy and Irrelevance would pass over their house if they scape-
goated the Tasaday. Even Richard Lee, who had exaggerated the
"isolation" of the !Kung San of the Kalahari, had stood up in Zagreb
and thrown his support behind Salazar's dubious genealogies. Today
some will tell you that anthropologists never took the Tasaday seri-

ously, and it's true that finding one today who admits anything but disbelief or skepticism at the time is like trying to find a baby boomer who admits to having voted for Richard Nixon. But anthropologist Leslie Sponsel, in an informal sampling of anthropology texts of the 1970s, found mention of the Tasaday in 35 percent of them. Not bad for a group that received so little scientific scrutiny. To the scientific community of the seventies, the Tasaday were a question mark, not, by any means, a laughingstock.

E ven in the most wide-open spaces, we can't truly know what's coming down upon us. In Hemingway's "The Snows of Kilamanjaro," a dying adventurer, a philanderer who has lost the ideals of his youth, imagines in delirium that he's flying in a plane toward the enormous mountain. The last image is the tiny plane, his soul, lost against the huge backdrop of the great mystery. Such a death, I think, would be a mercy, and perhaps Manda had similar thoughts in his final moments. Imagination sometimes is all that we're left with.

Bibang was the first man. There were no other people but Bibang. He carried his home, his cave, on his back, and a stone ax and his *tuyang*, when he suddenly came upon the place of the Tasaday. This man Bibang dropped his *tuyang*, and it ran off.

Bibang followed his *tuyang*, which was chasing a wild boar, and eventually Bibang grew tired and sat down to rest. He said, "This is my cave. I shall leave it here. I shall follow the sound of my *tuyang*."

He came to a stream where there was a spirit. Bibang wanted to pass over this river. The spirit wouldn't let him pass. He said, "We have to have a contest." Bibang dropped another cave from under his arm, and he won his contest with the spirit.

Bibang had two wives. Their names were Fuwéh and Sidakwéh. Like Bibang, they had unusual powers. One of the wives made people with noses that were so sharply upturned they drowned when it rained. The other fixed their noses. One was known as Bibang's good wife, and the other as his bad wife.

This is where they lived, in the special place. Their only thoughts were of food. "Our food is what we were looking for, the fruit of trees, the fruit of rattan. If it is eaten by monkeys, it is also eaten by us. If monkeys do not eat it, we also do not eat it." Their main food was *bik-*

ing, a type of wild yam. They had little metal or cloth, except for a few brass earrings and what they were able to trade for with the people they sometimes met in the forest. The main things they feared were *fugu*, a disease of which they had a vague memory, and *ngotngot*, witches or evil spirits that drank blood. There was a bird in the forest named *limokon* that warned them about such troubles. When they heard *limokon*, they did not venture from their caves. If they heard it in the morning, they delayed their trips until the afternoon. If they saw or heard it in the afternoon, they waited until the next day.[17] The thing they feared the most was thunder, which their ancestors heard sometimes, too, and when they heard it, they stayed in their caves and covered their ears. They did not know where it came from.[18]

There were two other small groups, the Tasafeng and the Sanduka, and the descendants of Bibang, Fuwéh, and Sidakwéh found wives among these other people. But one day the Tasafeng and Sanduka no longer came to the meeting place in the forest.

Their ancestors had foretold that someday a man, a bringer of good fortune, would come. The ancestors said they should live in the forest and "suffer" until the good man showed up.* They didn't know anything about this man except that they should wait for him.

Out digging *biking* one day, Salibuko met a man who called himself Mindal. He was with his son, Dafal. Over time this man and his son returned and gave Salibuko and the others things to wear in their ears and tools that were better than the ones they had always used. Mindal taught them how to hunt and make the food called *natek*, from the pith of the caryota palm, and he gave them betel nut. Then only Dafal came, and sometimes others from his village, and they traded *bui* vine with Dafal.

Dafal returned one day and said that a man wanted to meet them. This man would do good things for them. In order to meet this man, they would have to go to another place, but this man was special, so they should go. Some did not want to go. They told Dafal they would think about it, but when next they saw him, they said yes, they would

---

*"They said we would always have to live in our forest and suffer [this word was uncertain; Elizalde insisted it was one of Igna's or Mai's] until the good man came to us" (Nance, 57). This idea of the Tasaday suffering contradicts the overall picture of their Eden-like existence, and this is undoubtedly why Elizalde resisted the word.

go meet this special man. Some of them were so afraid they thought they might die, but they decided that everyone, even the youngest, would go with Dafal.[19] They brought their bows and arrows with them, to hunt along the way and to protect themselves. Most of the men and women wore cloth, though some of the children were naked or wore leaves.

When they finally reached this place, it was unlike any other they had known. Instead of trees, there was open ground and no protection. Four men went into the place where the eye sees too far and waited for the man's arrival.

A loud wind suddenly blew above them, and made the trees shake. In the distance, *limokon* was singing, but the wind, louder than thunder, drowned out its voice. The men could not hear their own breathing. Dafal had deceived them. There was no good man waiting, only something terrible descending upon them. They dropped their bows and collapsed. They cried for their lives. When the wind finally stopped, they looked up, their eyes wide, their mouths open as if to speak.

Notes

2: Protector of the Primitive

1. *Sports Review* (March 1953), 3.
2. This description of his college days is largely culled from John Nance's *The Gentle Tasaday: A Stone Age People in the Philippine Rainforest* (New York: Harcourt Brace Jovanovich, 1975).
3. Interview with anonymous friend and former business associate, Manila Golf Club, January 21, 1999.
4. Christopher Lucas, "Protector of the Primitive," *Reader's Digest* (January 1974), 91.
5. PANAMIN, *Protecting Man's Right to Choice* (1973), 17.
6. Nance, *Gentle Tasaday*, 7.
7. "Marcos Cronies Dominate Roster of Bad Borrowers," *Philippine Daily Inquirer*, October 30, 1992.
8. Interview with anonymous, Manila Golf Club.
9. A. Scott Berg, *Lindbergh* (New York: G. P. Putnam's Sons, 1998), 541.
10. Father John Doherty, S.J., Manila, "A Report on the Tribal Filipinos in Mindanao" (Manila: Research Office of La Ignacia Apostolic Church, 1978), 7.
11. Ibid., 45.
12. Ibid., 28.
13. Ibid., 15.
14. Anti-Slavery Society, *The Philippines: Authoritarian Government, Multinationals and Ancestral Lands* (London: Anti-Slavery Society Indigenous Peoples and Development Series, 1983), reprint no. 1, 126.
15. Nance, *Gentle Tasaday*, 46.

3: *The Center for Short-Lived Phenomena*

1. Nance, *Gentle Tasaday*, 31.
2. Manuel Elizalde, Jr., with Robert Fox, "Tasaday Forest People. A Data Paper on a Newly Discovered Food Gathering and Stone Tool Using Manubo Group in the Mountains of South Cotabato, Mindanao, Philippines" (Washington, D.C.: Smithsonian Institution, Center for Short-Lived Phenomena, July 1971), 2.
3. Ibid., 10.
4. Nance, *Gentle Tasaday*, 19.
5. Ibid., 16.
6. Ibid., 17.
7. Ibid., 17–18.
8. John Bodley, "The Tasaday Controversy, an Assessment" (Quezon City: Tasaday Commission, International Conference on the Tasaday Controversy and Other Urgent Anthropological Issues. Department of Anthropology, University of the Philippines, Diliman, 1986), 3.
9. Elizalde and Fox, "Tasaday Forest People," 3–4.
10. Richard B. Lee and Irven Devore, eds., *Man the Hunter*, 8th ed. (New York: Aldine, 1979), 86.
11. Elizalde and Fox, "Tasaday Forest People," 16–17.
12. Nance, *Gentle Tasaday*, 25.
13. Ibid., 18.

4: *Message from the Stone Age*

1. Nance, *Gentle Tasaday*, 28–29.
2. Ibid., 29.
3. Peter Arnett, *Live From the Battlefield: From Vietnam to Baghdad, 35 Years in the World's War Zones* (New York: Touchstone, 1994), 202.
4. Nance, *Gentle Tasaday*, 29–30.
5. John Nance, interview with author, November 14–15, Portland, Oregon, 1998. Much the same turn of events is described in *The Gentle Tasaday*.
6. Ibid. The story is also recounted on p. 31 of *The Gentle Tasaday*.
7. Ibid., 49–50.
8. Ibid., 52.
9. Jesus T. Peralta, "The Role of the National Museum of the Philippines in the Tasaday Controversy," in *The Tasaday Controversy: Assessing the Evidence*, ed. Thomas N. Headland (Washington, D.C.: American Anthropological Association, 1992), 158.
10. Nance, *Gentle Tasaday*, 67.
11. Fern Fox, "The Tasaday (The Way I See It)." Also, according to a list of personnel in a PANAMIN pamphlet, *Protecting Man's Right to Choice*, Oscar Trinidad and Janet Bauer, eds. 1972.
12. Robert Fox, "Time Catches Up with the Tasaday," *The Asian* 1 (October 24–30, 1971), 3, 7.
13. Teodoro A. Llamzon, "The Tasaday Language So Far," *Philippine Journal of Linguistics* 10, 2 (December 1971), 8.
14. Jack Foisie, "Philippine Tribe Goes Under the Microscope," *Washington Post*, July 22, 1972.

15. Robert Fox, "Time Catches Up with the Tasaday," 7.
16. Zeus Salazar, "Comments: Footnote on the Tasaday," *Philippine Journal of Linguistics* 2 (1971), 2, 34–38.
17. *Mindanao Résumé* 4 (October 1971), 6, 8.
18. Ibid.
19. Ibid.
20. Nance, *Gentle Tasaday*, 88.
21. Ibid.
22. Ibid., 92.
23. Fern Fox, "The Tasaday (The Way I See It)."
24. Nance, *Gentle Tasaday*, 108.
25. Kenneth MacLeish, "Stone Age Cavemen of Mindanao," *National Geographic*, 142, 2 (August 1972), 230.
26. Ibid.
27. MacLeish, "Stone Age Cavemen of Mindanao," 230.
28. Ibid., 232.
29. Ibid.
30. Nance, *Gentle Tasaday*, 110.
31. Ibid., 112.
32. Ibid.
33. Ibid., 123.
34. Ibid., 125.

5: Tourists in Paradise

1. Nance, *Gentle Tasaday*, 142.
2. Ibid., 130.
3. Ibid., 134.
4. MacLeish, "Stone Age Cavemen of Mindanao," 249.
5. Nance, *Gentle Tasaday*, 151.
6. Ibid., 146.
7. Trinidad and Bauer, eds., "Protecting Man's Right to Choose," 8.
8. Ibid.
9. Nance, *Gentle Tasaday*, 170.
10. Ibid., 171.
11. Ibid., 177.
12. Ibid., 187.
13. Ibid., 173–74.
14. Ibid., 198.
15. Carlos A. Fernandez II and Frank Lynch, S.J., "The Tasaday: Cave-Dwelling Food Gatherers of South Cotabato, Mindanao," *Philippine Sociological Review* 20 (October 1972), 3. Copublished as PANAMIN Foundation research paper no. 1, 21.
16. Nance, *Gentle Tasaday*, 229.
17. Ibid., 230.
18. Ibid., 225.
19. Ibid., 231.
20. Ibid., 234.
21. Ibid.

22. Ibid.

23. Ibid., 238.

24. Ibid., 236.

25. Fernandez and Lynch, "The Tasaday," 281.

26. Nance, *Gentle Tasaday*, 243.

27. Ibid., 244.

28. Ibid.

29. Ibid., 255.

30. Ibid., 258.

31. Ibid.

32. Ibid., 256.

33. Ibid.

34. Ibid., 287.

6: A New Society

1. Nance, *Gentle Tasaday*, 268.

2. Ibid.

3. Richard Elkins, phone conversation with author, August 5, 1998.

4. Nance, *Gentle Tasaday*, 292.

5. Douglas E. Yen, "The Tasaday Environment: Seventeen Years On," *Philippine Studies* 50 (First Quarter of 2000), 78.

6. Nance, *Gentle Tasaday*, 288.

7. Ibid.

8. David B. Baradas, Preface, *Philippine Sociological Review* 20, 3 (October 1972), 278.

9. Peggy Durdin, "From the Space Age to the Tasaday Age," *New York Times Magazine* (October 8, 1972), 85.

10. Nance, *Gentle Tasaday*, 364.

11. Tilman Durdin, "Violence Surrounding Filipino Tribe Is Reminiscent of America's Old West," *New York Times*, August 19, 1972.

12. Nance, *Gentle Tasaday*, 368.

13. Ibid., 281.

14. Manuel Elizalde, Jr., "Report to the President of the Philippines" (Manila: PANAMIN, September 1974), 1.

15. Manuel Elizalde, Jr., "Report and Recommendations on the Non-Muslim Minority Hill Tribes" (Manila: PANAMIN, March 21, 1975), 1.

16. Ibid., 10.

17. Yen and Nance, Preface to *Further Studies on the Tasaday*, reprinted in *Readings on the Tasaday*, ed. Virginia Dandan (Manila: Tasaday Community Care Foundation, Publication No. 1, 1988), 72.

7: Passion Play

1. James Hamilton-Paterson, *America's Boy: The Marcoses and the Philippines* (Manila: Anvil Publishing, 1998), 369.

2. Antonio "Tony" Cervantes, interview with author, Manila, June 24, 1999.

3. Hector R. R. Villanueva, "Manda Comes Home," *Manila Times*, August 27, 1987.

4. Oswald Iten, interview with author, Unterageri, Switzerland, November 25, 1999.
5. Hamilton-Paterson, *America's Boy*, 388.
6. Ibid., 395.
7. Iten, interview with author.
8. Oswald Iten, "The Tasaday and the Press," in *The Tasaday Controversy: Assessing the Evidence*, ed. Thomas N. Headland (Washington, D.C.: American Anthropological Association, 1992), 42.
9. Iten, interview with author.

8: "Crimed Up Very Badly"

1. *Captives on a Paradise Island*. Joey Lozano, producer. Videocassette.
2. Joey Lozano, *Fieldnotes*, 10, 2 (July–October 1998), 4.

9: A Smoking Gun

1. John Nance, "The Truth About the Tasaday: Return to a Stone Age Tribe," *Asiaweek* 12, 24 (June 15, 1986), 26–38.
2. Peralta, "The Role of the National Museum of the Philippines in the Tasaday Issue," 162.
3. Jerome Bailen, ed., *The Tasaday Controversy: Proceedings of the International Anthropological Conference on the Tasaday Controversy and Other Urgent Anthropological Issues* 1 (Quezon City, Philippines: Philippine Social Science Center, August 15–17, 1986), 135.

10: Quiet Understandings

1. Judith Moses, interview with author, December 5–7, 1998.
2. *The Tribe That Never Was*, 1986. Judith Moses, producer. Videocassette.

11: Heart of Grayness

1. By Margie Burgos in Kidapawan, Cotabato, August 7, 2000.
2. Nance, *Gentle Tasaday*, 13.
3. Lawrence Reid, personal communication, August 21, 2002.

12: Tribal Warfare

1. Bailen, *The Tasaday Controversy*, 106.
2. Ibid., 121.
3. Ibid., 130.
4. Michael L. Tan, "The Tasaday and Other Urgent Issues in Anthropology," *Social Science Information*, 14, 2 (July–September 1986), 20.

13: Return of the Native

1. Joey Lozano, e-mail to the author, March 21, 2000.
2. Ibid.

3. "El Controvertido Elizalde," *La Nación* (August 31, 1986). From a translation supplied by Judith Moses.
4. Papel de Oficio, No. 618763, San José, Costa Rica. Official transcript in investigation of Manuel Elizalde, Jr., recorded January 14, 1985. Original Spanish and English translation provided by Judith Moses. Recorded by Claudio Hernández.

14: Video Tribe

1. John Nance, et al. *Reply to 20/20.* 1987. Videocassette.
2. Roy de Guzman, "Britannica Deletes Tasaday," *Philippine Daily Inquirer*, October 17, 1987.
3. Cable from Bob McHenry of *Encyclopaedia Britannica* to Berton Woodward of *Asiaweek*, October 29, 1987.
4. "Savants Say Manda Prepared False Claims," *Philippine Daily Inquirer*, October 19, 1987.
5. "Geographic Drops Tasaday," *Philippine Star*, December 4, 1987.
6. *National Geographic* 174, 3 (September 1988), 304.
7. The statement was issued in October and was later republished in the *Philippine Daily Globe* with Father McDonagh's byline.
8. Sean McDonagh, "What About the Tasadays Themselves?," *Philippine Daily Globe*, December 9, 1987.
9. Edcel Lagman et al. to Hon. William Claver, chairman, Committee on Cultural Communities, House of Representatives, October 14, 1987.
10. Roy de Guzman, "Two Tasaday Witnesses Abducted," *Philippine Daily Inquirer*, November 15, 1987.
11. Roy de Guzman, "Critics Fear Ex-PANAMIN Boss Up to Something," *Philippine Daily Inquirer*, November 16, 1987.
12. "T'bolis Deny Kidnapping," *Philippine Star*, November 17, 1987.
13. "T'bolis Change Stand on Tasaday, Discovery," *Malaya*, November 17, 1987.
14. "Witness Says He Lied on Tasadays," *Manila Chronicle*, November 19, 1987.
15. Ibid.
16. Zeus Salazar, "Third and Final Footnote on the Tasaday," in *The Tasaday Controversy: Assessing the Evidence,* ed. Thomas N. Headland (Washington, D.C.: American Anthropological Association, 1992), 82–83.
17. From Dula's testimony in Lake Sebu, November 20–21, 1987.
18. "Manobo Woman Says Reports Malicious," *Malaya*, November 29, 1987.
19. "5 Savants to Testify on Tasaday," *Malaya*, December 3, 1987.
20. Roy de Guzman and L. Logarta, "Attempts to Manipulate Tasaday Probe Hit," *Philippine Daily Inquirer*, December 4, 1987.
21. Ibid.
22. Committee on National Cultural Communities, "Report on the Congressional Investigation Conducted on the Tasaday per House Resolution No. 405" (Quezon City: Republic of the Philippines House of Representatives, 1987), 15.
23. Ibid., 16.
24. Kristina Luz, phone conversation with author, March 3, 2001.
25. Seth Mydans, "From Forest to Manila, Stranger in a Strange Land," *New York Times*, December 27, 1987.

15: Loaded Words

1. "Court Orders Arrest of Missionaries in Tasaday Reservation," *Philippine Daily Globe*, February 5, 1988.
2. Ibid.
3. Iten, "The Tasaday and the Press," *Evidence*, 41.
4. Clayton Jones, "Tales from the Philippine Woods," *Christian Science World Monitor*, January 1989, 70.
5. Ibid., 71.

16: Trial in the Jungle

1. Jerome Bailen to Judith Moses, January 9, 1989.
2. "Prof in Tasaday Row in Hiding," *Philippine Daily Inquirer*, January 13, 1989.
3. John Nance, personal communication.
4. John H. Bodley, *Victims of Progress*, 3d ed. (Mountain View, Calif.: Mayfield Publishing Co., 1990), 186.
5. Lawrence Reid, "Another Look at the Tasaday Language." Paper presented as the keynote lecture to the Third Annual Conference of the Southeast Asian Linguistic Society, Honolulu, Hawai'i, May 10–13, 1993, 2.
6. Judith Moses, "The Tasaday," *Anthropology Today* 6, 1 (February 1990), 22.
7. Bettina Lerner, "The Tasaday," *Anthropology Today* 6, 3 (June 1990), 21.
8. Father Sean McDonagh, e-mail to the author, September 29, 2000.
9. Supreme Court, Republic of the Philippines, University of the Philippines v. Court of Appeals, G.R. No. 97827, *Supreme Court Reports Annotated*, 218, 9 (February 1993), 731.
10. Seth Mydans, "20th-Century Lawsuit Asserts Stone-Age Identity," *New York Times*, October 29, 1988.
11. "Tasaday Make Dramatic Entry at Tribal Meet," *Manila Standard*, November 28, 1988.
12. Ibid.
13. Resolutions on Cultural Survival and Integrity, International Festival and Conference of Indigenous and Traditional Cultures, Manila, Philippines, November 26, 1988.
14. "Blit-Tafitok Situationer," *Lunay S'bung, Newsletter of the South Cotabato Tribes* (Koronadal, South Cotabato: Santa Cruz Mission, n.d.), 4.

17: Your Own Private Tasaday

1. Thomas Headland, interview with author, Dallas, January 15–17, 1998.
2. Edith Terry, telephone conversation with author, September 30, 1999.
3. Terry to Headland, June 12, 1989.
4. Nance, *Gentle Tasaday*, 16.
5. Ibid., 21–22.
6. Headland interview, 1998.
7. Levita Duhaylungsod and David C. Hyndman, "Creeping Resource Exploitation in the T'boli Homeland: Political Ecology of the Tasaday Hoax," in *The Tasaday Controversy*, 68.

8. Ibid., 73.
9. Thomas N. Headland, "What Did the Tasaday Eat?" in *The Tasaday Controversy*, 130.
10. Ibid., 139.
11. Yen, "The Tasaday Environment," 89.
12. Gerald D. Berreman, "The Tasaday: Stone Age Survivors or Space Age Fakes?" in *The Tasaday Controversy*, 27.
13. Gerald D. Berreman, "The Incredible 'Tasaday': Deconstructing the Myth of a 'Stone Age' People," *Cultural Survival Quarterly* 15, 1 (1991), 17.
14. Ibid.
15. Berreman, "The Tasaday," 37.
16. Ibid.
17. Thomas N. Headland, e-mail to author, June 19, 1998.
18. Thomas N. Headland, interview with author, January 15–17, 1998.
19. Berreman, "The Tasaday," 32.
20. Ibid., 27.

18: Missing Links

1. Peralta, "The Role of the National Museum of the Philippines in the Tasaday Issue," 158.
2. Berreman, "The Tasaday," 35.
3. Reid, "Another Look at the Tasaday Language," 4.
4. Lawrence Reid, interview with author, Honolulu, Hawai'i, April 27, 1998.
5. Lawrence Reid, "The Tasaday Language, A Key to Tasaday Prehistory," in *The Tasaday Controversy*, 189–90.
6. Lawrence Reid, "Another Look at the Tasaday Language," 2.
7. Lawrence Reid, "Linguistic Archaeology: Tracking Down the Tasaday Language," in *Archaeology and Language*, vol. 1, *Theoretical and Methodological Orientations*, ed. Roger Blench and Matthew Spriggs (London and New York: Routledge, 1997), 192.
8. Ibid.

19: Good Men

1. Anonymous, interview with the author, Forbes Park, Manila, January 1999.
2. Associated Press, "Discoverer of Primitive Tribe Dies," Nando.net, May 5, 1997.
3. "Passages," *Seattle Times*, May 5, 1997.
4. "Cariño Brutal," *Philippine Daily Inquirer*, May 5, 1993.
5. Roy S. de Guzman, "Manda Says Raps Foul and Unfair," *Philippine Daily Inquirer*, September 27, 1987.
6. Letter dated May 4, 1997.
7. Dul, interview with the author, Kibang, Philippines, August 19, 2000.

20: Postcard from the Stone Age

1. Pascal Lays, *La Meuse Weekend*, Liège, Belgium, April 12–13, 1993. This of course is a translation from French.

2. Ibid.
3. Ibid.
4. Joey Lozano to "Bobbi V.," April 17, 1986.
5. Salazar, "Third and Final Footnote on the Tasaday," 85.
6. As told to me by Dul, August 19, 1999.
7. Helen Mabandos, "On Blit Proximity to the Tasaday." Typescript.
8. Salazar, "Third and Final Footnote," 84.
9. Amelia Rogel-Rara and Emmanuel S. Nabayra, "The Genealogical Evidence," in *The Tasaday Controversy: Assessing the Evidence,* ed. Thomas N. Headland, 99.
10. Ibid., 90.
11. Ibid.
12. Iten, "The Tasaday and the Press," 44.
13. Douglas E. Yen and Hermes G. Gutierrez, "The Ethnobotany of the Tasaday: I. The Useful Plants," in *Readings on the Tasaday*, ed. Virginia Dandan (Manila: Tasaday Community Care Foundation, Publication No. 1, 1988), 221.
14. Iten, "The Tasaday and the Press," 53.
15. Ibid., 52.
16. Nance, *Gentle Tasaday*, 101.
17. Iten, "The Tasaday and the Press," 42.
18. Lawrence Reid, e-mail to the author, September 24, 1999.

21: Confirmation Bias

1. Mariano Mondragon, "Sworn Statement," Makati, Philippines, September 23, 1988.
2. Thomas Headland, e-mail to the author, February 23, 2001.
3. Written November 28, 2000.
4. Headland, *Tasaday Controversy*, 183.
5. Nance, *Gentle Tasaday*, 51.
6. Berreman, "The Tasaday: Stone-Age Survivors or Space Age Fakes?," 34.
7. Nance, *Gentle Tasaday*, 301.
8. Ibid.
9. Ibid., 389.
10. Yen and Gutierrez, "The Ethnobotany of the Tasaday," 184.
11. Iten, "The Tasaday and the Press," 51.
12. Joey Lozano to "Bobby V.," April 17, 1986.
13. Joey Lozano to Judith Moses, November 16, 1988.
14. Iten, "The Tasaday and the Press," 57.
15. Rogel-Rara and Nabayra, "The Genealogical Evidence," 94.
16. Richard A. Shweder, *Thinking Through Cultures, Expeditions in Cultural Psychology* (Cambridge, Mass., and London: Harvard University Press, 1991), 9.
17. Nance, *Gentle Tasaday*, 99.
18. Ibid., 58.
19. Ibid., 9.

Selected Bibliography

ABC. *The Tribe That Never Was*. Documentary film for ABC-TV's 20/20 program. Judith Moses, producer. New York: American Broadcasting Company, August 14, 1986. A typescript of the narration was produced by Herman S. Jaffe Reporting and Transcribing Services, Inc., New York.

Adler, Christian. "The Tasaday Hoax: The Never-Ending Scandal." Paper presented at the International Conference on the Tasaday Controversy and Other Urgent Anthropological Issues. University of the Philippines, Diliman, August 15–17, 1986.

Anti-Slavery Society. *The Philippines: Authoritarian Government, Multinationals and Ancestral Lands*. London: Anti-Slavery Society, Indigenous Peoples and Development Series, Report No. 1, 1983.

Aquino, Corazon C. Keynote Address to the First International Festival and Conference on Indigenous and Traditional Cultures. Manila, November 23, 1988.

Arnett, Peter. *Live from the Battlefield: From Vietnam to Baghdad, 35 Years in the World's War Zones*. New York: Touchstone. 1994.

Azurin, Arnold Molina. "The Tasaday: Media Circus and Sci-Fi." *Diliman Review*, 36, 1 (1988), 19–24.

Bailen, Jerome, ed. *A Tasaday Folio*. Quezon City: UGAT, 1986.

———, *The Tasaday Controversy: Proceedings of the International Anthropological Conference on the Tasaday Controversy and Other Urgent Anthropological Issues*. Philippine Social Science Center, Quezon City, Philippines, August 15–17, 1986. Vol. 1.

Baradas, David B. Preface. *Philippine Sociological Review* 20, 3 (1972), 277–78. Copublished as PANAMIN Foundation Series No. 1.

Bendix, Regina. *In Search of Authenticity: The Formation of Folklore Studies*. Madison: University of Wisconsin Press, 1997.

Benedicto, Rey. *Reply to 20/20.* 1987. Documentary video, 30 minutes. Previewed at the December 10, 1987, congressional hearing on the Tasaday controversy, House of Representatives, Philippines.

Berg, A. Scott. *Lindbergh,* New York: G. P. Putnam's Sons, 1998.

Berreman, Gerald D. "The Incredible 'Tasaday': Deconstructing the Myth of a 'Stone-Age' People." *Cultural Survival Quarterly* 15 (1991), 2–45.

———. "The Tasaday: Stone Age Survivors or Space Age Fakes?" In *The Tasaday Controversy: Assessing the Evidence,* ed. Thomas N. Headland, 21–39. Washington, D.C.: American Anthropological Association, 1992.

Bodley, John H. *Victims of Progress.* Menlo Park, Calif.: Benjamin Cummings, 1975.

———. *Victims of Progress,* 3d. ed. Mountain View, Calif.: Mayfield Publishing Co., 1990.

———. "The Tasaday Controversy, an Assessment." Quezon City: Tasaday Commission, International Conference on the Tasaday Controversy and Other Urgent Anthropological Issues. Department of Anthropology, University of the Philippines, Diliman, 1986.

———. "The Tasaday Debate and Indigenous Peoples." In *The Tasaday Controversy: Assessing the Evidence,* ed. Thomas N. Headland, 197–99. Washington, D.C.: American Anthropological Association, 1992.

Bower, Bruce. "The Strange Case of the Tasaday: Were They Primitive Hunter-Gatherers or Rain-Forest Phonies?" *Science News* 135 (May 6, 1987), 280–81, 283.

Burch, Ernest S. Jr., and Linda J. Ellanna. *Key Issues in Hunter-Gatherer Research.* Oxford, Washington, D.C.: Berg, Exploration in Anthropology Series, 1994.

Carneiro, Robert L. "The Tasaday 'Stone Axes'—What Do They Tell Us?" In *The Tasaday Controversy: Assessing the Evidence,* ed. Thomas N. Headland, 172–79. Washington, D.C.: American Anthropological Association, 1992.

Central Independent Television. *Scandal: The Lost Tribe.* John Edwards, producer. Ian Taylor, director. Birmingham, U.K.: Central Independent Television, 1986.

Chagnon, Napoleon A. *Yanomamö: The Last Days of Eden.* San Diego, New York, London: Harcourt, Brace and Company, 1991.

Committee on National Cultural Communities. "Report on the Congressional Investigation Conducted on the Tasaday Per House Resolution Number 405." Quezon City: Republic of the Philippines House of Representatives, 1987.

Dandan, Virginia, ed. *Readings on the Tasaday.* Manila: Tasaday Community Care Foundation, Publication Number 1, 1988.

Doherty, Father John, S.J. "A Report on the Tribal Filipinos in Mindanao." Manila: Research Office of La Ignacia Apostolic Church, 1978.

Duhaylungsod, Levita, and David Hyndman. "Creeping Resource Exploitation in the T'boli Homeland: Political Ecology of the Tasaday Hoax." In *The Tasaday Controversy: Assessing the Evidence,* ed. Thomas N. Headland, 59–75. Washington, D.C.: American Anthropological Association, 1992.

———. *Where T'boli Bells Toll: Political Ecology Voices Behind the Tasaday Hoax.* Copenhagen: IWGIA, Document Number 73, 1993.

Dumont, Jean-Paul. "The Tasaday, Which and Whose? Toward the Political Economy of an Ethnographic Sign." *Cultural Anthropology* 3 (1988), 261–75.

Durdin, Peggy. "From the Space Age to the Tasaday Age." *New York Times Magazine* (October 8, 1972), 14–15, 85–92.

Elizalde, Manuel, Jr. "Report to the President of the Philippines." Manila: PANAMIN, September 1974. Typescript.

———. "Report and Recommendation on the Non-Muslim Minority Hill Tribes." Manila: PANAMIN, March 21, 1975. Typescript.

Elizalde, Manuel, Jr., with Robert Fox. "Tasaday Forest People. A Data Paper on a Newly Discovered Food Gathering and Stone Tool Using Manubo Group in the Mountains of South Cotabato, Mindanao, Philippines." Washington, D.C.: Smithsonian Institution, Center for Short-Lived Phenomena, July 1971. Typescript.

Elkins, Richard E. "The Tasaday: Some Observations." In *The Tasaday Controversy: Assessing the Evidence*, ed. Thomas N. Headland, 117–22. Washington, D.C.: American Anthropological Association, 1992.

Fankhauser, Barry. "A Nutritional Analysis of the Philippine Tasaday Diet." In *The Tasaday Controversy: Assessing the Evidence*, ed. Thomas N. Headland, 125–29. Washington, D.C.: American Anthropological Association, 1992.

Farquhar, Michael. "The Greatest Hoaxes of All Time." *Reader's Digest* (January 1998), 95.

Fernandez, Carlos A., and Frank Lynch. "The Tasaday: Cave-Dwelling Food Gatherers of South Cotabato, Mindanao." *Philippine Sociological Review* 20(3): 279–313, 328–30 [copublished as PANAMIN Foundation Series No. 1], 1972.

Fox, Richard G. " 'Professional Primitives': Hunters and Gatherers of Nuclear South Asia." *Man in India* 49 (1969), 139–60.

Fox, Robert. "Time Catches Up with the Tasaday." *The Asian* (October 24–30, 1971), 7.

———. "Notes on the Stone Tools of the Tasaday, Gathering Economies in the Philippines, and the Archaeological Record." In *Further Studies on the Tasaday*, ed. D. E. Yen and John Nance, 3–12. Makati, Philippines: 1976. PANAMIN Foundation, PANAMIN Foundation Research Series No. 2.

Freeman, Derek. *Margaret Mead and the Heretic: The Making and Unmaking of an Anthropological Myth*. Ringwood, Victoria, Australia: Penguin Books, Australia, 1996.

Gibson, Thomas. *Sacrifice and Sharing in the Philippine Highlands: Religion and Society Among the Buid of Mindoro*. London School of Economics, Monographs on Social Anthropology 57. London and Dover: Athlone Press, 1986.

Hamilton-Paterson, James. *America's Boy: The Marcoses and the Philippines*. London: Granta Books, 1998.

Headland, Thomas N. "The Wild Yam Question: How Well Could Independent Hunter-Gatherers Live in a Tropical Rainforest Ecosystem?" *Human Ecology* 15 (1987), 463–91.

———. Preface to *The Tasaday Controversy: Assessing the Evidence*. Washington, D.C.: American Anthropological Association, 1992.

———. Introduction to *The Tasaday Controversy: Assessing the Evidence*, Washington, D.C.: American Anthropological Association, 1992.

———. "What Did the Tasaday Eat?" In *The Tasaday Controversy: Assessing the Evidence*, 130–43. Washington, D.C.: American Anthropological Association, 1992.

———. Conclusion to *The Tasaday Controversy: Assessing the Evidence*. Washington, D.C.: American Anthropological Association, 1992.

————. "Tasaday Controversy." In *Encyclopedia of Cultural Anthropology*, ed. David Levinson and Melvin Embers, 1285–86. New York: Henry Holt, 1996. Vol. 4.

Headland, Thomas N., ed. *The Tasaday Controversy: Assessing the Evidence*. Washington, D.C.: American Anthropological Association, 1992.

Headland, Thomas N., and Lawrence A. Reid. "Hunter-Gatherers and Their Neighbors from Prehistory to the Present." *Current Anthropology* 30 (1989), 43–66.

Hyndman, David C., and Levita Duhaylungsod. "The Development Saga of the Tasaday: Gentle Yesterday, Hoax Today, Exploited Forever?" *Bulletin of Concerned Asian Scholars* 22, 4 (1990), 38–54.

Iten, Oswald. "The Tasaday: First a Hoax and Then a Cover-Up." Paper presented at the Twelfth International Congress of Anthropological and Ethnological Sciences, Zagreb, July 28, 1988.

————. "The Tasaday." *Anthropology Today* 6, 5 (1990), 24.

————. "The 'Tasaday' and the Press." In *The Tasaday Controversy: Assessing the Evidence*, ed. Thomas N. Headland, 40–58. Washington, D.C.: American Anthropological Association, 1992.

Iten, Oswald, and Joey R. B. Lozano. "A Swiss Journalist Says the Tasaday Could Be the Great Stone Age Hoax," Sunday magazine, *Malaya* 2, 47 (May 11, 1986), 3–7.

Johnston, E. Clay. "The Tasaday Language: Is It Cotabato Manobo?" In *The Tasaday Controversy: Assessing the Evidence*, ed. Thomas N. Headland, 144–56. Washington, D.C.: American Anthropological Association, 1992.

Jones, Clayton. "Tales From the Philippine Woods." *Christian Science World Monitor* (January 1989), 66–71.

Kloos, Peter. *The Akuriyo of Surinam: A Case of Emergence from Isolation*. Copenhagen: International Work Group for Indigenous Affairs, Document 27, 1977.

Kramer, Jane. Review of *The Gentle Tasaday* by John Nance. *New York Times Book Review*, June 1, 1975, 1–5.

Kummer, David M. *Deforestation in the Postwar Philippines*. Chicago: University of Chicago Press, 1992. Geography Research Paper No. 234.

Lays, Pascal. *La Meuse Weekend*. Liège, Belgium, April 12–13, 1993.

Lee, Richard B. "Making Sense of the Tasaday: Three Discourses." In *The Tasaday Controversy: Assessing the Evidence*, ed. Thomas N. Headland, 167–71. Washington, D.C.: American Anthropological Association, 1992.

Lee, Richard B., and Irven Devore, eds. *Man the Hunter*. New York: Aldine, 1979.

Lerner, Bettina. *Trial in the Jungle*. Script of program transmitted March 20 and repeated March 21. London: BBC, Horizon, 1989.

————. "The Tasaday." *Anthropology Today* 6, 3 (June 1990), 21.

Lévi-Strauss, Claude. *Tristes Tropiques*. New York: Penguin Books U.S.A., 1992.

Lindbergh, Charles A. Preface to *The Gentle Tasaday: A Stone Age People in the Philippines Rainforest* by John Nance. New York: Harcourt Brace Jovanovich, 1975.

Llamzon, Teodoro A. "The Tasaday Language So Far." *Philippine Journal of Linguistics* 2, 2 (1971), 1–30. Reprinted in *Philippine Sociological Review* 20, 3 (1972), 314–24.

Longacre, William A. "Cave Archaeology: A Possible Solution to the Tasaday Problem." In *The Tasaday Controversy: Assessing the Evidence*, ed. Thomas N. Headland, 194–96. Washington, D.C.: American Anthropological Association, 1992.

Lozano, Joey. *Fieldnotes*, 10, 2, July–October 1998, 4.

Lucas, Christopher. "Protector of the Primitive." *Reader's Digest* (January 1974), 85–92.

Lukesch, Anton. *Bearded Indians of the Tropical World: The Asurinâi of the Ipiaocaba.* Graz: Akademische Druck, 1976.

MacLeish, Kenneth. "Stone Age Cavemen of Mindanao." *National Geographic*, 142, 2 (1972), 219–49.

Malayang, Jerry P. "Elizalde's Tasadays: The Fame Syndrome. An Insider's Notes on an Alleged Anthropological Hoax." *Malaya*, May 6–9, 1986. Series of four articles on consecutive days.

Mansmann, Rex, C.P. "The Case for T'boli Rights to Their Ancestral Territory." *Dansalan Quarterly* 3, 4 (1982), 204–17.

Mindanao Résumé, 4, 6 (October 1971). Philippines: Davao City.

Molony, Carol H. "The Truth About the Tasaday: Are They a Primitive Tribe—or a Modern Hoax?" *Sciences* (September–October, 1988), 12–20.

———. "The Tasaday Language: Evidence for Authenticity?" In *The Tasaday Controversy: Assessing the Evidence*, ed. Thomas N. Headland, 107–16. Washington, D.C.: American Anthropological Association, 1992.

Molony, Carol H., with Dad Tuan. "Further Studies on the Tasaday Language: Text and Vocabulary." In *Further Studies on the Tasaday*, ed. John Nance and D. E. Yen, 13–96. Makati, Philippines: PANAMIN Foundation, 1976. PANAMIN Research Series No. 2.

Mondragon, Mariano. "Sworn Statement." Makati, Philippines, September 23, 1988. Typescript.

Moses, Judith. "The Tasaday." *Anthropology Today* 6, 1 (February 1990), 22.

Nabayra, Emmanuel S., and Amelia R. Rara, eds. "Dula's Testimony in Lake Sebu." November 20–21, 1987. T'boli original and translation by Fernando T. Lawi-an, Arturo M. Lawa, and Samuel Ganguso. Typescript.

Nance, John. *The Gentle Tasaday: A Stone Age People in the Philippine Rainforest.* New York: Harcourt Brace Jovanovich, 1975.

———. *The Tasaday: Stone Age People in a Space Age World.* New Rochelle, N.Y.: Pathescope Educational Media, Inc. and the Associated Press, 1975. Color filmstrip and accompanying 33⅓ rpm records (or cassettes). Narrated by Richard Kiley.

———. *The Tasaday: Stone Age People in a Space Age World.* New Rochelle, N.Y.: Pathescope Educational Media, Inc. and the Associated Press, 1975. Teacher's manual.

———. *Discovery of the Tasaday, A Photo-Novel: The Stone Age Meets the Space Age in the Philippine Rain Forest.* Manila: Vera-Reyes and Hong Kong: Toppan Printing, 1981.

———. *Lobo of the Tasaday: A Photographic Account for Young Readers.* New York: Pantheon, 1982.

———. *A Message from the Stone Age.* 1983. Film produced by Film Loft, Portland, Oregon. 30 minutes.

———. *A Message from the Stone Age.* 1983. Teacher's manual.

————. "The Truth About the Tasaday: Return to a Stone Age Tribe." *Asiaweek*, 12, 24 (June 15, 1986), 4, 28–38.

————. *The Gentle Tasaday: A Stone Age People in the Philippines Rainforest*. Boston: David R. Godine, 1988.

National Geographic Society. "First Glimpse of a Stone Age Tribe." *National Geographic*, 140, 6 (1971), 880–82b.

————. *The Last Tribes of Mindanao*. 1972. Dennis Azarella, producer-director. Documentary film.

NBC. *NBC Reports: The Cave People of the Philippines*. October 10, 1972.

NBC-TV. *Tasaday Contacted*. July 1971. Jack Reynolds, correspondent. Series of reports for *NBC Nightly News*. Available on videocassette from Vanderbilt University TV News Archives.

————. *The Cave People of the Philippines*. 1972. Gerald Green, producer. Documentary film.

————. "Tasaday Revisited and Authentic." June 1986. Jack Reynolds, correspondent. Reports on *NBC Nightly News* and *The Today Show*.

NDR-TV. *Ein Mann mit Vielen Namen [A Man with Many Names]*. Hamburg: Norddeutscher Rundfunk-TV. 1972. Documentary film.

Olofson, Harold. "Looking for the Tasaday: A Representation." *Philippine Quarterly of Culture and Society* 17 (1989), 3–39.

Peralta, Jesus T. "The Role of the National Museum of the Philippines in the Tasaday Issue." In *The Tasaday Controversy: Assessing the Evidence*, ed. Thomas N. Headland, 157–64. Washington, D.C.: American Anthropological Association, 1992.

————, ed. *Tau't Batu Studies*, Monograph No. 7. Manila: National Museum and the Presidential Assistant on National Minorities, 1983.

Reid, Lawrence A. "The Tasaday Language: A Key to Tasaday Prehistory." In *The Tasaday Controversy: Assessing the Evidence*, ed. Thomas N. Headland, 180–93. Washington, D.C.: American Anthropological Association, 1992.

————. "Another Look at the Tasaday Language." Paper presented as the keynote lecture to the Third Annual Conference of the Southeast Asian Linguistic Society, Honolulu, Hawai'i, May 10–13, 1993.

————. "The Tasaday Tapes." In *Pan-Asiatic Linguistics: Proceedings of the Fourth International Symposium on Languages and Linguistics*. Salaya, Thailand: Institute of Language and Culture for Rural Development, Mahidol University at Salaya, 1996. Vol. 4, 1743–66.

————. "Linguistic Archaeology: Tracking Down the Tasaday Language." In *Archaeology and Language*, vol. 1, *Theoretical and Methodological Orientations*, ed. Roger Blench and Matthew Spriggs, 184–208. London and New York: Routledge, 1997.

————. *The Tasaday*. http://aa2411s.aa.tufs.ac.jp/~reid/Tasaday/index.html. 1999.

Reid, Lawrence, with assistance from Belayem Salibuko. "Preliminary Tasaday Lexicon." June 1994. Typescript.

Rocamora, Joel. "The Political Uses of PANAMIN." *Southeast Asia Chronicle* 67 (1979), 11–21.

Rogel-Rara, Amelia, and Emmanuel S. Nabayra. "The Genealogical Evidence." In *The Tasaday Controversy: Assessing the Evidence*, ed. Thomas N. Headland, 89–106. Washington, D.C.: American Anthropological Association, 1992.

Salazar, Zeus. "Footnote on the Tasaday." *Philippine Journal of Linguistics* 2 (1971), 34–38.

———. "Second Footnote on the Tasaday." *Asian Studies* 11, 2 (1973), 97–113.

———. "Third and Final Footnote on the Tasaday." In *The Tasaday Controversy: Assessing the Evidence*, ed. Thomas N. Headland, 76–85. Washington, D.C.: American Anthropological Association, 1992.

Schoen, Ivan. "Contact with the Stone Age." *Natural History* 68, 1(1969), 10–18, 66.

———. "Report on the Second Contact with the Akurio (Wama) Stone Age Tribe, Surinam, September 1968." Washington, D.C.: Smithsonian Institution, Center for Short-Lived Phenomena, 1969. Typescript.

Schweder, Richard A. *Thinking Through Cultures: Expeditions in Cultural Psychology*. Cambridge, Mass., and London: Harvard University Press, 1990.

Solway, Jacqueline S., and Richard B. Lee. "Foragers, Genuine or Spurious? Situating the Kalahari San in History." *Current Anthropology* 31, 2 (April 1990), 109–47.

Sponsel, Leslie. "An Anthropologist's Perspective on Peace and Quality of Life." In *Peace and Development: An Interdisciplinary Perspective*, ed. D. S. Sanders and J. K. Matsuoka, 29–48. Honolulu: University of Hawai'i School of Social Work, 1989.

———. "Our Fascination with the Tasaday: Anthropological Images and Images of Anthropology." In *The Tasaday Controversy: Assessing the Evidence*, ed. Thomas N. Headland, 200–212. Washington, D.C.: American Anthropological Association, 1992.

Stiles, Daniel. "The Hunter-Gatherer Revisionist Debate." *Anthropology Today* 8, 2 (1992), 13–17.

Supreme Court, Republic of the Philippines. "University of the Philippines v. Court of Appeals, G.R. No. 97827." Manila: Supreme Court Reports Annotated, February 9, 1993, 728–42.

Tan, Michael L. "The Tasaday and Other Urgent Issues in Anthropology." *Social Science Information* 14, 2 (July–September 1986), 20, 26.

Trinidad, Oscar, and Janet Bauer, eds. *Protecting Man's Right to Choice*. Manila: PANAMIN, 1972. Pamphlet.

Yen, Douglas. "The Ethnobotany of the Tasaday, II: Plant Names of the Tasaday, Manobo Blit and Kemato T'boli." In *Further Studies on the Tasaday*, ed. John Nance and D. E. Yen, 137–38. Makati, Philippines: PANAMIN Foundation, 1976. PANAMIN Foundation Research Series No. 2.

———. "The Ethnobotany of the Tasaday, III: Notes on the Subsistence System." In *Further Studies on the Tasaday*, ed. John Nance and D. E. Yen, 159–83. Makati, Philippines: PANAMIN Foundation, 1976. PANAMIN Foundation Research Series No. 2.

———. "The Tasaday Environment: Seventeen Years On." *Philippine Studies* 50 (First Quarter of 2002), 76–91.

Yen, Douglas, and John Nance, eds. *Further Studies on the Tasaday*. Makati, Philippines: 1976. PANAMIN Foundation Research Studies No. 2.

Yen, Douglas E., and Hermes G. Gutierrez. "The Ethnobotany of the Tasaday: I. The Useful Plants," *Philippine Journal of Science* 103 (1974), 97–139. Reprinted in *Further Studies of the Tasaday*, 97–136, and in *Readings on the Tasaday*.

Acknowledgments

This book truly would not have been possible if not for the generosity and expertise of a number of people. Thomas Headland of the Summer Institute of Linguistics was of immeasurable help throughout the writing of this book, giving good counsel, supplying reams of documents, and answering my many questions. Lawrence Reid was equally generous, lending me his unparalleled knowledge of Austronesian languages, as well as reading and commenting upon the manuscript of this book. There's much about the Tasaday that would remain a mystery if not for his intellectual curiosity and determination. John Bodley was gracious to get me started in my research on the subject and to read through the manuscript upon its completion. Amy Rara gave me invaluable assistance in the Philippines.

Jennifer Hengen and Rebecca Kurson helped spark this book, and I'll always be grateful to them for that. My agent, Chris Calhoun, kept me focused and optimistic, and my editor, Ethan Nosowsky, helped me shape the manuscript and make it into a book. Throughout the writing, he was patient yet demanding in a way that one wishes all editors could be. I also want to thank Cecily Parks for her diligence and good humor.

Patrick and Peter Parsons opened doors for me in the Philippines that would otherwise have remained closed. In the process, they have become good friends. Jim Brotherton was my *brod* and helped me survive and negotiate some difficult moments.

Many others contributed their time and energies to this project. Some granted me interviews, their views, their time. Some provided me with important documents. Many helped me with both. They include: John Nance, Douglas Yen, Carlos Fernandez, David Baradas, Jesus Peralta, Leslie Sponsel, Oswald Iten, Jim Turner, Father Jack Walsh, Rex Mansmann, Dul, Belayem Salibuko, Toto' Dudim, Mefalu Dudim,

329

Mai Tuan, Fludi Tuan, Yani Tuan, Dad Tuan, Lobo, Lolo', Bilengan, Adug, Gintuy, Wilfredo Ronquillo, Kristina Luz, John Bell, Karl Hutterer, Gerald Berreman, Ross Errington, Meg Fraiser, Douglas Fraiser, Judith Moses, Bion Griffin, Jo Lynn Guiness, Rebecca Cann, Richard Elkins, Antonio Cervantes, Dulce Baybay, Bruce Young, John Hicks, Joey Lozano, Bob Heins, Clay Johnston, Jerome Bailen, Zeus Salazar, Levita Duhaylungsod, Vicente Mondragon, Edith Terry, Helen Mabandos, Father Sean McDonagh, and David Givens.

At various times during this long project, others assisted me in various ways, and I'm indebted to them. These people and organizations include: Kim Lau, Meg Brady, Mark West, Rebecca Saxton, Amanda Tysowski, Bruce Beasley, Suzanne Paola, Brenda Miller, Boy Arendain, Rick Emmerson, J.D. Dolan, Benjie Abellera, Natalia Singer, Maria Lourdes Burgos, Robert Cowser, Al Viebranz, Pam Race, Stuart Culver, Richard Snelsire, Victoria Smith, the Bureau of Faculty Research at Western Washington University, and the English departments of the University of Utah and St. Lawrence University.

Grateful acknowledgment is also made to John Nance for permission to quote from *The Gentle Tasaday*.

And finally, my daughters, Olivia and Isabel, have shown me nothing but love and unwavering support.

Index

ABC, 85, 190; *20/20*, 8, 99, 117–19, 141, 159, 160, 161, 171, 177, 301, 305

Adler, Christian, 147, 148, 149, 154, 181, 190, 303

Adug, 56, 119, 173, 235, 236, 269, 270, 303; Yabes, hoax proponents claim as name, 152

Agta group, 15, 17, 202

America's Boy (Hamilton-Paterson), 90, 91, 147

American Anthropological Association (AAA): D.C. conference on Tasaday, 8, 202, 205–7, 210–14, 220

Aquino, Benigno "Ninoy," 82, 83, 87, 88, 147, 164

Aquino, Corazon "Cory," 88–92, 166, 179, 190, 196, 212, 232

Arienda, Roger "Bomba," 167, 168

Associated Press (AP), 32, 34, 35, 44, 56, 81, 160, 232

Azurin, Arnold, 150, 151, 168, 173, 192

B'laan group, 15, 49

Bailen, Jerome, 84, 148, 150, 165, 168–71, 173, 186, 187, 189, 190, 192, 195, 211, 242

Bantay Tasaday (Tasaday protectors), 144, 145, 276, 277, 284, 299

Baradas, David, 74, 77, 80, 84, 163, 190, 209, 213, 271, 276, 294, 296, 298; field study among the Tasaday, 61–63, 65–73, 130, 131, 267, 290, 297

BBC, 8, 185, 187, 191–93, 209

Belayem, 26, 63, 76, 77, 80, 97, 108, 172, 219, 227, 228, 244, 255, 261, 263, 277, 278, 303–4; Hemley and, 250, 260, 266, 270, 275; hoax theories regarding, 152; libel suit of, 195, 242; meetings with outsiders, 25, 38, 41, 45–47, 49–50, 271, 272; missing boy and, 296–97; origin story, telling of, 225–26, 243, 252–54; Reid and, 217, 223–26, 245; Sindi' and, 56, 58, 60, 62, 107, 222; tool making and, 217, 268, 291, 292

111; Sanduka or Tasafeng origins of, 103, 255; stabbing of, 236–37, 239–42

Dula, 56, 172, 173, 175, 176, 177, 195, 225

EDSA Revolution, 90–92
Eggan, Fred, 212, 213, 214
Eibl-Eibensfeldt, Irenäus, 85, 151
Elizalde, Freddy, 10, 11, 13, 163, 166, 272
Elizalde, Manuel, Jr. "Manda," 133, 167, 177, 193, 211, 225, 226, 253, 308; caves, request for Tasaday to remain at, 113, 138, 298; clothing of Tasaday and, 201–2; contact with Tasaday barred by, 85, 111, 151; D.C. conference and, 205–8, 212; death of, 8, 231–33, 295, 303; *diwatà* (deity) of the Tasaday, 5; drinking, 13; exile, life in, 147, 164–66, 183; exploitation of indigenous peoples, 79, 96, 100, 169, 216; fondness of Tasaday for, 39–40, 80, 87, 108, 218–19, 241, 242, 246, 254, 272; Fox and, 74; hoax proponents, role assigned by, 94, 95, 98, 119, 148–50, 153, 162, 172, 296, 300, 304; indigenous tribes, policies toward, 17–20, 59; intimidation techniques of, 189–91; libel suit of, 195, 242; Mansmann's opinions of, 180–82; marriage and children of, 12, 13, 190; meetings with the Tasaday, 37–40, 137, 258, 271, 294, 296; misappropriation of PANAMIN funds by, 175, 179, 233; naming of Tasaday and, 203; Nance and, 31, 45, 60; PANAMIN and, 16, 179, 287; parents of, 10, 11; Peralta's opinion of, 111–14; political ambitions of, 43–44, 82, 196, 217; primitivism of, 58; protector of the Tasaday, 64, 219–20, 297; publicity and, 21, 28, 36, 56, 57, 228; representation in *Trial in the Jungle*, 194–95; reputation, 21, 43, 59, 71, 88, 149, 163, 164, 170, 176, 190, 233, 285; research, scientific and, 55, 60, 62, 64–70, 73, 74, 75,

78, 213, 229, 294; response to hoax proponents, 173–75; Sison and, 17, 18, 247; Tasaday, early visits to, 23–28, 32, 34, 45–47, 49–53, 103, 104, 105; tribal affairs director, 4, 15, 169; womanizing and, 20, 165–66, 181; Yen and, 74; youth of, 9–12

Elizalde-Fox report, 36, 104, 113, 203, 266
Elkins, Richard, 74–78, 163, 186, 224, 255, 279, 289, 294, 297; authenticity of Tasaday, belief in, 205–6, 296
Enrile, Juan Ponce, 82, 90, 91
Errington, Ross, 285, 289
Etut, 26, 56, 79

Families of Victims of Involuntary Disappearances (FIND), 147
Fernandez, Carlos, 60, 84, 107, 255, 266, 298; authenticity of Tasaday, belief in, 149–51, 187, 296; Baradas, fieldwork with, 61–63, 65–69, 73, 78, 79, 209, 290, 297; congressional testimony, 174; Elizalde, mistrust of, 70–71, 190, 233, 296; Lynch, report co-authored with, 80; Reid and, 220–21; shooting at caves and, 67–69, 276, 294; Tasaday, first visits to, 48, 52, 53, 56, 57; *Tasaday* (co-authored with Lynch), 33; at UP conference, 149–51
First International Festival and Conference on Indigenous and Traditional Cultures, 196
Fox, Robert, 4–5, 17, 25–28, 36, 37, 39, 42, 43, 48, 59, 60, 61, 74, 75, 104, 149–51, 201, 202, 213, 220, 296; *see also* Elizalde-Fox report
fugu (smallpox), 24–25, 43, 103, 223, 308

Galang, Datu', 130, 131, 133, 135, 137, 235, 236, 261, 305; bribed and coached by Lozano, 171, 176–77, 262, 282, 300–301, 303; bribes Tasaday, 174, 254; Central TV and, 161, 162; Hemley conducts interviews at

PANAMIN (Presidential Assistant on National Minorities and Private Assistance for National Minorities), 60, 96, 127, 130, 136–37, 150, 176, 208, 218, 241, 251, 256; Baradas' resignation from, 84, 213; Blit region, development of, 23; Civilian Home Defense Forces and, 83, 95, 145, 164; collapse of, 179, 183, 286; donations to for Tasaday filming rights, 57, 74; Elizalde and, 16, 179, 232, 287; exploitation of Tasaday, accusations of, 169; Filipino scientists and, 61, 71; founding of, 12, 14; Fox's resignation from, 149, 151, 213; hiring of Tasaday poseurs for march, 85; hoax proponents accusations against, 148, 149, 163, 171, 209, 287; Lynch's resignation from, 151, 213; Mansmann, animosity with, 180, 182; Marcos and, 12, 73, 83, 84, 148, 181; misappropriation of funds by Elizalde, 175, 179, 233; *National Geographic* special about, 26; policy of holding land in trust, 81; publicity possibilities of Tasaday for, 28, 84; research department of, 25, 66–68, 78–80, 294; reservations and settlements and, 19–20, 37, 102, 249–50; shooting at Tasaday caves and, 67–70; Tasaday expeditions, 37, 42, 47, 201, 210, 272; weapons distribution and, 118, 144–45

People Power Revolution, 90–92

Peralta, Jesus, 37–39, 107, 109–15, 150, 151, 174, 206, 211, 212, 217, 220, 237, 255, 278

Philippine Association for Intercultural Development (PAFID), 99, 100

Philippine Daily Inquirer (newspaper), 168, 170, 173, 175, 232–33

Philippines: Commission on Elections, 90; Congress of, 14, 82, 168, 169, 170, 172, 175, 176, 305; constitution, 82; ethnolinguistic groups of, 15 (*see also* Agta; B'laan; Manadaya; Manobo; T'boli; Ubu); National Mu-

seum of the, 76; newspapers, 33, 80, 168, 179, 196, 231 (*see also Philippine Daily Inquirer*); Senate of, 43, 151

Presidential Decree 1017, 85

Presidential Proclamation No. 995, 59, 195

Ramos, General Fidel, 90, 91

Ramos, Salvador, 227, 228

Rara, Amy, 71, 102, 105, 125, 206, 221, 226, 227, 243, 249, 252, 267, 278–80, 282, 283; ancestral domain law, explains to Tasaday, 274; authenticity of Tasaday, belief in, 101; death of Elizalde and, 233, 250; Dul, visits in hospital, 239, 241, 242; early visits to Tasaday and, 60, 64, 211; fieldwork of, 207, 261, 303; Hemley, visit to Tasaday area with, 257–64, 266, 267, 269, 270, 272, 275; Igid, Joe, suspicions of, 251; resigns from Elizalde's employ, 228; *Reply to 20/20* and, 173–74; returns to Kematu with Dul and Hemley, 246–48; translator, acts as Hemley's, 242, 244–46, 253–56, 262, 264, 271, 273, 276, 277; Zagreb conference and, 186–88

Reader's Digest, 12, 14, 33, 36, 37, 39

Reid, Lawrence, 15, 39, 205, 253, 255, 268, 270, 281, 285, 288, 290, 291; DNA study and, 228–29; fieldwork with the Tasaday, 221–28, 243, 252; lexicons of Blit Manobo and Tasaday created by, 134, 140, 245, 264, 279; tapes recorded at Tasaday caves and, 217, 219, 220, 289; translates tapes made of Hemley's first Bilengan interview, 136, 138, 141, 142; at Zagreb conference, 191, 193

Reply to 20/20 (video), 173, 174, 176

Reynolds, Jack, 3, 4, 6, 36–37, 39, 56, 73, 74, 99, 107, 109, 159, 244, 271, 275

Rivero, Ching, 48, 56, 68, 271